WITHDRAWN
UTSA LIBRARIES

CHINA UNDER HU JINTAO:

Opportunities, Dangers, and Dilemmas

Series on Contemporary China (ISSN: 1793-0847)

Series Editors

Joseph Fewsmith (Boston University)
Yongnian Zheng (East Asian Institute, National University of Singapore)

Advisory Board Members

Tun-jen Cheng (College of William and Mary)
Jane Duckett (University of Glasgow)
James Tang (University of Hong Kong)
Gungwu Wang (East Asian Institute, National University of Singapore)
Lynn White (Princeton University)
Dali Yang (University of Chicago)
Ji You (University of New South Wales)

Published

Vol. 1
Legitimacy
Ambiguities of Political Success or Failure in East and Southeast Asia
edited by Lynn White

Vol. 2
China Under Hu Jintao
Opportunities, Dangers, and Dilemmas
edited by Tun-jen Cheng, Jacques deLisle & Deborah Brown

Series on Contemporary China – Vol. 2

CHINA UNDER HU JINTAO:
Opportunities, Dangers, and Dilemmas

edited by

Tun-jen Cheng
College of William and Mary, USA

Jacques deLisle
University of Pennsylvania, USA

Deborah Brown
Seton Hall University, USA

NEW JERSEY • LONDON • SINGAPORE • BEIJING • SHANGHAI • HONG KONG • TAIPEI • CHENNAI

Published by

World Scientific Publishing Co. Pte. Ltd.
5 Toh Tuck Link, Singapore 596224
USA office: 27 Warren Street, Suite 401-402, Hackensack, NJ 07601
UK office: 57 Shelton Street, Covent Garden, London WC2H 9HE

British Library Cataloguing-in-Publication Data
A catalogue record for this book is available from the British Library.

CHINA UNDER HU JINTAO: OPPORTUNITIES, DANGERS, AND DILEMMAS

Copyright © 2006 by World Scientific Publishing Co. Pte. Ltd.

All rights reserved. This book, or parts thereof, may not be reproduced in any form or by any means, electronic or mechanical, including photocopying, recording or any information storage and retrieval system now known or to be invented, without written permission from the Publisher.

For photocopying of material in this volume, please pay a copying fee through the Copyright Clearance Center, Inc., 222 Rosewood Drive, Danvers, MA 01923, USA. In this case permission to photocopy is not required from the publisher.

ISBN 981-256-347-4

Typeset by Stallion Press
E-mail: enquiries@stallionpress.com

Printed in Singapore by World Scientific Printers (S) Pte Ltd

Contents

China under Hu Jintao: Introduction   1
Tun-jen Cheng, Jacques deLisle, and Deborah Brown

Part I

1. Political Succession: Changing Guards and Changing Rules   27
Joseph Fewsmith

2. Is the Chinese State Apparatus Being Revamped?   47
Yanzhong Huang

3. Who Does the Party Represent?: From "Three Revolutionary Classes" to "Three Represents"   75
Bruce J. Dickson

Part II

4. Jiang Zemin's Successors and China's Growing Rich-Poor Gap   97
Edward Friedman

5. Information Technology in China: A Double-Edged Sword   135
Tun-jen Cheng

vi *Contents*

6. The Future of SOEs: From Shortage Economics to "Enron–omics"? 165
   Xiaobo Hu

7. The Evolution of Elections in China 185
   Amy E. Gadsden

8. What Does Buyun Township Mean in the Context of China's Political Reform? 199
   Yawei Liu

Part III

9. China and the WTO: Evolving Agendas of Economic Openness, Domestic Reform, and International Status, and Challenges of the Post-Accession Era 229
   Jacques deLisle

10. China's Accession into the WTO and China's Financial Markets 293
    K. Thomas Liaw

11. China-ASEAN Relations: The Significance of an ASEAN-China Free Trade Area 311
    Alice D. Ba

12. New Leadership Team, New Approaches toward Taiwan? 349
    Chih-cheng Lo

13. China's Relations with the United States and Japan: Status and Outlook 373
    Robert Sutter

Contributing Authors 407

Index 413

China under Hu Jintao: Introduction

Tun-jen Cheng, Jacques deLisle, and Deborah Brown

Held in November 2002, the Sixteenth Chinese Communist Party (CCP) Congress marked the official ascension of China's fourth generation of leadership — headed by Hu Jintao — the new general secretary and ranking member of the Politburo Standing Committee.[1] Several months later, in March 2003, the National People's Congress took the next steps in this formal generational transition, in part by conferring the premiership on Wen Jiabao and the presidency of the state on Hu.

These developments were unusual in the history of the People's Republic in two ways: the transfer of power was the first to occur

---

[1] For distinction and designation of leadership generation, see Cheng Li, *China's New Leaders: The New Generation* (Lanham, MD: Rowman & Littlefield, 2001). The "third generation" leadership, Jiang Zemin, Zhu Rongji and their cohorts, were born at the turn of the 1930s, and grew up during the Civil War and the founding decade of the People's Republic, while the members of the new "fourth generation" leadership, under Hu Jintao, were born around the time of the Civil War and came of age during the Cultural Revolution.

without the guiding hand of a "founding father" of the regime; and the transition was achieved without crisis or purge. Yet, the changing of the guard remained less than clear-cut. Jiang retained the chairmanship of the Military Affairs Commission of the party through most of 2004, and his protégés seemingly hold a majority of the Politburo. Moves by Hu and Wen early in their terms — including their handling of the Severe Acute Respiratory Syndrome (SARS) crisis — suggested that a relatively rapid consolidation of the transition might occur. But the shadow of the Jiang era was far from dispersed nearly two years after the formal transfer of offices began.

An incomplete or protracted political succession in China is hardly unprecedented. Jiang himself had to struggle to emerge from the shadow of Deng Xiaoping, the enduring preeminent leader in post-Mao China. Given that Jiang seemingly tried hard to preserve his influence (retaining the military committee chairmanship, stacking the Politburo in his favor, and at one point, prompting rumors of a possible delay in holding the party congress due to unsettled personnel matters), Hu faced a challenging process of establishing his leadership.

The challenges confronting Hu — and the post-Sixteenth Party Congress leadership more generally — during and after leadership transition are made all the more daunting by the issues and agendas the fourth-generation leaders have inherited from their predecessors. Some of these matters (addressed in Part I of this volume) are primarily questions of changes "within" the party-state: Can the members of the fourth-generation leadership work out a *modus vivendi*, maintain a political equilibrium, and perhaps reform or institutionalize the rules of the game in elite politics? Will the party be able to revamp and retool as its old ideologies and functions seem more and more irrelevant, especially to the most dynamic and increasingly influential elements in a market-oriented society that is led by rising middle classes and entrepreneurs? Can the party and state find effective ways, including institutional restructuring, to deal with rampant corruption and unresponsiveness among officials who rob the regime of legitimacy and imperil its efficacy?

Other challenges (on which Part II of this book is centered) arise primarily from the domestic environment: How will the leadership respond to the grievances of the growing underclass in China's booming coastal cities and its still undeveloped hinterland — groups that provide a potential constituency for criticism of the reform policy agenda that the regime has pursued for a quarter century? How will China's rulers handle an increasingly — if very unevenly — "wired" society that has access to unorthodox information on the Internet, and the trade-off between the pursuit of higher-tech economic growth and the resulting erosion of controls over information? What lies ahead regarding the limited and uneven foray into elections and democracy at the village level and any popular expectations that those processes have created? How will the leadership address the dangers of financial meltdowns and asset-stripping in state industries that continue to be major employers and recipients of state investment even as their share of the economy shrinks?

A final set of concerns (which forms the focus of Part III of this book) comes from China's external environment: Will China's post-Jiang leadership be able and willing to meet China's World Trade Organization (WTO) obligations and satisfy international expectations for economic liberalization and openness, given that most grace periods for implementing WTO commitments are five years or less and that required or expected changes are costly and possibly wrenching for China? After the at least nominal retirement of the third-generation leadership, how is the new, incompletely consolidated leadership approaching China's complex international relationships, including the perennially crisis-ridden question of Taiwan (and its pivotal place in the Sino-American relationship), relations with the region's two other great powers (the United States and Japan), and the political implications and dimensions of the People's Republic of China's (PRC's) deepening economic ties to Southeast Asia (including the pursuit of an ASEAN-China Free Trade Area)?

The current phase of the post-Sixteenth Party Congress political succession provides an opportune moment to assess these broad questions of policy and political change in China. Such regime transitions can provide occasions for uncommonly open policy debates, openings for unexpected, extensive political reorientation, and opportunities for unusually penetrating glimpses of how power is exercised in China.

Moreover, Hu with other members of China's post-Jiang leadership, and the regime they head, face considerable pressure to move forward in addressing the challenges that confront them now, in advance of the next party congress which is scheduled for 2007. If Hu is to be more than a Hua Guofeng-like designated but short-term successor (a fate many had expected for Jiang when Deng drafted him for the heir-apparent post in 1989), he will have to pursue a second term from a position of having managed the lingering power and possible interventions of Jiang or other elders, and the complex relationship of rivalry and interdependence with Zeng Qinghong and other fourth-generation leaders.[2] In addition, Hu's and his near-colleagues' prospects for a successful second term will depend greatly on how well or how badly they have handled, during their first years in office, questions of reform within the party-state and challenges arising from domestic and international contexts.

Finally, the current leaders' successes and failures may be particularly illuminated in the months surrounding the Seventeenth Party Congress since 2008 is also the year that Beijing will host China's first Olympic Games. Such events can have great symbolic and political importance, as the precedents set by two prior Olympics on Asian soil underscore. Recall the Tokyo Games of 1964, the first held in Asia. Having achieved a doubling of national income, secured entry into the Organization for Economic Cooperation and Development (OECD), and pursued an initiative to establish an Asian Development Bank (with a leading role for itself), Japan saw the games ratify and emphasize its entry into the ranks of major, establishment powers and its return to the family of responsible

---

[2] For assessments of the Hu-Zeng and Jiang-Zeng relationships, see, respectively, Li Cheng and Lynn White, "The Sixteenth Central Committee of the Chinese Communist Party: Hu Gets What?" *Asian Survey* 43, no. 4 (July–August 2003): 553–597, especially 590–597. See also, Andrew J. Nathan and Bruce Gilley, *China's New Rulers: The Secret Files* (New York: New York Review of Books, 2002).

nations after the partial ostracism that followed World War II. Consider also the Seoul Games of 1988. In the end, they shone a spotlight on South Korea as an economy that had industrialized rapidly from postwar backwardness, a democratic polity that had emerged from decades of dictatorship, and an emerging source of outbound investment and foreign aid. The preceding period was another matter, however, marked by street protests and international pressure forcing open political space for brisk democratization, and by trade partners' concerns with Korea's huge trade surplus that contributed to a massive and sudden revaluation of the country's currency for the first time in the postwar period. In Japan, too, street protests — triggered by the renewal of the U.S.–Japan Security Treaty — had created a political crisis a few years before the Olympics.

Constituencies inside and outside China will likely expect or demand from the Olympics-hosting PRC accomplishments analogous to those of Japan, which China increasingly rivals as a regional economic and military power, and those of South Korea, a smaller nation formerly in the Middle Kingdom's orbit. The remarkable record of economic growth during two and a half decades of reform, China's ascension as a regional power, and China's accession to the WTO and deepening engagement with the international order on many fronts echo the pre-Olympic accomplishments of Japan and Korea, conferring similar gains in global influence and prestige on the early post-Jiang PRC. Thus, as the Olympics near, it will be an especially pressing concern for China's leaders to minimize — and for critics of the government to highlight — difficulties that cast doubt on the sustainability of China's economic miracle, the security of social and political order, and the appropriateness of the PRC's rehabilitation from the international opprobrium that followed the Tiananmen "Incident" of 1989 (which loosely paralleled Japan's postwar situation and which likely cost Beijing the 2000 Olympics).

THE PARTY-STATE

Part I of this volume focuses on the pressures and possibilities for change within the Chinese party-state itself during the post-Sixteenth

Party Congress era. In his chapter, Joseph Fewsmith addresses the vital issue of elite politics, asking whether the process of succession surrounding the Sixteenth Party Congress shows significant and durable institutionalization. Fewsmith concludes that the post-Sixteenth Party Congress PRC remains in a deeply ambivalent and, therefore, ambiguous position between weakly institutionalized, charismatic (in Weber's terms) and personalistic authority, on the one hand, and institutionalized, legal-rational (again in Weber's terms) and, ultimately, more constrained authority, on the other hand.

Fewsmith identifies several long-term factors favoring the platform of institutionalization that Jiang embraced in his political report to the Sixteenth Party Congress, including: commitments to restore party organizational norms after the Cultural Revolution, calls to enhance the role of legal rules in politics, efforts to staff the party with technocrats and to impose rules governing retirement, and acceptance of "objective" economic laws as a basis for policy-making and fundamental economic policies that restrain the discretion of the party, such as acceptance of market principles, globalization, and the demands of WTO membership. Fewsmith further argues that the generational transition at the top may provide a further impetus toward institutionalization, bringing to power leaders with a technocratic (and therefore rational) perspective, a Cultural Revolution-bred aversion to institutional chaos, and a relative dearth of the personal or ideological authority and cross-*xitong* personal networks that earlier generations of top leaders enjoyed. In addition, Fewsmith notes that institutionalization at the top elite level could build upon the progress of institutionalization at levels below the Central Committee, limited experiments with inner-party democracy, or precedents set by Jiang Zemin's use of institutionalizing rules, such as a mandatory retirement age to secure the removal of rivals, including Qiao Shi (even though the rule was deployed selectively and instrumentally in that seminal case).

However, Fewsmith stresses that such prospects are not enough to guarantee institutionalization. Hu's grip on the top post in part reflects Deng's attempt to anoint both his successor (Jiang) and his successor's successor — a process that reflects much personalistic authority and little institutionalization. The persisting weakness of formal institutions at the top has meant that the third- and fourth-generation leaders have turned to personal connections and networks and clientele practices, rather than to institutions and rules in efforts to replace the authority that ideology and founding-generation status once provided. Moreover, Fewsmith describes how Jiang engaged in extensive and protracted institutionalization-undermining means to try to secure his hold on power from "behind the screen" after his formal retirement.[3] Even where Jiang and others have turned to rules that seemingly could be institutionalized (such as mandatory retirement age), they have seen these rules in highly instrumental terms. More broadly, Fewsmith argues that the party's refusal to renounce the right to penetrate society — in private enterprises, nominally democratically self-governing villages, and so on — badly undermines the purported agenda to remake the CCP from a "revolutionary" party guided by Leninist logic into a "ruling" party constrained by principles and norms of legal-rational authority. While it might ultimately mark an important milestone in the political evolution of the CCP and the PRC, the Sixteenth Party Congress did not adopt an agenda of fundamental reform of political structures that could secure lasting institutionalization of China's political system.

Fewsmith's account suggests a number of interesting additional issues, including what might be called the question of "uneven institutionalization," which occurs not just across "levels" of the political system (as Fewsmith notes) but also across "aspects" of the elite process. The latter is illustrated by the relatively extensive introduction of rules governing "exit" and the relatively limited development of rules governing "selection."[4]

---

[3] For constraints imposed on Jiang, see David Bachman, "Succession, Power, Retirement, and the Chinese Political Elite," in Deborah A. Brown and Tun-jen Cheng, eds., *New Leadership and New Agenda: Challenges, Constraints, and Achievements in Taipei and Beijing* (Jamaica, NY: Center for Asian Studies, St. John's University, 2002), 43.
[4] Frederick C. Teiwes, "Normal Politics with Chinese Characteristics," *China Journal*, no. 45 (January 2001): 76.

While politics at the apex of the party-state thus remains in a state of institutional ambiguity and ambivalence, the demands of economic development have underpinned an ambitious, some would say desperate, effort to improve the quality and effectiveness of the state apparatus. The core agenda has been largely Weberian: shifting recruitment and promotion toward meritocracy (increasingly defined in technocratic terms) and away from virtuocracy (with political attitude, class, and revolutionary background being the key virtues); and making clearer the distinction between office holder and office, and the obligations of officeholders to stay within the rule-defined powers and fulfill the rule-defined responsibilities of office. A third related aim has been the creation of a state bureaucratic structure that has the capacity to regulate a market economy efficiently and to implement central policies effectively.

In the account offered in Yanzhong Huang's contribution to this volume, the post-Sixteenth Party Congress leadership faces an extremely difficult task in achieving the above goals, despite its initial reaffirmation of their importance and commitment to their achievement. Despite nearly two decades of rationalization and reform efforts, the Chinese state bureaucracy remains plagued by rampant political patronage and corruption: lines of accountability that run primarily upward and thus promote systematic neglect of public needs (as well as preferences) and periodic lapses into campaign-style politics to implement some selected policies, and a policy process in which the fragmentation of authority among numerous ministerial and local government actors impedes policy formulation and undermines regulatory capacity.

Huang argues that administrative reforms have done little to ameliorate the stated problems and, worse yet, that reform-era policies have made perennial difficulties worse or added new ones. Decentralization of appointment authority to lower levels in China's nomenclatura-based bureaucratic personnel system has increased the spoils available to relatively low-level officials and reduced the transaction costs for office- or promotion-seekers willing to pay bribes (and for appointing officers who solicit such payments).⁵ Continued growth in government employment and, as a result of tax reform, the shifting of the burdens of local government finance to locally-raised off-budget fees have in recent years soured local state-peasant relations, eroded the provision of local public welfare goods, and prompted government entities to pursue economic activities that weaken administrative capacity. Such "commercialization" or "industrialization" of government and the reform-era decentralization of authority have deepened the problems of fragmented authoritarianism.

The handling of the SARS crisis, the implementation of population control policies, and the pursuit of "strike hard" anti-crime campaigns provide recent examples of selective, unresponsive, and ineffective bureaucratic behavior that show China's failure to solve the dual-agency problem of the Chinese state — accountability to the party leadership that sets policy and to the citizenry whose interests are in theory being served and whose acquiescence, in practice, is necessary. Efforts to address the first agency problem have encountered high monitoring costs as well as corruption and parochialism among the entities that are charged with doing the monitoring.

Huang's analysis suggests that solving agency problems of the second sort — and achieving the broader agenda of bureaucratic rationalization and building state regulatory capacity — may call for political reforms that simply are not on the post-Sixteenth Party Congress leadership's agenda.⁶

In addition to the relatively limited and unsuccessful moves to remake the state, the party also has undertaken a significant

---

[5] Kevin O'Brien and Lianjiang Li have insightfully shown that well-liked policies, such as expansion of government services, are put on backburners, while unpopular policies, such as tax extraction and family planning, are implemented with abusive measures. See their "Selective Policy Implementation in Rural China," *Comparative Politics* 31, no. 2 (January 1999): 167–186. Huang's chapter in this volume uncovers the perverse incentives and the condition (decentralization) that have greatly contributed to the pervasive problems of policy implementation.

[6] For the initial formulation of the agency problem in China's party state, see Susan Shirk, *The Political Logic of Economic Reform in China* (Berkeley, CA: University of California Press, 1993), chap. 4.

redefinition of its social base and its recruitment pool. To retain its legitimacy and perhaps its ability to rule, the party leadership in the years surrounding the Sixteenth Party Congress has perceived a need to adapt its ideology and institutions to cope with the vibrant, albeit still developing economy, and with an increasingly heterogeneous, though not yet fully pluralistic society.

In his contribution to this volume, Bruce Dickson addresses a vital aspect of the process of accommodation, specifically the party's relationship with the new elite of entrepreneurs, professionals, and technology specialists that the party's own reform policies have helped to create. Dickson argues that the party has been pursuing a relatively promising strategy of co-opting these new elites, especially during the final years of Jiang's incumbency and the initial phases of Hu's. The process has included several elements: shifting the basis of the party's legitimacy to economic modernization, which required the party to rely upon and accommodate members of the new economic elite; sanctioning the creation of voluntary associations, such as chambers of commerce and professional associations; revising party ideology to incorporate the "Three Represents," which declare that the party speaks for the "advanced productive forces" (a code word for the new economic elite), which Jiang adumbrated in 2000 and which was written into the party charter at the Sixteenth Party Congress; and increasing recruitment of entrepreneurs into the party, with a *de facto* relaxation of, and at the Sixteenth Party Congress, the formal reversal of, a ban against them that was imposed after the Tiananmen "Incident."

While such measures have begun to change the social composition of the party, Dickson notes that they remain part of a largely defensive or conservative strategy that seeks to maintain the party's monopoly of organized politics and to preempt potential opposition. Signs of limitation abound. The party's claim to legitimacy continues to rest significantly on its nationalist accomplishments and asserted unique ability to maintain order. The civil society-like associations for the new elite are subject to party penetration and steering and remain far more corporatist than pluralist. Jiang had to struggle long and hard with more "leftist" elements in the party (and endure allegations that he was a Gorbachev-like or Lee Teng-hui-style traitor to his Leninist party) in order to win acceptance of the "Three Represents," which remain burdened by ideological strictures insisting that only entrepreneurs with the correct or transformed proletarian outlook belong in the party. Finally, many of the "Red Capitalists" now swelling party ranks were preexisting party members who became entrepreneurs.

Dickson's analysis concludes by suggesting two divergent paths as the party's strategy for incorporating the rising reform-era elites: successful cooptation of these groups and diversification of the party and politics without transformation of the party or the acceptance of true pluralism; or a "soft landing" scenario by which cooptation of diverse emerging elites eventually produces a qualitative change, legitimating divergent interests and providing a foundation for genuine pluralism from which could follow expansion of political participation to include broader social groups. The latter scenario, Dickson suggests, is not immediately likely, as the newly incorporated entrepreneurial, professional, and technical elites generally favor the status quo, having benefited from reform policies, party membership as a route to greater or more secure riches, and the market economy that party policies have helped to create.

The chapters in Part I suggest that, while significant changes in elite and institutional politics may be underway, unless the party system is effectively changed and political reform is seriously pursued, the Chinese party-state apparatus is unlikely to rid itself of corruption or become accountable and responsive to a broader public.[7]

DOMESTIC CONTEXTS

Part II of this volume analyzes the changed social, economic, and political settings that the party-state and its leaders face in the post-Sixteenth Party Congress period. While the reform policies of the

---

[7] Cf. Gang Lin, "Ideology and Political Institutions for a New Era," in *China after Jiang*, ed. Gang Lin and Xiaobo Hu (Washington, DC, and Stanford, CA: Wilson Center Press and Stanford University Press, 2003). Lin is sanguine about intraparty pluralism. See also, Cheng Li, "The New Bipartisanship in the CCP," *Orbis* 49, no. 3 (2005): 387–400.

last twenty-five years have been wildly successful, especially (some would say almost exclusively) in the realm of economic development, the domestic environment that they have produced for the regime now formally headed by Hu is challenging, complex, and, in many respects, hostile.

In his chapter, Edward Friedman assesses the implications of the radically and increasingly uneven distribution of the fruits of "reform and opening to the outside world" in contemporary China. The post-Sixteenth Party Congress leadership faces challenges borne of huge disparities between rural and urban areas; inland and coastal regions; and insecure or laid-off employees of old-style state-owned enterprises and sought-after and well-compensated staffers of newer, often private or foreign-invested, firms. Friedman perceives a China that has become so deeply divided by the consequences of reform that there are now several distinct and conflicting political cultures. The "winners" under reform include the highly prosperous and globalized coastal east and south, and the relatively prosperous and "super-patriotic" north centered on Beijing. The "losers" consist of a vast "central" China that includes the underdeveloped southwest, the rustbelt northeast and poor rural hinterlands, and a "western" China that includes frontier regions with significant, discontented, and potentially unruly non-Han populations.[8]

As Friedman sees it, the "losers" are a constituency for a potential "New Left" in Chinese politics, one that is harshly critical of the reforms and the pre- and post-Sixteenth Party Congress leaderships. This possibility stems not only from the losers' being left behind economically but also from a clash of political cultures. Possessed by a post-socialist Social Darwinism, the winners view their own power and material success as well-earned and the losers' plight as a product of their own laziness and backwardness. In contrast, the losers view the winners' gains as the product of corruption, self-serving

---

[8] Cf. Richard Madsen, "One Country, Three Systems: State-Society Relations in Post-Jiang China," in *China after Jiang*, ed. Gang Lin and Xiaobo Hu (Washington, DC, and Stanford, CA: Wilson Center Press and Stanford University Press, 2003).

policies, exploitation of the hinterland, comprador-like collaboration with foreigners, and betrayal of the values of solidarity and sacrifice that characterize the Chinese heartland.[9]

On Friedman's account, there is little prospect for addressing these problems in the Jiang and post-Jiang era leaderships' approaches. Despite Hu's likely sincere concern for the problems of the less well-off, the regime remains committed to a strategy of high growth, with a tolerance for inequality and a reliance on trickle-down economics to address the problems of those left behind — a policy that will do little to alleviate many of the losers' grievances and material foundations. The leadership also has turned increasingly to a strong and militant nationalism that has much resonance among the losers but that also threatens to inflame central China's discontent with its overly internationalist leaders' performance and to forge a problematic alliance between central China and the patriotic north. China's leaders have shown little taste for fundamental political reforms that might address the potential New Left's critiques — measures such as reforming the Brezhnevian party apparatus that rules a resentful central China, implementing elections to give the vast population of reforms' losers a political voice, or foregoing knee-jerk reassertions of central authority and centrally-designed "messages" that seek to counter, but often exacerbate, divergent local political cultures.

Yet, Friedman concludes that the threat of political instability under the Hu-Wen leadership remains small, absent a bursting of the economic bubble, a conflict over Taiwan, or other similar shock. Much of the populace has become deeply cynical about politics and focused on pursuing wealth, and is thus unlikely to turn to organized opposition. Where dissent and discontent threaten to coalesce, the regime still has powerful tools of repression.

---

[9] Many have exposed the plights of the "losers." See, for example, He Qinglian, *The Pitfalls of China's Modernization* [Zhongguo xiandaihua de xianjing]. Friedman's chapter shows how the "winners" perceive the "losers."

As Friedman's account underscores, the third-generation leadership's economic accomplishments have been skewed toward the "high end" of China's economy. In his contribution to this volume, Tun-jen Cheng examines the most "high end" segment of China's economy, the information technology (IT) sector, and the political challenges that its rapid development pose for the fourth-generation leadership. Cheng attributes the explosive development of this sector to substantial infusions of investment and support by the state and by foreign investors. The economic result has been the rapid development of the information technology industry that has become a significant sector in its own right, an important export industry, and (with the emergence of a more "wired" China) a source of efficiency and productivity gains for the wider economy.

Information technology, Cheng emphasizes, is a double-edged sword for China's leadership. With the economic gains come threats to political control, especially those from broadened Internet access, including: the erosion of the regime's monopoly on information; the provision of new venues and pathways for the dissemination of dissident or foreign ideas; the creation of space for the formation of virtual political communities with their own identities; the escalation of costs to the regime of blocking or monitoring troublesome content; and the risk that ideas and information initially spread via IT media will jump the digital divide and reach broader Chinese audiences.

Still, Cheng argues, the regime has so far been relatively successful in containing the political risks. The state has maintained control over the handful of portals for access to foreign sites and developed powerful monitoring and censoring tools with the help of foreign technology. The regime has also put in place an extensive legal framework to register and identify Internet users, monitor their patterns of use, and threaten them with punishment under vague criminal law provisions. The authorities have also engaged in preemptive strikes to deter organized dissident use of the Internet, including the detention of suspected fomenters of cyberdissent. All of this has produced, Cheng concludes, an effective culture of self-censorship.

Yet, Cheng asserts, such previously effective methods may not suffice for the fourth-generation leadership. Sophisticated users and new technology permit evasion of the state's barriers. The collateral economic costs imposed by crude means of restricting information flows on the net may rise prohibitively, as may the administrative costs of monitoring the rapidly expanding volume of communications and the agency costs of overseeing a growing number of monitors scattered about a fragmented bureaucracy that is charged with policing China's cyberspace. The effective "audit rate" may fall so sharply that previously effective levels of deterrence will decline sharply.

Cheng concludes that the regime may have to pursue a Singapore-style strategy, mimicking the People's Action Party's approach of engaging and competing in the Internet marketplace of political ideas. However, Cheng notes that the contemporary Chinese regime lacks several key advantages enjoyed by its Singaporean counterpart, including a highly capable and respected government, and the legitimization — and perhaps the refinement — of its messages that come from competition in a political marketplace that is — for all its limits — more open than China's.

Xiaobo Hu's chapter turns our attention to the difficult legacies that the Jiang Zemin-era leadership's approach to enterprise reform has left for the post-Sixteenth Party Congress regime. Hu traces the origins of "Enronomics" or "crony capitalism" with Chinese characteristics to three aspects of enterprise reform that took hold sequentially in reform-era China. First, decentralization of control and related disaggregation of ownership rights in relatively "traditional" state enterprises produced a problematic form of "state corporatism." Decentralization took the forms of separating the party-government structure from management, shifting the locus of state control to more local levels of the state, and shifting authority from the state to individual state-owned enterprises, which had the effect of separating underlying rights to own or formally dispose of state assets from rights to use such assets or extract rents from them. This fragmentation of ownership and continuation of state authority and entanglement meant that enterprise decisions were made on personal and political bases rather than on purely economic ones.

Second, the emergence of township and village enterprises — particularly in the service sector — generated a new "bureaupreneurial class" that possessed a distinctive type of human capital. In some cases, local bureaucrats used state assets to establish enterprises which they then ran. In other cases, local entrepreneurs, facing an environment that offered weak protections for property rights and from arbitrary state exactions, sought protection from local officials by bringing them in as economic partners. Either way, the same problems emerged, with the relevant enterprises operating outside the strictures and monitoring of the state plan, with deep quotidian entanglement of government and enterprise managerial roles and personnel, and with *de facto* property rights allocated or protected through means that left such rights fragmented and informal and that had little foundation in (and sometimes conflicted with) relevant law and policy.

Third, a series of policies and practices led to the alienation of state-owned enterprises or their assets. The means have included conversion to share-issuing companies, merger, bankruptcy, and (especially after the Fifteenth Party Congress) selling off small- and medium-sized state enterprises. Such transfers of ownership or less formal stripping of assets from state-owned enterprises has usually meant transfers to insiders — the politically connected and party-state-appointed former managers of enterprises who constitute another subspecies of bureaupreneur, eliding and melding political power and economic pursuits.

Hu concludes that these phenomena have moved China from the familiar "shortage economics" of a Soviet-style economy to Chinese "Enronomics." The latter is marked by problems that parallel those associated with Enron-like scandals in the very different economies of the fully capitalist developed world: economic decisions made on the basis of personal or political connections, weak protection of the rights of owners (whether shareholders or the state), absence of objective, honest, and effective regulation, and resulting massive transfer of value to politically-connected managers. Hu sees remedies to this situation as a tough task for the fourth-generation leadership, one made harder by the third-generation leadership's parting shot: the embrace of the "Three Represents" and, with it, the legitimation and inclusion in the party of the bureaupreneurs, state corporatists, and crony capitalists who are at the heart of the problem.

Two other chapters, by Amy Gadsden and Ya-wei Liu, analyze the patterns and post-Sixteenth Party Congress prospects for electoral democracy in China, focusing on the implications of developments in China's villages and rural townships. Gadsden surveys the relatively rapid development and institutionalization of elections for villagers' committees, from the unauthorized experiment in Guozuo, Guangxi province, in 1980, through the adoption (under Peng Zhen's stewardship) of a 1982 constitutional provision recognizing the committees as the basic unit of rural governance and 1987 legislation on villagers' committee elections, to the universal if uneven and much-debated implementation of village elections during the last decade and a half. Gadsden depicts how the Ministry of Civil Affairs (led by officials who had been relatively sympathetic to the 1989 Democracy Movement) overcame political opposition and daunting technical and organizational challenges to foster the holding of elections, adoption of secret ballots, and development of candidate selection, campaigning, and election-monitoring procedures. She attributes these successes in significant part to dogged determination, extensive training of election officials (with foreign assistance) and education of local officials and publics, and skillful cultivation of support and endorsement from senior Chinese leaders and influential foreign leaders and organizations.

Beyond the village level, elections have made little progress. Liu's chapter details the widely known "experiment" with election for township magistrate in Buyun in Sichuan province in 1998 and its limited reprise in 2001, on the eve of the fourth-generation leadership's formal succession. In both rounds, Liu finds much to be optimistic about, including opportunities for unofficial candidates to reach the final rounds, contentious and issue-focused campaigning for voters' support, respect for secret ballots, and reasonably high turnout. There were, to be sure, troublesome shortcomings, including factors that strongly favored the incumbent, such as: an effective bye in the 1998 primary; retention of the final formal power to select the magistrate by the township people's congress in 2001; superior access to material resources in the campaign phase; and the use of established village leaders to help illiterate residents mark their ballots.

Arguably, the more troubling and clearly the more systemically significant limitations reflected by Buyun lay elsewhere. Although the 1998 balloting won praise from the electorate (who welcomed the chance to vote), academic commentators (who favored political reform and also saw opportunities to reduce state-society tensions and official corruption in the countryside), local officials (who perceived a valuable monitoring function), and some official commentaries (which drew upon official endorsements of democratization), the party center clearly declared that the 1998 vote was illegal (although not to be overturned) and not to be repeated.

Gadsden describes how advocates of the expansion of elections and democracy, thus stymied in their efforts to replicate the Buyun township magistrate elections, have turned to other targets, such as: direct elections to township people's congresses (which ratify the selection of magistrates and which the constitution indicates are to be elected), direct elections to community committees in the urban areas (which have been nonthreatening powerless entities), cultivation of inner-party democracy (which the top leadership has endorsed as a means of checking cronyism and increasing transparency), and the development of "elections" for positions in nongovernmental entities and organizations.

Gadsden and Liu offer slightly divergent assessments of the prospects for elections in post-Sixteenth Party Congress China. They variously see reasons for optimism in Buyun's defenders' ability to invoke: the democratic rhetoric offered by Jiang Zemin at the Fifteenth Party Congress; the more strongly democratic proclamations offered by Jiang in his Sixteenth Congress valedictory; Hu Jintao's emphasis on inner-party democracy; the "space" for bottom-up political reform created by the Buyun experiment; the possibly shifting perceptions within the party as it sees incumbents winning elections and fears increasingly violent discontent from a disenfranchised society displeased with the party-state; the possibility that even limited opportunities to cast ballots may instill in Chinese citizens a "voter's mentality"; and a new approach in Chinese foreign policy that seeks international acceptance which the expansion of elections at home might help to secure. On the other hand,

Gadsden cautions, the post-Sixteenth Party Congress leadership has shown little interest in significant departures from the electoral policies and practices of the Jiang era, and the outcomes of elections held since the congress show a continued determination to exclude mavericks from office.

EXTERNAL FACTORS

Part III of this book turns to the external environment and other international factors that confront the post-Sixteenth Party Congress leadership. The reform era and the Jiang Zemin years, in particular, witnessed a profound transformation in China's relations with the outside world, with much of the change being of China's own making. While China's rise as a regional and at least incipient great power and its vastly deepened engagement with an increasingly globalized economy (including WTO membership) count as major accomplishments, these developments also pose significant challenges and difficult choices for new Chinese leaders. So, too, do less felicitous aspects of China's reform-era interaction with other states and the international order. The chapters in Part III take up several important aspects of this complex area.

In his chapter, Jacques deLisle examines the prospects for China's engagement with the WTO in the post-Sixteenth Congress Party era. During this period, China will face much international scrutiny of its implementation of — or failure to implement — its WTO commitments, as China's partners evaluate the first several years of experience with obligations that took effect upon accession, and as the last, and some of the most difficult, phased-in commitments come fully into effect. The same period will provide the first indications of how China will behave in Geneva — that is, as a WTO member participating in the rule-making and adjudicative procedures of the WTO.

DeLisle argues that the principal motivations for China's pursuit of WTO membership during the 1990s derived from expectations that joining the regime would help to: secure and expand access to export markets; expand the foreign presence in China's economy and its contributions to China's growth and development; deepen market-oriented domestic economic and legal reforms in line with the demands imposed by WTO rules and China's accession protocol; and confirm China's status as a normal and emerging great power that was not to be excluded (or warrant exclusion) from one of the most important, powerful, and nearly universal international organizations. He maintains that these legacies of the Jiang-Zhu leadership's successful drive to enter the WTO are likely to continue to shape China's interaction with the WTO well beyond the leadership transition launched by the Sixteenth Party Congress.

Nonetheless, deLisle further argues, several emerging factors suggest that China's interaction with the WTO in the middle 2000s and beyond very well may take new turns, just as China's motives for seeking accession evolved considerably from the 1980s to the 1990s. He points to several factors that suggest that WTO accession and commitments may bring discontents in the post-Sixteenth Party Congress era, including: foreign concern over chronically problematic implementation of some WTO obligations and accession protocol commitments (giving rise to conflicts over how much China has fallen short and whether China has been unable or merely unwilling to do better); domestic backlash against the economically dislocating effects of implementing some WTO commitments (which may become part of the broader social and political problem of discontent among reform's "losers" in China); Chinese resistance to obligation-expanding WTO "mission creep" (which may emerge from efforts from many quarters to expand the reach of the WTO and the definition of "trade-related" to include issues such as the environment and human rights with respect to which the PRC's views are more out of step with the emerging international norms); China's reluctance to engage with Taiwan on a fully equal basis as a fellow WTO member (which will be a difficult issue to avoid, given the density of trade relations between the two and the Taiwanese regime's incentives to use the WTO to assert and confirm Taiwan's high levels of international political, economic, and legal status); and Beijing's likely pursuit of more of a "regime-shaper" role in the WTO and outside the WTO (as befits its image as a great power and major economy, and as a means of asserting China's interests and preferences in areas of international economic activity).

Thomas Liaw's chapter continues the discussion of China's WTO accession and its consequences, with a focus on the financial services sector. Liaw argues that China's commitments in this area pose particularly difficult issues for the post-Sixteenth Party Congress leadership and are likely to be sources of friction with China's fellow WTO members. PRC commitments to put this sector on a more market-based footing and to open it to a much larger foreign presence and foreign competition pose especially grave threats of disruption. Simply, in comparison with many other sectors of the economy, industries such as banking, insurance, and securities in China variously suffer from especially limited prior market-oriented reform, weak financial positions, human capital, internal structures, and management mechanisms, and underdeveloped regulatory oversight. In addition, there is a strikingly imperfect fit between China's goals and its WTO partners' goals in pursuing liberalization and international openness in these sectors. The PRC side primarily seeks foreign capital to strengthen Chinese firms' financial positions, joint-venture partners to provide experience and expertise to Chinese banks, insurance companies or securities firms, and a foreign presence to establish new types of sophisticated entities (particularly in the investment sector). Foreign parties, on the other hand, want maximum access and flexibility in terms of the range of financial services, geographic areas, and legal forms of investment. Finally, Liaw's account suggests, the long prehistory of China's accession to the WTO may have left a residue of resentment, with some in China believing that China was required to promise too much.

Such factors portend post-Sixteenth Party Congress behavior that is likely to include a good deal of foot-dragging in implementation and moves to create new obstacles for foreigners to replace those that fall through the implementation of WTO-related financial sector deregulation.

Alice Ba's contribution to this volume analyzes China's relations with its near abroad, specifically the ASEAN states. Ba assesses these relations through the prism of a key initiative in this area that the post-Fifteenth Party Congress leadership bequeathed to the post-Sixteenth

Party Congress leadership: the plan for an ASEAN-China Free Trade Area (ACFTA) by 2010 (expanding to include all members by 2015). She sees China's turn toward closer ties with Southeast Asia (through the ACFTA and other means) as motivated by economics and, even more strongly, by politics. On the economic side, China's growing economic clout and openness gave it a greater stake in extensive and smoothly functioning economic ties with a region that had shown itself vulnerable to considerable disruption in the Asian financial crisis. An ACFTA or similar arrangement also provided a defensive economic response to the regionalism or "bloc-ism" that China saw as growing in Europe and North America. And China would reap some direct economic benefits from the lowering of trade barriers that would come with an FTA. Because the net economic gains would flow primarily to ASEAN states (which would have expanded access to China's large and growing markets and which would become more attractive to foreign investors seeking to reach those markets), Ba argues that China's principal reasons for pursuing the ACFTA and closer economic ties with Southeast Asia have been political.

Initially, the political appeal to China of an economic turn to ASEAN lay in part in such Asian states' not joining strongly in the chorus of criticism that came from China's trade and investment partners in the West. Later, and especially amid the Asian financial crisis, economic and related policy cooperation with ASEAN gave China opportunities to demonstrate its willingness and ability to function as a regional leader. Similarly and more broadly, China's becoming a principal economic and economic policy partner with ASEAN underscored China's rise as a regional power and helped to make that rise seem more peaceful and wedded to a commitment to interdependence and, thus, less threatening to smaller states that had reasonable fears of domination by their giant neighbor. Ba details Chinese leaders' impressive success in assuaging or overcoming the concerns that the FTA proposal raised among ASEAN members, including worries about the long-term implications of China's rise, the sectoral dislocations that an FTA with China would create in some ASEAN economies, the special risks of disruption that an ACFTA might pose for ASEAN's newest and least developed members, and the suddenness of the proposal itself. Suggesting another measure of the political success of China's initial ACFTA gambit, Ba also points to contrasts with the generally less ambitious, less well-designed, less effective, and largely reactive FTA proposals for the region floated by Japan and the United States.

Chih-cheng Lo turns to an aspect of China's external relations that most would see as less obviously successful and that China regards as not a matter of external relations at all: cross-Strait relations. In contrast to the predictions of volatility or repeated crisis that characterize many accounts of PRC-Taiwan relations, Lo finds strong foundations for continuity in the PRC's Taiwan policy in a period of transition from the Jiang era to the post-Jiang era. In terms of policy substance, he sees a stable commitment to the framework set forth in Jiang's Eight Points, formulated in 1995 to address the problems raised by Lee Teng-hui's securing a visa to the United States, Washington's F-16 sales, and Jiang's own need to enhance his leadership stature. Lo emphasizes the durability of the Jiang era's substantive commitments to the "one China principle," the "one country, two systems" formula, and the preference for peaceful reunification. In his view, even the tensions and conflicts arising during the Chen Shui-bian presidency on Taiwan have brought only tactical adjustments to a stable strategy that the fourth-generation leadership is not likely to be willing and able to change soon.

In terms of policy process, Lo predicts continuity with the Jiang-era patterns of a relatively institutionally fragmented and consultative pattern in which the top leader, the Taiwan Affairs Leading Small Group, the Politburo Standing Committee, the People's Liberation Army, and other interested but smaller and weaker bureaucratic actors all play some role. Such a pattern of policy-making and policy-revising, Lo plausibly suggests, is not conducive to sudden and radical change. Lo adds that the fourth-generation leadership is not likely to depart from this Jiang-era pattern because the rising group of leaders lacks the Mao- and Deng-era founding-generation leaders' personal authority, is generally pragmatic in its orientation, seeks good relations with the United States which would be jeopardized by confrontation over Taiwan, and believes that time is generally on its side in cross-Strait relations.

Moreover, the current and near-future PRC leadership's preoccupation with economic growth and its need to cope with WTO-induced dislocations, discontent-producing socioeconomic inequality, the challenges from further economic reforms, and pressures for political reform all, in Lo's analysis, weigh generally against measures that would produce destabilizing discontinuity in China's Taiwan policy, unless some exogenous crisis forces a response or changes the leadership's calculus.

In this volume's final chapter, Robert Sutter examines the legacy that the post-Sixteenth Party Congress leadership inherits in relations with the region's two great powers, the United States and Japan. Like many analysts and participants, Sutter regards U.S.-PRC relations as exceptionally smooth during the period surrounding China's recent formal leadership transition. But Sutter attributes this largely to the George W. Bush administration's taking a generally firm and tough line in dealing with Beijing, affirming American strength and confidence in the region and globally, expressing a firm commitment to backing Taiwan's autonomous status quo, generally downgrading China's importance relative to Asian democratic allies in American foreign policy, limiting military exchanges with China, using the considerable economic leverage of the United States where necessary and pursuing a strategy of asking and demanding little from China. In Sutter's view, China has acquiesced because it recognizes the limits of its own power in the face of American might and resolve, and because it is preoccupied with such matters as reform, development, stability and leadership succession at home, maintaining an external environment that secures "space" for "comprehensive national development," and facing international pressures and expectations on issues ranging from the WTO to the Olympics.

Sutter attributes relatively satisfactory Sino-Japanese relations to a similar mix of power and policy. Both sides recognize the long-term relative decline of Japan and rise of China as regional powers. But the instability that such a shifting balance might generate is checked by China's accurate perception of the currently strong state of Japan's ties to the sole superpower, and by the pragmatic agendas of Chinese and Japanese leaders who have seen the mutual benefits of a good economic relationship and who have focused primarily on domestic political and economic concerns.

The implications of Sutter's analysis for United States–China–Japan relations in the post-Sixteenth Party Congress period and under the fourth-generation leadership are ambiguous. The factors underpinning Chinese acceptance of the recent status quo are relatively durable, as are some of the elements upholding the ability of the United States to shape the relationships in recent years. But Sutter also attributes much of the current state of United States–China–Japan relations to the far more changeable ingredients of the policies and will of the American leaders and, to a lesser extent, Japanese leaders as well.

Collectively, the contributors to this volume portray a China under Hu Jintao that stands at many crossroads, more than has been the case at any time since the Tiananmen "Incident" and the relaunching of reform in 1989–1992, and perhaps more than has been the case at any time since the dawn of the reform era in the late 1970s. While the transition from Jiang to Hu may, or may not, reflect and advance the transformation of the long poorly institutionalized process of succession, Hu and other post-Jiang leaders face, on every front, difficult choices in grappling with challenges borne of past economic, political, and diplomatic successes, and their sometimes problematic consequences. The chapters that follow offer a guide to the magnitude of the task, the likely or possible approaches the regime might take, and the prospects for success and failure.

Part I

Chapter 1

Political Succession: Changing Guards and Changing Rules

Joseph Fewsmith

The question of whether political succession — changing guards — promotes institutionalization — changing rules — is an important one. More precisely, one should speak of the "reinstitutionalization" of China, that is, what one is talking about is the destruction of one form of institution — the Leninist party and the state structures associated with it vis-à-vis the creation of another form of authority — bureaucratic authority embedded in a market economy. In terms of those who staff party and government structures, this is a transformation from cadres, whose job is to mobilize people, to functionaries, whose job is to administer society. In Weberian terminology, it is a transformation from charismatic authority to legal-rational authority (which differs from the routinization of charisma).

Although the central question that is to be dealt with in this chapter is the impact of political succession, that factor is clearly embedded in other factors, many of which have been operating throughout the reform period. Thus, it will be helpful to begin by enumerating, but not exhaustively discussing, the trends that appear to have pushed the Chinese system in the direction of institutionalization.

First, in the wake of the Cultural Revolution, there was a very strong desire on the part of party elites to restore party norms. It can be objected that the Chinese Communist Party (CCP) violated whatever norms it had tried to establish throughout its history, but many party veterans shared a belief that there was a core of norms governing personal behavior, party procedures, and party-society relations. There was a renewed stress in the early reform period on the CCP as an *organization* governed by procedures in which the exercise of authority would not be so arbitrary. This was reflected in the party's adoption of the "Guiding Principles for Political Life Within the Party" in 1980.[1] Clearly, there was a tension between personal authority, which concentrated power in the hands of party secretaries at various levels, and organizational procedures, which called for party committees to discuss policy collectively. This tension has by no means disappeared, though party procedures appear to be somewhat more consultative these days.

Second, there was a discussion opened on the relationship between the party and the legal system. The 1982 constitution called for "all political parties" to "take the constitution as the basic norm of conduct."[2] This declaration, even if honored mostly in the breach, nevertheless marked a conscious break with Mao's defiant assertion that he was "a monk holding an umbrella," unrestrained by law or

---

[1] "Guanyu dangnei zhengzhi shenghuo de ruogan zhuze" [Guiding principles for political life within the party], in Zhonggong zhongyang wenxian yanjiushi, ed., *shiyiju sanzhongquanhui yilai zhongyao wenxian xuuandu* [Selected readings in important documents since the third plenary session of the eleventh central committee], 2 vols., (Beijing: Renmin chubanshe, 1987), vol. 1, 163–184.

[2] "Xuyan" [Preamble] to *Zhonghua renmin gongheguo xianfa* [Constitution of the People's Republic of China], in *Shi'er dayilai zhongyao wenxian xuanbian* [Important documents since the Twelfth Party Congress], 3 vols., ed. Zhonggong zhongyang wenxian yanjiushi (Beijing: Renmin chubanshe, 1986), vol. 1, 219.

heaven.³ The Sixteenth Party Congress in November 2002 strengthened this admonition, saying, "We must operate strictly in accordance with the law. No organizations or individuals are allowed to have the privilege of overstepping the Constitution and other laws."⁴ For his first public appearance following the Sixteenth Party Congress, Hu Jintao, the new general secretary of the CCP, chose the twentieth anniversary of the promulgation of the 1982 constitution, emphasizing how that document has promoted socialist democracy, law, and human rights.⁵

Third, there was a tension over the basis for making party policy. As an exclusive political party based on a solipsistic claim to truth, the CCP traditionally did not admit (at least openly) considerations other than Marxist-Leninist doctrine to influence its decision-making. But in the wake of the Cultural Revolution, there was a clear recognition that there were "truths" in the world that were not encompassed by Marxism-Leninism as traditionally understood. There were "objective" economic "laws" that, if violated, would exact a cost on the party and the nation.⁶ Ambiguity was reintroduced through the argument that Marxism is a methodology, not a dogma, so Marxism could grow and develop as it came to understand these "objective" truths and thus incorporate them into

---

³ Tang Tsou, "Reflections on the Formation and Foundations of the Communist Party-State," in *The Cultural Revolution and Post-Mao Reforms,* ed. Tang Tsou (Chicago: University of Chicago Press, 1986), 313–315.

⁴ All citations from Jiang's work report are from Jiang Zemin, "Quanmian jianshe xiaokang shehui, kaichuang Zhongguo tese shehui zhuyi shiye xinjumian" [Comprehensively build a comparatively well-off society, open up a new phase in socialism with Chinese characteristics], http://news.xinhuanet.com/newscenter/2002-11/17/content_632239.htm.

⁵ Xinhua, "Speech by Hu Jintao at Beijing Gathering of People of Various Circles on 4 December to Mark the 20th Anniversary of the Promulation of the PRC Constitution," trans. Foreign Broadcast Information Service (FBIS), December 4, 2002.

⁶ The most authoritative statement of this position was Hu Qiaomu, "Act in Accordance with Economic Laws, Step Up the Four Modernizations," Xinhua, October 5, 1987, trans. FBIS, *China Daily Report,* October 11, 1978, pp. E1–22.

Marxism-Leninism.⁷ However, the "Marxism as methodology" argument introduced two other tensions. First, "reformers" (those seeking to "develop" Marxism) parted ways from more orthodox upholders of the Marxist tradition, thus introducing tensions between "reformers" and "conservatives" into the party. Second, the Marxism as methodology argument no doubt slowed the absorption of Western economic understandings into China by suggesting that they could not be right until they were properly explained in Marxist-Leninist terms. Thus, it was not until Deng Xiaoping's 1992 trip to the south that arguments about markets and plans being characteristics of capitalist and socialist societies, respectively, were finally squelched, if in fact they were fully muted. One hears echoes of this debate in the argument about whether private entrepreneurs can become members of the CCP. One also wonders whether contemporary arguments about the standing of neoliberal economics and globalization are not, at least in part, echoes of these earlier arguments. In any event, the argument would be that, on the one hand, the admission that there were "objective truths" "out there" paved the way for incremental reform and institutionalization, while, on the other hand, the need to reinterpret such "truths" in Marxist-Leninist terms stretched this process out and even today inhibits institutionalization of the system.

Fourth, almost from the beginning of the Dengist period there was an effort to rejuvenate the body of party cadres. This was in part because the group of veteran cadres who returned to power following the Cultural Revolution really was aged (like Deng himself who was seventy-three in 1978) and lacked the physical vigor needed to rule. It was also because many in that veteran cadre cohort were considerably more conservative than Deng Xiaoping

---

⁷ An early statement of this position was Hu Yaobang's speech at the centennial anniversary of Marx's death. See Hu Yaobang, "The Radiance of the Great Truth of Marxism Lights Our Way Forward," Xinhua, March 13, 1983, trans. FBIS, April 15, 1983, pp. K1–15. With the Sixteenth Party Congress' admonition to "keep pace with the times" (*yushi jujin*), this interpretation of Marxism as methodology rather than dogma has become orthodoxy.

and did not share his vision of marketization and reform. And it was also because Deng wanted a younger and more professionally competent group of cadres to replace the veteran revolutionaries. In selecting younger cadres, educational criteria were given great weight in part because these were relatively apolitical criteria upon which people could agree. Technocrats had an advantage in this competition largely because their backgrounds were apolitical. People from different groups could agree on technocrats because they had no obvious political leanings.

Thus, generational succession became a part of reform and institutionalization. By the early 1990s, revolutionaries had been replaced by technocrats.[8] Part of this process of generational succession was the gradual institutionalization of retirement norms. Retirement norms are universal features of bureaucratic systems, and the recruitment of younger, better educated, and more professionally competent people began to establish professional bureaucratic norms.[9] Thus, there were the beginnings of a civil service reform, though those hopes were snuffed out, at least temporarily, by the reversal of Zhao Ziyang's reforms in the wake of the Tiananmen crackdown in 1989.

Fifth, there was the changing relationship between the party and the economy. The story of China's economy "growing out of the plan" is too well-known to be repeated here;[10] what needs to be emphasized is that, as the market orientation has taken hold, there has been an effort (by no means fully implemented) to develop secondary markets, standardize laws, implement accountancy regulations, and free

---

[8] Hung Yong Lee, *From Revolutionary Cadres to Party Technocrats in Socialist China* (Berkeley, CA: University of California Press, 1991), and Cheng Li, *China's Leaders: The New Generation* (Lanham, MD: Roman and Littlefield, 2001). Whether China's new leaders should be considered technocrats is problematic. Many can be considered technocrats, but most, even if their education was technical, quickly transferred to party work and had little to do with their original technical fields.

[9] Melanie Manion, *Retirement of Revolutionaries in China* (Princeton, NJ: Princeton University Press, 1993).

[10] Barry Naughton, *Growing Out of the Plan: Chinese Economic Reform, 1978–1993* (Cambridge, UK: Cambridge University Press, 1995).

enterprises from government control. As price competitiveness has increased, opportunities to collect rents have been reduced. In and of themselves, such trends would support and, to a certain extent demand, increased institutionalization.

Finally, there is globalization, in general, and the WTO, in particular. The degree to which globalization brings about institutionalization is hotly debated, but certainly many proponents of China's accession to the WTO believe that it is an important factor. Globalization, particularly the rules of the WTO, will force enormous changes in Chinese governance because the WTO demands transparency and an end to government subsidies in most instances. Most of all, because globalization enlarges the scope of competition, various areas in China will be forced to compete with each other (and with cities in other countries) to create the best investment environment. Those areas in which there is less government interference in business, less corruption, and more service provided to business will do better. Globalization also means a competition to recruit and retain the best people, precisely those who are most mobile. So those areas that make life more comfortable for skilled personnel will do better over the long run — and that generally means the government is becoming more responsive to the demands of the emerging middle class.[11]

Although these and no doubt other factors facilitate and, to some extent, propel institutionalization, or reinstitutionalization, they do not appear to be enough, in and of themselves, to bring about legal-rational authority embedded in a market economy. In part, this is because these changes are partial. A partially reformed economic system in a dubious legal environment has spurred the money-power nexus described so well by He Qinglian in her *Pitfalls of Modernization*.[12]

---

[11] Chen Qingtai, "Jingji quanqiuhua xia de zhengfu gaige" [Reform of the government under economic globalization], *Neibu canyue* [Internal reference], no. 10 (March 15, 2002): 2–6.

[12] He Qinglian, *Xiandaihua de xianjing: Dangdai Zhongguo de jingji shehui wenti* [The pitfalls of modernization: The economic and social problems of contemporary China] (Beijing: Jinri Zhongguo chubanshe, 1998).

Mostly, however, the fact that the reinstitutionalization of the system is only partial stems from the continuing role of the party. The party inhibits and distorts the creation of institutions because the party remains more important than the state (so there cannot be real civil service reform), because the party remains more important than the law (so the constitution and other laws remain goals more than realities), and because the party, by granting power to its cadres, prevents the economy from becoming fully independent. Moreover, reforms have corroded traditional norms within the party without inhibiting the abuse of power. As the CCP comes more to resemble Tammany Hall and less the Leninist party of Mao, corruption becomes not so much a by-product of the operation of the party as essential to its functioning. And corruption is anathema to institutionalization.

Listing these dysfunctionalities makes the picture look bleaker than it is. The bureaucracy has clearly become better, as better educated and more professional cadres have been promoted to positions of responsibility. The economy, while cultivating the support of cadres (the cost of doing business), has managed to do quite well. Further, the legal system has begun to play a positive role, at least in some areas of the economy and society.[13] And even the degeneration of the party has a bright side — the social protests that it unintentionally sets off have started the party on a course of reform that *might* reduce the worst abuses.

One element of party rule that is important to consider in its own right is that of political succession, and it is to that factor that this chapter now turns.

POLITICAL SUCCESSION

Political succession might be divided into two large topics, that of generational succession and that of political succession at the

---

[13] Stanley Lubman, *Bird in a Cage: Legal Reform in China after Mao* (Stanford, CA: Stanford University Press, 1999), and Randall Peerenboom, *China's Long March toward Rule of Law* (Cambridge, UK: Cambridge University Press, 2002).

highest reaches of power. Generational change, of course, is a product of the decisions to rejuvenate the cadre force and to enforce retirement ages. Each generation brings a different experience based on its formative experiences and educational background. In the case of China, the major split was between the revolutionary generation (which included both Mao and Deng) and the postrevolutionary generation (headed by Jiang Zemin), though there are obviously differences with each generation. The revolutionary generation was distinguished, among other things, by an extraordinary self-confidence. Mao launched the country into the Great Leap Forward and Cultural Revolution, apparently without concern that he might unleash forces he could not control. Similarly, Deng was bold enough to launch dramatic economic reforms, without fearing that he could not deal with the consequences.

The generational experiences of Jiang Zemin and Li Peng were quite different from those of the revolutionary generation. Rather than engage in heroic action in the course of founding a new state, they and others of their generation had to climb the bureaucratic ladder, rung-by-rung. Their careers advanced because of their caution, not their boldness. It is not surprising that policy over the past decade, though not without its share of success, has been guided by a more cautious policy-making style (Zhu Rongji is a bit of an exception here!).

The generation of Hu Jintao and Wen Jiabao is marked by somewhat different characteristics. First, this is the first generation to rise to the top rungs of political power without any personal memory of pre-1949 China. Second, these leaders have traveled very little outside of China; they were too young to study in the Soviet Union and too old to study in the West. Third, their careers were delayed by the Cultural Revolution (those, like Hu and Wen, who were graduated from college before the Cultural Revolution, basically stood to one side while that event coursed through the body politic; those who are younger members of this "fourth generation" were Red Guards and gained in political sophistication but also in ideological disillusionment). Fourth, their careers are associated with promoting economic reform, and they no doubt have drawn lessons from the traumatic events of 1989, though it may be some time until we are sure of precisely what those lessons were.[14]

These generational characteristics can and do influence the exercise of political power, though how and to what extent are difficult to pin down. Leaders such as Hu Jintao and Wen Jiabao — technocrats who had their careers delayed by the Cultural Revolution and then rose because of their administrative skills, are likely to be cautious about political reform, fearing that it may unleash forces that they are unable to control — but they are also likely to be rather open-minded regarding policy options. They are, after all, technocrats and they seek solutions that "work." But both seem to be "systems builders" — people who are trying to systematize the system *within* the confines of the basic structures of the party and state (see below). Interestingly, although the top leadership of the CCP is now officially in the hands of technocrats such as Hu Jintao and Wen Jiabao, they are joined by others of their own generation who, while also technocrats, have nevertheless had substantially different experiences. Those born after 1948 (in other words eighteen-years-old at the start of the Cultural Revolution) are likely to have had substantial involvement in the Cultural Revolution. However, this political experience probably makes them, like the elder members of their own generation, abhor the ideological struggles and social chaos of the Cultural Revolution. Their organizational experience in "linking up" (*chuan lian*) to share their "revolutionary experiences" is apt to make them bolder and more self-confident, somewhat like the revolutionary generation (though by no means to that extent). This could bring about an interesting combination of caution and risk-taking.

Nevertheless, another characteristic of the new leadership is that their experience and contacts are limited. Although they have generally had wider career experience than the "third generation" of leaders, they, too, have had to climb the career ladder step-by-step,

---

[14] Joseph Fewsmith, "Generational Transition in China," *Washington Quarterly* 25, no. 4 (Autumn 2002): 23–35.

generally within a single *xitong* (system). This has limited their exposure to other xitong and the personal contacts that they would have developed if they had participated in the work of other bureaucracies. This limitation is particularly true with respect to the military.[15] The new leadership has not served in the military, though some, such as Zeng Qinghong, appear to have widespread connections with the military by virtue of their education and elite family backgrounds.

Elite succession creates a dynamic that is related to generational succession but also distinct from it. The fundamental problem, of course, is that there is no legitimate way to transfer power from one leader to another. Mao, it seemed, had the authority to pass his power on, but his last-minute efforts to give authority to Hua Guofeng were overturned by the party and by Deng Xiaoping, who criticized such a personal bequest of power as a "feudal" practice.[16] That criticism notwithstanding, it appears that Deng tried to pass on power not only to Jiang Zemin (who may not have been his first choice) but also to Hu Jintao, thus attempting to institutionalize a new pattern of leadership succession. The first point that should be made is that, although there have been clear attempts by political leaders to name their successors, the party has not been altogether comfortable with that practice and has increasingly tried to institutionalize political succession. The second point is that weak institutions and the continuation of traditional political culture have so far limited efforts to institutionalize leadership succession.

The effort to institutionalize political succession at the highest level grows out of the increasing institutionalization of political transfers at lower levels. Efforts to rejuvenate the cadre force in the 1980s led to the gradual acceptance of retirement ages for cadres at the ministerial level and below. Moreover, the membership of the Central Committee has been increasingly composed of the occupants of

---

[15] David Shambaugh, *Modernizing China's Military: Problems, Progress, and Prospects* (Berkeley, CA: University of California Press, 2003).

[16] Deng made this accusation in 1980. See "Answers to Italian Jouranlist Oriana Fallaci," http://english.peopledaily.com.cn/dengxp/vol2/text/b1470.html.

specific positions (i.e., all provincial party secretaries and governors are now named to the Central Committee, approximately 22 percent of the seats are reserved for the military, and so forth). This, of course, does not mean that promotion to those positions cannot be manipulated by personal clientalism and other factors, but at least it seems to regularize and limit political competition to some extent.

However, efforts to institutionalize political procedures above the Central Committee level, particularly at the Politburo and Central Military Commission (CMC) level, have been notably less successful. The CMC, the source of ultimate power in the system, has been highly personalized. Even when Deng Xiaoping tried to spread political benefits around to different groups within the party, the CMC was nevertheless packed by veterans of the Second Field Army (in which Deng served as political commissar). When Jiang Zemin took over, he assiduously cultivated support within the military, handpicking those to be promoted to the highest level. Although observers of the military note that strong professional norms have gained ground in the military in recent years, the civilian party leadership still seems unable to ignore this important political resource.

Nevertheless, succession has increased efforts to define political rules at the highest level of the political system. For instance, when Jiang Zemin wanted to oust Qiao Shi from the leadership at the Fifteenth Party Congress in 1997, he set the retirement age at seventy. Jiang himself, then seventy-one, was excused from following this rule because he was the "core" leader. One is no doubt correct to view such political maneuvers in a cynical light, but setting a rule, which may become institutionalized, is certainly better than exercising arbitrary power, or accusing one's political opponent of being a "capitalist roader" or of some other such political error.

What are the incentives for a political leader such as Jiang Zemin to endorse a general rule — retirement age — in order to oust a rival such as Qiao Shi rather than to simply remove him through the exercise of raw power? This has to do with both succession and the overall evolution of the political system. As a leader of the postrevolutionary generation, it would have been difficult for Jiang to claim the right to purge a political rival on the basis of ideology. This speaks not only to the fading of ideology over time but also to the inability of successor generations to embody the ideological legitimacy of the revolutionary generation. Then, too, there was the specific political atmosphere of the post-Tiananmen period. Ironically, the ideological excess of the immediate post-Tiananmen period created an atmosphere in which expression of ideology was less legitimate; the regime was able to rebuild legitimacy precisely because it moved away from the rhetoric of Marxism-Leninism. By the mid-1990s, it would have been unacceptable for Jiang openly to criticize Qiao for committing a "political" error, so a nonpolitical "crime" (age) was chosen.

In other words, given that their own backgrounds limit their experience in different areas of party work and that the party structure of which they are now in charge has degenerated in terms of ideological conviction and organizational discipline, new leaders who come to power through succession must find different levers through which to exercise control. One possibility is to increase the role of personal connections (by promoting friends and protégés), a possibility that would increase the role of personal (as opposed to ideational) factionalism in the party. Another is to increase the role of institutions. Just as generational succession created incentives to institutionalize retirement norms and at least begin efforts to create a professional civil service, leaders such as Jiang have an incentive to establish rules in order to deal with political rivals. It appears that, indeed, there are incentives both to rely on personal factionalism and to create institutional norms, and one of the very real problems that the CCP faces today is the tension between these conflicting imperatives.

The example of Jiang's ouster of Qiao Shi (other examples could be cited) nevertheless suggests an instrumental use of rules and institutions, and the results of the Sixteenth Party Congress very much reflect the ongoing tension between the need to legitimize power through general rules and institutions and the realities that such norms are not strong enough (at least yet) to genuinely channel the conduct of politics.

The political dynamic over the year or two preceding the congress suggested that Jiang Zemin very much hoped to emulate Deng Xiaoping's model of formally retiring but exercising ultimate authority from "behind the screen." Thus, he trumpeted his theory of the "Three Represents" (which were enshrined in the party constitution at the Sixteenth Party Congress) and built something of a personality cult around himself. It was frequently argued that "Jiang Zemin is no Deng Xiaoping," meaning that his personal prestige was never on a par with that of his predecessor, but the results of the congress suggested that Jiang, in fact, was able to maintain considerable personal authority. First, he continued to head the party CMC (and was elected to head the state CMC at the National People's Congress [NPC] the following spring). Second, he expanded the size of the Politburo Standing Committee to accommodate two additional protégés, and third, the Politburo Standing Committee was packed with five or six of Jiang's closest associates (depending on who is doing the counting). Thus, even while Jiang presided over a congress that called for the "standardization, institutionalization, and the procedualization" (*guifanhua, zhiduhua, chengxuhua*) of the system, his desire to maintain his own authority — and perhaps the broader requirements of the political system — led him to engage in the politics of personalism.[17]

THE POLITICAL REPORT OF THE SIXTEENTH PARTY CONGRESS

The same tension between institutionalization of the political system and the continued exercise of noninstitutional, or at least nonlegal-rational forms of political power was reflected in the political report that Jiang Zemin delivered to the congress. If the words of Jiang Zemin's political report can be taken at face value, the political leadership was trying to implement the call in Jiang's July 1, 2001 speech

---

[17] Joseph Fewsmith, "The Sixteenth National Party Congress: The Succession that Didn't Happen," *China Quarterly*, no. 173 (March 2003): 1–16.

to transform the CCP from a revolutionary party into a ruling party. That meant institutionalizing party affairs, regularizing the party's relationship with the state, placing the operations of the party within the scope of the law, and regularizing the party's relations with society by recruiting (co-opting) "advanced elements" from social sectors that had emerged in the course of reform (i.e., private entrepreneurs).

Indeed, a significant part of the work report was written as if the drafters had had Max Weber's work on bureaucracy at hand. It demanded:[18]

- "Party members and cadres, especially leading cadres, must be models in abiding by the constitution and law." Indeed, the report called, as others have in the past, for exercizing the CCP's authority through the law. In this regard, the report called for improving the judicial system so that it would be "impartial in enforcing the law."
- Changing the functions and behavior of government so that they would be characterized by "standardized behavior, coordinated operations, fairness, transparency, honesty, and high efficiency."
- Improving the cadre and personnel system so that it would become "scientific, democratic, and institutionalized." In this regard, Jiang called for expanding "the rights of party members and the masses to know, participate in, select, and supervise" the selection of cadres.
- Building a mechanism for the exercise of power, marked by a reasonable structure, scientific distribution, rigorous procedure, and effective restraints. In this regard, the political report, which hardly discussed political reform, nevertheless called for the building of "socialist political civilization," which many take as a code word for political reform. In discussing socialist political civilization, Jiang called for "strengthening supervision over power in decision making, execution, and other areas."

---

[18] Jiang Zemin, "Quanmian jianshe xiaokang shehui, kaichuang Zhongguo tese shehui zhuyi shiye xinjumian."

Such prescriptions seem to indicate recognition of the need to create a better, more efficient bureaucracy that is subject to effective constraints and "public" supervision. This is not a new recognition in China but rather it follows the line of thinking of numerous policy documents over the past two decades that push in the same direction. Nevertheless, one might argue that the social problems facing China and the imperatives of succession politics are imparting a new urgency to this bureaucratic rationalization.

Nevertheless, just as there are forces at the highest political level that push back against efforts to institutionalize the political system, there are also political forces that slow and distort this effort to reinstitutionalize administrative authority. The single biggest problem is easily stated: The logic of legal-rational authority is quite different from the logic of Leninist systems, and the CCP resists giving up its prerogatives as the pervasive political organization, penetrating as many arenas of society as possible. Granted, the enormous changes in Chinese life over the last two decades, particularly the erosion of the *danwei* (work unit) and *hukou* (household registration) systems have made this more difficult, but the party has not given up the struggle. Indeed, there is at least as much attention being paid to party building these days as in years past.

The political report to the Sixteenth Party Congress, not unexpectedly, placed a great deal of emphasis on the "Three Represents" in its section on party building, and certainly the emphasis on ideology in party building is not new. The "Three Represents" suggests that the nature of the party may change (as liberals hope and conservatives fear) as private entrepreneurs are recruited into the party (though the number of entrepreneurs who have joined the party is actually quite small). Potentially, the biggest changes may derive from changes in the way the party operates. If "inner-party democracy" were genuinely expanded so that the party "fully reflect[ed] the will of party members and organizations" that would be a fundamental change in the CCP's "democratic centralism," and for that reason is not likely to happen. Indeed, early experiments are not altogether encouraging. Change may also come with establishing party delegates as some sort of permanent organ, rather than convening solely for quinquennial party congresses. Such changes, likely to come slowly if at all, are intended to make the party more effective, not to change its role in Chinese life.

Indeed, perhaps the most surprising aspect of the CCP's effort to remake itself as a "ruling" party rather than as a "revolutionary" party is its refusal to withdraw from various areas of social life. It seems plausible that, if the CCP really desired to act as a "ruling" party and to govern the country through law and a legal-rational bureaucracy, it would begin to withdraw from certain areas of Chinese life, or at least not push into those areas that have emerged in recent years outside of party control. This applies first and foremost to the private economy. If the party really wanted to exercise political control as a ruling party, it would move away from the traditional model of controlling society through the penetration of danwei and exercise control geographically and through the use of law. That is to say, a form of political power that would be much more compatible with legal-rational authority would be to adopt consciously a model that would accept the nonexistence of CCP party branches in private enterprises, believing that, as long as such enterprises obeyed the law, they should be left alone and otherwise unsupervised. Such a model would give greater play to the role of law, impartial administration, and economic efficiency.

It is possible that such a model may yet emerge; the CCP has not been notably successful in penetrating private enterprises, and where it is successful, it seems to play a very nontraditional role (this is particularly true if the enterprise head is the secretary of the party branch, making the party branch a means of enforcing worker discipline within the enterprise). But clearly the party hopes to maintain its traditional control through the danwei system; thus, in his report to the Sixteenth Party Congress, Jiang called for "strengthen[ing] party-building in nonpublic enterprises," as he had done before.

One is also confronted by the anomalous situation of the CCP carrying out yet another rectification campaign, even as the party stresses the role of law. In January 2005, the CCP launched a campaign to "uphold the advanced nature of Chinese Communist Party

Members."[19] This campaign is the third such rectification campaign launched since the start of the reform era. Although rectification campaigns in the contemporary period lack the fury of campaigns in the Maoist period, they still use the old methods of studying documents, writing expositions on one's thoughts, and criticism and self-criticism in an effort to enhance ideological control and reinforce party organization and authority. They also seem intimately related to the consolidation of leadership control and political interpretations. Thus, the first rectification campaign was launched in 1983 and was connected with the consolidation of the Dengist "line" of "building socialism with Chinese characteristics," while the second campaign (known as the "Three Stresses" (*sanjiang*) was launched in 1998 and consolidated the authority of Jiang Zemin. It seems no coincidence that two years after Hu Jintao became general secretary of the party (and three months after Jiang Zemin stepped down as head of the powerful Central Military Commission) that this latest campaign was launched (though party documents say that it was approved by the Sixteenth Party Congress). Campaigns are obviously a legacy of the party's revolutionary years and their continued existence, no matter how attenuated by comparison with earlier campaigns, suggests that a logic other than institutionalization remains at work.

One could make the same argument regarding China's villages. Villages in China's administrative system are formally "self-governing." It is on that basis that they have been allowed to have elections over the past decade for village heads, but not, generally speaking, for party secretaries. If the party wants to continue to exercise control as a ruling party, it could either allow direct elections of party secretaries at the village level (something that has happened in a few places) or withdraw to the township level (or perhaps even the county level, since there has been extensive discussion about abolishing or curtailing the role of the township level of government). But the desire to penetrate society remains strong, and Jiang Zemin called again in his

---

[19] Joseph Fewsmith, "CCP Launches Campaign to Maintain Advanced Nature of Party Members," *China Leadership Monitor*, no. 13 (Winter 2004), www.chinaleadershipmonitor.org.

report to the party congress to strengthen party organizations at the village level.

The same tendency to move toward the rule of law while not giving up the traditional prerogatives of party control can be seen in the "Religious Affairs Regulations" that went into effect on March 1, 2005. Although the regulations place the management of religious activities on a legal basis (recognizing the "legitimate" rights of worshippers), authoritative commentary on the regulations states explicitly that the new regulations "will not weaken party leadership over religious work." On the contrary, the commentary continues, the regulations are "an important guarantee for, and a way of, strengthening and improving leadership over religious work in the new situation."[20]

What should we make of the outwardly smooth transition in power from Jiang Zemin to Hu Jintao? As noted above, Jiang Zemin enlarged the Standing Committee of the Politburo, packed it with his supporters, and retained chairmanship of the CMC — seemingly leaving Hu Jintao weak and potentially vulnerable. However, Jiang Zemin stepped down from the military commission in September 2004. Does this indicate that institutions are stronger than apparent from the outside and the political system can now be properly described as "institutionalized"?[21]

This is a question that needs to be explored as more details of the transition become known. There were considerable public indications of tension between Jiang Zemin and Hu Jintao in the period after Hu succeeded as general secretary.[22] The decision for Jiang

---

[20] "Religious Affairs Regulations," Xinhua, December 8, 2004, trans. FBIS, CPP20041220000193, and Wang Zuoan (deputy director of the State Bureau of Religious Affairs), "Promote Management of Religious Affairs According to Law and Uphold Party Leadership over Religious Work," *Zhongguo Zongjiao*, October 26, 2004, trans. FBIS, CPP20041122000250.

[21] Zhiyue Bo, "Political Succession and Elite Politics in Twenty-First Century China: Toward a Perspective of Power Balancing," unpublished manuscript.

[22] Joseph Fewsmith, "China's New Leadership: A One-Year Assessment," *Orbis* 48, no. 2 (Spring 2004): 204–216.

Zemin to retire as head of the military commission appears to have been reached rather suddenly in August 2004, perhaps indicating that his decision was not altogether voluntary. If this scenario is borne out, then the question is: How did Hu Jintao acquire sufficient power to pressure his predecessor to leave office? Institutionalization is no doubt part of the answer — incumbency confers leverage in all political systems, and Hu Jintao appears to have been able to use the institutional levers of power to his advantage in the two years between becoming general secretary and Jiang Zemin's leaving his last post. But institutionalization does not appear to be the complete answer. As with other senior leaders in China, Hu Jintao has enjoyed considerable informal power, conferred by his relations with retired party leaders and those currently serving at various party and governmental levels. He also had access to information on the business activities of various leaders and their families. Some of this information might have reflected poorly on either Jiang Zemin or some of his close associates. Whether Hu used such resources remains speculative, but the possibility suggests that institutionalization is not the only possible explanation for the transfer of power.

CONCLUSION

Over the past two decades, there have been many forces that have been tempering the CCP's Leninist approach to political control and fostering a more "normal" relationship between state and society; mobilization has been giving way to administration. Yet, before we assume that political reform can occur in a seamless, incremental fashion, we have to take into account those forces that push in the opposite direction, that oppose the institutionalization of political life. Indeed, we need to consider that such forces might even increase at the same time that there are pressures pushing in the direction of institutionalization. As the mobilizational aspects of the CCP's Leninist past are reduced, so, too, is party discipline; and with the relaxation of party discipline, there are new incentives and opportunities to find other ways of controlling political power. Clientalism is one of them. Thus, whereas a model of incremental change would posit the gradual replacement of Leninist political structures with bureaucratic rationality, it seems that political actors try to develop informal political strategies to hold together the form of Leninism and resist the pressures for bureaucratic rationality.

Political succession is one area in which we see conflicting imperatives generating different responses to the problem of political control. On the one hand, it creates incentives — legitimacy for the new leader, means for ameliorating political conflict, and better control over the administrative machinery of the state — to push for stronger political and bureaucratic institutions. On the other hand, because the political system is not yet well institutionalized, succession creates anxieties for rulers. Rulers in such situations often resort to nonbureaucratic means to enhance leverage. Thus, Hu Jintao has employed ideological agenda-setting, a rectification campaign, and the promotion of protégés to enhance his power. Such efforts, however, erode the very institutionalization that succession seems to promote and that the political system very much needs.

The Sixteenth Party Congress appears to be the product of such tensions. The articulation of demands to create strong administrative institutions and the succession of the designated successor, Hu Jintao, suggest a strengthening of institutional norms, while the extraordinary lengths Jiang Zemin went to preserve his influence suggests the continued power of informal, personalistic norms. The fact that Jiang Zemin retired from the CMC two years after the Party Congress suggests that Hu Jintao was able to combine institutional resources with enhanced informal influence. The result of the Sixteenth Party Congress and its aftermath indicate both the need to reform political structures so that they can support the increasing institutionalization of the system and the difficulty of doing so.

Chapter 2

Is the Chinese State Apparatus Being Revamped?

Yanzhong Huang

While the rise of administration is "a necessary part of capitalism and capitalist society,"[1] bureaucracy is not unique to capitalist states. The tasks of socialist construction require revolutionary cadres to co-opt technical experts into the ruling elite. However, rejecting the Soviet model in which techniques and cadres prevail, China under Mao for decades suppressed and denied bureaucratic authority. Quite often, it was party-sponsored mass mobilization, rather than the contributions of technical specialists, that played a key part in the policy process.[2]

This situation did not change until after the end of Cultural Revolution. In the post-Mao era, while the principle of the party leadership is still protected from any open challenge, reform seems

---

[1] Theodore Lowi, *The End of Liberalism: The Second Republic of the United States* (New York: W. W. Norton, 1979), 21.
[2] See, for example, David M. Lampton, *The Politics of Medicine in China: The Policy Process, 1949–1977* (Boulder, CO: Westview Press, 1977).

to have generated a more favorable atmosphere for state rebuilding. Deng Xiaoping, himself a victim of noninstitutionalized Cultural Revolution politics, concluded in 1980 that it was not appropriate to overconcentrate power in party committees, for "the party's monist leadership often led to a personalistic leadership."[3] While party-state dualism continued under Deng, the national agenda change (from "politics in command" to "economic development as the focal point") generated pressures to separate political and economic societies,[4] to redefine the role of the state, and to tap the expertise of professional-based bureaucrats. As the party delegated more authority to the government bureaucracy, attempts to integrate a disciplined party, based on a binding ideology, with a bureaucratically-structured governmental apparatus were diluted in the policy process. The political resources were further decentralized with the implementation of fiscal and administrative reforms. While market-oriented economic reform produced alternative sources of power and authority, fiscal and administrative reforms decentralized control over fiscal resources, and, in some cases, devolved supervisory and management control to regional and local oversight. Consequently, it became increasingly difficult to skew the distribution of capabilities in favor of *one* superordinate actor. The reasserted bureaucratic authority, in conjunction with the post-Mao decentralization and the restructured state-society relations, has expanded the space of real politics, which, instead of revolving around inner party struggles, is increasingly

---

[3] Deng Xiaoping, *Deng Xiaoping wenxuan, 1978–1982* [Selected works of Deng Xiaoping, 1978–1982], vol. 2 (Beijing: Renmin chubanshe, 1983), 289.

[4] "Political society" refers to those core institutions by which society constitutes itself politically (e.g., the party committees at each level, the military apparatus, the law-enforcement apparatus), while "economic society" calls attention to "a set of socio-politically crafted and socio-politically accepted norms, institutions, and regulations that mediates between state and market." See Juan J. Linz and Alfred Stepan, *Problems of Democratic Transition and Consolidation: Southern Europe, South America, and Post-Communist Europe* (Baltimore, MD: Johns Hopkins University Press, 1996).

characterized by the interplay of bureaucrats, the local state, and social forces.

Perhaps equally important, there has been growing functional differentiation within the bureaucracy. This began with post-Mao state rebuilding, which led to a rapid growth of the number of departments and personnel within existing "line ministries," the establishment of "stand-alone" administrative capacities by previously latent bureaucratic sectors (such as the State Family Planning Commission), and the creation of new regulatory agencies (such as the National Bureau of Statistics). In addition, state cadres were disaggregated into a business elite, government officials, and employees of nonprofit institutions, with different management methods developed for each sector.[5] The coexistence of the growing functional differentiation and the prevalent diffusion of influential resources in a hierarchically-ordered political realm eroded the patterns of bandwagon politics (in which functional differentiation is low and political power is tightly concentrated in the hands of superior actors) and balance-of-power politics (in which differentiation of functions among the units is generally retarded) that had characterized Chinese politics and policy processes during 1949–1966, and 1966–1978, respectively.[6]

The changing political and institutional landscape has important implications for the quality of China's bureaucracy. As the regime shifted its main task from revolutionary transformation to economic development, a large number of revolutionary cadres who were poorly educated and had little specialized knowledge were replaced by professionally more competent technocrats.[7] Since 1993, civil servants in China, once again, have been selected through open

---

[5] John P. Burns, "The People's Republic of China at 50: National Political Reform," *China Quarterly* 159, no. 1 (September 1999): 588.

[6] Avery Goldstein, *From Bandwagon to Balance-of-Power Politics: Structural Constraints and Politics in China, 1949–1978* (Stanford, CA: Stanford University Press, 1991).

[7] Hong Yung Lee, *From Revolutionary Cadres to Party Technocrats in Socialist China* (Berkeley, CA : University of California Press, 1991).

competitive examinations. This change in the composition and recruitment of cadres has resulted in a shift of the Chinese bureaucracy away from "virtuocracy," which emphasizes an individual's correct political attitudes and heritage, to "meritocracy," where individual ability or achievement counts.[8] Given the reduced use of purges, labeling, and demotions against those who propose ideas that eventually are rejected, bureaucrats now possess a longer time horizon and more focused policy goals. The emphasis on expert opinion, in turn, has given rise to salience of consultancy in policymaking, as evidenced by the establishment of various new policy research organs at different levels, and the frequent use of national surveys and case work carried out by governmental, nongovernmental, and international agencies. Further, China has moved away from gerontocracy by institutionalizing mandatory retirement (which prescribes age requirements for leading officials at both central and local levels). The transition to a younger and more educated cadre corps continued throughout the 1990s, when an increasing number of official positions became subject to open competition. By the end of 2000, 350,000 positions, including 179,000 section-chief (*ke*) or division-chief (*chu*) positions in twenty-nine provincial units were open to competition among 800,000 candidates.[9] As a result, not only did the average age of party-state cadres drop, but also the proportion of college-educated officials rose significantly. By the end of 2001, 54.4 percent of the cadres were college-educated, and 75.9 percent of them were below the age of forty-five.[10]

The dramatic change in the demographics of the cadre corps is only part of the efforts to restructure the state so that it can match the changes in the nature of China's economic system. In the light of continued market-oriented economic reform, fiscal, monetary, and industrial policies have increasingly replaced direct administrative

---

[8] See Susan Shirk, *Competitive Comrades: Career Incentives and Student Strategy in China* (Berkeley and Los Angeles, CA: University of California Press, 1982).

[9] *Xinhua News* (in Chinese), October 10, 2002, http://www.people.com.cn/GB/news/8410/20021010/839239.html.

[10] *Renmi Ribao* [People's Daily], October 9, 2002.

fiat as the government's preferred mode of affecting the economy. In 1994, the government kicked off a major fiscal reform, which demarcated the taxation powers between the central government and the local states. That reform constituted an important measure to establish a modern, genuinely independent, central tax system, and, more importantly, it was a significant step toward beefing up state capacities over the long run. Since the end of the Mao era, China also has made a remarkable effort to reconstruct a legal code and build a system of laws through the National People's Congress. In addition, the reform era features attempts to provide the foundations for the pursuit of a regulatory state through the reestablishment of several regulatory and enforcement agencies that are expected to play vital roles in ensuring market order, fair competition, and sustained economic development.[11]

Post-Mao state rebuilding, therefore, has expanded the scope for "normal politics" in China.[12] This general trend toward "regime institutionalization" seems to have accelerated since the late 1990s. In March 1998, the government launched an ambitious reform of its administrative system. Unlike the previous reform attempts, the new plan focused on redefining the core functions of the state organs and creating a leaner and more efficient state.[13] The changes were poised to continue with the emergence of new leadership from the Chinese Communist Party's Sixteenth Party Congress in November 2002. Premier-to-be Wen Jiabao hinted in January 2003 that administrative reform would be deepened in the forthcoming year in order to build a "fair, transparent, honest, and efficient" government that "behaves rationally and operates coordinately."[14] This seems to

---

[11] See Dali L. Yang, "State Capacity on the Rebound," *Journal of Democracy* 14, no. 1 (January 2003): 43–50.

[12] See Frederick C. Teiwes, "The Paradoxical Post-Mao Transition: From Obeying the Leader to 'Normal Politics,'" *China Journal*, no. 34 (July 1995): 55–94.

[13] Kjeld Erik Brødsgaard, "Institutional Reform and the *Bianzhi* System in China," *China Quarterly* 170 (June 2002): 361.

[14] *Xinhua News*, January 24, 2003, http://www.people.com.cn/GB/shizheng/16/20030124/914171.html.

partially vindicate the claim that reforms will eventually make China's political system "more open, more rational, more responsive, and more accountable."[15]

Given that a modern political system is essentially "bureaucratic" — characterized by "the rule of officials"[16] — one of the most important issues facing the leadership that came to power in 2002 is the "usability" of its bureaucracy. Is China's state apparatus being revamped? To some scholars, the answer is yes. Emphasizing the positive changes in the policy structures, for instance, Dali Yang suggests that,

> The reconstitution of the central state is...not just a rebuilding of the old state that had an iron fist but short and weak fingers. Instead, with the reconstitution, the central state may finally possess elaborately constructed arms, hands, and fingers that could play in coordination to produce good music.[17]

Other scholars are less optimistic. In his analysis of organizational involution and corruption in China, Xiaobo Lu concluded: "Chinese officialdom will more likely remain neotraditional in the near future, nurtured by a 'booty capitalism' — a fragmented but administratively managed market economy."[18]

While the question of whether the Chinese state apparatus is being revamped is ultimately an empirical one, a more complete understanding of China's bureaucracy requires us to examine not only its character traits but also its effectiveness in policy administration. The reason is very simple: reinvigorating public institutions

---

[15] Harry Harding, "The Halting Advance of Pluralism," *Journal of Democracy* 9, no. 1 (January 1998): 17.

[16] Robert D. Putnam, "The Political Attitudes of Senior Civil Servants in Britain, Germany, and Italy," in Matei Dogan, ed., *The Mandarins of Western Europe* (New York: Sage Publications, 1975), 87.

[17] Dali L. Yang, "Economic Transformation and State Rebuilding in China," in *Holding China Together*, ed. Barry Naughton and Dali L. Yang (New York: Cambridge University Press, 2004), 143.

[18] Xiaobo Lu, *Cadres and Corruption: The Organizational Involution of the Chinese Communist Party* (Stanford, CA: Stanford University Press, 2000), 257.

means reigning in entrenched corruption and subjecting state institutions to greater competition, on the one hand, and increasing the performance of state institutions, making the state more responsive to people's needs, on the other.[19] Accordingly, this chapter will contribute to the debate by exploring two interrelated questions inherent in bureaucratic rejuvenation. First, is the Chinese bureaucracy increasingly operating within professional norms? Second, have members of the state apparatus increased their efficiency and enhanced their responsiveness to the people in public policy administration?

CORRUPTION AND POLITICAL PATRONAGE IN CHINA

Is Corruption in Decline?

An ideal typical Weberian bureaucracy is built upon, among other things, two important principles: "separation of person from office" and "promotion on the basis of merit." Indeed, building a modern bureaucracy that operates on rational legal terms is one of the main objectives of China's administrative reform. Official policy requires civil servants to conform to a code of conduct laid down in the Provisional Regulations on Civil Servants (article 6), which includes "execution of public duties in accordance with laws, regulations and policies of the state," and "being fair and honest and working selflessly in the public interest."[20] Needless to say, cronyism, favoritism, and corruption are clear violations of these professional norms.

Despite its existence long before the post-Mao reforms, the market-oriented economic transition has presented new opportunities for corruption, making it "more pervasive, serious, and regime-threatening than in previous decades."[21] Chinese leaders are keenly aware of this problem. Indeed, attempts to rationalize the bureaucracy were initiated in tandem with the economic transition in the

---

[19] World Bank, *World Development Report 1997: The State in a Changing World* (New York: Oxford University Press, 1997), 3.
[20] People's Republic of China, Ministry of Personnel, *Provisional Regulations on Civil Servants*, August 14, 1993, http://www.mop.gov.cn/zcfg/content.asp?id=5.
[21] Lu, *Cadres and Corruption*, 235.

early 1980s. If these administrative reform measures (as well as repeated efforts to tighten controls against corruption) were effective, we should witness a drop in the level of corruption in China.

According to Transnational International, an anticorruption organization which compiles an annual Corruption Perceptions Index (CPI), China scored 3.4 in 2003, compared with 2.16 in 1995 (when the index was first compiled).[22] This seems to suggest that the Chinese bureaucracy is becoming increasingly "clean." Yet, the comparison between 1995 and 2003 should be taken with a grain of salt. The index primarily provides an annual snapshot of the views of business people, with less focus on year-to-year trends. Moreover, year-to-year change of a country's score reflects changes in the sample and methodology in compiling the index. The 2003 index used thirteen surveys, compared with only four in 1995. This makes meaningful comparison difficult because, only on the basis of data from sources that have consistently been used for the index, can one confidently identify actual trends. In fact, the 2003 index has a standard deviation of 1.0 (as opposed to 0.28 in 1995), suggesting a high degree of deviation of opinions among the thirteen polls.

Indeed, more and more evidence seems to suggest that corruption has become intolerable in China, especially since the 1990s. An internal report prepared by the Chinese Academy of Sciences and Tsinghua University studied sixty-six graft cases that involved provincial- or ministerial-level government officials during the reform era. It found that none of the pre-1992 cases involved more than 100,000 *yuan* (U.S. $12,050) in graft; but after 1992, twenty-seven cases did, of which twelve involved more than one million yuan, and four more than ten million yuan.[23] A prominent Chinese

---

[22] CPI is a composite index, drawing on different polls and surveys from independent institutions carried out primarily among business people. It ranges between 0 and 10. Ten indicates an entirely clean country, while zero indicates a country where business transactions are entirely dominated by kickbacks, extortion, and so on. See http://www.transparency.org/cpi.

[23] *21 Century Economic Herald*, September 15, 2003, http://www.nanfangdaily.com.cn/jj/20030915/jd/200309150475.asp (accessed March 9, 2004).

scholar, Hu Angang, estimated the cost of corruption to China's economy in the late 1990s at 13 to 17 percent of the country's GDP.[24] Reckoning that some 80 percent of officials are corrupt, he and another scholar assert that corruption is systematic and increasingly becoming China's "greatest economic blight, its biggest social pollutant and an important political challenge."[25] The growing difficulties in containing corruption are recognized by a World Bank Institute report, which suggests that the percentage of countries worldwide that rate below China in controlling corruption dropped from 58.7 in 1996 to 42.3 in 2002.[26] A recent public opinion survey on the performance of government officials shows that only 19.6 percent of rural residents and 26.3 percent of urban residents believe their local leader is not corrupt.[27]

In comparison with other East Asian countries, the cancer of corruption embeds itself deeper in China's body politic. In the transition to a market economy, China suffers from what Max Weber called "political capitalism," meaning the accumulation of wealth through political power rather than by means of economic enterprise and open competition. Although the government has been ordered by Beijing to cast away its business interests, bureaucrats at almost every level — from central government ministries to local authorities — can assure themselves a privileged position in the

---

[24] Hu Angang, "Fubai yu fazhan" [Corruption and development], in *Zhongguo: Tiaozhan fubai* [China: Fighting against corruption], ed. Hu Angang (Hangzhou: Zhejiang renmin chubanshe, 2001), 60.

[25] James Kynge, "China's Future: Cancer of Corruption Spreads throughout Country," *Financial Times*, November 1, 2002.

[26] Daniel Kaufman, Aart Kraay, and Massimo Mastruzzi, "Governance Matters III: Governance Indicators for 1996–2002," *World Bank Policy Research Working Paper 3106*, 2003, http://www.worldbank.org/wbi/governance/pubs/govmatters3.html (accessed March 9, 2004).

[27] The survey was carried out by Beijing-based Horizon Research, a private market research company. It polled 5,613 urban and rural residents, asking them what they thought of their local mayor or county leader. For more information, see http://www.horizonkey.com/ (accessed March 9, 2004).

emerging market economy by being the owners of key corporations and/or the regulators of market competition. Given the relatively low salary level of bureaucrats and the absence of effective rules and restraints to keep arbitrary state action in check, an environment exists that facilitates government officials' exercising their political power for private gain.[28] To some extent, this problem may have been intensified in recent years by an ill-defined property rights system, growing social discontent, and the party's "dual crises of identity and legitimacy."[29] Realizing that the game may end soon, corrupt officials have rushed to "steal the state" and transfer their ill-gotten gains abroad. Official sources revealed that capital flight amounted to 53 billion dollars between 1997 and 1999; the amount increased to 139 billion between 2000 and 2001.[30] In October 2001, managers of a Bank of China branch in Guangdong Province were found to have stolen more than U.S.$483 million.[31] All the suspects fled China with their loot. This is just the tip of the iceberg. According to the Beijing-controlled newspaper in Hong Kong, *Wen Wei Po*, in the first six months of 2003, a total of 8,371 party members and cadres fled overseas; nearly half of them held a bureaucratic rank at or above levels of county head or division chief.[32] How to contain rampant official corruption is a critical challenge facing China's new leadership.

---

[28] When the author was having a lavish dinner (paid for by a businessman) with some central government officials during the summer of 2002, one official from the Central Disciplinary Inspection Commission (who, himself, apparently was corrupt) said: "Corruption is widespread for two reasons. First, the government officials are poor. Second, they are too powerful." It is interesting to note that, despite a series of large-scale pay raises for state officials under Jiang Zemin and Zhu Rongji, the increasing income gap in China has heightened a sense of deprivation even among government officials.

[29] David Shambaugh, "Will the Party Lose China?" *New York Times*, November 7, 2002, A31.

[30] *China Youth Daily*, October 19, 2002; *Financial Times*, November 1, 2002.

[31] Minxin Pei, "The Long March against Graft," *Financial Times*, December 9, 2002.

[32] *Wen Wei Po* (Hong Kong), January 20, 2004.

Political Patronage

While power and corruption go hand-in-hand even in advanced democracies,[33] the problem is made worse in China by its personnel management system. Under the nomenclatura system, *all* personnel power (appointing, transferring, and dismissing leading civil servants) is concentrated among the upper-level party bosses in order to make certain that the civil service implements party policy. The system change in 1984 placed greater personnel power in the hands of local governments. Under the 1984 system, leaders at each level have full authority to appoint major officials at the immediate lower level — which means that, in personnel appointment, they no longer need to gain approval from an upper-level party organizational department. The hope was that the decentralization of personnel management would reduce the workload of territorial party committees so that bureaucrats at each level could be managed more efficiently. Yet, in the absence of effective monitoring of the cadre recruitment and promotion process, the 1984 system provided enormous personnel power to a handful of party leaders that was easily abused for private gains. On the demand side, this provided more incentives to subordinate cadres to set up patron-client ties with their immediate superiors. Ironically, the transaction cost of establishing such a relationship was reduced because now a politically ambitious cadre needed to please only his or her immediate superiors, especially the party secretary (rather than government officials at two levels above), who were also easier to access given their spatial proximity. The increased incentive for rent seeking and reduced transaction costs of political patronage have led to the rise of the *paoguan* phenomenon: government officials are preoccupied with pursuing higher positions by lobbying higher authorities. Not surprisingly, bribery and sale of official

---

[33] The most recent example in the United States is Jim Traficant, who, as a former congressman from Ohio, was convicted of ten counts of bribery, racketeering, and corruption in April 2002. See Seth Mnookin, "Do the Traficant Rant," *Newsweek*, August 5, 2002.

positions have been a major concern since the 1980s. Party bosses sell official positions under their control in this "political market." In early 1999, a county party secretary of Shanxi Province even "wholesaled" official positions by promoting and adjusting 420 positions within two months. In exchange, he accepted bribes worth three million yuan.[34] This type of corruption appears so routinized in China's officialdom that there is even a sliding scale of payments for posts.[35] Since at any time the number of positions available is limited while the demand for them is always high, this is by all accounts a seller's market. The personalized personnel management system means that, in deciding how much to pay for an available position, political aspirants are caught in a situation similar to the prisoner's dilemma. While a candidate prefers a low payment, he is also aware that, if his competitors pay a higher price, his chance of being offered the position will be smaller. To avoid being a "sucker" (i.e., failing to be promoted because a competitor pays a higher price), each candidate will pay a price that is as high as possible.[36] This significantly raises the price for any marketable official position. Thus, it is not surprising that, even in some poor counties, buying a township head position (the lowest bureaucratic rank) can cost as much as 100,000 yuan.[37] Given the extremely high price and the relatively low salary level of government officials, it is safe to conclude that, in most cases, the money used for bribery comes either from the public coffers and/or from bribes taken from lower levels. Lack of effective monitoring and control evidently worsened the problem.

---

[34] *Nanfang Zhoumu* [Southern Weekly], October 7, 2002.

[35] The payment allegedly varied from as little as 30,000 yuan for a village party head's job to one million for a county party secretary's position. See Melinda Liu, "Stirring up a Hornet's Nest," *Newsweek*, November 17, 2003, 37.

[36] The assumption, here, is that a candidate does not know how much his potential competitors are going to pay. This does not exclude the possibility of communication among potential competitors. Similar to what happens in the prisoner's dilemma, allowing potential competitors to reveal to each other the amount of money he or she is going to pay will not bring down the price due to the problem of cheating.

[37] *Nanfang Zhoumu*, August 23, 2002.

Is the Chinese State Apparatus Being Revamped? 59

As a matter of fact, China did not introduce any formal regulations focusing on internal party supervision until 2004.[38] Quite often, the higher the bureaucratic rank of a cadre, the less strictly he is supervised. The result is a vicious cycle in China's officialdom: money → promotion → more money from subordinates and/or the public coffers → promotion to a higher level. It is reported that some position buyers sold an entire state-owned factory for higher positions to manage more factories, only to sell them for even higher positions.[39]

China, of course, does not fall short of monitoring institutions. In addition to the regular judicial and law-enforcement departments (e.g., the police, the People's Procurate, and the People's Court), China has created half a dozen specialized monitoring institutions (e.g., the Central Disciplinary Inspection Committee, an antigraft and bribery bureau) since the early 1980s. What makes these monitoring institutions largely ineffective is that, as part of the patronage system, they themselves are creatures of the level of government they are to supervise. Judges, for example, rely on the local government for their appointments and for the financing of their courts. Any judge knows that, if he rules against the government's interests, he may not be a judge for much longer. That explains why, despite pervasive corruption, only 10 to 20 percent of the corrupt officials are ever detected. Of those detected, only 6 to 10 percent are ever punished.[40]

The personalized selection process creates other problems that affect the quality and capacity of the civil service. Despite the procedural requirements for public participation in the recruitment of leading cadres, the entire process is still monopolized by the party committees. In the absence of effective input from the general public in the cadre selection process, it is difficult for the party bosses to gain thorough knowledge of the candidate who "happens" to catch their attention. In other words, the cadre selection system remains

---

[38] *Xinhua News*, February 17, 2004.
[39] *Nanfang Dushi Bao*, September 4, 2002.
[40] Kynge, "China's Future."

one that is "of the few, and by the few." The use of education credentials and age as criteria in promotion helps to alleviate the problems of information asymmetry, but these credentials can be easily circumscribed for lack of public participation and monitoring. A poorly-educated but politically-ambitious person can land a government position using a fake diploma. The 2000 national census recorded at least 600,000 more college or university graduates than the actual number of degrees conferred.[41] This does not include a large number of "fake real diplomas" (e.g., an advanced degree conferred to a government official by a prestigious university, despite the recipient's failure to complete course studies). Even worse, these "objective" criteria are often not as important as *guanxi*, or personal connections, in the recruitment process. A candidate who is favored by his superiors is often chosen despite his or her well-known reputation for mediocrity and/or corruption. Consequently, cronyism, nepotism, and favoritism are rampant in China's officialdom. This begets further problems, because corrupt and incompetent officials tend to select equally (if not more) corrupt and incompetent ones to staff the state apparatus. Ultimately, gains from post-Mao institutional building are watered down. In a recent article, one Chinese scholar warns of the emergence in some regions of "sultanistic" local regimes, based purely on personal loyalties.[42]

In July 2002, the Party Center issued *Working Regulations on Selection and Appointment of Party and State Leading Cadres* in order to assure effective management and control of bureaucratic leaders. A set of new institutional arrangements was introduced, including publicity before taking office (*zhiqian gongshi*), probation

---

[41] Shaoguang Wang, "The Problem of State Weakness," *Journal of Democracy* 14, no. 1 (January 2003): 39.

[42] Xiao Gongqin, "Zhongguo houquanneng quanwei zhengzhi"[China's post-totalist authoritarian politics], in *Zhanlue yu guanli* [Strategy and management], no. 6 (2002). According to Weber, sultanism is an extreme case of patrimonialism. See Max Weber, *Economy and Society: An Outline of Interpretive Sociology*, vol. 1, ed. Guenther Roth and Claus Wittich (Berkeley, CA: University of California Press, 1978), 231–232.

period (*shiyong qi*), engagement (*pinren*), open competition for leading posts (*gongkai xuanba jingzheng shanggang*), resignation to take the blame (*yinjiu cizhi*), and supervision responsibility on the part of party leaders in cadre management. Given that most of the institutional measures enshrined in the 1995 provisional regulations, such as the systems of resignation and demotion, the avoidance system, and the leadership exchange system, have already proved unable to rein in the corruption and patronage problems, there is no reason to believe that the new regulations necessarily will fare better. Moreover, while the new document sought to expand the public's rights of "being informed, participation, selection and monitoring," it retained the nomenclatura system by reiterating the principle of the "party managing cadres," which is the root cause of corruption and political patronage in China.[43]

ACCOUNTABILITY, RESPONSIVENESS, AND STATE EFFECTIVENESS

Merit, Upward Accountability, and Policy Enforcement Problems

To be sure, bribery, connections, age, and educational credentials are not the only factors determining upward mobility. One's ability and work-related achievements (*zhengji*) matter. Yet, they matter only when they serve to please superior leaders. In the words of a former vice provincial governor, "Performance can lead to promotion; but what matters is not to let people, but the superiors see the performance."[44] Because government officials in China are all politically appointed,[45] they are held accountable only to their superiors, not to the general public. This upward accountability means the

---

[43] For the full text of the old and new regulations, see http://www.people.com.cn/GB/shizheng/19/20020805/792361.html.

[44] Cao Yong, "The 'Performance' View of a Vice Governor," *Nanfang Zhoumu*, August 23, 2003, http://www.people.com.cn/GB/8410/20020823/806461.html.

[45] Villages and urban neighborhoods are not part of the state apparatus.

government will always be more sensitive to something that comes from the top down, rather than from the bottom up. According to a 2004 survey conducted by Horizon Research, 54 percent of the respondents believed that government officials cared more about currying the favor of their superiors than working for ordinary people, and only 24.5 percent of them said otherwise.[46] In order to demonstrate to the political masters their ability and achievement and to secure quick promotion, local leaders spend large sums of public funds on grand extravagant projects or programs. While some of these vanity projects or programs (e.g., upgrading infrastructure facilities) benefit local economic development, many are infeasible or unmarketable. Worse, they tend to aggravate local economic woes and burden local residents with various fees and levies. In addition, the spread of these showcase projects means that less money is spent on improving social welfare, thus exacerbating the public financing problems at the local level. In this way, the upward accountability leads to problems of "shirking" or the pattern of "selective implementation": cadres conscientiously enforce unpopular policies, while refusing to carry out other measures that local residents welcome.[47] This gap between bureaucratic capacity and responsiveness is suggested by the Horizon survey, in which only 27.5 percent of the respondents thought local governments cared about the people, even though more than half of them agreed that local officials were "very knowledgeable."

The upward accountability also exacerbates the information asymmetry problems inherent in a hierarchical structure. While in any political system bureaucratic agents tend to distort the information that they pass to their political masters in order to place themselves in a good light, the problem is alleviated in democracies through "decentralized oversight," which enables citizen interest groups to check up on administrative actions. Since China still

---

[46] Horizon Research, http://www.horizonkey.com (accessed March 9, 2004).
[47] Kevin J. O'Brien and Lianjiang Li, "Selective Policy Implementation in Rural China," *Comparative Politics* 31, no. 2 (January 1999): 167–186.

refuses to enfranchise the general public in overseeing the activities of government agencies, lower-level officials can fool higher authorities more easily than their counterparts in liberal democracies.[48] During the 2003 Severe Acute Respiratory Syndrome (SARS) crisis, for example, Beijing municipal authorities hid the actual SARS situation in the city from the Party Center until April. Initial deception by lower-level officials led the central leaders to misjudge the situation. On April 2, Premier Wen Jiabao chaired an executive meeting of the State Council to discuss SARS prevention and control. Based on the briefing given by the Ministry of Health, the meeting erroneously declared that SARS had "already been brought under effective control."[49]

To overcome the above agency problem in the delegation relationship (in which the upper-level party-state is the "principal" and the subordinate government agencies are the "agent"), the cadre responsibility system has been implemented from the provincial level down since the mid-1980s. Under this system, the upper-level local state employs specific performance criteria (*kaohe zhibiao*) to determine each official's level of remuneration, tenure of office, and opportunities for advancement.[50] This is hardly an institutional innovation, because the former Soviet Union introduced similar systems and failed to solve the agency problem in policy enforcement.[51] Moreover, in implementing the system, the government seeks to make certain that all significant social power goes through the party's command structure, rather than have corporately coherent Weberian bureaucracies collaborating with active civil associations in seeking collective goals. Without engaged civil society groups to

---

[48] For the problem of oversight in different political systems, see Susan L. Shirk, *The Political Logic of Economic Reform in China* (Berkeley, CA: University of California Press, 1993), 57.

[49] Joseph Fewsmith, "China and the Politics of SARS," *Current History* 102, no. 665 (September 2003): 251.

[50] Susan Whiting, *Power and Wealth in Rural China: The Political Economy of Institutional Change* (New York: Cambridge University Press, 2001), 110–118.

[51] See Steven L. Solnick, *Stealing the State: Control and Collapse in Soviet Institutions* (Cambridge, MA: Harvard University Press, 1998).

serve as a source of discipline and information for government agencies, the state capability is often used in conflict with society's interest. In order to secure their own career success, bureaucratic leaders often assign impractical targets to their subordinates. In implementing the government's birth control policy, for instance, surgery quotas in some localities were so high that a large number of women approaching menopause age nevertheless were required to undergo operations.[52] Perhaps more importantly, quotas ultimately create a results-oriented bureaucracy in which only closely monitored targets are met and all other considerations are secondary to the attainment of assigned targets. Indeed, once the party-state intervention is translated into specific quotas and disseminated, local cadres may have to resort to unusual, sometimes extreme measures in order to produce desired results. Bureaucratic cadres seek to please their superiors through cheating. Beginning in 1998, China has suffered an epidemic of false reporting in economic information, including official measures of provincial and national growth. According to an article that appeared in an official Chinese journal:

> Some of the targets that come down from the higher levels are objectively impossible to reach, but since the leaders demand high speed, then the operating departments split up the responsibilities, and, in order to ensure the achievement of the result specified by the upper levels, the lower levels apply more pressure.... plan indicators that are based on the requirements sent down by the upper levels in reality are forced on the lower level statistical figures and then returned upwards.[53]

Similar problems can be identified in other policy areas. Under the pressures of achieving assigned population targets, program officers in some regions have relied on deception to please their

---

[52] Jiang Zhenghua, *Yijiu jiuer nian zhongguo shengyulu chouyang diaocha lunwen ji* [The collection of research papers of 1992 fertility sampling survey in China] (Beijing: Zhongguo renkou chubanshe, 1996), 6.

[53] Gan Xinmin and Li Tongyin, "To Control Falsification, We Must Control Its Foundations," *Zhongguo tongji* [China statistics] (November 1998): 21, in Thomas Rawski, "China's GDP Statistics — A Case of Caveat Lector," unpublished paper, Department of Economics, University of Pittsburgh, 2001.

superiors. In order to conceal actual births, for instance, one township government in Anhui Province even distributed documents to villages enumerating methods for fooling the inspection teams sent by higher authorities. The attempts to conceal "excess" children have led to significant underreporting of births. The underreporting rate in some rural areas, according to the State Family Planning Commission, might be as high as 30 percent. [54] Between 1991 and 1998, the underreported population in Sichuan Province alone was over 400,000, approximately the population of a mid-sized county.[55] This has created serious problems for policy and planning and forced government agencies such as the National Bureau of Statistics to work hard on strategies to annually adjust for such statistical "errors."

Alternatively, policy enforcers rely on campaigns or other mobilization approaches to fulfill state-assigned targets. By highlighting the government's determination, mobilization helps to overcome the constant public resistance. Moreover, by placing political pressure on reluctant local cadres to fulfill targets, mobilization is a convenient bureaucratic tool for overriding fiscal constraints and bureaucratic inertia, while prompting grass-roots cadres to behave in ways that reflect the priorities of their superiors. The latter role is especially important against the background of an inadequate legal and administrative program structure.[56] Yet, during campaigns, the emphasis is on producing immediate and practical results. Since 1983, for example, China has mounted periodic "Strike Hard" campaigns to keep crime in check. Many police stations are given arrest and conviction targets that they are expected to meet. By creating a results-oriented implementation structure, deliberate and methodical mobilization often leads to widespread coercion. The "Strike Hard" campaigns sweep up tens of thousands of suspects, rush them through abbreviated trials, and send thousands of them to death,

---

[54] State Family Planning Commission, *Zhongguo jihua shengyu nianjian* [China yearbook of family planning], 1996, 18.
[55] *Sichuan Daily*, July 13, 2000.
[56] Tyrene White, "Postrevolutionary Mobilization in China," *World Politics* 43, no. 1 (1990): 53–76.

regardless of the likelihood that some are innocent. According to Amnesty International (AI), in regard to only officially publicized cases, over forty people a week are sentenced to death in China; the country executes more people every year than the rest of the world put together.[57] From April to early July 2001, AI recorded 2,960 death sentences and 1,781 executions, a rate of execution not seen since a previous campaign in 1996.[58] In July 1999, the government launched a campaign against the Falun Gong spiritual movement. After a year and a half of difficulties in suppressing the movement, the government sanctioned the systematic use of violence against its members. By February 2003, some 526 followers allegedly had died in government custody.[59]

On the surface, through widespread coercion, the post-Mao Chinese state obtains high "infrastructural power" to penetrate its territories and enforce control on a recalcitrant society.[60] The problem is that, without genuine civic engagement in the policy process, this externally-imposed authority will not easily take hold. For instance, there is actually little long-lasting deterrent from the "Strike Hard" campaigns: as the intensity of the crackdown inevitably wanes, old practices return. Similarly, years of government crackdown still have not entirely extinguished the Falun Gong movement. Followers of the movement repeatedly hack into China's official TV networks and play footage promoting the movement. What we have seen, here, is an extension of the state into the space its prior retreat created, but in a fashion that suppresses popular demands rather than being responsive to them.

---

[57] "Bang, You Are Dead," *Economist*, June 2, 2001.
[58] Amnesty International, *Amnesty International Report 2002: China*, http://web.amnesty.org/web/ar2002.nsf/asa/china!Open.
[59] Falun Gong, http://media.minghui.org/gb/death_report.html. Also see, John Pomfret and Philip P. Pan, "Torture is Breaking Falun Gong: China Systematically Eradicating Group," *Washington Post*, August 5, 2001, A1.
[60] See Michael Mann, *The Sources of Social Power, Volume II: The Rise of Classes and Nation-States, 1760–1914* (New York: Cambridge University Press, 1993), 59.

Bureaucratic Overexpansion and Public Financing Problems

Without an effective control mechanism, increased autonomy and functional differentiation also have led to bureaucratic overexpansion. According to the World Bank, between 1991 and 1995, employees in both central and subnational governments in China (excluding police and education and health personnel) accounted for 1.7 percent of the population, compared with 0.9 percent in India and the average 1.2 percent in middle-income countries. By this measurement, China was virtually on a par with Brazil, which was notorious for its bloated bureaucracy.[61]

In order to streamline government agencies, the Chinese government conducted major organizational reforms in 1982, 1988, 1993, and 1998. Among these reform attempts, administrative streamlining in 1982 was reversed soon by the creation of new organs at the central level. The 1988 administrative restructuring was aborted in the wake of the 1989 democracy movement, which saw the purge of Zhao Ziyang, the mastermind of the reform. The 1993 round of administrative reform had a significant effect on the number of provincial administrative personnel, but failed to fundamentally reverse the trend of bureaucratic expansion.[62] Between 1993 and 1998, the number of civil servants as a share of the total population continued to increase, from 1:131 to 1:129.[63] The 1998 reform appeared to be more successful in reining in the bloated bureaucracy. According to *People's Daily*, four and a half years of restructuring reduced the number of ministries from forty to twenty-nine, the average number of provincial administrative organs from about fifty-five to forty, and the average number of county administrative organs from twenty-eight to eighteen. Yet, the number of cadres on the state payroll was reduced by only 1.15 million, rather than the

---

[61] World Bank, Public Sector Employment & Wage Data by Country, http://www1.worldbank.org/publicsector/civilservice/development.htm.
[62] See Brødsgaard, "Institutional Reform and the *Bianzhi* System in China."
[63] Ibid.

five million originally envisaged. (The reduction of five million civil servants is essential if China wants to downsize its civil service to the 1.2 percent average for middle-income countries). The reform was far less successful at the subprovincial level, which claimed 98 percent of all cadres. Only 19.4 percent of the government employees at this level were laid off.[64]

A direct result of this sustained growth of government employment is the dramatic increase of the costs of administration, mostly wage bills. Official statistics suggest that, between 1978 and 2001, administrative costs as a percentage of total fiscal expenditure increased from 4.7 percent to 18.6 percent.[65] According to the official *Procurate Daily*, of the 800 billion yuan annual fiscal income, 640 billion yuan, or 80 percent, are spent on office cars and wage bills.[66] The increasing costs of administration were not matched by rising budgeted revenues. The aggregate government revenues remained at 30 percent of GDP, although off-budget revenues rose to 10 to 15 percent of GDP in the late 1990s. Off-budget revenues are more subject to abuse and corruption because of the lack of transparency and control.[67] To a large extent, the problem has been caused by the 1994 tax reform. Under the current tax arrangements, the central government scoops up most of the lucrative taxes, leaving to the local governments the low-revenue-bearing taxes, which are costly to collect. This has forced subnational governments to turn to various fines, administrative fees, and other forms of nontax contrivances to make their ends meet. The problem is even more precarious at the subprovincial level. While the central and

---

[64] *Renmin Ribao*, October 25, 2002, http://www.people.com.cn/GB/shizheng/19/20021025/850695.html.

[65] National Bureau of Statistics of China, http://210.72.32.26/yearbook2001/indexC.htm (accessed March 10, 2004).

[66] Du Gangjian, "Separation of the Party and the State Is Essential for a Thorough Administrative Reform," http://www.jcrb.com/zyw/n6/ca12185.htm.

[67] Minxin Pei, "Beijing Drama: China's Governance Crisis and Bush's New Challenge," *Policy Brief*, Carnegie Endowment for International Peace, no. 21 (November 2002).

provincial governments siphon away the lion's share of the local revenue, overbloated bureaucracies and increasing financial responsibilities further drain the local government's meager coffers.[68] In 1999, counties generated revenue barely equal to two-thirds of their spending, and about 40 percent of them could pay for only half of their expenditures.[69] Bad as it is, most township governments do not have access to a steady revenue flow because they are financed directly by farmers through fees rather than taxes. Given farmers' nearly stagnant income growth since 1997, it has become very difficult for rural governments to collect these fees. Not surprisingly, rural government debts have ballooned in recent years. According to an estimate, the accumulated total debt of 600 billion yuan (U.S. $72.6 billion) means that rural governments also have to pay an annual interest of 80 billion yuan (U.S. $9.7 billion).[70] If this is true, the Chinese government is in a crisis similar to that experienced by many African states.[71]

Because local governments today are expected to provide most social services such as education and health, the dysfunctional fiscal system has negative implications for an important function of the state apparatus — the provision of public goods and services. From 1990 to 2000, for example, government spending on education as a percentage of GDP dropped from 3.04 percent to a mere 2.87 percent, which is even below the average of 4 percent for developing countries in the mid-1980s.[72] Insufficient government contribution

---

[68] "Fragile Financial Base of the Bureaucratic Pyramid: China's Concern," *People's Daily Online*, December 16, 2002, http://www.peopledaily.com.

[69] Minxin Pei, "China's Governance Crisis," *Foreign Affairs* (September-October 2002): 106.

[70] Li Changping, *Wo xiang zongli shu shihua* [I tell the truth to the premier] (Beijing: Guangming ribao chubanshe, 2002).

[71] Nicholas Van de Walle, *African Economies and the Politics of Permanent Crisis* (New York: Cambridge University Press, 2001).

[72] Ministry of Education, http://www.moe.gov.cn/jytouru/zlwenxian/01.htm, and http://www.moe.gov.cn/jytouru/zlwenxian/jfzxqk_3.htm (accessed March 10, 2004).

led to the commercialization and privatization of public sectors, transforming the latter into revenue-making machines, rapidly raising the level of private spending. Take public health, for example. Between 1978 and 2001, the private share of health spending increased from 20.8 percent to 60.5 percent.[73] This is appalling because, even in least developed countries, the average private share of total health spending was only 40.7 percent.[74] The rising private spending has deterred many from seeing doctors except in extreme emergencies. According to a recent report by the Chinese Consumer's Association, about 50 percent of people who are sick do not see a doctor because of the extremely high out-of-pocket payments.[75] Inadequate public funding also explains the failure to enact some popular public health programs. China is the only one of the thirty-seven nations in the Western-Pacific region that requires its people to pay for routine childhood immunizations.[76] Lack of money is also thwarting efforts to provide compassionate care for those who are infected with HIV/AIDS. Until recently, China spent only a fraction of the money Thailand devoted to education and prevention.[77] Unlike advanced industrial democracies, where bureaucratic expansion accompanied welfare state development, bureaucratic overexpansion in China actually led to the withdrawal of the state from the provision of basic services.[78]

---

[73] See *Zhongguo weisheng nianjian* various years. Since 1987, public health spending has not included funding for traditional Chinese medicine and medical research.

[74] Wang Shaoguang, "The Crises and Turning Points in China's Public Health" (Zhongguo gonggong weisheng de weiji yu zhuanji), *Bijiao* [Comparison], no. 7 (2003).

[75] *Zhongguo Jingji Shibao* [China Economic Times], November 5, 2003.

[76] Hannah Beech, "Unhappy Returns," *Time*, December 8, 2003, http://www.time.com/time/asia/magazine/article/0,13673,501031208-552154,00.html.

[77] *New York Times*, August 23, 2002.

[78] Strong states are likely to produce strong welfare states, with state strength defined in terms of institutional cohesion and governmental administrative capacities. See Hugh Heclo, *Modern Social Politics in Britain and Sweden* (New Haven, CT: Yale University Press, 1974); Ellen Immergut, *Health Politics: Interests and Institutions in Western Europe* (New York: Cambridge University Press, 1992).

Bureaucratic Fragmentation and the Problems of Coordination and Regulation

In a state apparatus where any major policy initiative needs to gain the active cooperation of many bureaucratic units that are themselves nested in distinct chains of authority, the policy process is often protracted, disjoined, and incremental. In the 1980s, David Lampton, Kenneth Lieberthal, and Michel Oksenberg brought forward the "fragmented authoritarianism" model to study China's policy process. The model posits that, as authority below the very peak of the Chinese political system becomes fragmented and disjoined, a bogged-down policy process appears that is characterized by extensive bargaining.[79] While the model offers only a static description of how the core state apparatus worked,[80] it correctly points out the coordination problems in China's policy process. In reality, the lines of crisscrossing authority become exceedingly complex and cumbersome. Because Chinese decision-making emphasizes consensus, the involvement of more actors with equal status in decision-making only increases the time and effort needed for policy coordination and compromise. Since units (and officials) of the same bureaucratic rank cannot issue binding orders to each other, it is also relatively easy for one actor to frustrate the adoption or successful implementation of important policies.[81] This is often complicated by the fact that the primary leadership over a functional bureaucratic agency (*tiao*) resides with the horizontal piece (*kuai*), with the latter determining the size, personnel, and funding of the former. In addition to the tensions between functional departments and territorial governments, coordination problems exist among different levels of functional departments, and

---

[79] David M. Lampton, *Policy Implementation in Post-Mao China* (Berkeley and Los Angeles, CA: University of California Press, 1987); Kenneth G. Lieberthal and David M. Lampton, *Bureaucracy, Politics, and Decision Making in Post-Mao China* (Berkeley, CA: University of California Press, 1992).

[80] Michel Oksenberg, "China's Political System: Challenges of the Twenty-First Century," *China Journal*, no. 45 (January 2001): 28.

[81] Kenneth G. Lieberthal and Michel Oksenberg, *Policy Making in China: Leaders, Structures, and Processes* (Princeton, NJ: Princeton University Press, 1988).

between civilian and military institutions. This fragmentation of authority constitutes a major problem for a bureaucratically weak sector, such as public health. As one senior health official admitted, before anything can be done, the Ministry of Health must negotiate with other ministries and governmental departments.[82] The lack of interdepartmental cooperation ostensibly delayed any concerted efforts to address the initial SARS outbreak. In fact, while it is evident that as early as January 20, 2003, the Ministry of Health was aware that a dangerous new type of pneumonia existed in Guangdong Province, the Chinese government waited more than three months before taking any decisive action.[83]

Bureaucratic fragmentation also has been responsible for the lack of progress in building a regulatory state during China's transition to a market economy. The Chinese reform experience suggests that, while decision makers have been remarkably successful in creating the conditions for a basic market economy, they have been far less successful in changing the functions of the state to actively monitor markets for goods, services, and capital to ensure that they perform competitively and effectively.[84] True, the state has taken on market regulatory functions that are entirely new (in organizations such as the China Securities Regulatory Commission), yet it has difficulty in transforming the function of existing state institutions from controller and producer to architect of a more self-regulating and self-adjusting type of system. According to a World Bank

---

[82] John Pomfret, "China's Crisis Has a Political Edge," *Washington Post*, April 27, 2003.

[83] For a political analysis of the absence of effective response to the original outbreak, see Yanzhong Huang, "The Politics of China's SARS Crisis," *Harvard Asia Quarterly* (Fall 2003): 9–16.

[84] As Steinfeld's study of Chinese state-owned enterprises shows, reform measures seeking to encourage market behavior by transferring property rights, such as decentralization, privatization, and enterprise contracting, fail because the basic institutions needed to make them exist—foremost among them a stable regulatory environment—are simply absent. See Edward S. Steinfeld, *Forging Reform in China: The Fate of State-Owned Industry* (Cambridge, MA: Harvard University Press, 1998).

Institute report, the percentage of countries worldwide that rate below China in terms of regulatory quality dropped from 48.1 in 1996 to 40.2 in 2002.[85] One reason for this is that the government in China is deeply involved in economic activities. The Beijing municipality, for example, has stakes in about 16,000 local businesses, making it extremely difficult to disentangle its commercial interests from its roles as "industry regulator, paymaster for courts, tax collector and economic policymakers."[86] Furthermore, under the current system, all companies have to submit their purchasing plans to local governments, whose stakes in local business create a natural bias toward local suppliers. This may explain why China's efforts to integrate into the international market have accompanied domestic market disintegration. According to a recent study, regional trade barriers within China are as high as those between countries of the European Union, and interprovincial trade barriers have risen steadily since the 1980s, even as barriers to imports have fallen.[87] Another factor that inhibits sound regulation is fragmentation of authority between functional departments, under which strengthening the regulatory power of a bureaucratic agency hinges on the "acquiescence" (*liangjie*) of other bureaucratic departments.[88] Instead of having a unified United States-style Food and Drug Administration (FDA), for example, the regulative power on food and drugs is shared among health, agricultural, public security, and industrial and commercial departments. The lax government regulation accounts for the prevalence of false or unqualified drug-related advertisements.[89] In fact, food, health, drug, and cosmetic products top the list of fake and shoddy products in China.[90] Cases of mass poisoning are often heard, especially in the countryside.

---

[85] Kaufman, Kraay, and Mastruzzi, "Governance Matters III."

[86] James Kynge, "China's Burden," *Financial Times*, January 3, 2002.

[87] Bruce Gilley, "Provincial Disintegration: Reaching Your Market Is More Than Just a Matter of Distance," *Far Eastern Economic Review*, November 22, 2001.

[88] *Jiankang Bao*, March 26, 1989.

[89] *Renmin Ribao*, overseas edition, April 30, 2002, 2.

[90] *Renmin Ribao*, overseas edition, September 25, 2001, 5.

CONCLUSION

An examination of the quality and capability of China's bureaucracy reveals that, despite some positive developments, two decades of administrative reform have failed to fundamentally rationalize or revamp China's state apparatus. China continues to be plagued by a combination of problems that are typical of a Third-World country: high levels of corruption, widespread political patronage, low efficacy, and lack of responsiveness to the people. This is so, in large part because some fundamental aspects of China's civil service system have remained intact during the reform era. While the nomenclatura system precludes the rise of a bureaucracy operating within professional norms, the upward accountability inherent in the civil service explains why the bureaucratic power is not used in the society's interest. Furthermore, some reform measures have exacerbated the existing problems while creating new ones in China's state apparatus. Bureaucratic and fiscal decentralization, for example, not only have aggravated political patronage and corruption, but also have contributed to problems of public financing and further bureaucratic fragmentation in policy implementation. Recent reform measures aimed at a solution have yet to prove their effectiveness to significantly enhance the "usability" of China's bureaucracy.

In *The Advancement of Learning* (1605), Francis Bacon taught us the virtue of "a mature suspension of judgment." Administrative reform is still unfolding in China — and there is indication that the new leadership, which emerged from the Sixteenth Party Congress, is seriously considering separation of decision-making, implementation, and monitoring powers in the state apparatus.[91] Perhaps the reform path is "rough and fatiguing in the entrance, but soon after fair and even." The conclusion, here, may be prematurely drawn, but so far we have not seen any fundamental change in China's state apparatus that justifies a healthy dose of optimism.

---

[91] *Duowei News*, February 15, 2003, http://www.chinesenewsnet.com.

Chapter

3

Who Does the Party Represent?: From "Three Revolutionary Classes" to "Three Represents"

Bruce J. Dickson

The continued survival of the Chinese Communist Party (CCP) has stymied many observers. Some have expected it to go the way of other communist parties, which collapsed in rapid succession in 1989, just months after the CCP leaders decided to repress popular demands for change in Tiananmen Square and elsewhere around the country. Many have noted the incongruity of a Leninist party presiding over a market-oriented economy and predicted that political reform will eventually have to catch up to economic reform. In recent years, the troubles encountered in the midst of economic privatization, in particular massive layoffs, unpaid wages, excessive taxation and fees, and rampant corruption, have triggered sporadic protests, raising questions about the stability of the country and the CCP's ability to maintain control. Whether the issue is the party's popularity, the compatibility of the political and economic systems, or proper policy implementation, the problems facing the CCP are daunting.

While the details may be novel, the basic issues have plagued the CCP for years. Knowing on whom to rely for popular support and political and technical skills has been a cause of concern and political struggle from the early 1950s to the present. Throughout the post-Mao period, the party has wrestled with the need to open up the economic system without also losing political control. Labor unrest, cadre corruption, and the center's inability to monitor and enforce the local implementation of policy also were recurrent problems, with varying degrees of intensity, long before the twenty-first century. As this chapter will show, however, the CCP has a variety of political and practical advantages that have allowed it to survive, despite these challenges.

When listing the problems confronting the CCP, most people do not think ideological inconsistency is a cause of concern, especially when pragmatism has been raised to almost an ideological doctrine by itself. But the CCP, or at least some of its leaders, continue to believe that the party requires an ideological rationale for its continued rule and the economic, political, and organizational reforms it has undertaken. During the Maoist era, when ideological issues helped determine political survival and even personal well-being, Chinese citizens and outside observers paid careful attention to ideological debates and propaganda formulations. Since class struggle was renounced as the party's top goal and communist goals were abandoned in all but name, interest in ideology has waned and rightfully so. It is no longer a guide to policy, but primarily a justification for what the leaders have decided to do. Nevertheless, the party expends a great deal of effort to propagate ideological innovations, emphasizing how its reform agenda is consistent with its traditional goals and the collective benefit of the country, despite appearances to the contrary. In addition, the attention paid to ideology also offers a window on basic conflicts within the party. As will be shown below, while most in the party insist that adaptation is necessary for its survival, a small but stubborn fraction asserts that such changes are weakening the party and undermining its legitimate claim to rule.

The CCP finds itself confronted with competing claims for attention. Its response varies, depending on the nature of those claims. On the one hand, the party has been tolerant of demands that are economic in nature. It has created organizations for various professions, particularly industry and commerce, as a way to integrate itself with individuals and groups who contribute to the economic modernization of the country. In addition to these institutional ties, it also has pursued a co-optive strategy of recruitment of new members into the party. No longer simply a vanguard party of the "three revolutionary classes," that is, peasants, workers, and soldiers, the party now claims to represent three key interests: the "advanced productive forces" (primarily the growing urban middle class of businessmen, professionals, and high technology specialists), the promotion of advanced culture (as opposed to both "feudal" and materialist values), and the interests of the majority of the Chinese people. This depiction of the party's new relationship with society, known as the "Three Represents," was first introduced by Jiang Zemin in spring 2000, and then propagated through an extensive media campaign. In one of the key developments of the Sixteenth Party Congress, the "Three Represents" slogan was enshrined in the revised party constitution. As a corollary to this change, the party congress also lifted the ban on recruiting private entrepreneurs into the party, which had been in effect since 1989. These two changes have been criticized from both the left and the right, some arguing that they betray the party's traditions and weaken party unity, others that they are window dressing at best, and hypocritical at worst. Nevertheless, they reflect the party's efforts to adapt itself to the changed economic and social environment in China. At the same time, the CCP continues to suppress other demands for political reform and liberalization that it perceives as threats to its ruling party status. For the vast majority of Chinese, the political atmosphere is more relaxed and less obtrusive than in the Maoist period, but for political activists who resist the party's authoritarian rule and challenge restrictions on personal and political freedom, the CCP's hand can still be quite heavy.[1]

---

[1] This distinction between economic and political demands is derived from Yanqi Tong and Gordon White, Jude Howell, and Shang Xiaoyuan, who make similar distinctions about the different dynamics and sectors of civil society. See Yanqi Tong, "State, Society, and Political Change in China and Hungary," *Comparative Politics* 26, no. 3 (April 1994): 333–353, and Gordon White et al., *In Search of Civil Society: Market Reform and Social Change in Contemporary China* (Oxford: Oxford University Press, 1996).

In short, the party's strategy of accommodation reflects what Jowitt described as the phase of "inclusion" for Leninist regimes.[2] Without surrendering its monopoly on legitimate political organization, the party has attempted to be more inclusive, drawing in a wider range of social groups, reducing its emphasis on its traditional bases of support, and embracing the modernist paradigm, while continuing to pay lip service to the goals of socialism. However, it is not open to all groups and goals within Chinese society. The party continues to exclude and repress those who pose a challenge to its authority and seek fundamental political change.

It is the multifaceted nature of the CCP's approach to state-society relations that merits better understanding and appreciation. While coercion and repression remain a part of the political reality in contemporary China, it is only a part of the reality. The party has abandoned its attempt to control all aspects of economic and social life, and, with the liberalization of the post-Mao era, it also has relinquished the tools that would allow it to do so.[3] Instead, it has adopted a more flexible approach, permissive in some respects but still repressive in others. The irony is that the party's efforts at adaptation may, in fact, be counterproductive. This is the dilemma often faced when undertaking organizational reform: Will the changes lead to rejuvenation or further deterioration?

This chapter addresses these issues in the following order. It begins with a discussion of the factors that have allowed the CCP to endure as the ruling party of China. It then describes the evolution of the party's relationship with society. It looks at changes in party recruitment, which reflect this evolving relationship with society, and its efforts to create new institutional links with certain sectors of society. Following from this, the chapter then looks more closely at the "Three Represents" slogan, both as a reflection of the party's

---

[2] Kenneth Jowitt, "Inclusion," in *New World Disorder: The Leninist Extinction* (Berkeley, CA: University of California Press, 1992), 88–120.
[3] Andrew G. Walder, "The Decline of Communist Power: Elements of a Theory of Institutional Change," *Theory and Society* 23, no. 2 (April 1994): 297–323.

strategy and as a guide to its policies. Finally, it briefly discusses the implications for political stability, a perennial concern for China's leaders.

WHY IS THE PARTY STILL IN POWER?

The CCP's continued status as the ruling party of China is based first and foremost on its monopoly on legitimate political organization. Leninist organizational principles prohibit the formation of competing organizations that could challenge the CCP, and the party enforces this prohibition strictly. This was seen most vividly in the party's refusal to recognize autonomous associations for students and workers in 1989, and in its repeated suppression of aspiring autonomous labor unions, the Chinese Democracy Party, and spiritual and religious groups, such as Falun Gong and house churches. The inability to organize in opposition to the state significantly raises the cost of collective action and lowers the likelihood of a successful challenge.[4]

The party's survival is not just a result of coercion, however. It has other assets which allow it to remain in power. First of all, the CCP's victory in the 1949 revolution may have less legitimizing force in a time when the goal of economic growth has supplanted most other party goals. However, it still has a residual impact. Whereas ruling communist parties in Eastern Europe were mostly imposed by the Soviet Union, and therefore lacked legitimacy in the eyes of many of the people they governed, the CCP came to power via an indigenous revolution that ousted a discredited and unpopular government. The CCP was not tainted with the image of an outside occupying force, as was the case for Eastern European parties and even for the Kuomintang (KMT) on Taiwan.[5] The result is that it

---

[4] Sidney Tarrow, *Power in Movement: Social Movements and Contentious Politics*, 2d. ed. (New York: Cambridge University Press, 1998).
[5] Bruce J. Dickson, *Democratization in China and Taiwan: The Adaptability of Leninist Parties* (Oxford and New York: Oxford University Press, 1997).

does not have to adapt itself in order to "sink roots" into society, although it is increasingly alarmed about the health and viability of its roots. While the party's policies and practices may not be popular today, it came to power with demonstrable popular support.

In addition to the residual value of its indigenous origins, the CCP also benefits from the apparently widespread belief that it is the best and only safeguard against national disunity and political instability. These are both prominent and deeply-felt fears among members of both the state and society. Political protest and regime change inevitably entail disruption and uncertainty. The CCP can utilize the cultural preference for stability to discredit those who would challenge its monopoly on power. This is one reason why the CCP has stoked nationalistic feelings throughout society: At a time when it no longer promotes class struggle or other communist goals, it can claim to promote nationalistic aspirations, beginning with the maintenance of national unity and order.

The CCP also enjoys material resources that can engender support. For instance, it is an effective patronage machine. It still controls many key jobs, not just in government but also in the financial and academic worlds. With the privatization of the economy, the CCP may not control as many managerial positions in enterprises as it did before, but the number which it controls is still considerable. Party membership also can smooth access to important resources, such as business and investment opportunities and permission to travel abroad. This is a double-edged sword: While this power encourages some people to join to obtain their slice of the pie, it also contributes to the party's image as a corrupt and self-serving machine, with little regard for collective well-being.

Recognizing that the party is the only game in town and that party membership is beneficial to many career goals, growing numbers of young intellectuals and private entrepreneurs are applying for party membership. This may seem surprising, because these select people enjoy the educational and entrepreneurial credentials to succeed on their own. While some are unwilling to join the CCP out of principle or concern that party membership could constrain their options, others are willing to join for practical reasons because membership still provides important privileges, especially for administrative careers.[6] In recent years, the combination of higher learning or entrepreneurial acumen with a party card has had tangible benefits for the careers of many professionals and businesspeople. These kinds of people are not the traditional sources of support for the party, but the party recognizes that they are necessary partners in its goal of achieving economic modernization. The CCP publicizes the growing number of applications to join the party and the profiles of those who seek admission as evidence of the party's continued popularity. While this may be a self-serving misreading of the data, there is no question that the party continues to grow, from almost 40 million in 1982 to almost 70 million in 2005.

In short, the CCP remains in power because it enjoys a political monopoly, is an indigenous party, can provide tangible benefits to its members, and successfully attracts new members from the modernizing sectors of the society. These are not static factors, and the CCP has not been passive in trying to remain relevant. As will be seen in the sections below, the CCP has been transforming its organization and its relations with society in order to adapt itself to the economic and social environment its reforms are bringing about. Its future prospects largely depend on the success of this transformation.

THE PARTY AND THE PEOPLE

As the CCP entered the post-Mao period, it abandoned the class struggle policies and campaigns that characterized the Maoist era, particularly the Cultural Revolution, in favor of the promotion of economic modernization. With that shift in the basic work of the

---

[6] Andrew G. Walder, "Career Mobility and the Communist Political Order," *American Sociological Review* 60, no. 3 (June 1995): 309–328; Bruce J. Dickson and Maria Rost Rublee, "Membership Has Its Privileges: The Socioeconomic Characteristics of Communist Party Members in Urban China," *Comparative Political Studies* 33, no. 1 (February 2000): 87–112; and Andrew G. Walder, Bobai Li, and Donald J. Treiman, "Politics and Life Chances in a State Socialist Regime: Dual Career Paths into the Urban Chinese Elite, 1949 to 1996," *American Sociological Review* 65, no. 2 (April 2000): 191–209.

party came commensurate changes in the party's organization and its relationship with society. Whereas party recruitment and job assignments in the Maoist era had emphasized mobilization skills and political reliability, the new focus on economic modernization placed a premium on practical skills and technical know-how for party members, especially cadres. Beneficiaries of the Cultural Revolution were removed from their posts, and even the victims of the Cultural Revolution were quickly eased into retirement to make way for younger technocrats.[7]

The shift in the party's priorities for its members and key personnel had a dramatic impact. The proportion of party members with high school or higher levels of education rose from 17.8 percent in 1984 to 52.5 percent in 2002. In the CCP's central committee, the percentage of those with college degrees rose from 55.5 in 1982 to 98.6 in 2002. Among cadres at the county level and above, those with a college education rose from 16.4 percent in 1981 to 87.9 percent at the end of 2001.[8]

The most remarkable sign of the party's transformation is this: Whereas peasants and workers formerly were the mainstay of the party and the basis for its popular support, they now comprise a minority of party members. Their numbers dropped from 63 percent of party members in 1994 to only 44 percent in 2003. This was a drop not only in relative terms, but absolute numbers as well, from approximately 34 million to less than 30 million in just those few years. New recruitment among peasants and workers is not keeping pace with retirements and deaths among existing members. The CCP no longer gives priority to the subordinate classes for whom it fought the revolution, but instead reaches out to the technological, professional, and entrepreneurial elites who have emerged in the wake of the party's *gaige kaifang*

---

[7] Hong Yung Lee, *From Revolutionary Cadres to Party Technocrats in Socialist China* (Berkeley, CA: University of California Press, 1991); Melanie Manion, *Retirement of Revolutionaries in China: Public Policies, Social Norms, Private Interests* (Princeton, NJ: Princeton University Press, 1993).
[8] Xinhua, June 12, 2002, in Foreign Broadcast Information Service (FBIS), June 13, 2002.

(reform and opening up) policy. As a consequence, the CCP has redefined its relationship with society to reflect its current priorities.

By declaring the end of class struggle at the outset of the post-Mao era, the CCP implied that its relationship with society would be more harmonious. Rather than relying on the familiar Maoist instruments of ideological mobilization and coercion, the party adopted a two-pronged strategy of adaptation: creating new institutions to link state and society, and co-opting new elites into the party.[9] The party no longer viewed society as rife with class enemies who were determined to overthrow the CCP, but as the source of talent and ambition needed to modernize the economy. While it continued to suppress those it deemed as "counterrevolutionaries" or in other ways hostile to its regime, the CCP sought to cooperate with others who shared its economic goals.

The first element of the CCP's new policy of inclusion was the creation of new institutional links with society. Beginning in the 1980s, and accelerating in the 1990s, China experienced the formation of myriad types of social organizations, including chambers of commerce, professional associations, sports and hobby clubs, and so on. The growing density of these organizations has led some observers to speculate about the potential for civil society emerging in China. However, for the most part, these organizations do not enjoy the type of autonomy expected of a civil society. Instead, their relationship to the state is more akin to a state corporatist perspective: they are sanctioned by the state and granted a monopoly on the interest they represent, at least in their locality; many even have party or government officials in their leadership. This corporatist strategy was designed not to abandon party control but to accentuate it with more flexible instruments. As the party reduced its penetration into the daily life of most of its citizens, these organizations substituted the direct and coercive control over society that characterized the Maoist era with more indirect links.

---

[9] The following analysis is based on my *Red Capitalists in China: The Party, Private Entrepreneurs, and Prospects for Political Change* (New York: Cambridge University Press, 2003).

The second element of the CCP's strategy of adaptation was co-opting newly emerging social elites, in particular, professional and technical elites and private entrepreneurs. Given the party's focus on economic modernization, this was an appropriate strategy. It let the party be connected directly to the kinds of people who were primarily responsible for the growth and modernization of the Chinese economy. The success at recruiting better educated members was noted above. Although the party banned the recruitment of private entrepreneurs in August 1989, local officials found ways to dodge the ban. In some cases, they claimed the entrepreneurs were managers of individual, collective, or joint stock enterprises and, therefore, were not, technically speaking, private entrepreneurs. In other cases, local officials simply ignored the ban, arguing that it was unfair to exclude people who were succeeding due to the party's own policies. Because the promotion of economic growth was a key criterion for evaluating the work performance of local officials, many were eager to cooperate with the entrepreneurs who could provide that growth. The percentage of entrepreneurs who belonged to the party grew from 13 percent in 1993 to over 30 percent by 2004. Not all of these "red capitalists" were co-opted, however; many party members, especially party and government officials, went into business for themselves after joining the party. Without the ban, the numbers of entrepreneurs seeking to join the party undoubtedly would have been higher. After Jiang Zemin proposed lifting the ban in his speech marking the eightieth anniversary of the founding of the party, the rate of recruitment among entrepreneurs was expected to grow. That did not happen immediately, however. Jiang's proposal sparked renewed controversy over the propriety of capitalists within a communist party. Local officials adopted a wait and see attitude and even some entrepreneurs expressed their reluctance to join the party.[10] After the Sixteenth Party Congress formally lifted the ban, a renewed effort to recruit entrepreneurs and publicize their admission was expected to occur,

---

[10] Henry Chu, "Chinese Capitalists Cool to Party Invite," *Los Angeles Times*, August 3, 2002.

but (as of the end of 2004) did not.[11] The numbers of red capitalists continued to grow, but not because private entrepreneurs were joining the party. Instead, the growth was almost entirely the consequence of the privatization of state-owned enterprises: the new owners were formerly managers of the state-owned enterprise, almost all of whom were already party members. Interest in joining the CCP among other private entrepreneurs waned sharply despite the party's new willingness to admit them, but the reason is not very clear. Anecdotal evidence suggests that some entrepreneurs did not want to belong to a party that was increasingly identified with corruption; others were being appointed to official posts even without party membership, so they were being co-opted in other ways. It is also true that many local officials continued to resist recruiting entrepreneurs, despite the new policy.

This strategy of corporatism and co-optation over the last two decades has served to weaken the party's traditional emphasis on party building. The CCP experienced declining recruitment from the "three revolutionary classes" (peasants, workers, and soldiers) and its party organizations in the cities and countryside atrophied. In the mid-1990s, the party declared that half of its rural organizations were inactive. An estimated 2.5 million party members joined the "floating population" of migrant workers, further weakening the party's presence in the countryside. Of the estimated 1.2 million private enterprises in 1998, less than one percent had party organizations and only 14 percent had party members among their workers.[12] In short, the party's presence was shrinking in the countryside, where roughly 70 percent of the population still live and work, and virtually

---

[11] Although the CCP lifted the ban on the recruitment of entrepreneurs, it limited their presence in the top echelons. Only one private entrepreneur — Zhang Ruimin, head of the Haier Group — was chosen as an alternate member of the central committee at the Sixteenth Party Congress, and his name appears at the end of the namelist, which is arranged according to the number of votes received. The limited support he received from the delegates to the party congress, and the absence of other private entrepreneurs on the central committee, reflects the continued ambivalence toward red capitalists.

[12] *Renmin ribao*, September 12, 2000, 11.

nonexistent in the private sector, the most dynamic part of the Chinese economy. As the party shifted its attention toward new professional, technical, and entrepreneurial elites, its ties to the rest of society were allowed to weaken.

As will be seen below, however, the shift in the party's work, especially regarding its recruitment priorities, was contested by those in the CCP who opposed the abandonment of party traditions. While some in the party felt adaptation was necessary for the party's survival and popular legitimacy, others feared the inclusion of such diverse — and nonproletarian — interests into the party could destroy the party's unity and ultimately lead to its dissolution.

WHO DOES THE PARTY REPRESENT?

As China's economic reforms have transformed its social structure, leading to the emergence of new social strata, the CCP has altered its relationship to society. In the past, the CCP has claimed to be the vanguard of the proletariat, but this claim seems quaint amid the rapid marketization of China's economy and the accompanying transformation of its social structure. In order to remain relevant, the CCP has redefined its relationship with society by means of the so-called "Three Represents" slogan, as noted earlier. Jiang unveiled the slogan during his spring 2000 inspection tour of several key economic cities in southern China. He visited joint ventures, private enterprises, township and village enterprises, as well as state-owned enterprises, and investigated party-building efforts in these different types of firms. For example, he met several private entrepreneurs in Zhejiang, all of whom reportedly expressed interest in joining the party, even though they were prohibited from doing so by the party's own policy. This experience reportedly inspired the "Three Represents" slogan, because Jiang recognized that the party could not represent the estimated 130 million workers in the private sector if private firms did not have party organizations in them.[13] Nearly

---

[13] You Dehai, "The Background of the Launch of the 'Three Represents,'" *Xuexi yu shijian* (Wuhan), September 2000, 18–20, 45; the author was president of the party school in Wuhan. See also Xinhua, February 25, 2000, in FBIS, February 29, 2000.

overlooked when he first used the slogan in February 2000, he re-emphasized and elaborated the concept in a May speech at the central party school, which was treated to extensive media coverage for months.

Jiang Zemin did not change the definition of the proletariat, as Deng Xiaoping had done in 1978 by adding intellectuals to the working class. Instead, he advocated incorporating into the party new social strata whose interests were equivalent to those of the working class. In essence, the "Three Represents" slogan was intended to broaden the mass character of the party, without abandoning its class foundation. The CCP replaced its claim to be the vanguard of the proletariat with a "two vanguards" thesis: It represented the interests of both the working classes (comprised of workers, farmers, intellectuals, party and government officials, and those in the military) and the vast majority of the people, especially entrepreneurs, professionals, and high-tech specialists. While this sleight of hand kept the party's propaganda writers busy for years, the careful parsing of the "Three Represents" slogan and its implications also served to point up the discrepancy between the ideological needs of the party and China's dynamic society.

Jiang's efforts to popularize the "Three Represents" slogan was hampered by the party's ban on the recruitment of entrepreneurs into the party. This ban was enacted in August 1989 out of concern that some entrepreneurs had supported the Tiananmen demonstrators (particularly Wan Runnan, founder of the Stone Corporation) and that the presence of entrepreneurs in the party was compromising its class character. It is easy to find an ideological rationale to support the ban. Lin Yanzhi, a member of Jilin's provincial party committee, made a succinct argument against co-opting entrepreneurs:

> If we allow private entrepreneurs [to join the party], it would create serious conceptual chaos within the party, and destroy the unified foundation of the political thought of the party that is now united, and destroy the baseline of what the party is able to accommodate in terms of its advanced class nature.... A pluralistic political party would certainly fragment.... The party name, the party constitution, and the party platform all would have to be changed.... Therefore, we not only cannot permit private entrepreneurs to

join the party, we must encourage those members of the Communist Party who have already become private entrepreneurs to leave.[14]

While the ban on recruiting entrepreneurs made good ideological sense, it was increasingly out of step with the party's goal of promoting economic development and also with the growing complexity of China's society. If the party was basing its legitimacy largely on economic growth, it made little sense to exclude the people who were needed to create that growth and whose success was the result of following the party's policies. Also, traditional class divisions were breaking down as a result of economic reform, as workers moved between jobs in the state-owned, collective, and private sectors, and as former farmers, intellectuals, and party and government officials took the chance to "plunge into the sea" (*xiahai*) by opening their own businesses. As *People's Daily* noted, the new social strata "were originally farmers, intellectuals, managerial personnel of state-owned enterprises, cadres of party and government institutions, scientific and technical personnel, and students who had returned from their studies abroad."[15] Excluding such people was clearly not in the party's long-term interests.

Co-option of entrepreneurs and other new social strata into the party was designed not only to benefit the party by tapping new sources of support, but also to preempt a potential source of opposition. Jiang Zemin reportedly acknowledged in January 2001 that the party was considering lifting the ban on entrepreneurs, perhaps to prevent them from aligning themselves with the prodemocracy political activists.[16] Along these same lines, Wang Changjiang of the Central Party School argued that, if the party did not embrace the vast majority of the Chinese people, they would seek to organize themselves outside the political system. Inclusion was intended,

---

[14] Lin Yanzhi, "How the Communist Party Should 'Lead' the Capitalist Class," *Shehui kexue zhanxian* [Social Science Battlefront], June 20, 2001, translated in FBIS, July 14, 2001. This article, written by a deputy party secretary of the Jilin Provincial Party Committee, originally was published in the May 2001 issue of *Zhenli de zhuiqiu*.
[15] *Renmin ribao*, September 17, 2001, in FBIS, September 17, 2001.
[16] Kyodo News International, January 15, 2001.

at least in part, to prevent organized opposition to the party and to maintain political stability and party leadership.

Finally, Jiang Zemin publicly recommended lifting the ban on entrepreneurs in his July 1, 2001 speech marking the eightieth anniversary of the founding of the CCP. In reviewing the consequences of the reform and opening policies, he noted that private entrepreneurs, free-lance professionals, scientific and technical personnel employed by Chinese and foreign firms, and other new social groups had emerged. He observed, "Most of these people in the new social strata have contributed to the development of productive forces and ... are working for building socialism with Chinese characteristics." While claiming that the workers, farmers, intellectuals, servicemen, and cadres would remain the "basic components and backbone of the party," Jiang claimed the party also needed "to accept those outstanding elements from other sectors of the society."[17]

The party's propaganda machine actively promoted Jiang's "Three Represents" slogan and his recommendation to incorporate China's new social strata into the party. Several themes were prominent in this campaign to square the "Three Represents" with the party's traditions. First, the class nature of the party was not determined solely by the economic class of its members. Historically, workers were not the majority of party members, but rather peasants, intellectuals, soldiers, and students. Yet, they all were said to represent proletarian interests. Second, there was no necessary conflict between the party's claim to represent both the proletariat and the vast majority of the people. According to this syllogism, because the majority of Chinese are workers and farmers, if the party represents the interests of the majority of the people, it thereby represents the interests of workers and farmers. One conclusion from this was

---

[17] Jiang's speech was carried by Xinhua, July 1, 2001. See FBIS, July 1, 2001. See also John Pomfret, "China Allows Its Capitalists to Join Party: Communists Recognize Rise of Private Business," *Washington Post*, July 2, 2001, and Craig S. Smith, "China's Leader Urges Opening Communist Party to Capitalists," *New York Times*, July 2, 2001.

that the party could maintain its proletarian class nature, even if it recruited from other social strata. Even nonproletarians allegedly could have a proletarian outlook. But what if the other classes want to represent their own interests, or those of their professions? Membership in the party supposedly will change those interests:

> Like a big furnace, the party can melt out all sorts of non-proletarian ideas and unify its whole thinking on Marxist theory and the party's program and line. Today, in admitting the outstanding elements from other social strata into the party, so long as we uphold the principle of building the party ideologically and require all party members to join the party ideologically, we will surely be able to preserve the ideological purity of the party members and the advanced nature of the party organizations.[18]

The "Three Represents" recognizes that diverse interests now exist in China, but the rationale used to justify the slogan only legitimizes proletarian interests.

A third theme of the "Three Represents" propaganda campaign was that the party's claim to represent the interests of the majority of the Chinese people was nothing new. At the Wayabao conference in 1935, the party passed a resolution asserting that it was the vanguard of both the proletariat and the whole nation. This is a very weak precedent, however, because it ignores the next sixty-five years of the party's history, and also ignores the historic context of that resolution: the party's appeal to nationalism in the face of Japanese invasion. Despite the claims that the CCP always represented the interests of most Chinese, the media also emphasized the need to conduct extensive education and training of incumbent cadres and the selection of new cadres on the basis of these claims. Apparently, this party tradition was not clear to all.[19]

Commentators also were careful to distinguish Jiang's call to recruit "the outstanding elements from all social strata into the party" from the reviled concept of a party of the whole people

---

[18] *Jiefangjun bao*, August 15, 2001, quoted in FBIS, August 15, 2001.
[19] See for example *Qiushi*, June 1, 2001, and *Renmin ribao*, December 2, 2001, 1, in FBIS, December 3, 2001.

(*quanmindang*), first advanced by Nikita Khrushchev. The distinction is that not all people in each stratum deserve to join the party; only the truly outstanding ones who also meet the other criteria of party membership are qualified. Wang Changjiang of the central party school focused on this point in several articles. In *Liaowang* [Outlook], he argued:

> When the party expands its social foundation to various social strata and groups, it doesn't mean that all the people in these strata and groups can join the party.... What we want to absorb are the outstanding elements of these strata and groups. Possessing the political consciousness of the working class and willingness to fight for the party's program constitutes the common characteristics of these outstanding elements and also the qualifications they must meet in order to join the party.... There is no connection between this kind of party and the so-called... "party of all the people."[20]

In a journal for party cadres, he argued that "since the elements [i.e., party members] influence the nature of the party *to some extent*, we cannot just throw open the doors of the party and welcome everyone.... Allowing entrepreneurs into the party is not the same as saying that any entrepreneur can join the party."[21] Other party media repeated this warning. According to *People's Daily*, "We allow the worthy people in the new social strata to join the party. However, this does not mean that we keep our doors wide open in an unprincipled manner. Still less should we drag into the party all those who do not meet our requirements for party membership."[22] *Qiushi* [Seeking Truth] advised against "using erroneous methods to measure the new criteria for party membership, such as admission based on economic strength, on the amount of donation to society, and on personal reputation."[23] These easily determined criteria — as opposed to the more abstract considerations of supporting the party's program and "standing the test of time" — were undoubtedly

---

[20] *Liaowang*, August 13, 2001, quoted in FBIS, August 22, 2001.

[21] *Zhongguo dangzheng ganbu luntan* (Beijing), January 6, 2002, quoted in FBIS, February 4, 2002 (emphasis added).

[22] *Renmin ribao*, September 17, 2001, quoted in FBIS, September 17, 2001.

[23] *Qiushi*, November 16, 2001, quoted in FBIS, November 29, 2001.

the ones used by many local committees in recruiting from the new social strata.

Although *People's Daily* claimed the "Three Represents" slogan had joined the pantheon of Mao Zedong Thought and Deng Xiaoping Theory as hallmarks of the "sinicization" of Marxism, not all in the party were so enamored of it.[24] *Zhanlue yu guanli* [Strategy and Management] criticized the notion of the "interests of the whole body of the people" as illusory because interest groups need to be checked and balanced in order to avoid "many calamities and difficulties."[25] The party's orthodox leftists used a series of open letters to rebuke Jiang's proposal to admit entrepreneurs into the party. Not only did they challenge the ideological propriety of admitting capitalists into a communist party, but also they attacked the personal leadership style of Jiang Zemin. They accused him of violating party discipline by making such a significant recommendation without obtaining formal approval from the party's central committee or Politburo. They even compared him to Mikhail Gorbachev and Lee Teng-hui, leaders who are widely criticized in China for betraying their parties' interests.[26] Jiang Zemin responded to these attacks by ordering *Zhenli de zhuiqiu* and *Zhongliu* to cease publication. Resistance to Jiang's proposal did not end there, however. Given the prolonged debate and strong emotions generated by this issue, criticism of the political influence of red capitalists and passive resistance to the new policy of recruiting entrepreneurs into the party is likely to continue.

In a more oblique critique of the "Three Represents," the Chinese Academy of Social Sciences (CASS) published a lengthy report on China's social strata in December 2001. It reportedly was prepared at the behest of CASS president Li Tieying, widely seen as skeptical of economic reforms and their political implications. It

---

[24] *Renmin ribao,* November 8, 2001, 9, in FBIS, November 8, 2001.
[25] *Zhanlue yu guanli,* April 30, 2002, in FBIS, June 7, 2002.
[26] A text of the letter identified with Deng Liqun was translated by FBIS, August 2, 2001.

noted the inevitable choice of the CCP to tilt toward the new social strata, especially management, technical personnel, and private entrepreneurs, to promote the party's economic developmental goals. But the consequence was a weakening of the workers and farmers in the party's social base. A commentary on this report in *Zhanlue yu guanli* focused on the polarization and corruption caused by twenty years of reform, which would lead to a crisis of legitimacy if not corrected. Furthermore, it accused private entrepreneurs of buying political power, asserting, "While the new capital stratum is rising into becoming a vested interest group in the reform, it goes further in buying the power-holders with cash so as to consolidate and strengthen its position." Including such people in the CCP only would further undermine the already corrupt political system.[27] The CASS report also described industrial workers, agricultural workers, and the unemployed as comprising the bottom three strata in Chinese society and accounting for over two-thirds of the work force. In contrast, the beneficiaries of the "Three Represents" slogan — private entrepreneurs and technical specialists — are near the top of the pyramid. It was reported that this revelation was something of an embarrassment to party leaders, and contributed to the slowdown in recruiting these new social strata into the party.

Although economic modernization has not yet changed China's political system, it may be changing the party. The diversification of classes and fluidity of social structure is leading the party to change whom it recruits and whom it claims to represent. This is not quite equivalent to pluralism, characterized by competition among fully autonomous interest groups and opposition parties, a development that the CCP still is unwilling to allow. The CCP continues to retain its political monopoly, but tries to be more inclusive and, therefore, more representative. But the idea that the party can represent the vast majority of the people may expose it to even greater criticism and cynicism. It continues the traditional view that societal interests and state-society relations are generally harmonious, unlike the

---

[27] *Zhanlue yu guanli*, April 30, 2002, in FBIS, June 7, 2002.

Western perspective of a society made up of diverse and often conflicting interests. The reform era in China has revealed a variety of competing interests, not just among social strata (the conflict between labor and capital being among the most obvious) but also among regions, nationalities, genders, and other structural factors. These interests need not be incompatible, but they normally desire, even demand, that their own organizations represent their interests before the state and do not want to grant that responsibility to a vanguard party.

The co-optation of private entrepreneurs and other new social strata is a result, not a cause, of recent trends in China, particularly of economic reform. Therefore, their presence in the party is not likely to lead to a dramatic change in the party or the political system more generally, but to reinforce the current policy direction. They are the primary beneficiaries of the party's policies, and, consequently, are unlikely to push for change. Further, previous research on entrepreneurs and technocrats have found them to be in favor of continued liberalization but not enthusiastic about democratization.[28] This also would suggest that their presence in the party would not necessarily pose a challenge.

In addition, greater differentiation in the social strata and policy preferences within the CCP need not lead to fragmentation. Instead, it may create the basis for future pluralization by legitimizing diverse interests.[29] Moreover, the increased possibility for legitimate participation within the party may further enhance the prospects for stability.

---

[28] See, for example, David Wank, "Private Business, Bureaucracy, and Political Alliance in a Chinese City," *Australian Journal of Chinese Affairs*, no. 33 (January 1995): 55–71, and Margaret Pearson, "China's Emerging Business Class: Democracy's Harbinger?" *Current History* 97, no. 620 (September 1998): 268–272. For technocrats, see Hong Yung Lee, "China's New Bureaucracy," in *State and Society in China: The Consequences of Reform*, ed. Arthur Lewis Rosenbaum (Boulder, Co: Westview, 1992).

[29] For a description of the changing attitude toward competing interests during the reform era, see Lucian Pye, "Factions and the Politics of *Guanxi*: Paradoxes in Chinese Administrative and Political Behavior," in *The Nature of Chinese Politics: From Mao to Jiang*, ed. Jonathan Unger (Armonk, NY: M.E. Sharpe, 2002), esp. 55–57.

Dahl and Huntington note the benefits of increased participation within elite circles before expanding more broadly to other groups in society.[30] If that observation holds true for China, then the prospects for political stability, and even a smooth transition from the still nominally communist political system, will be enhanced. At the same time, the prospects for regime continuity are diminished by the growing diversification of the political elite. As Huntington noted in a later work, one of the main threats to a one-party regime is the "diversification of the elite resulting from the rise of new groups controlling autonomous sources of economic power, that is, from the development of an independently wealthy business and industrial middle class."[31] Therein lies the dilemma of reform for the CCP: It needs to adapt to its changing economic and social environment, but adaptation also creates new challenges and risks to the party's hold on power.

CONCLUSION

The CCP is neither monolithic in its relationship with society nor in its attitude toward adaptation. Instead, it has forged multidimensional relationships, depending on the sector of the society and how it fits into the party's modernization strategy. As Stepan argued, a state can pursue a combination of inclusive and exclusive policies at the same time, and that certainly has been the case for the CCP.[32]

The merits and logic of these multidimensional relationships also have been a source of continued debate within the party. Some

---

[30] Robert A. Dahl, *Polyarchy: Participation and Opposition* (New Haven, CT: Yale University Press, 1971), and Samuel P. Huntington, *Political Order in Changing Societies* (New Haven, CT: Yale University Press, 1968).
[31] Samuel P. Huntington, "Social and Institutional Dynamics of One-Party Systems," in *Authoritarian Politics in Modern Society: The Dynamics of Established One-Party Systems*, ed. Samuel P. Huntington and Clement H. Moore (New York: Basic Books, 1970), 20.
[32] Alfred C. Stepan, *The State and Society: Peru in Comparative Perspective* (Princeton, NJ: Princeton University Press, 1978).

argue that the relationships are necessary to preserve the party's right to rule and to promote its economic program. Others argue they are a betrayal of the party's traditions and *raison d'être*. Rather than bolstering the party's legitimacy, critics allege the party's policies of inclusion will undermine the party's authority, both by abandoning its traditional bases of support and by admitting new members who are likely to further divert the party from its original mission and dilute its organizational coherence.

The inherent risk of the CCP's efforts at adaptation is that the transformations may undermine rather than enhance the party's right to rule. The organizational and personnel changes that are necessary to accommodate developments in the economy and society may run counter to the needs of efficient governance and preservation of the one-party state. However, the economic and professional elites whom the CCP is now courting seem not to have a coherent political agenda and are willing to be embedded in the state rather than to seek autonomy from it. Incorporating them into the CCP is likely to have the intended effect of stabilizing the political order, at least in the short run. If so, the emergence and strengthening of civil society will not be an organized opposition, as it was in Eastern Europe, but a cooperative set of groups focused on economic rather than political issues. This would frustrate those who see civil society as an inherently democratizing force. Nevertheless, the growing diversity of Chinese society and party membership presents a challenge to the party's claimed vanguard status and monopoly on political organization. The party's strategies of creating corporatist links and co-optation of new elites may be necessary for its successful adaptation, but provides no guarantee for long-term survival.

Part II

Chapter 4

Jiang Zemin's Successors and China's Growing Rich-Poor Gap

Edward Friedman

Hu Jintao, the 2002 successor to Jiang Zemin, was, at first, sometimes characterized as a partner of the Shanghai-based Zeng Qinghong and a cheerleader for the Shanghai group seen as representing the rich coastal regions of China. A "great number of leaders in the inland provinces have been concerned about Jiang's Shanghai-based favoritism and nepotism," which Professor Cheng Li finds have allowed people in the south to benefit "far more than those in the inland areas largely due to the favorable policies" of the regime in the north.[1] "Business in the large coastal cities is thriving.

---

[1] Cheng Li, "Emerging Patterns of Power Sharing: Inland Hu vs. Coastal Zeng," *Asia Program Special Report*, no. 105 (September 2002), Woodrow Wilson Center, 30. In contrast, Yehua Denis Wei finds that "regional development no longer relies on the policy of the central government but has to consider local effort and global change." See Yehua Denis Wei, *Regional Development in China* (London: Routledge, 2000), 207. For other economic, noncultural approaches to Chinese regionalization, see C. W. Kenneth Keng, "China's Future Economic Regionalization," *Journal of Contemporary China* 10, no. 29 (2001): 587–611, and

Those who know how to operate in China's casino capitalism are getting richer. The educated middle class is doing all right. But huge numbers of workers and peasants are being exploited, thrown out of work or driven out of their homes."[2]

Yet, successor Hu was also portrayed as the voice of the hinterland poor since he earlier served in worst-off regions. In his report to the Sixteenth Party Congress, Shanghai's President Jiang was virtually silent on the growing number of dispossessed, whereas successor Hu, soon after the congress, stressed representing all China's people and voiced initiatives in that direction. Since studies show that the rich-poor gap in China is already worse than in Russia or in India, that the gap between China's regions is similar to that between the world's industrialized democracies and the world's poorest nations,[3] and since rulers in China worry that this economic chasm can be politically destabilizing, it matters greatly whether successor Hu is committed to reducing the still widening gap between prospering and hurting regions.[4]

"China has a two-track economy. One is the booming outward-focused one that is primarily coastal and southern. The other is... the sickly rural old-industry interior...."[5] Chinese analysts Wang Shaoguang, Hu Angang, and Ding Yuanzhu find that, because of expanding inequality, intensifying societal dissatisfaction could unleash violence from below and wipe out the growth of the reform

---

Carolyn Cartier, "Origins and Evolution of a Geographical Idea: The Macro Region in China," *Modern China* 28, no. 1 (January 2002): 79–143. The focus of this article, however, is political culture, not economics. Cheng Li's view captures Chinese cultural consciousness.

[2] Ian Buruma, *Taipei Times*, August 4, 2002.

[3] David Zweig, "Open-door Policy Leaves Successors with Serious Dilemmas," *South China Morning Post*, October 7, 2002, 16.

[4] Indeed, it is likely that the rich-poor gap is larger than found in official statistics because from 1997 to 2001 there was a tremendous over-reporting of the income of the rural poor in China's center. See Thomas Rawski, "Measuring China's Recent GDP Growth," *China Economic Quarterly* 2, no. 1 (October 2002): 53–62.

[5] David Murphy, "Two-Track System," *Far Eastern Economic Review*, December 19, 2002, 49.

era, as occurred in Indonesia during the Asian financial crisis of 1997–1998.[6] Minxin Pei finds a "near collapse of local public finance ... in the populous rural interior provinces...." Bloated local bureaucracies in the nation's center coercively extract revenue from farmers, leading to local rage, a warning to rulers in the north of how rural regions "historically ... generated large-scale peasant rebellion."[7] These observers advise rulers in Beijing to get the Chinese Communist Party (CCP) out of the corrupt state-run economy where it produces a gross misallocation of capital and instead to begin to redistribute wealth and also ensure fair market-oriented competition or face surging forces of instability and fragmentation.

But following his assumption of power when the former paramount leader Deng Xiaoping declined, Jiang Zemin ignored reform pioneer Deng's policy of separating the CCP from business, of getting the CCP out of the job of running enterprises. In addition, rather than following through on Premier Zhao Ziyang's 1980s commitment to building a professional civil service to administer the country, President Jiang reasserted party prerogatives. He acted as the representative of the ruling CCP. Jiang's goal was to build a rule-based administrative CCP that would facilitate economic growth and allow people to pursue their own happiness, supposedly as in Singapore.[8] Successor Hu seems committed to going further in this direction of reforming the ruling party. Jiang's achievements have already won the CCP performance legitimacy in the rising south.

Yet, at the same time, Jiang's policies have further entrenched an ever more brutally corrupt, Brezhnev-like CCP, a political reality which is a world apart from relatively corruption-free Singapore. The CCP is generally seen in China's geographical center as a vehicle for grabbing power for the members' personal or clique/patronage

---

[6] Wang Shaoguang, Hu Angang, and Ding Yuanzhu, "Behind China's Wealth Gap," *South China Morning Post*, October 31, 2002.
[7] Minxin Pei, "The Chinese Governance Crisis," *Foreign Affairs* (September/October 2002): 106.
[8] On the Singapore model, see Economist Intelligence Unit, "Why Reforms Safeguard the Status Quo," January 14, 2003.

enrichment. Successor Hu Jintao eventually will have to choose whether to continue President Jiang's priorities or to do more to close the rich-poor gap, imagined by the poor as a result of CCP greed, theft, and corruption, a policy by, of, and for the ruling few and their clients in the favored south.

This chapter explores how the major economic beneficiaries of post-Mao reforms in China's north and south legitimate to themselves the suffering of those at the bottom percentiles of income distribution, especially people in the center, in a country which since 1984–1985 has seen the gap between rich and poor grow to extraordinary proportions. Minxin Pei finds that, because of this societal chasm, Shanghai feels little in common with suffering Chinese elsewhere in the country.[9] Shanghai, the richer coastal areas, the south, and rulers in the capital in the north legitimate this fragmentation based on regional cultural communities which marginalize China's center by using popular cultural stereotypes. This chapter will both explore how letting the marginalized suffer is imagined within Chinese political culture and project what this means for growth, equity, and stability in a post-Jiang era.

Thinking in Marxist terms, the prospering north and south are imagined by Chinese as the middle class, with the relatively impoverished center as the lower class and the non-Han west as lumpen, a criminally dangerous class. Imagining democratization as the empowerment of the lower classes, a dynamic which supposedly caused the disintegration and decline of Soviet Russia, people in the prospering north and south prefer reliance on the party dictatorship to a threatening democracy, understood as the empowerment of the angry center. The peripheralized center is imagined in the south as the enemy of national prosperity. "The middle classes see themselves as superior to the lower classes in...level of knowledge, intelligence, vision, legal-political consciousness, governing capability, and life style."[10]

---

[9] Minxin Pei, "A Soul Searching Mission in Beijing," *Financial Times*, October 8, 2002.

[10] An Chen, "Capitalist Development, Entrepreneurial Class, and Democratization in China," *Political Science Quarterly* 117, no. 3 (2002): 417.

The prospering in the south and north have earned the right to rule authoritatively. The middle classes do not seek democracy.

What follows is an explanation of the methodology of political culture which focuses on regional symbols as foci of political contestation, followed by data on this conflict among regional communities and its conceptualization in China entering the twenty-first century, concluding with alternative scenarios. These scenarios follow from this political culture approach to the politics of growth and polarization in China looking toward a post-Jiang era. This requires entering the discourse within China about the conflicts among the various regions, where regions are imagined as embodiments of economic and moral forces, urban and rural, coast and hinterland, those plugged into state resources and those excluded, beneficiaries of reform and losers because of reform. This means discussing the north, south, center, and west.

METHODOLOGY

Political culture studies the cognitive mind-sets which people carry into the political realm. Data is obtained either by measuring attitudes displayed in survey responses to questions or by seeking to interpret meanings, often preconscious or seemingly apolitical, which shape one's map of the political. In exploring how political culture informs political dynamics, an analyst can seek to comprehend what makes any particular nation special or different, or, instead, comprehend politics as a clash (of interests, groups, institutions, and ideals), with political culture offering interpretations of conflicting identities that infuse the fissures and debates within a nation.

The first perspective, presuming that national political cultures are different, seems to most travelers obviously true. Someone from the United States going to China has to adapt. Chopsticks are used, not forks and knives. Tea is drunk, not coffee. Rice and noodles supplant bread and potatoes. The language is different. So is the humor. People mourn and marry differently. They stand at a different distance when they chat. Family relations are imagined in different ways.

Patriots embrace what makes their own nation beloved, worthy of their commitments and sacrifices. Consequently, treating each modern nation as a uniquely loveable entity is ubiquitous. This approach leads to national character studies. A famous Chinese scholar of race and society, Zhang Junjun, concluded, "The Mexicans are tumultuous, the Moroccans like to fight (a trait shared by all north Africans), the Arabs are robbers, the Jews are thieves, the Persians are prone to suspicion, the Indians are deluded, the Burmese are treacherous."[11] Pundits opine about America as a cowboy culture, Japan as a samurai culture, Indians as other-worldly, or Chinese as amorally self-centered.[12]

Understanding a national political culture as a uniform unchanging entity, not as an ongoing contestation over how to respond to ever-changing challenges, is often a matter of choosing sides in a political debate within a country, a framing which allows one side to use the "othering" tactic of labeling alternative positions as alien. Essentializing the momentarily hegemonic obscures the ongoing struggle over alternative futures, which never ends.[13] This chapter clarifies political struggles and alternative futures in post-Jiang China by exploring clashing notions of region and community at the turn into the twenty-first century.

When one naturalizes the victors of the moment, one cannot ask questions such as why many Chinese in the era of the New Democracy understood their political culture as familistic and individualistic such that Chinese would never embrace a Soviet-style collectivist project. United States Secretary of State Dean Acheson, in a White Paper on policy to China, hoped, upon Mao's CCP conquering power, that "ultimately the profound civilization and democratic

---

[11] Quoted in Lung-kee Sun, *The Chinese National Character* (Armonk, NY: M.E. Sharpe, 2002), 175.

[12] Alastair Iain Johnston, *Cultural Realism: Strategic Culture and Grand Strategy in Chinese History* (Princeton, NJ: Princeton University Press, 1995). On Chinese national character, also see the numerous works of the prolific Lucian Pye.

[13] Lisa Wedaen, "Conceptualizing Culture: Possibilities for Political Science," *American Political Science Review* 96, no. 4 (December 2002): 713–728.

individualism of China will reassert themselves and she [China] will throw off the foreign [Russian Bolshevik] yoke." In response, Mao agreed that Chinese intellectuals "are the supporters of what Acheson calls 'democratic individualism.'" To discredit that popular quest for democratic freedoms and instead legitimate the importing of Czarist Leninist institutions, the CCP portrayed America as a land where democratic individualism brought empty lives (seen in Hollywood films), racism, the exploitation of labor, and the oppression of progressives (McCarthyism).[14]

By 1960, however, observers were insisting that Chinese always put the collective good ahead of family. That supposedly explained enthusiasm for Mao's Great Leap. In the post-Mao era, however, families decry the Maoist attempt to turn children against parents. That Maoist project was un-Chinese, very un-Confucian. It would also be difficult to defend the proposition that Mao's embrace of conflict and chaos is a reflection of dominant Chinese values. China's historic national narrative has changed in the post-Mao period.

In the Mao era, the monstrous Nanjing massacre of December 1937/January 1938 perpetrated by Japan's Showa Era Imperial Army was hardly commemorated. To his death, Mao never uttered a sentence of sorrow about the Nanjing massacre. In the post-Mao era, however, the suffering of the Chinese nation during prior periods of weakness was used to legitimate the north's priority of economic modernization to build strength. In the Mao era of "the people" building socialism and defeating the "enemies of the people" who supported capitalism, no progressive people, that is, CCP members, were martyred in Nanjing, and there were therefore no "people" to mourn.

Nanjing had been the capital of Generalissimo Chiang Kai-shek's force of counterrevolutionaries. The German Rabe who heroically saved Chinese lives in Nanjing was a Nazi who subsequently was rewarded by an "enemy of the people," Madam Chiang. As with

---

[14] For the politics of Mao's anti-Americanism starting in the late 1940s, see Chen Jian, *Mao's China and the Cold War* (Chapel Hill, NC: University of North Carolina Press, 2001).

contrasting imaginings of Nanjing in the Mao and post-Mao eras, national identity actually is malleable. Myths can and do change, even though, at any moment, one narrative may seem hegemonic and alternatives, misleadingly, do not seem possible.

Entering the 1980s, Singapore's government began to try to persuade its people that Singapore's future success depended on learning to see all Singaporeans as common beneficiaries of Asian values in contrast to a culturally decadent, and, hence, declining America, an understanding soon welcomed for China by many Chinese after the Soviet socialist system of Czarist Leninism imploded in 1991. But what many Singaporean Muslims instead experienced in being force-fed Confucian ethics was an imposition of alien Chinese ways. Similarly, Chinese leaders, after the implosion of Suharto's Indonesia in 1997–1998, were not so enamored of so-called Asian values underpinning Asian developmental authoritarianism.

The Singapore government by 1995 had rethought its civic education aim. Entering the twenty-first century, Singapore became more open to and respectful of multiculturalism. It was willing to adopt the best from all parts of the world, noticing that America was not in decline. Yet, Singapore still worried — as did France — about how to deal with Muslim girls who would come to school wearing head scarves or veiled. Was communalism undermining national unity?

All governments committed to a common national identity must deal with great internal diversity — region, language, religion, economic geography, ethnicity, gender, generation, and so on. The cultural interpretation of societal differentiation helps shape diverse paths and possibilities of political mobilization. China is a large nation with a long and rich history. No matter how much CCP patriots in Beijing insist on finding a commonality of national feeling (*minzu ganqing*) premised on a common past of unique yet shared tribulations offering a promise of a more glorious national destiny, there actually are many ways to be patriotic. This chapter sketches contending regional cultural narratives. The different political projects are vitally important for a better or worse fate for the citizenry. For example, rich southern cities want to have the power to fund their own pensioners, while the rust belt central cities demand a national government bailout for impossible-to-meet pension commitments.

Each group presents itself as uniquely capable of guiding the nation away from what has kept it weak or poor. Each community claims to be the real patriots with the true solution to the nation's dilemmas. Conflicting notions of national political culture mobilize citizens to different patriotic projects. Political cultural alternatives are bitterly contested. The conflicts attendant to transiting to a modern nation state tend to be prolonged and painful, with their successful resolution requiring heroic effort, including a contesting of a once sacred national mythos. China's Mao Zedong was a supporter in the 1960s of the dissolution of the inherited ancient czarist empire. He saw the Russian communist imperium as a continuation of the czarist empire, known as the prison house of nationalities. Yet, most Chinese experienced Russia's peaceful liberation of imprisoned nationalities during the 1990s as a catastrophe.

One social scientific approach to this change and diversity is to understand societal divisions through public opinion surveys. But people surveyed in politicized authoritarian societies with hegemonic nationalist discourses tend to live on two levels.[15] At one level, the public transcript, they have imbibed an official story. In addition to the official level of patriotic loyalty and complicit caution in authoritarian systems, people live at an unofficial level where they are bound by ties of trust and local notions of justice. At that level, as expressed in graffiti, jokes, popular songs, gossip, and critical rhymes, people express a less censored view of the world, one which reveals other political potentials than scripted in the official or hegemonic discourse. Analysts can decipher and decode what is encrypted in unofficial discourses. They can unpack condensation symbols. They can take the unofficial story seriously. This chapter treats seriously how diverse communities of Chinese struggle for a better future.

---

[15] James C. Scott, *Domination and the Arts of Resistance: Hidden Transcripts* (New Haven, CT: Yale University Press, 1990).

DATA

All people imagine themselves complexly. Identities are infused by family, birthplace, language, and region. When I go to market with residents of the southern Hebei village where I have done research for a quarter of a century, they hear bidding for an item not by a person but by a particular village. They hold stereotypes of each of the neighboring villages. They also can tell by accent which sellers are outsiders, that is, not from their own county. Here, too, historic stereotypes prevail, reflecting an intensifying localism.

Inside the village, residents discuss lineages. But villagers refer to those from the nation's capital, Beijing, a northern city, as "them." Given the large number of particularistic ways Chinese characterize the diversity that is China, there is no one true set of groups and groupings which uniquely and accurately captures the rich variety within a diverse political culture.

Province-level identification has also intensified in the reform era. This is not just a matter of province-level propaganda socializing provincials to proud self-identities. To be sure, that process is ongoing. But beyond top-down socialization, there is a lived experience. Stories spread of the mistreatment of the province's outward migrants by those who are not our fellow provincials. Public Security vehicle drivers are secure in their own province but fair game for thieves and hold-up artists once they cross their own province boundary. Shandong criminals do not respect or fear a Public Security vehicle from Hebei. And the Hebei driver knows it. People generally agree on the good qualities of their province-level unit and wish it (themselves) well.

There are over thirty province-type units in China between the capital in the north and the hundreds of thousands of variegated villages. That number is too many for mental manipulation by Chinese trying to comprehend the story of their nation. Consequently, even though there are numerous, conflicting, and overlapping ways by which Chinese see their political culture, from millions of lineages to various binaries (e.g., Han and non-Han) and the thirty-plus provincial-type identities, this chapter will focus on the dominant way, in the late 1990s and into the twenty-first century, by which Chinese reduced their complexity to four over-simplified communalist categories by which they could apprehend the future of justice and injustice in China.

These four cultural groupings can, of course, change in the future. Indeed, they only have recently congealed so as to seem, at least temporarily, real. Contestation over a complex and ambiguous Chinese culture, naturally, continues. However, this chapter will explore how notions of north, south, center, and west are put together to tell a story in which the prospering coastal urban middle class is understood as the south. Neither north nor south is much troubled by the plight of the poor, understood as the center and the yet poorer west, home to minorities who are voiceless. The non-Han west is imagined as troublesome border region minorities who have to be kept from fostering disorder. What is called the west is a somewhat "C"-shaped region running from non-Han areas in the northeast through Xinjiang and Tibet in the west to Guangxi in the southeast. Injustice is seen in the center as concentrated in the north, where reside the corrupt, greedy, and useless rulers whose capital is Beijing, but who nonetheless are indispensable for order. These seemingly precise locations are actually condensed symbols of social forces. The notion of four regions distorts in making manageable a far more complex reality.

Personally, I find no Chinese at all in China. What I see when I am privileged to visit are young and old, men and women, officials and nonofficials, educated and noneducated, migrants and residents, military and nonmilitary, richer and poorer, coastal and hinterland, retired and working, and so on *ad infinitum*. When people at home ask me what I think of *the* Chinese, I respond, "which one?" I know prejudiced and tolerant, conservative and liberal, dull and fun to be with, drinkers and tea-tollers. But that is not how Chinese imagined themselves to tell stories about themselves at the turn into the twenty-first century.

To them, there are four conflicting regions: (1) a super patriotic north (the capital city region and those tied to it) committed to reform through more centralization; (2) a south and east coastal region (including Dalian in the northeast as well as Shanghai and Xiamen) more open to globalization and decentralization; (3) a center, actually imagined as a somewhat "s"-shaped region running from the rust belt in the northeast down through the long marginalized southwest, a region whose people see themselves as not sufficiently benefiting from reform, Han Chinese who see themselves as having fought throughout the millennia, including during the anti-Japan war, to save the nation and now find no commensurate reward for their sacrifices. They tend to be supercentralizers and suspicious of the reform project, even as treasure and people flow out of the center to the richer south and north in order to seek a better future. And, (4) a trouble-making west is imagined as having to be kept quiet.

In the 1980s, I began gathering data on the rise of a southern identity which represented a popular Chinese vision of an open and reformist future in contrast to an old-fashioned, conservative north.[16] By the late 1990s, north and south had been reimagined. The north now symbolized political power, the south wealth. Culture moves and is impelled by human agency. Regional notions reflect changing realities, anxieties, and aspirations.

Intellectuals in the 1980s directly contested the official national mythos in the television series *River Elegy* and the movie *Yellow Earth*. Both deride the Maoist notion that illiterate and miserably poor villagers of the center were China's salvation, claiming that Mao's project actually left the center in stagnant misery. By the twenty-first century, that center had been reimagined as tradition-bound and backward. Voice was granted to the modern which rightly held "authority over the periphery," with the center "stubbornly resistant to enlightenment or modernity.'"[17] Political culture changes.

In the 1980s, from the point of view of the patriotic north, there was nothing good to be said about the outward-facing south, represented by the major metropolises of Canton (Guangzhou) and

---

[16] Edward Friedman, *National Identity and Democratic Prospects in Socialist China* (Armonk, NY: M.E. Sharpe, 1995).
[17] W. K. Cheng, "Imagining the People: 'Yellow Earth' and the Enigma of Nationalist Consciousness," *China Review* 2, no. 2 (Fall 2002): 48, 56.

Shanghai. As popular doggerel verse (*shunkouliu*) then had it, "Beijing people are patriots, while Shanghai people go abroad, and Cantonese are traitors."

The characterization of north and south had changed by the end of the 1990s. Beijing people's patriotism no longer seemed unambiguously wonderful. It threatened war with Taiwan. Shanghai had risen as paradigmatic. With the CCP telling Chinese that incorporating the autonomous island of Taiwan was a life or death matter, Xiamen, a southern port city across from Taiwan which was benefiting from large Taiwanese investment, replaced Canton in a popular rhyme which this time claimed, "Beijing is the source of war; Shanghai is the source of peace; and Xiamen is the source of surrender." Shanghai was now paradigmatic.[18]

The verse found that time was on Shanghai's side, that is, China's side, in dealing with Taiwan and that the war threats emanating from Beijing in the north were counterproductive. A rapidly growing

---

[18] Which does not mean that the south was homogeneous or uniformly moral. In one popular adage, "Beijing was where one found oneself lacking in power, [while in the south] Shenzhen was where one found oneself lacking in wealth, and Sanya [in Hainan, flush with prostitutes] was where one found oneself lacking for physical stamina." In the patriotic north, gossip about prostitutes focused on Chinese success and Russian failure as indicated by the Russian women fleeing to China to engage in sex work. But because communalist identities are ambiguous and contested, at the very same moment that Tibetans in the west imagine Chinese from the north and south destroying the good mores of the Tibetan people, those Chinese imagined Tibetans as sexually loose. See Charlene Makley, "On the Edge of Respectability: Sexual Politics in China's Tibet," *Positions*, no. 103 (Winter 2002): 576–630. Because massive prostitution has been a symbol of illegitimate governance, the ridiculing of the regime in terms of prostitution is significant. In one doggerel verse,

> Furloughed women don't cry.
> Into the barrooms they fly.
> Drinking, singing, shaking their asses,
> Screwing for free the top four classes.
> Screwing for free all the top men,
> Women's wages soar by a factor of ten.
> Paying their share of the state tax bill.
> Who says women are lacking in skill?

Shanghai's policy of serving as a home to hundreds of thousands of Taiwanese wanting to do business was a better way to maintain peace with prosperity, and thereby benefit the nation. The Shanghai-Beijing split as a peace-war split, a win-win approach to the world versus a zero-sum view of the world, has large policy implications. "As late as 1998 and 1999, some Chinese continued to claim that American power was illusory.... It has only been in the last year [2000–2001] that a few fairly brave individuals have voiced a different view. These writers tend to live away from... Beijing (most of them are based in Shanghai)."[19] The Shanghai Cooperation Organization promising win-win relations with Muslim republics of central Asia offered a better future than did the social Darwinist vision of a world in which I live only if you die, a perspective which prevailed in the north.

The center, as is the case with the west, has no purchase on China's future in the consciousness of the advanced regions. Neither center nor west exists in the popular adages just quoted. They are objects of enlightened despots and not agencies of their own destinies. The subaltern is presumed to be incapable of speaking of its own and the nation's interest. For the west, China's security forces speak of what to do to maintain unity and stability. But the plight of the center, a region of suffering Han Chinese, is palpable in both north and south.

Studies of late twentieth-century collective protest find that "the provinces that experienced the most turmoil were mostly interior provinces in central China, including Sichuan, Hunan, Shaanxi, and Henan. These provinces have a high concentration of strategic and heavy industries...."[20] This is China's rust belt, dinosaurs of the age of Stalinism.

---

[19] Kurt Campbell, "Hegemonic Prophesy and Modern Asia," in *The Rise of China in Asia*, ed. Carolyn Pumphrey (Carlisle, PA: Strategic Studies Institute, U.S. Army War College, 2002), 55.

[20] Ching Kwan Lee, "Pathways of Labor Insurgency," in *Chinese Society*, ed. Elizabeth Perry and Mark Selden (London: Routledge, 2000), 41–61; Antoine Kernan, "State Employees Face an Uncertain Future," *China Perspectives*, no. 40 (March/April 2002): 22.

The center also has the nation's worst gender ratios. There are not enough young women for men to marry.[21] Such "bare sticks" were Mao's preferred village recruits for revolution. The single men have least to lose and are most deeply outraged by how unjust life is. They tend to aggressive violence more than any group. They are full of nostalgia for an idealized past. They also are extreme male chauvinists, feeling that women are too powerful, able to pick and choose which male to marry.

The demonstrations of late July 1999 by Falun Gong in response to a crackdown on Li Hongzhi's group, which began in his hometown of Changchun in the northeast (the center, as regions are imagined in China), were strongest in central China, including Hubei, Anhui, Hunan, and Guizhou. AIDS is spreading in the nation's center. Also in the center, according to Chinese Public Security reports, reactionary religious sects figured "most prominently in the provinces of Henan, Shaanxi, Sichuan and Yunnan."[22] Religious sectarianism is a standard indicator of social discontent.

The popular view in the center is that the growing income gap between residents of Shanghai and those of the center reflects not a market-regarding logic but rather how the head of the Shanghai Gang, President Jiang, unfairly disbursed the nation's wealth to peripheralize the center and privilege Shanghai. While Shanghai imagines itself as deservedly taking the lead in China, having risen by its energy, intelligence, skill, and entrepreneurial abilities, the center ascribes Shanghai's rapid rise to subsidies from Beijing in the north. That is, favoritism unjustly builds up Shanghai. The clash among regions is sharp. It pits the deserving against the undeserving.

People and rulers agree that order is precarious. There is "trepidation about the ability of the CCP to maintain national integrity."[23]

---

[21] Paul Wiseman,"China Thrown Off Balance as Boys Outnumber Girls," *USA Today*, June 19, 2002.
[22] Stephen Feuchtwang, "Religion as Resistance," in Perry and Selden, *Chinese Society*, 169.
[23] Geremie Barme, "The Revolution of Resistence," in Perry and Selden, *Chinese Society*, 206.

A consequent obsession with order produces a Hobbesian legitimacy in which no one wants to do or say anything that would destabilize China. The incomplete effort to reform out of Leninist trammels leaves behind much explosive social dynamite, "fertile soil for widespread social unrest that could threaten the stability of the communist regime."[24] This unofficial discourse is captured in doggerel verse that rural analyst Cao Jinqing found in central China on the people's relation to the CCP:

> During the revolution, it was fish and water.
> When reform began, it was oil and water.
> Now it's fire and water.
> [Next it will be fire and oil.]

That is, a big conflagration may be in the offing. Such unofficial opinion is at odds with the public transcript in which people accept the official northern story that the regime guarantees stability.[25] The unofficial transcript, however, is in line with the anxieties over stability explored by Wang Shaoguang, Hu Angang, and Minxin Pei.

Another rhyme captures the fraud of trying to limit local tax rip-offs by distributing cards declaring the maximum burden since, in fact, officials are said to grab, in the unofficial story, whatever they want in order to enjoy a corrupt good life. Xian ka,\hou na\Zaihou O.K.\zhei jiu jiao Karaoke. (First you're given a card.\Still your money is taken anyway.\Everything's said to be O.K.\It's what's meant by Karaoke.)

But for residents getting ahead in the south and north, people in the center and west who are impoverished, marginalized, and silenced are seen as deservedly suffering because they are lazy and backward. Rural migrants who do the dirty work for low wages that dynamizes urban growth are disparaged as "urban peasants," "outsiders," "hoodlums," and "vagrants" who are sources of crime, dirt, and disorder. Demolishing their neighborhoods is imagined as pure

---

[24] David Zweig, "The 'Externalities of Development,'" in Perry and Selden, *Chinese Society*, 191.
[25] Martin Whyte, "Chinese Social Trends," in *Is China Unstable?* ed. David Shambaugh (Armonk, NY: M.E. Sharpe, 2000).

progress.[26] Chinese analysts see intrinsic causes for the poverty of the hinterland: "traditional and anti-market ideas, and corruption," "predatory and wasteful habits, inefficiency, and unfamiliarity with the market," "old habits and ways of thinking," and a "conservative" "unwillingness to take less respectable jobs."[27] The center is to blame for its misery.

Beijing people in the north imagine themselves as the top-quality people in China, as Shanghai people in the south think of most others, including Taiwanese, as bumpkins. The excluded are imagined as inherently lacking what it takes to make it in today's world.

For the post-modern knowledge economy, it is talent that matters. If others score higher on the national college entrance exam than Beijingers, they are dismissed as just nerds. Consequently, villagers and rural migrants from the center and those thrown out of work, in sum, the poor in Beijing (many from Henan Province), are imagined as having no one to blame but themselves. People doing well tell each other exemplary stories of how the lazy do not even know how to turn free rickshaws into good cash, but college students of the south did.

By the start of the twenty-first century, disparaging Henanese was a preferred way of putting down the center. The most populous province in central China is Henan. Attitudes of people in the more economically successful north and south toward Henan people were replete with virtually racist contempt.

In reality, time after time, disasters had been imposed on Henanese by China's rulers. In the late 1930s, a retreating Nationalist Army ruptured the dikes on the Yellow River, intending to slow the advance of invading troops from Hirohito's imperial Japan, thereby killing and uprooting tens of millions of Henanese and destroying the land. In the early 1940s, after Japan's brutal "three all" campaign, millions of Henanese died of famine. During Mao's Great Leap

---

[26] Maurizo Marinelli, "Floating Images," *World History Bulletin* 18, no. 2 (Fall 2002): 17–20.
[27] Hongyi Harry Lai, "China's Western Development Program," *Modern China* 28, no. 4 (October 2002): 459–460.

Forward catastrophe of 1959–1961, there were more famine deaths in Henan than in any other Chinese province. And in the 1990s, a corrupt provincial CCP devastated the province by spreading HIV-AIDS and covering up the CCP's crime.

The Henan AIDS crisis is described as coming from "clever" and "crafty" people in biological products companies in southern metropolises who took advantage of China's racist purism (Chinese don't have HIV. Our blood is clean. Foreigners will pay a good price for it.) But the victims did themselves in. The "simple" farmers of the central plain will do anything "to escape poverty along with some lazy people."[28] The unaccountable ruling CCP's corrupt patron-client networks which killed poor Henanese and protected their murderers went unmentioned.

The new left play, *Che Guevara*, which damned market reforms as a source of inhuman polarization, was staged without government interference in poor Henan Province in 2000 and 2001 but banned in rich Shanghai. The center and the south seemed opposing moral universes.

The center is imagined by the south as inherently and laughably a failure. The media presents Henan as a leader in putting shoddy goods on the market. People in the north and south are made to feel leery of being cheated by low-quality Henan frauds. Henan people are imagined as spouters of nonsense who are unreliable and totally incapable of imagining how to get out of their difficulties, consequently, as responsible for their painful suffering.

In a mocking 2002 jibe at Henan stupidity, Henanese are said to have ridiculously opted for four major and four minor projects to lift themselves out of poverty. The four big and useless items were (1) tiling over the Great Wall, (2) fencing in the Yellow River, (3) putting a lid over the Pacific Ocean, and (4) gilding the globe with gold. The equally ridiculous four minor projects were (1) gauze masks for mosquitoes, (2) gloves for flies, (3) shackles for bedbugs, and (4) condoms for cockroaches. These attitudes are manifest in two

---

[28] He Aifang, "Revealing the 'Blood Wound' of the Spread of HIV AIDS in Henan Province," November 28, 2000, http://bbscity.com/news/rdxw/forum.html.

recent books on the people of Henan Province. The first book asked, *Henanren re shei le?* that is, *Whom have the Henanese offended?*[29] Henan Province is imagined as a historically poor place, full of crooked and inept folk who flee to the rich coastal cities, made prosperous by middle-class mental workers, where the Henanese spread disease and crime. If these most miserable poor are suffering, it is because they are low-quality people. The responding volume, *Henanren shei ye meire* [Henanese haven't offended anyone],[30] accepts that crime and disorder in the cities are, indeed, caused by Henanese but asks that not all Henanese be judged by the evil deeds of the bad Henanese.

In interviews of people in Beijing about the best-selling book, *Whom Have Henan People Offended?*, Henan is dubbed "the fountain of thieves." Jobless Henanese are seen as the source of urban thefts and muggings. They are said to be lazy. A Beijing resident comments, "They are ungenerous, dishonest and spiteful. Henan migrants never do their work properly. Their mindset is unbalanced so they are apt to cause trouble." They suffered the most famine deaths in Mao's Great Leap Forward because they [alone?] doctored statistics. It seems natural that they should now suffer AIDS and tragedies such as discotheque fires. Their barren "hills and turbulent waters produce nefarious people."[31]

While they complain that they suffer discrimination worse than African-Americans in the United States, Henan people from central China are expected to acknowledge the accuracy of the prejudices toward them and to change their ways.[32] As the United States

---

[29] *Henanren re shei le?* [Whom have Henanese offended?] (Haikou: Hainan Publishing House, 2002).

[30] *Henanren shei ye meire* [Henanese haven't offended anyone] (Beijing: Contemporary World Press, 2002).

[31] David Hsieh, "'Dishonest, Spiteful…' Henanese Try to Dispel Poor Image," *Straits Times* (Singapore), May 28, 2002.

[32] I suspect that the frequency with which urban Chinese visitors to the United States from the prospering north and south tell Americans that they now understand white America's supposedly negative attitude to black Americans is a projection of racist-like prejudices toward the people of central China.

supposedly rose by ignoring whining minorities, so, in the north-south view, should today's China.

As social analyst He Qinglian notes in an essay on "China's Listing Social Structure," "one often reads comments in the media to the effect that the real problem is that laid-off workers have been spoiled and are too choosy about the jobs they will take." This notion that the poor are a burden on the state also came through in a question and answer session by then reformist Premier Zhu Rongji's aide, Wen Jiabao, with Hebei deputies on March 7, 2002, in conjunction with a meeting of the National People's Congress. When a local finance official complained about low farm incomes, Wen shot back, "Do you know how much the government pays out for a *jin* of wheat? It's 3,163 RMB [about U.S. $395] a ton. And the governments in America and Australia, what do they pay? In America, $135; Australia, $128."[33] In short, China's rural poor were a burden.

This hard-heartedness may be overdetermined. It reflects the dog-eat-dog cynicism of postsocialism in which it is assumed that all have learned what it takes to climb the greasy pole. Those who were ahead had earned their good fortune. There was little common bond between groups in a polarizing China to impel the better-off to empathize with, aid, or learn from those abandoned and injured by the system. Public opinion in north and south is reflective of a political culture not committed to equality.

Already in the 1980s, intellectuals in urban centers in both the north and the south began to discredit the egalitarian project. As post-Leninist reformers in Europe, they found wisdom in neoliberal attacks on the wasteful socialist state that had long mired the people in stagnant misery. The failures of Soviet-type systems bred mistrust of rationales for sharing. As those inside the Leninist state system in the Mao era talked about socialism while they actually "pursued private gain.... the commitment to the public good...eroded...."[34] In both Europe and China, reformers at first accepted the neoliberal view that a socialist quest for equality undermined economic

---

[33] *Shijie ribao*, March 8, 2002.
[34] Robert Cottrell, "Big Money in the New Russia," *New York Review*, June 13, 2002, 17.

efficiency. Growth, therefore, became the master legitimist of economic policy. In former Leninist states in east and central European democracies, however, the neoliberals could be voted out of power in the next round of elections and replaced by the former communists, now democratic socialists, who promised to stop layoffs and restore the social safety net. Inequality intensified in China because it lacked the accountability institutionalized in democracy. In China, the marginalized lack voice and agency.

Only the rising regions have voice. This elitism seemed in prospering areas of China to be reason incarnate. What were the alternatives? Ignorant masses would ruin things or old-line Stalinists would keep running things into the ground. Embracing economist Joseph Schumpeter on entrepreneurships' inevitable creative destruction and economist Milton Friedman on state spending on social welfare as counterproductive, reform economists in China were not merely not focused on delivering social equity, they felt disdain for the egalitarian project.

This assent to extreme inequality is comprehended in Marxist terms as the inevitable price of growth. The regime's description of the present age as the "initial stage of socialism," a notion swiftly embraced by President Jiang's successor Hu Jintao, is taken by politically conscious people to mean an era of "primitive capitalist accumulation," a painful epoch described in Engels' *The Making of the English Working Class*. Dickensian inhumanity is rationalized by alleged iron laws of stages of economic development. There is little China supposedly can do about it if it wishes to rise, although the consensus of economists internationally is that inequality slows growth because it wastes talents and fosters instability.[35]

While Hu Jintao and others in the new leadership favor "loosening the limits on internal migration," an evolutionary tendency which, indeed, allows hundreds of millions in the center and west gradually and painfully to escape poverty,[36] the rulers' first economic

---

[35] Jeff Madrick, *Why Economies Grow* (New York: Basic Books, 2002).
[36] Of course, opening up rich nations to immigration from the world's rural poor would do most to reduce the rich-poor gap.

priority is "breakneck...growth" at any cost. This means that the regime cares in its heart about China's disadvantaged, that such people will be verbally embraced because the rulers know the rage in the center has "come to the boiling point."[37] But when mere calls to change the ruling party's work style actually change little that might swiftly reduce the growing rich-poor gap, then all that will be left is repression. Beijing will pay that price to maintain China's rapid rise.

Egalitarianism increasingly seems a residual value of the elderly and illiterate.[38] America's economic achievement is theoretically linked to its income inequalities. Sometimes people mention the Kuznets curve, a famous economic hypothesis that a newly industrializing economy inevitably polarizes for a prolonged period of time before moving in the direction of equality as the middle class slowly grows. In short, income inequality is both necessary and good for growth in China. There is no CCP commitment to address the rich-poor gap as a top priority.

The rhetoric of justification seems almost self-consciously that of social Darwinism.[39] Whatever the inevitable pains, the world simply is bloody fang and claw. There is no other way for China to climb the mountain but to accept nasty realities. In contrast, China's center sees itself as committed to charitableness and shared sacrifice which is legitimated by a revived Confucian notion that it is moral behavior "to suffer before the whole world does and to enjoy life the last of all people." The richer regions are immoral, undeserving.

---

[37] See Andrew Nathan and Bruce Gilley, *China's New Rulers* (New York: New York Review of Books, 2002), 29, 68, 88, 110, 117, 173, 175, 193.

[38] Zhou Xiaohong, "The Social Psychology of Rural Chinese during the Present Period of Social Transformation: A Comparison of Zhouzhuang Township and Beijing's 'Zhejiang Village,'" in *Progress in Asian Social Psychology*, vol. 2, Proceedings of the 2nd Conference of the Association of Social Psychology 1997, Kyoto, ed. Toshio Sugiman, Minoru Karasawa, James H. Liu, and Collen Ward (Seoul: Kyoyook Kwahak Sa, n.d.), 22.

[39] Pierre Hagmann, "Reflections on the Official Discourse Pertaining to China's Accession to the WTO," *China Perspectives*, no. 40 (March/April 2002): 28–36.

From the south's perspective, China's economic polarization is not only inevitable, but also it is a positive factor, a source of capital accumulation, of high investment and of rapid growth. Yet, many Chinese fear that their nation's polarization is also a cause of social instability, a force pitting advanced regions against laggards. The extreme inequality is hated by the center and west, seen as stemming not from the ineluctable logic of growth economics but as rooted in selfish, greedy, limitless official and regional corruption and patron-client networks.

The ripoff of public wealth by powerholders will continue. That is a given. President Jiang's successful struggle to entrench his group leading up to the Sixteenth Party Congress in November 2002, in which a younger generation wished for a genuine transfer of power that did not happen, is taken as a green light, an open sesame for the corrupt who are still entrenched.

The clash between the center and the south-north pits those favoring an amelioration of reform and a stoppage of the high-growth policies in order, instead, to limit inequality against those who prefer continuation of the policies of high growth, despite plunder by officialdom which polarizes society, hoping that there is sufficient growth so that all rise somewhat such that polarization reflects relative poverty, not absolute poverty — in short, polarization without "immiserization." This hope could be realized since reform economics have already lifted hundreds of millions of the rural poor out of stagnant misery.

These regional disparities are painfully manifest in the Chinese debate over building the mammoth Three Gorges Dam which benefits urbanities in Wuhan, Nanjing, and Shanghai but harms vulnerable people in the nation's heartland. "People in the dam region... have difficulty accepting the great disparity in living standards between their region and benefiting regions." In general, "Since the 1980s, the disparity among regions has increased and become a sensitive nerve for the nation."[40]

---

[40] Wei Yi, "Major Problems and Hidden Troubles in the Relocation of Three Gorges Project," *Strategy and Management* (May 28, 1999).

Worried about fragmentation, there is a leadership consensus to promote nationalist feelings privileging unity, defined in the categories of the prospering region as a glue to hold society together and overcome the tensions inherent in polarizing regionalism. But that policy commitment, that discourse, is pregnant with dangers. It raises patriotic expectations on policies toward Japan, Taiwan, and America that the national leadership in Beijing cannot meet. It produces not only feelings that the leaders are insufficiently patriotic in not standing up to and defeating alien adversaries but also a belief that strong action is needed against foreign enemies, whatever the impact on reform. The view is spreading in the center that leaders do not take such actions because they are virtual traitors (Li Hongzhangs), selling out to the enemy, preferring that their kin and network of clients get rich in foreign-related business whatever the negative impact on ordinary Chinese suffering from polarization, corruption, and no social safety net.

This chauvinistic outrage is intensified by romanticized nostalgia for prereform, Mao-era policies, creating thereby the poisoned elements required for a red-brown coalition in China, similar to how the French military opposed the "treasonous" political class and challenged the fifth republic on military action to hold the overseas province of Algeria. It is the same with Zhirnovsky in Russia and Milosovic in Yugoslavia, both popular figures in the Chinese northern-central patriotic discourse.

Far from there being a deep emotional bond among members of a Chinese nationality, a united multinational entity forged over the millennia that should share equally and actually, the CCP has never confronted the painful reality of communalist and regional tensions. There is little empathy among the major beneficiaries of today's CCP system for those who are marginalized by polarizing system dynamics. Instead, a strong, almost biological, basis is tacitly embraced to legitimate little practical concern for the losers in a system of an extremely inegalitarian distribution of wealth, power, and status, with the losers seen as having no one to blame but themselves and, also perhaps, anti-China alien imperialists. Contestation within political cultural communities and symbols is sharp and deep.

PROJECTIONS

This chapter has presented a clash of political cultures which can be overly simplified as the prospering north-south against a center-west which is falling ever further behind the advanced. It has tried to make audible the voice of the center. Given this political culture of clashes over China's better future, what can one expect from China's post-Jiang successors?

President Jiang committed himself by 1999 to doing more for what he called the west. So much national investment then poured into the far western province of Xinjiang that, at the start of the twenty-first century, only rich Shanghai grew faster. Yet the rich-poor gap within the west did not shrink because the ruling party and its state enterprises in Xinjiang so monopolized the burgeoning wealth that Turkish-speaking Muslims, the bulk of the poor in the region, were largely excluded from the growing wealth and consequently experienced themselves ever more as virtually apartheid victims of greedy Han Chinese reformers. Communalist tensions were not tamped down because the rich-poor gap is institutionalized by a hierarchical, caste-like political system which deflects the best efforts of economic reformers.

Since rapidly reducing the rich-poor gap requires fundamental political reform, China is not likely soon to shrink the growing rich-poor gap and, therefore, already extant pervasive fears of instability will greatly intensify. Such factors increase the likelihood of an eventual strong backlash against the reform project from the center, with reform imagined as the cause of the pains Chinese now suffer and with the backlash in the nation's center (Han people not benefiting from reform) legitimated as saving the nation from an American imperialist project and plot aimed at weakening China by disuniting China, thereby blocking a hoped for return to greatness of a long-suffering, humiliated, and victimized Chinese people. In short, patriotism, especially in the center, will try to counter reform.

The leaders in Beijing and Shanghai, north and south, will be seen as betraying working people. This condemnation of President Jiang Zemin's reform agenda of closing money-losing enterprises and throwing workers into the streets in the suffering center was captured in the 2002 adage, "Mao wanted people to work in the countryside (xia xiang); Deng wanted people to do business in the cities (xia hai); Jiang wants people not to work (xia gang)," that is, to be furloughed or cashiered by money-losing enterprises or forced off insufficiently productive land.

To protect its hold on power through policies of a rapid economic transition and militant nationalism, the ruling CCP has unleashed forces which threaten China with destabilization. Students of transitions to democracy find that, to prevent national disintegration, a government committed to political reform should hold national elections before regional elections. National mobilization for electoral contestation would then focus attention on the national center as a solution to pressing problems, legitimating the central government as the focus for resolving national issues, intensifying a shared national identity.

But in China the CCP, a narrowly corrupt group experienced as not caring about poor villagers, has begun instead with village elections so as to put in place trusted administrators who can win compliance from villagers for national policies. Local identities, very local identities, are consequently growing stronger. Rural dwellers, almost two-thirds of all Chinese, think of themselves as members of a county, a village, or a lineage. They see others, very different, if not antagonistic others, in just such parochial terms, too. Conflict, even violent conflict, has sharpened in response to the surging localism.

The ruling CCP acts counterproductively on its commitment to a unitary, authoritarian order. The state insists that all regions run the party center's news program, including national advertising, with the revenues going to the center. One might assume that national-level propaganda successfully knits the country together. But the regions resist this national grab of advertising revenue by the capital in the north and increasingly run programs in the local language focused on local culture. Localized identities increasingly gain more solid material and political bases. International firms who manufacture and source in China find that they regularly have to export from one province to Hong Kong and then back into another province because of provincial protectionism. Quite naturally, ruling groups in Beijing — as recounted by Wang Shaoguang, Hu Angang, and Minxin Pei — worry about fragmentation. They scapegoat America for supposedly supporting separatist forces in Taiwan, Tibet, and Xinjiang, "arguing that the United States has been trying to fragment, weaken and westernize China ... to inhibit China from becoming powerful and beyond America's control."[41]

In order to legitimate itself so it can hold on to power, the number one priority for the ruling group in Beijing, the CCP leadership promotes an ever-stronger nationalism to keep the surging disintegrative forces in China in check. Since most Chinese fear hellish consequences from national disintegration, the response to nationalistic appeals is extraordinarily positive and passionate.

The discourse of dominant groups renders invisible internal victims. Attempts by Xu Liangying to commemorate the victims of the 1957–1958 antirightist movement failed. The regime, at the eightieth anniversary of the 1921 founding of the CCP, both in museum exhibits and publications, hid the death toll of Mao's Great Leap Forward. Ba Jin's attempt to found a museum to remember the victims of the Cultural Revolution was vetoed. Attempts to publish Russian archival documents on China's complicity in North Korea's 1950 invasion of South Korea were halted and censored. Buried and explosive truths are reminders of the shallowness and volatility of public opinion which is captured in surveys and too often "essentialized" as reflective of abiding passions.

That a people is socialized not to know the truth about the history of their mistreatment of innocents is not peculiarly Han. But Chinese also are taught only the glory of war, never its brutality. Chinese texts do not highlight the number of Chinese casualties from thirty-four months in Korea or two weeks in Vietnam. These silences hint at how much change in attitude is possible once people hear

---

[41] Zhu Feng, "The American Debate Over China Policy," in *China Cross Talk*, ed. Scott Kennedy (Lanham, MD: Rowman and Littlefield, 2003), 301.

previously repressed narratives.[42] Still, what I hear from mid-level officials among fourth-generation super-patriotic northerners is that, when they get to power and do what a supposedly pro-American President Jiang was too afraid to do, the world will finally see what Chinese with real nationalist passions are capable of achieving.

The regime has unleashed dangerous forces. It is riding on the back of a tiger. It has given birth to a beast that could devour the fruits of reform and throw off its back the narrowly-greedy and self-serving CCP. That is, opposition to the rulers who are situated in the north, imagined as a clique which unfairly benefits the south, is igniting fires of rage in China's center, experiencing itself as impoverished because the rich south and north would rather make deals with foreigners than care for China's poor in the nation's center.

Too many views of Chinese attitudes ignore the communalist contestation, and merely generalize from opinions in the northern capital, Beijing. Interpretations of public opinion polls tend not to emphasize regional diversity. They privilege Beijing (and omit its recent immigrants).[43] Beijing actually is quite distinctive. Leninism enriches the national capital. Studies tend to show that Moscow, the capital, absorbed far more of the Soviet Union's national propaganda story, the public-transcript, than did other sites.[44] That is, Beijing residents, excluding the huge number of recent and temporary migrants from the center and west, are far more likely to treat the official story as their genuine opinion than people who live in other regions. The attitudes in peripheries tend to be far more volatile, shallow, and conflicted.

Consider the Ukraine. A year before the USSR imploded, an anonymous survey of the Ukraine found 80 percent of the people affirming that, if given a free choice, they would choose to stay in the

---

[42] Edward Friedman, "Preventing War between China and Japan," in *What If China Doesn't Democratize?* ed. Edward Friedman and Barrett McCormick (Armonk, NY: M.E. Sharpe, 2000), 99–128.

[43] Pei, "China's Governance Crisis," p. 102 for migrant opinion.

[44] Richard D. Anderson, Jr., "The Discursive Origins of Russian Democratic Politics," in *Postcommunism and the Theory of Democracy,* ed. Richard D. Andersun, Jr., et al. (Princeton, NJ: Princeton University, Press, 2001), 96–125.

Soviet Union. But as the USSR imploded, when the people of the Ukraine could actually freely opt for independence, 90 percent voted to leave the Russian empire. In general, the discursive practices of post-Leninist discourse are extraordinarily different from those of the Leninist era because opinion shifts rapidly and by huge amounts. Public opinion under authoritarian regimes promoting ideological conformity is unusually volatile. Actually, Chinese are acutely aware of the faddish and fleeting nature of opinion and refer to it as "fevers."

Should a survey question touch on politically sensitive issues, the respondent's tendency is to give the "correct" answer. Consequently, surveyors will find Chinese publicly supportive of the regime and therefore conclude that China is stable[45] and find no basis for the informed opinion of Wang Shaoguang, Minxin Pei, et al., about intensifying forces of instability. Throughout the 1990s, although support levels for the regime continued to be incongruously high, given people's belief that ruling officials were corrupt and self-serving, support percentages kept falling. Delegitimization and change based on declining popular support may be more likely than the high support numbers would suggest.

Given the volatility of attitudes in nations with ruling communist parties, it might be useful to think of popular political passions, no matter how sincerely expressed, more as sentiment than as opinion. One day the Cultural Revolution will save the nation. The next day it seems a national catastrophe. Lin Biao goes from hero to villain in an instant. Opinion lacks grounding. It has no staying power. Survey questionnaires do not readily capture the unofficial transcript, the latent. This is largely because of the dilemmas of popular cautionary complicity combined with the framing power of the official story, especially in the capital city. The Chinese government seems far superior to that of the former Soviet Union in making its narrative momentarily persuasive. That is, opinion surveys touching politically sensitive issues can be most misleading.

---

[45] Wenfang Tang, "Political and Social Trends in Post-Deng Urban China: Crisis or Stability," *China Quarterly* (2001): 890–909.

In a Leninist system where the state still controls not only much of the economy but also access to a great deal of housing, jobs, passports, education, administrative service, and the like, people, much as in a conquered land, in order to protect the futures of family members, are structurally compelled to collaborate with the regime even if they find ruling groups illegitimate or singularly self-serving. Citizens have to find ways to give themselves good consciences for their complicity since few anywhere imagine themselves as hypocrites. A standard way to be loyal while criticizing corruption and selfishness, which most Chinese do, indeed, criticize, is to imagine oneself as a real patriot. This means becoming a 110 percenter on matters touching national survival. Consequently, the popular adages which imagine Shanghai people entering the twenty-first century as not seeing the world as humiliated victims who are full of resentment and who would therefore seek revenge may be profoundly significant. A most positive change is brought to light by this political culture approach that may lie just beneath the surface of the public transcript.

Super-patriotism pervades Leninist regimes. Prisoners in the Siberian Gulag volunteered to fight in the front lines to prove their loyalty to the Soviet party dictatorship which had brutally mistreated them. Cursing Mao's post-Great Leap dearth, hungry people invented stories of Soviet perfidy and China's integrity in paying debts to the USSR to explain China's man-made famine so that Mao was innocent and foreigners were guilty.

In like manner, in north and central China after the April 1, 2001 collision of USA and PRC military aircraft over international waters off Hainan Island, patriots "knew" that an evil America was attacking an innocent China, that the American plane had invaded Chinese territory, and that President Jiang was too soft in his treatment of the American side. This sentiment spread even though the PRC government never falsely claimed that the tragic accident had occurred over Hainan Island and even though, internally, the ruling CCP quietly allowed criticism of the martyred Chinese pilot's individual heroics (*geren yingxiongzhuyi*) and of the behavior of the Hainan military command.

In like manner, among northern and central patriots, it is "known" that on May 9, 1999, the US bomber flying for NATO whose missiles hit the Chinese embassy in Belgrade, tragically killing three Chinese officials, aimed those missiles with the intent of hitting sovereign Chinese territory, fully cognizant that it was the Chinese embassy that had intentionally been targeted. Of course, President Jiang knew that the Clinton administration, trying to improve United States-China relations, did no such thing. But President Jiang would not dwell on those facts. Hence, the very different southern view of the world, a win-win view, is not the result of informed public debate in China. Why is it that President Jiang never visited the Nanjing site commemorating the victims of the massacre? Is it possible that Shanghai is not infused with the center's and north's "victimization, vengeance" type of nationalism? The south's openness to win-win games reflects a regional experience, one contesting for national hegemony. Political culture truly matters.

Students at prestigious Qinghua University induced to ask United States President Bush embarrassing questions during his February 22, 2002 visit were themselves upset by the trivialness of the questions proffered by the CCP, believing that the students would have done a better job of standing up for the nation if given the freedom to do so. Chinese compete in patriotism. The norm in the north and the center is to not let anyone be more patriotic than you. Consequently, no matter how ill-informed, ever more chauvinistic public sentiment can and does have a major impact in shaping policy options, especially since military officers tend to identify with the plight of people in the nation's center. It matters whether the north and center predominate or the south.

The north does not recognize its chauvinism as such. The dominant tendency in the north in Beijing is to imagine a happy swing in opinion from a 1980s, when people romanticized the Euro-American West, to a 1990s in which Chinese lost their illusions about foreigners and became realistic. Liberal Zhu Xueqin and neoconservative Xiao Gonqin in Shanghai in the coastal south, on the other hand, find that the late 1990s conjuncture of forces in Beijing facilitated among northern young men the rise of a potentially antireform and destabilizing radical left nationalism combining super-conservative and new left tendencies. This dangerous trend is not the realism that northern intellectuals tout. Rather than an informed public opinion, senior liberal theorist Li Shenzhi noted, there is a potential high cost from distorting the past as the chauvinists in power in the north and in agony in the center do in their embrace of a singular myth of victimization which ignores such things as the trauma imposed on India by China's 1962 border war against India. The result of such self-delusion "is the national loss of memory and the loss of the ability to think logically."[46] The north legitimates militaristic revenge as justice but then, since China's rise is impossible without continuing rapid growth, acts on the south's economic orientation, making the leaders in Beijing seem to people in China's center to be soft and hypocritical. Consequently in the center,

> the Chinese see their government and the nation's elite as conspiring to sell them out to imperialists, *aka* the Americans.... Little wonder that the rabidly xenophobic Mao Zedong is increasingly popular.... Once again shouting "Long live Chairman Mao," they see foreign investors stealing China's wealth, China's rich mingling freely with expatriate business men and China's elite sending their children and cash to the United States.[47]

People in the center share a discourse which discredits the rich in the south and the rulers in the north. They grow nostalgic for an anticapitalist project. A villager in central China suffering from AIDS, asked, on being offered free medicine, if it were a gift from Mao. As a refinery worker in central China put it, "That Jiang Zemin is a traitor.... Jiang Zemin did nothing after the Americans bombed our embassy in Belgrade! Jiang Zemin did nothing after the

---

[46] Cited in Joseph Fewsmith, *China Since Tiananmen* (New York: Cambridge University Press, 2001), 222.
[47] Xueqin Jiang, "Letter from China," *The Nation*, March 4, 2002, 23.

Americans destroyed our plane! He's selling out the Chinese people!"[48] Such nostalgia for the prereform Mao-era policies in the nation's center, if mobilized, threatens the international openness which allows China to rise.

Since Mao was not "rabidly xenophobic" and since Jiang actually acted as a strong Chinese patriot, surveys of public opinion should be sensitive to the diverse regional interpretations and try to capture the unofficial story. How should one understand the work of opinion surveyors in Beijing in the north led by the able Martin Whyte that shows, while the rich gained their wealth by connections and corruption, people like me get ahead by hard work and skill? The analysts find in public opinion proof of social stability. Despite corruption, effort counts. Merit will be rewarded. But people in the center or west do not see merit rewarded. They experience a caste-based apartheid society whose rulers invest in the north and the south while ignoring the center. What the hidden transcript reveals is that, when people in the north and south assert that merit and hard work are rewarded, they mean the suffering poor in the center are lazy, low-quality people who have only themselves to blame for their plight.

Yet, despite gross and growing inequality, most Chinese also see opportunities to get ahead. They are far more likely to grasp those opportunities than to protest *en masse* against the entrenched system. In addition, the corrupt nature of self-serving patron-client networks leaves people extremely cynical about the political realm, almost depoliticized, again, not a situation easily engendering vocal and public opposition to the government. In sum, repression against small and isolated pockets of resistance here, there, and everywhere could well succeed. This analysis suggests that, rather than the projection of Wang Shaoguang and Minxin Pei that China could fragment if it does not make ending growing inequality a top priority, and rather than the happy projection of analysts who imagine successor Hu Jintao as successfully addressing the rich-poor gap, in fact, the gap and authoritarian repression are both likely to persist.

---

[48] Ibid., 24.

As with President Jiang's initiatives to reduce poverty in the west, successor Hu Jintao's policy reforms to benefit the rural poor of the center are sincere. Over a long period of time, the consequences of treating Chongqing as a national city, investing heavily in infrastructure, permitting internal migration, and upgrading health and education in rural China should have a major impact. But that is the long run.

The entrenched geographical hierarchy of the ruling party meanwhile functions to favor the capital in the north and the commercial metropolises of the south. People, therefore, will continue to flee from the center to the south. Investment moves internally in the same direction. In sum, successor Hu's sincerity to end the growing rich-poor gap is not enough. Given the belief that the most rapid possible growth is the single best way to accumulate the means to achieve global power and, eventually, to shrink the rich-poor gap, prosperous regions likely will continue to grow in ways which intensify the pain of the marginalized for quite a time to come, unless the poor are given a political voice.

Victims in the center, despite a burst of last-gasp protests, believe that little can be done about this entrenched and growing rich-poor gap. Idealists and ultra-leftists in the ruling CCP might curse its leaders for only representing wealthy business interests and ignoring "workers and families," but what was the point of denouncing "the new rich and the princelings" as the result of "capitalism?"[49] Surely Mao's revolutionary model of Soviet socialism was not an alternative. As the poet Yi Sha put it, all the losers could do was think "of the Soviet Union/with bitter nostalgia."[50] There seemed no realistic alternative. The cries of outrage by the abandoned within China go unheeded. In responding to the imperatives of global economic competition, the logic of contemporary science and technology, and the realties of military security and international power distribution, China had to learn from the

---

[49] Mark O'Neill, "Party Foils Mass Resignations over Jiang's Capitalist Stance," *South China Morning Post*, August 7, 2002.
[50] Quoted in Ronald James, "What History Cannot Write," *Critical Asian Studies* 34, no. 2 (2002): 273.

advanced and make a priority of catching-up with those ahead of China by competing in the global market. There was no alternative. Given elite consensus on this plus a willingness to repress protesters, the rich-poor gap need not be destabilizing.

There is a political regime entrenched in China with tremendous inertial forces at work so that the rulers protect themselves and their base of power. "China is...more right-wing even than Chile under Pinochet...China...has raw capitalism...no independent trade unions, let alone political parties...the party bosses operate like corrupt chief executives, doling out money, concessions and franchise to cronies, family members and favored minions."[51]

The political cultural approach of this chapter buttresses the Minxin Pei and Wang Shaoguang view of a clash between the nation's center, angry and marginalized, versus the south, prospering and confident. It differs from Pei and Wang in not projecting the country falling apart or declining. The racist way the prospering, in the regional culture analysis just presented, stigmatize the peripheralized for their unhappy fate is a virtual guarantee that the regime in the north will swiftly use force to crush scattered popular resistance from below.

Repression can succeed. By banning publications on official corruption, social injustice, and the rich-poor gap and by not publicizing demonstrations against these ills, the regime hopes that each problem will seem to the sufferers as isolated and that all locales will appeal to the national capital for succor, such that the regime will appear not as the source of these problems, which it is, but as the solution.

So far the tactic seems to be working. As it was said of HIV victims in Henan, "View the caskets but do not cry."[52] In addition, the marginalized, as represented by the Henanese, will absorb the negative stereotypes held about them and prefer migration to the coast over resistance. Loyalty to local ancestral soil is declining.[53]

---

[51] Buruma, *Taipei Times*.
[52] He Ai-fang, "Revealing the 'Blood Wound' of the Spread of HIV AIDS in Henan Province."
[53] Zhou, "The Social Psychology of Rural Chinese during the Present Period of Social Transformation."

The "educated elite viewed the rest of the population as illiterate, backward and superstitious."[54] "China's upwardly mobile" turn "a blind eye" to the suffering center. Local officials dismiss protesters as lazy and greedy. "They're lying scoundrels, always trying to get more money than they deserve." Generally, villagers "fearful of retribution — will keep their door closed and their mouth shut."[55]

Politics, however, is not a realm where futures can be confidently projected. Contingent and conjunctural factors along with leadership clashes can change the nation's trajectory. It is possible to imagine, in a context of economic bubbles bursting, tensions growing over Taiwan, and leadership groups fighting for their political lives, change in a more militaristic and fascistic direction. In that scenario, the palpable pain of so many could lead idealistic young in the prospering cities to scapegoat both corruption and the lesser-quality people in the periphery for the rich-poor gap. Politically speaking, it is the dissatisfaction of "frustrated achievers," not the marginalized center, which is likely to influence policy.[56] The idealists could be attracted to a tough, purifying nationalism of a more fascist variety. But they would reject democracy as an alien plot that would empower China's lesser-quality people of the center, thereby splitting the nation and ending its rapid rise.[57] Since that is utterly illegitimate, the idealists will instead embrace their own glorious cultural tradition, understood as disciplined rule by a culturally-qualified southern elite.

Social stability, meaning protecting the entrenched party dictatorship, remains the top priority of both the prospering south and

---

[54] Frank Dikotter, "Penology and Reformation in Modern China," in *Crime, Punishment, and the Prison in Modern China, 1895–1949*, TMs.
[55] Jiang Xueqin, "'You Betrayed the Motherland,'" *Far Eastern Economic Review*, August 8, 2002, 48.
[56] Carol Graham and Stefano Pettinato, *Happiness and Hardship: Opportunity and Insecurity in New Market Economies* (Washington, DC: Brookings Institution Press, 2002).
[57] For a more optimistic reading of the democratic potential of reform era cultural dynamics, see Yijiang Ding, *Chinese Democracy after Tiananmen* (Vancouver: University of British Columbia Press, 2001).

the northern regime. Successor Hu Jintao may be sincere in wanting to help the rural poor and power-broker Zeng Qinghong may be seriously committed to grass-roots democracy, but the leadership still gives no sign of challenging the local party power structure which is a burden on the rural poor, acts for narrow career enhancement, and puts the interests of villagers last because the local party's set of patron-client networks — "decentralization without accountability"[58] — remains the base of the party dictatorship's pyramid of power. Consequently, in a village, when the elected village committee clashes with the party committee, higher levels almost invariably support the local party and abandon the local people. Local rage against local officials is so great that villagers, despite everything, imagine the national government in the north as their final hope. These factors favor political continuity. In sum, a projection from the political cultural analysis of communalisms of this chapter suggests that, at a great cost in gratuitous human suffering, China will hold together and continue to rise in the era of successor Hu Jintao.

---

[58] Minxin Pei, "A Soul Searching Mission in Beijing."

Chapter

5

Information Technology in China: A Double-Edged Sword

Tun-jen Cheng

China belatedly but boldly embraced information technology (IT) in the mid-1990s.[1] In less than a decade, it became a major IT producer, an electronically connected polity, and an increasingly wired society. However, IT is a double-edged sword; it may enhance China's economy and national power, but it also may "shift power from the state to citizens"[2] and threaten the Chinese Communist Party's (CCP's) authoritarian rule. Indeed, IT has permitted political dissidents within China and abroad to break Beijing's information blockade. It also has helped social dissents to undertake collective action, as vividly exemplified by the formation of the Chinese Democratic Party in 1998 and a large-scale protest in 1999 by Falun Gong members in front of Zhongnanhai, the headquarters of the CCP regime.

---

[1] Regarding the decision to "cross the Rubicon," see Peggy Pei-chen Chang and Tun-jen Cheng, "The Rise of the High-Tech Sector in China," *American Asian Review* 20, no. 3 (September 2002): 125–174.

[2] Nina Hachigian, "China's Cyber-Strategy," *Foreign Affairs* (March-April 2001): 118.

The regime is not prepared to surrender its grip on society. In fact, the Central Government in Beijing has implemented many countermeasures to cope with the IT revolution and, at least in the short run, has succeeded in cultivating self-censorship among Internet users and service providers within China and deflecting or dampening much of the offense by overseas dissidents.³ The crackdown in cyberspace before and after the Sixteenth Congress of the Chinese Communist Party in 2002 suggested that the regime was likely to continue to make every effort to sanitize information flow on the net. However, in the long run, the IT revolution may pose immense challenges to Beijing's authoritarian rule, especially when the density of China's Internet population reaches a high threshold and rapid economic growth begins to taper off.⁴ Singapore offers a clue to the balancing act between maintaining effective authoritarian political control and achieving full-fledged IT development. Yet, such a Singaporean solution to reconciling the two conflicting goals is not readily applicable to China.

The first section of this chapter identifies the progress China has made in the past few years in developing its IT sector. Section two shows how IT can pose a threat to political control. Section three analyzes the approach of China's leaders in Beijing to the management of political risk that IT entails. Finally, section four conjectures about the cyberspace strategy that the authoritarian regime in Beijing may use in the future.

BECOMING WIRED

Efforts for IT development were embedded in the national quest for the modernization of science and technology in post-Mao China. Various IT projects were included in four successive national science and technology plans — the 863 plan, Torch, Star Lit, and the Climb,

---

[3] Michael Chase and James Mulvenon, *You've Got Dissent! Chinese Dissident Use of the Internet and Beijing's Counter-Strategies* (Santa Monica, CA.: RAND, 2002), 49–86.

[4] Hachigian, "China's Cyber-Strategy," 131–132.

all of which were based on governmental budget allocation and handled by academic research institutes. But it was under the leadership of Jiang Zemin and Zhu Rongji when China plunged into the IT revolution with a big splash. In the second half of the 1990s, the government designated some fifty-three science and technology parks, funded the development of a dozen of them to house IT enterprises, and encouraged institutions of higher education, research laboratories, and high-tech firms to become integrated. To unleash entrepreneurship, the government permitted the technology providers to be awarded 30 percent of a corporation's paid-in capital in credit, turned some 242 research institutes into corporations (beginning in May 1995), and established venture capital firms (in 1999) to support small- and medium-size enterprises in high-tech sectors.[5]

In orchestrating an all-out effort to establish a nationwide, hierarchical IT structure, the government funded a series of infrastructure projects, encouraged capital inflow, and reluctantly promised to gradually open up the IT sector after China entered the World Trade Organization (WTO). As Foster and Goodman aptly describe, the top-down approach to IT development in China was in dire contrast to the completely market-driven, and somewhat inordinate approach in India, the other leading IT nation in the developing world.[6] However, as Mueller and Tan argue, the Chinese government astutely exploited the pent-up demand for telecommunications and funneled the proceeds from phone sales into the massive development of China's IT infrastructure.[7] China built eight north-south and eight east-west high-capacity cable and optic lines, the ground foundation for telecommunications and data-transmission. The government also wove together a number of key information networks. The main frame of this emerging cobweb is the much acclaimed Golden Bridge that connects ministries and state-owned enterprises

---

[5] *Da-gong-bao,* August 25, 1999, A3.
[6] William Foster and Seymour E. Goodman, "The Diffusion of the Internet in China," report, Center for International Security and Cooperation, November 2000.
[7] Milton Mueller and Zixiang Tan, *China in the Information Age* (Westport, CT: Praeger, 1997), chap. 1.

through an Internet protocol (IP) network, and provides support for other Golden projects.[8] One Golden net links educational institutions, enterprises, and local networks. Another one connects science and technology research units nationwide. Higher education research institutions also share a net. A national information service net is either in use or being completed, while there soon will be a net that links health care, tax, customs, banking, and economic information bureaucracies.[9]

The government has actively induced Western and Taiwanese corporations to invest in China's electronics industry. As Table 5.1 shows, foreign direct investment (FDI) in China slipped slightly during the 1997–1998 Asian financial crisis. However, when investment rebounded in 1999, electronics and communication clearly emerged as the favorite sectors for China-bound multinationals. Capital inflow into these sectors is expected to grow, as China promised to open up these sectors within five years after its entry into the WTO (see Table 5.2). High-tech firms in electronics, electrical appliances, computers, and precision machinery also have become the mainstay of Taiwan's new direct investment in China, accounting for 64 percent of Taiwan's direct investment in China in 2000 (43 percent, 37 percent, and 20 percent during 1999, 1998, and 1997, respectively).

As a result of the intensive state-led development and massive FDI, China quickly became a major IT producer, a wired polity, and an increasingly wired society. In 1997, textiles and garments were China's leading export items, but since 2000, IT products, most notably computer, and to some extent telecommunications equipment, though not yet semiconductors, have become the top category

---

[8] Foster and Goodman, "The Diffusion of the Internet in China," 11.
[9] Wei Guo, "Yinzhao Zhongguo de wanglu daxichan" [Creating big Internet markets in China], *Liao-wang* [Outlook], October 5, 1998, 38; Frederick S. Tipson, "China and the Information Revolution," in *China Joins the World: Progress and Prospects*, ed. Elizabeth Economy and Michael Oksenberg (New York: Council on Foreign Relations Press, 1999), 250–253; *Economist*, July 22, 2000, 25; Wendy Frieman, "The Understated Revolution in Chinese Science and Technology," in *China's Military Faces the Future*, ed. James R. Lilley and David Shambaugh (Washington, DC: American Enterprise Institute and M. E. Sharpe, 1999), 252.

Table 5.1-a: FDI in China — by Industries

Industries	US $Millions				
	1997	1998	1999	2000	2001
Farming, Forestry, Animal Husbandry & Fishery	630	624	710	676	899
Excavation	940	578	557	583	811
Manufacturing	28,120	25,582	22,603	25,844	30,907
Textile	n.a.	n.a.	1,371	1,368	1,917
Chemical Raw Materials and Products	n.a.	n.a.	1,919	1,795	2,199
Medicine	n.a.	n.a.	684	523	622
Ordinary Machinery	n.a.	n.a.	977	1,043	1,327
Special Use Equipment	n.a.	n.a.	510	527	774
Electronics and Communication Equipment	n.a.	n.a.	3,146	4,594	7,092
Production and Supply of Power, Gas and Water	2,070	3,103	3,703	2,242	2,272
Construction	1,440	2,064	917	905	807
Transportation and Telecom Services	1,660	1,645	1,551	1,012	909
Commerce	1,400	1,181	965	858	1,169
Banking and Finance	0	0	98	76	35
Real Estate	5,170	6,410	5,588	4,658	5,137
Other	3,820	4,432	3,623	3,855	3,921
Total	45,250	45,620	40,315	40,709	46,867

Source: CEIC Data Company Limited (Associate of the McGraw-Hill Companies), CFIC database.

(see Table 5.3). When Deng Xiaoping toured South China to rekindle the torch of economic reform in 1992, China was not even on the world's list of IT producers. By 2000, China had emerged as the third largest IT producer in the world, following only the United States and Japan (see Table 5.4). As of November 2003, every ministry — with the conspicuous exception of Public Security and State Security — of the central government and most provincial governments had homepages. Major policy announcements are posted instantly, and

Table 5.1-b: The Distribution of FDI in China — by Industries

	1997	1998	Unit: % share 1999	2000	2001
Farming, Forestry, Animal Husbandry & Fishery	1.39	1.37	1.76	1.66	1.92
Excavation	2.08	1.27	1.38	1.43	1.73
Manufacturing	62.14	56.08	56.07	63.48	65.95
Textile	n.a.	n.a.	3.40	3.36	4.09
Chemical Raw Materials and Products	n.a.	n.a.	4.76	4.41	4.69
Medicine	n.a.	n.a.	1.70	1.28	1.33
Ordinary Machinery	n.a.	n.a.	2.42	2.56	2.83
Special Use Equipment	n.a.	n.a.	1.26	1.29	1.65
Electronics and Communication Equipment	n.a.	n.a.	7.80	11.28	15.13
Production and Supply of Power, Gas and Water	4.57	6.80	9.18	5.51	4.85
Construction	3.18	4.52	2.27	2.22	1.72
Transportation and Telecom Services	3.67	3.61	3.85	2.49	1.94
Commerce	3.09	2.59	2.39	2.11	2.49
Banking and Finance	0.00	0.00	0.24	0.19	0.07
Real Estate	11.43	14.05	13.86	11.44	10.96
Other	8.44	9.72	8.99	9.47	8.37
Total	100.00	100.00	100.00	100.00	100.00

Source: CEIC Data Company Limited (Associate of the McGraw-Hill Companies), CFIC database.

homepages often are updated on a daily basis. IT not only permits decentralized decision-making in a reforming economy, but also it enables tighter and more efficient central control over localities.[10] Consider that all tax bureaus, customs offices, and police units are

---

[10] Peter Lovelock, "E-China: Why the Internet Is Unstoppable," *China Economic Quarterly* 3, no. 1 (1999): 19–35.

Table 5.2: A Timetable for Market Opening in the Information Sector

Time	Ceiling for Foreign Ownership	Cities
ICP		
Upon entry to WTO (2001)	30%	Beijing, Shanghai, Guangzhou
2002	49%	The above, plus additional 14 cities
2003	50%	The whole nation
ISP		
2004	25%	Beijing, Shanghai, Guangzhou
2006	35%	The above, plus additional 14 cities
2007	49%	The whole nation

Source and Note: Pyramid Research. The additional fourteen cities are Chengdu, Chongqing, Dalien, Fuzhou, Hangzhou, Nanjing, Ningbo, Qingdao, Wuhan, Shengjun, Xiamen, Xian, Taiyuan, and Shengyang. The original table used 2000 as the base year. However, China joined the WTO in late December 2001.

linked. The number of Internet users has grown by leaps and bounds (see Table 5.5). China is still lagging behind some other nations in the use of cellular phones, personal computers, and Internet use on a per capita basis, but its rankings in the world in terms of market size for these products have drastically ascended.

POLITICAL RISK

IT may offer a fast track to economic competitiveness and military modernization. First, IT provides economic agents with low-cost networking and eliminates paper work and inventories. Second, IT enhances operational flexibility and productivity; the basic data-processing unit — the computer — has been shrinking in size, while becoming more powerful, and the proliferation of software applications permits innovation.[11] Indeed, information is simply indispensable to modern commerce and economic activities. China had missed a number of postwar economic development trains in Asia that had

---

[11] Tipson, "China and the Information Revolution," 235.

Table 5.3: The Structure of China's Exports by Commodity — Share and Growth Rate, 1996–2000

Year	2000		1999		1998		1997		1996	
Industry	Share (%)	Growth rate (%)	Share (%)	Growth rate (%)	Share (%)	Growth rate (%)	Share (%)	Growth rate (%)	Share (%)	Growth rate (%)
Raw Materials	9.7	28.7	9.6	−6.1	10.8	−13.6	12.6	9.1	14.0	3.3
Textiles	19.8	19.7	21.2	1.9	22.0	−6.3	23.6	23.5	23.1	−2.5
Footwear	4.8	13.3	5.4	2.8	5.6	0.9	5.6	19.1	5.7	4.3
Metals	7.7	26.8	7.7	3.3	8.0	−3.6	8.3	29.8	7.7	−15.5
Machinery & Electrical Equipment	29.2	39.9	26.7	19.4	23.7	14.0	20.9	23.2	20.6	12.3
Miscellaneous & Others	7.3	24.4	7.5	6.4	7.5	5.5	7.2	25.9	6.9	6.6
Total	100.0	27.8	100.0	6.1	100.0	0.6	100.0	20.9	100.0	1.5

Source: *China Customs Statistics*, various years.

Table 5.4-a: Leading Computer Hardware Producing Countries (output value in $million), 1994–2000

Country	Year						
	2000	1999	1998	1997	1996	1995	1994
United States	98,489	95,085	90,630	94,180	71,541	65,132	60,307
Japan	45,468	44,051	42,558	92,167	70,706	63,551	61,107
Taiwan	23,081	21,023	19,240	18,889	16,414	14,156	11,579
China	25,535	18,455	14,196	10,920	n.a.	n.a.	n.a.
United Kingdom	16,167	16,007	15,398	14,438	11,490	9,668	8,952
German	12,001	10,910	8,844	8,874	7,305	7,492	7,135
South Korea	9,925	8,862	8,169	9,660	6,795	5,079	4,320
Malaysia	10,638	8,865	n.a.	n.a.	n.a.	n.a.	n.a.
Mexico	10,281	8,568	n.a.	n.a.	n.a.	n.a.	n.a.

Sources: Electronic Industries Association of Japan, Nomura Research Institute of Japan, Electronic Industry Association of Korea, and Market Intelligence Center, Institute for Information Industry, www.iii.org.tw, various years.

Table 5.4-b: Leading Computer Hardware Producing Countries (percent of growth rate), 1995–2000

Country	Year					
	2000	1999	1998	1997	1996	1995
United States	3.6	4.9	−3.8	31.6	9.8	8.0
Japan	3.2	3.5	−53.8	30.4	11.3	4.0
Taiwan	9.8	9.3	1.9	15.1	16.0	22.3
China	38.4	30.0	30.0	n.a.	n.a.	n.a.
United Kingdom	1.0	4.0	6.6	25.7	18.8	8.0
Germany	10.0	23.4	−0.3	21.5	−2.5	5.0
South Korea	12.0	8.5	−15.4	42.2	33.8	17.6
Malaysia	20.0	n.a.	n.a.	n.a.	n.a.	n.a.
Mexico	20.0	n.a.	n.a.	n.a.	n.a.	n.a.

Source: Computed from Table 5.4a.

Japan and other nations on board. Therefore, the leadership in Beijing was not prepared to forgo participation in the IT-based economic growth cycle. After all, economic performance is the most important ingredient of political legitimacy in post-Mao China. After

Table 5.5: Internet Users and Computer Hosts in China (millions)

Year/month	Users (millions)	Computer hosts (millions)
1998/1	0.62	0.3
1998/7	1.17	0.54
1999/1	2.1	0.75
1999/7	4	1.46
2000/1	8.9	3.5
2000/7	16.9	6.5
2001/1	22.5	8.92
2001/7	26.5	10.02
2002/1	33.7	12.54
2002/7	45.8	16.13
2003/1	59.1	20.83
2003/7	68	25.72
2004/1	79.5	30.89
2004/7	87	36.3
2005/1	94	41.6

Source: http://www.cnnic.net.cn/develst/.
Note: Fifteen survey reports have been posted. The users are defined as Chinese citizens who, on average, use the Internet an hour or longer per week. The number of computer hosts indicates the total number of computer units with Internet capacity. The growth rates of the Internet population were 100 percent for every six-month period between 1998 and 2000; 30 percent for every six-month period between 2000 and 2002; and 30 to 20 percent per year afterward.

the Tiananmen massacre in 1989 and in the wake of the collapse of communism in Eastern Europe and the Soviet Union, China's leaders recrafted a social contract in which the "promise" of prosperity was exchanged for the public's acquiescence to authoritarianism.

However, embracing IT, a key girder of the promised economic growth, can be politically unnerving. IT makes it easy for a political dissident to disseminate ideas and news, without the CCP regime's seal of approval. It is penetrative, making national borders more permeable and undermining the CCP regime's monopoly of information in China. IT may reinforce the "invasion of ideas" and the public's aspiration, if not demand, for political liberalization, which, after two good decades of economic growth and market reform, are somewhat discernable. Indeed, the proliferation of Western ideas and the growth of independent-minded views in China led the leadership to warn against the prospect of a "peaceful evolution" away from the party dictatorship to some sort of soft authoritarianism and eventually to liberal democracy. The IT revolution may amplify the call for civil liberty, as information flow becomes freer and broader, enhances political awareness, and facilitates collective action. IT's political impact may be particularly pronounced among intellectuals who are more well-informed than the general public. New mechanisms of communication open new sources of information not controlled or sanctioned by the party-state, permitting immense opportunities for learning, which lead to new ideas that forge new identity, undermine officially-endorsed or traditionally-held values, discount political loyalty, and ultimately threaten political control.[12]

IT facilitates interactive communications, undercutting the state's ability to prohibit the development of associations and collective action. IT users may try to remain anonymous (capital and money are not difficult to trail, but information flow is). Further, IT permits individuals to transcend the constraints and structures of organizations and authority. It is public knowledge that fax machines performed a crucial role in the 1989 student uprising. Ten years later, Internet and e-mail links enabled the Falun Gong, a religious organization that promotes both physical development and moral teachings, to organize a 10,000-member protest directly outside the government's central compound, and to ominously challenge the regime's mandate of heaven.[13]

Thus, the IT revolution has complicated the CCP regime's efforts to control one-way and two-way communications. Before the recent information revolution, foreign radio broadcasts were a vital source

---

[12] Bates Gill, "Information Technology, Social Order and Regional Security: The Case of China," paper presented at the Asia–Pacific Security Forum conference, December 17–18, 1999.

[13] Jacques deLisle, "Appeal of Falun Gong Puts Strain on Beijing," *Free China Journal,* August 13, 1999, 7; see also, Julia Ching, "The Falun Gong: Religious and Political Implications," *American Asian Review* 19, no. 4 (Winter 2001): 1–18.

of uncensored news for Chinese, and for that matter, for the people of pre-1989 Eastern Europe and the Soviet Union. They remain important to China's public today. The Voice of America is the primary source of news for 60 percent of China's educated population,[14] and reaches more than ten million Chinese per week on the mainland. The prior-consent principle for radio broadcasts from one country into another is a rule that is virtually impossible to enforce. As Frederick Tipson states, the only option for a host government is to deny revenue to providers and to penalize users if they are caught.[15] Jamming is possible, but not effective. Not only is there a wide range of frequencies for radio broadcasting, but also, when jammed, the news can be posted on the Internet — as done by Voice of America. If the Internet service is blocked, the news can spread via e-mail transmission.[16]

Satellite-based TV broadcasts have posed a new problem to the CCP regime. Rupert Murdoch's Star-TV began in 1992, but was kept out of China, even in Beijing's hotels. Nevertheless, by 1999, about thirty million households had installed dishes to receive Star-TV.[17] CNN is available only in tourist hotels; meanwhile, special programs on sensitive topics are blocked to households and nontourist overnight facilities. Ironically, any occupant of a tourist hotel, including Chinese citizens, can have access to CNN news. The number of domestic tourists has grown drastically as the government aggressively promotes consumption through a variety of measures, including the creation of long holiday weeks. It is also possible for Fujian residents to receive TV broadcasts from Taiwan, and for Guangdong residents to watch programs aired in Hong Kong. While the government has required disk users to register, verification that all

---

[14] Joseph S. Nye, Jr., and William A. Owens, "American Information Age," *Foreign Affairs* (March-April 1996): 30. In the 1960s, one-sixth of the Soviets tuned in to Western broadcasts.

[15] Tipson, "China and the Information Revolution," 240.

[16] Sanford J. Ungar, speech to Foreign Policy Association and Overseas Press Club of America, December 13, 1999.

[17] Tipson, "China and the Information Revolution," 249.

persons owning disks have registered is not an easy task — and, furthermore, it is a costly undertaking.

For two-way communication, basic services — mainly regular phones and faxes — have increased drastically since 1989, and other services — cellular phones and Internet — have come into being. A survey released by the Ministry of Information Industry in December 2002 showed that there were seventeen fixed telephone lines per one hundred people and fifteen cellular phone lines per one hundred people. In 2003, the density of cellular phones had exceeded that of fixed lines. Phone- and fax-based communications go through a state-controlled switchboard, and therefore can be easily intercepted or monitored. Satellite transmission requires a ground-based station or some type of antenna to support phone communications. While it is easy to eavesdrop on analog-based phones, a digitalized system (for example, Sprint's PCS) can be encrypted. Indeed, Teledisic offers a worldwide mobile phone system, which does not require the support of ground stations and, hence, allows a subscriber to reach anywhere in the world — completely bypassing existing ground installations (ducking border controls, such as international short-wave broadcasting).[18] It is not clear whether it is technologically possible to monitor information flow on this worldwide mobile phone system, but if it is possible, perhaps China does not have the expertise to do it. However, if China does have the capability, it might not be able to absorb the enormous administrative and economic costs without creating implosions of its economy and bureaucracy.

Even more difficult to control than fax and phone communications is the Internet, which is fast, cheap, and, most importantly, sweeping and capable of instantly reaching numerous receivers. Moreover, the Internet is not only a potent one-way communicator, capable of dispatching information (via mass e-mailing, postings on Web sites, and Web-based magazines), but also it allows two-way communications and coordination (e-mail exchange, discussions on bulletin-board sites (BBS), and in chat rooms). The Internet has been the most potent weapon in the hands of political dissents

---

[18] I thank Nicco Mele, telecommunication specialist, for this point.

inside China and abroad. Michael Chase and James Mulvenon catalogued 30 Web sites established by dissidents in China's democracy movement, 27 Tibetan Web sites, 8 Uyghur and Mongol Web sites, and 33 Falun Gong Web sites worldwide. Many of them are maintained by technology-savvy engineers who are engaged in "Internet guerrilla warfare" with China to destroy the CCP regime's censorship.[19] VIP Reference is said to have 250,000 to 300,000 e-mail addresses on its list.[20] It is estimated that Falun Gong has 100 million followers (70 million in China, a country of 1.3 billion, and 30 million elsewhere), and it is believed that many of them are directly or indirectly connected through electronic messages from Falun Gong's leader, Li Hong-zhi, who fled to the United States.[21] The Internet permits one to access and structure information, and is arguably the most cost-effective way of organizing social and political action. It also allows grievances to "accumulate" in cyberspace, and permits activists to transcend the limits of geography. When the public is informed, one can anticipate contagious behavior under the influence of "informational cascade."[22] And when the public is organized, one-party rule may be endangered, as vividly witnessed in the 1996 Internet-mediated Serbian uprising.[23]

A recent survey shows that most of China's Internet users are educated urban dwellers, primarily in the age cohort of eighteen to thirty years old. The IT revolution also may indirectly affect other age cohorts and rural dwellers, as local tabloids — typically initiated and edited by educated urban IT users — emerge as important sources of

---

[19] Chase and Mulvenon, *You've Got Dissent!* 91–100.

[20] Ibid., 30. Based in Northern Virginia, VIP Reference — a dissident-run organization — compiles news sources not available to the public in China and e-sends them weekly (in the form of an e-mail magazine) and daily (in the form of news clippings).

[21] Ching, "The Falun Gong: Religious and Political Implications," 4.

[22] M. Stephen Walt, "Fads, Fevers, and Firestorms," *Foreign Policy* (November–December 2000): 36. Information flow may be as important as the distribution of power in shaping domestic and international order.

[23] For information on this episode, see David S. Bennahum, "The Internet Revolution," *Wired Magazine,* April 1997, 122–130.

information for the general public.²⁴ Left unregulated, cyberspace could be an arena where antiregime discourse gains momentum and antiregime action is easily agitated. The regime is concerned with polemics targeted on problems associated with China's development, such as corruption and inequality. While figures reflecting income inequality in China have been reported and debated in Internet forums, they rarely are compared to international data. Cases of corruption are widely covered, but mainly used to demonstrate the government's efforts to combat bureaucratic dishonesty; however, international comparison using popular indicators, such as the Transparency Index, is not made available. Consider this scenario: A group of political activists is committed to educating the public about the three measurements of income inequality (Gini coefficient), liberty (the Freedom House scale), and corruption (Transparency Index) by using real cases and real names that are familiar to every household. The public would be restive if it knew that (1) the Gini coefficient was zero right after the massive land reform in the early 1950s, (2) the coefficient revealed that all the wealth accrued to the princelings' party, and (3) the coefficient for China increased from 0.28 in 1981 to 0.43 in 2000. Particularly unnerving to the regime is investigative reporting on serious events that directly affect the livelihood of the man on the street, such as food poisoning and explosions. The government is unable to prevent such tragedies, yet it also is unwilling to release any information about them. Not only can these episodes undermine the regime's credibility, but also they can cast doubt on its ability to maintain national stability. If the public's political knowledge were altered, the probability of political action would increase. As Dilli Carpini and Scott Keeter contend, political knowledge and political action are strongly linked, and in modern democracy, the Internet has clearly contributed to the mushrooming of advocacy groups and citizens' participation in

---

²⁴ China's news media are becoming more concerned with business interests and market share. Market competition typically results in aggressive and risk–taking reporting.

politics and policy-making because it lowers the cost of mobilization for entrepreneurs and activists.[25] In an authoritarian polity, the form of political action is unpredictable, volatile, and potentially violent.

GOVERNMENT MONITORING AND SANITIZING

Because IT is economically necessary but politically risky, it behooves the authoritarian regime in Beijing to manage the dangers of cyberspace. Essentially, the government monitors IT users and sanitizes the information available in cyberspace in order to keep the public from accessing information that is unfavorable to the government and threatens to subvert its authoritarian control in China. The architecture of IT risk management has three components. First, the government has established a two-tiered network structure and monopolizes the upper tier of this structure in order to control links to the outside world. Second, the government has developed a comprehensive legal framework through which violators can be severely punished. Third, the government uses preemptive strikes to deter potential Internet-based collective action.

The two-tiered network structure is comprised of an "access network" at the lower deck and an "interconnection network" at the upper deck. The lower deck of the structure is for Internet service providers (ISPs), such as AOL or Earthlink; no ISP is directly connected to any net beyond national borders. The upper deck of the structure allows the state to control the switchboard to the immense international databases. The lower deck screens users, while the upper deck edits the content of foreign data sets. As Marcus Franda summarizes, the government in Beijing used to channel "almost all Internet participation at the International level through one small physical and bureaucratic bottleneck controlled by a single government monopoly

---

[25] Michael X. Delli Carpini and Scott Keeter, "The Internet and an Informed Citizenry," in *The Civic Web: Online Politics and Democratic Values,* ed. David M. Anderson and Michael Cornfield (Lanham, MD: Rowman & Littlefield Publishers, 2003), 147–148.

telecommunication provider, China Telecom."[26] The monopoly has been broken because China Telecom has been sliced into two entities, and also two additional smaller telecommunication providers have been licensed. However, all four providers are state-owned, and are staffed by high-level officials from the Ministry of Information Industry and other ministries. Foreign capital can be invested in an ISP up to 49 percent of its ownership (for Internet Content Providers, or ICPs, such as Yahoo-China or Google-China, up to 50 percent of ownership; see Table 5.2). However, the linkage between China and the outside world remains firmly in the hands of the government. By establishing an Internet firewall between itself and the rest of the world, China, like Saudi Arabia and a few other countries, has established a circuit switch to block certain international Internet traffic. It is debatable whether this device is fail-safe or whether the export-dependent Chinese economy can function smoothly if the Internet circuit is switched off. Still, it is clear that very few nations are as intent as China in maintaining a gate for all external connections and as persistent in monitoring international electronic traffic.

The government did not build a great wall to seal the borders; rather, it attempts to screen politically sensitive Web sites and direct Chinese browsers away from any database that may contain "unhealthy or inappropriate contents." Ironically, in patrolling this firewall, the rulers in Beijing have been adroit in enlisting many multinationals for technical support.[27] Cisco, known for building corporate firewalls to screen viruses and hackers, developed "a router device, integrator, and firewall box especially designed for the government's telecom monopoly" and "IBM arranged for the

---

[26] Marcus Franda, *Launching into Cyberspace* (Boulder, CO: Lynne Rienner, 2002), 189.

[27] Building a wall was not the only option that the Ming Dynasty had in dealing with the nomads. The other options — arguably the better ones — were a military offensive, diplomacy (playing the balance of power game among the competing nomads by using subsidies, treaties, and royal martial ties), and opening frontiers for trade. See Arthur Waldron, *The Great Wall of China: From History to Myth* (Cambridge, UK: Cambridge University Press, 1990), chaps. 6–8.

'high-end' financing" for the Chinese government to purchase many thousands of firewall boxes. Multinationals have the technological edge, hence, should have some leverage over Chinese authorities. Yet, foreign firms outbid one another for business opportunities in China and, thus, are willing to "go it alone" to strike a deal with the CCP regime, rather than cooperating with fellow companies to safeguard technology that might be used for censorship. AOL, Netscale Communications, and Sun Microsystems backed the Chinese Internet Corporation (part of the state-controlled New China News Agency) and consequently helped to disseminate government propaganda, while Canadian Sparkice provides state-sanctioned news on its site. Nortel provides software for voice and closed-circuit camera recognition, a technology that the Public Security Bureau (PSB) is using. Indeed, Yahoo has even disabled searches for select keywords, such as Falun Gong and Chinese democracy.[28]

Every Internet user is required to register and provide full biographical data to authorities, whether the connection is through a home computer, an Internet café, or any other public facility, such as those located in institutions of higher education. Internet users, the ICPs, Internet cafés, and the ISPs all must promise to comply with state regulations that govern cyberspace. The ISPs and Internet cafés may even be required to verify the identity of a user and retain a record of Internet surfing for a certain period of time (that is, finger-print the use of Internet).[29] The government not only has its own patrol — a 30,000 Internet police force housed in the Ministry of Public Security (MPS) — but also it has obliged the ISPs, Internet cafés, and ICPs to monitor the traffic and edit the information content in cyberspace.[30]

---

[28] Information on multinational corporations in this paragraph came from Ethan Gutmann, "Who Lost China's Internet?" *Weekly Standard,* Internet version, February 25, 2002, 1–4.

[29] Geremie R. Barme and Sang Ye, "The Great Firewall of China," *Wired Magazine,* June 1997.

[30] The number of Internet police is reported in Ethan Gutmann, "Who Lost China's Internet?" State Council Order 147, promulgated in 1994, authorizes the MPS to enforce Security Regulations for the Computer Industry.

The legal framework for cyberspace is comprehensive but ill-defined. Since 1993, the year that the Ministry of Post and Telecommunication (MPT) decided to open computer information services and e-mail to non-MPT entities, the State Council, Ministry of Information Industry (or its predecessors, including the MPT) and MPS have promulgated a thicket of legal documents to supervise the development and use of cyberspace. Taking the form of orders (*faling*), regulations (*fagui*), provisions (*banfa; zhangxing guiding*), and implementation procedures (*zhixing size*), these documents are not laws or statutes (which can only be enacted by the National People's Congress). However, most of these documents are substantive, unlike the administrative decrees in the Anglo Saxon system that have to do with procedure. Moreover, these documents are legally binding, even though some of them bear the label "temporary provisions."[31] The defining feature of these documents is that they all give the government *carte blanche* in implicating a legal or natural person for violation of state regulations. A classic document widely cited in the literature is the January 25, 2000 Regulations Regarding the Release of State Secrets through the Internet, a document released by the State Council's State Information Office and implemented by the Bureau for the Protection of State Secrets. This regulation prohibits any Chinese computer or information system from transmitting state secrets on-line. One clause stipulates, "No individuals or danwei [work unit] can pronounce, discuss, convey, relay, disseminate, or copy any state secret in any electronic mail, bulletin, chat room, or Internet news forum." What constitutes a state secret is never defined. Other regulations which prohibit content that "subverts state power, disturbs social order, undermines unification efforts with Taiwan, spreads rumors, preaches the teachings of evil cults, distributes salacious materials, dispenses pornography, slanders others, or harms the 'honor' of China," also give the state nearly unlimited legal discretion in indicting users of cyberspace.[32]

---

[31] Note that China has a continental legal system in which legality is based on codification rather than precedents.
[32] Hachigian, "China's Cyber-Strategy," 123–124.

It is not shocking, therefore, that self-censorship is prevalent.[33] Internet traffic is heavy, and it is impossible for the Internet police to monitor every use, or every site, at every moment. However, a search of the sensitive topic of state censorship is itself a tripwire, setting off a fire alarm and catching the attention of the Internet police. Aside from the strategic use of their surveillance time, the Internet police also reduce the cost of monitoring by hiring informants, rewarding whistle-blowers, and gaining the support of Internet service and content providers. Random checks of various Web sites are a very effective reminder that no one is excluded from the drag net. In addition to the probability of being detected for violations, Internet users also need to take note of the government's broad legal discretion in defining law-breaking and assigning punishment. The logic of self-policing in cyberspace is no different from that of deterring tax evasion. Taxpayers are likely to follow the tax codes if they know that they are under surveillance and that a heavy penalty is awaiting violators. Indeed, savvy IT users may even assume that the IT revolution has enhanced the government's ability to monitor the populace and that an IT society can be transparent under the eyes of big brother. As mentioned in section one above, a national information infrastructure of fiber, satellite, and microwave facilities is being built to link ministries of the central government to their provincial counterparts and to link various functional units of the governments, from banks, to customs, to law enforcement. Parallel to this Golden Dragon project is the proposed Golden Card system.[34] This smart card system reminds Internet users of the *hukou* (household registration) or *danwei* (work unit) system to which all citizens were previously bound — and some still are.

In addition to nurturing a culture of self-censorship, the government has also taken counter-measures to forestall cyber activism, especially on the eve of important occasions, such as visits by foreign dignitaries and the anniversaries of key events. Dissidents

---

[33] *Economist,* July 22, 2000, 25.
[34] Ibid., 243.

active inside China have been apprehended, including the founders and activists of the Chinese Democratic Party, as well as those who have collected e-mail addresses for foreign-based organizations. The counter-measures against overseas dissidents include freezing Web sites that the government regards as subversive, blocking all e-mails from those ISPs suspected of serving as conduits for dissidents, hacking the dissident Web sites, and using disinformation and deception to pit dissidents against each other.[35] Overseas dissident movements are fraught with factional rivalry, mutual suspicion, and relentless accusations, and their idealism and political devotion dissipate easily.[36] The Internet probably intensifies, rather than alleviates, the internal tension and "line struggle" within the dissident community. In a democracy, on-line activism and advocacy regarding particular issues stimulate political participation, but generally do not decrease political fragmentation and reconcile diverse interests and world views harbored by homogeneous but separate communities.[37] Internet seems to permit the authoritarian regime to discredit and drive wedges among exiled political dissidents.

Nearly all observers agree that the government's monitor-and-sanitize approach to IT risk management is working, at least in the short run. But there are problems with this approach. First, encryption technology remains a major hurdle to effective monitoring of users and screening of information. Prior to the September 2002 "Google incident," the government shut off any Web site deemed subversive or unhealthy, and, in doing so, effectively suppressed the stream of data from that source. The approach was essentially a

---

[35] See Chase and Mulvenon for a cataloguing and exposition of these counter-measures.
[36] See Ian Buruma, *Bad Elements: Chinese Rebels from Los Angeles to Beijing* (New York: Random House, 2001). Buruma interviewed twelve well-known dissidents exiled in the United States. Among them, two are in corporate America, three preach the gospel, two are studying (literature and history), one teaches, one has retired, one is a disk jockey, one continues to write, and one works for Radio Free Asia.
[37] William A. Galston, "If Political Fragmentation Is the Problem, Is the Internet the Solution?" in *The Civic Web: Online Politics and Democratic Value,* ed. David M. Anderson and Michael Cornfield (Lanham, MD: Rowman & Littlefield Publishers, 2003), 39.

hardware solution to the problem of policing cyberspace, namely, blocking an Internet protocol (IP) which was assigned to a Web site owned by an individual or an institution, such as a university or a marketing company. The blockade inevitably disrupted communications and economic activities. For example, the MIT Web site once was not accessible because it contained announcements of Falun Gong activities. A less disruptive way to monitor information flow is to allow access to databanks stored in servers outside China, but to monitor data transmission, download the information into a supercomputer, store it, and then edit it. The government appears to be shifting to this more refined *modus operandi*, which is essentially a surgical strike at what the government views to be undesirable content. The intercepted database, however, is not easily deciphered, especially if it is wrapped with strong encryption. Software encryption techniques are used in all servers, personal computers, cellulose phones, and cable television. In early 2000, the Chinese government had ordered all firms, foreign and domestic, to register and file their encryption software used in Internet service. However, Western firms, led by Microsoft, refused to surrender their underlying codes, as they are related to their intellectual property rights, patents, legal obligation to protect the privacy of their clients, and other vital commercial interests.[38] China can and will enhance its encryption techniques. However, to effectively censor information, it must be one step ahead of foreign data transmitters, a very challenging task.

Even if such technical problems can be overcome, limited administrative resources will continue to constrain the state's effort to monitor and sanitize information flow. The Internet police force is 30,000 strong, but its density is low and will become even lower. As of January 2005, China had an Internet population of 94 million, far exceeding the number of party cadres. There is only one member

---

[38] The pending sale of a supercomputer — subsequently approved by President Clinton — and the Cox report on China's alleged illicit acquisition of American high technology probably also dissuaded the Chinese government from enforcing the order.

of the Internet police per 3,134 Internet users.[39] As Table 5.5 reveals, the Internet population doubled every six months from 1998 through 2000. The growth rate decelerated to 30 percent per six months during 2001 and 2002, and declined further to 15 percent and 10 percent per six months during 2003 and 2004, respectively. At the current rate, the number of Internet users will double by the end of 2008, the year the Olympic Games will be held in Beijing. The ratio of China's Internet population to the national population was about one percent in 2000. This ratio will increase from 7 percent in 2005 to 11 percent in 2008. It is unlikely that the Internet police force will be able to expand correspondingly. New recruits for the cyberspace police will have to be highly educated, constantly trained, consistently loyal, and well paid, in keeping with the technical and social demands of the job: technology is steadily evolving and there is a social cost one must pay in working for a much feared, if not bitterly disliked, ministry in the fastest growing economy in the world. In addition, policing cyberspace is not the government's only urgent task. Following China's entry into the WTO, the protection of intellectual property rights and even the maintenance of consumer safety also require high-skilled state employees.[40] When state resources are strained, law enforcement is likely to be compromised. As Tipson reported, the government was aware of thirty million illegally installed disks tuned to Star-TV, but crackdown has been sporadic and uneven.[41] Identifying and penalizing these households would incur a high administrative cost that the government simply cannot afford to pay.

The third problem pertains to "agency cost." The leadership obviously cannot directly monitor and control cyberspace. It must

---

[39] The density is low if compared with the CCP membership. As of the Fifteenth CCP Congress in 1997, there were 58 million party cadres in a country with a population of 1.2 billion: there was one cadre per 20.68 people. As reported in the Sixteenth CCP Congress in late 2002, the party had 66 million cadres: one per 18.2 people.

[40] See Dali Yang, "Can the Chinese State Meet Its WTO Obligations? Government Reforms, Regulatory Capacity, and WTO Membership," *American Asian Review* 20, no. 2 (Summer 2002): 191–221.

[41] Tipson, "China and the Information Revolution," 249–250.

delegate the authority to do so to its agents (line ministries), which in turn employ their own agents (such as Internet police) to guard cyberspace. Agency loss — the discrepancy between the principal's goal and the agent's performance — can be very extensive. Because of rapid technological innovation in the IT sector, the jurisdiction of line ministries related to information technology can never be delineated in a clear or timely way. Aside from the Ministry of Information Industry and Ministry of Public Security, at least seven bureaucracies also have a stake in the IT sector: the Ministry of Railways (which controls cable networks along the railways), the Ministry of State Security (responsible for intelligence gathering), the Ministry of Broadcasting (which oversees the development of broadband technology), the State Administration for Radio, Film and Television (also involved in broadband communications), the State Education Commission (engaged in the prominent presence of students in cyberspace), the National Commission on Encryption Code Regulation, and the Ministry of Science and Technology. In China's environment of great multiplicity of agencies, policy-making is expectedly slow.[42] Further, policy for Internet security tends to be loose and vague because no player wants to assume sole responsibility and blame. Thus, policy is often made after the existing regulatory regime has failed. Internet police began to monitor Internet cafés only after a large fire broke out in one of numerous underground Internet cafés in Beijing. ICPs were barred from hiring reporters only after their on-line investigative reporting — legally not covered by the code for newspaper and TV reporting — had exposed a series of scandals. Policy implementation is as problematic as policy-making. As the "owners" of the party-state, China's top leaders may have a strong desire to monitor all Internet traffic to uncover every political dissident. However, not sharing the leadership's zeal, state functionaries on the front line, such as the Internet police, have little incentive

---

[42] The leadership will review a new policy proposal when its agents reach a consensus, but consensus is slow to emerge when everyone is a veto player. See Susan Shirk, *Political Logic of Economic Reform in China* (Berkeley, CA: University of California Press, 1992), chap. 7.

to do their utmost to outwit the Internet users and every incentive to passively monitor the Web sites to which the political leadership is particularly allergic. Moreover, although state functionaries probably suppress 95 percent of the Web sites that the government deems to be undesirable — a record that would be impressive if seen on paper — the other 5 percent may be the more "unhealthy" element. State functionaries may be able to deter 95 percent of China's Internet users from testing the limits of the law, but history may be made by the 5 percent of the users who are not deterred. In addition, in monitoring the traffic, state functionaries may themselves "internalize" the information and the values it carries, or may enjoy viewing specific sites, such as pornography. Who guards the guardians?

ENGAGE AND IMMUNIZE?

The three problems analyzed above, encryption technology, limited administrative resources, and agency cost, would vanish should the regime in Beijing decide to embark on political liberalization and democratic transition. However, if the regime persists in exercising authoritarian control over society, it will have to find a new way to manage the political risks that IT entails, as the current approach of monitoring and sanitizing IT does not appear to be sustainable in the long run. In the existing cat-and-mouse game, the regime is on the defensive, trying to stop political activists who seek to penetrate the firewall, while the Internet police attempt to fend off guerrillas and prevent bona fide users from joining the insurgency. The defensive position is frustrating and exhausting and not necessarily more effective than the offense. As the Internet sprawls, defense will become even more costly. There are signs that the authoritarian regime in Beijing is contemplating a Singaporean approach to managing the political risks that IT poses. However, does Singapore provide a good model to emulate?

The ruling party in Singapore, the People's Action Party (PAP), encourages the use of information technology in the commercial and financial sectors. Information flow is crucial to Singapore, which, as a city-state, is utterly dependent on external trade and service to the region for its economic well-being. Information technology has permeated the entire society and economy. Bandwidth is mandatory, not based on subscription. Every house has a coaxial connection to a national fiber optic network, which, in turn, is linked by satellites and undersea cables to every corner of the world. Every teacher has a notebook and every two school children have one computer.[43] More than half of the households have PCs and access to the Internet. In early 2000, Singapore further liberalized its information and telecommunication industries at a pace that was faster than any other Asian nation. Singapore also has had remarkable success in turning itself into a publishing and broadcasting center of the Asia-Pacific region.

However, senior minister Lee Kuan Yew seemed to assume that only 2 or 3 percent of Singapore's people could handle the clash of values in cyberspace, and that the rest of the population would need help. Thus, young PAP cadres formed a vibrant battalion to help the government mainly by debating with anyone who cared to challenge the paternalistic rule of the PAP in cyberspace.[44] The assumption remains that the populace cannot be insulated from the information and free-floating ideas in international cyberspace, but they can be persuaded that clean politics, stability, and prosperity under PAP governance are a very acceptable political package for Singaporeans. Betting on the support of middle-class conservatism, the PAP regime is not as concerned with containing subversive Web sites as with losing its leadership in the cyberspace discourse. Censorship did occur, but more as a punishment to the foreign press for allegedly distorting the government's view than as an attempt to deny Singapore's citizens access to the information flow in cyberspace. Self-censorship probably exists, as no one fails to realize that surveillance is easy in a tiny nation. However, the PAP regime seems to be less focused on cultivating

---

[43] These were goals announced in a speech entitled "Information Technology and Singapore's Future," by then Minister of Information George Yeo, at EMASIA, Los Angeles. These goals have been reached.

[44] Gary Rodan, "Internet and Political Control in Singapore," *Political Science Quarterly* 113, no. 1 (Spring 1998): 63–90.

self-censorship among its citizens than shaping their minds. The entire party regime is engaged in public discourse: Lee contended with former Korean President Kim Daejung in a *Foreign Affairs* forum on Asian values; numerous ministers have defended the Singaporean way from many foreign podiums; and young PAP stalwarts are active in both citizens' associations and Internet chat rooms.[45] By engaging in a battle for minds, the PAP regime hopes to enhance the immunity of its citizens to what it views as a Western liberal democratic virus.

Assessing the effectiveness of the engage-and-immunize approach is difficult, as there has been no public opinion survey on democratic values in Singapore. The latest general elections show that the votes for opposition parties and abstention ballots have decreased, while the sliding trend for the PAP's vote share has been reversed. In addition, the exodus of liberal-minded professionals and intellectuals has slowed; indeed, Singapore has had a net gain in terms of talent flow. The migration of skilled workers is primarily a function of employment opportunity. In their engagement with their fellow citizens in cyberspace, PAP young cadres have never failed to highlight Singapore's economic prospects. Election results and immigration statistics do not allow us to conclude that the PAP regime has prevailed in the cyberspace discourse, but they may suggest that the regime is not losing the battle in this arena.

On a few occasions, the regime in Beijing permitted, if not actively injected, nationalism to deflect Internet users' attention away from information that might foment desires for liberal democracy. But spurring nationalism could and did backfire. The *People's Daily*'s *Qiangguo luntan* [Strong Country Forum] repetitively was replete with postings criticizing the government for being too soft on the Belgrade embassy bombing in May 1999, the inauguration of Taiwan President Chen Shui-bian in May 2000, and the China-United States aircraft collision near Hainan Island in April 2001. These outcries of

---

[45] Diane Mauzy, "Explaining the Political Longevity of the PAP in Singapore," paper presented at a workshop on One Party Dominant Systems, East–West Center, March 8–9, 2002.

nationalism threatened to destabilize some of China's delicate relations in the international sphere. Thus, fostering middle-class conservatism would seem to be a better strategy for the regime in its dialogue with Internet users.

Indeed, creating an olive-shaped society with a bulging middle class might well be on the wish list of China's leadership, now that it has decided to gradually and subtly transform its proletarian, exclusionary party into an all-inclusive catchall party. The expansion of the middle class may blur the rich-poor cleavage and serve as a stabilizer in a society that has been under the duress of rapid transformation. Moreover, as David Goodman shows, the newly emerging middle class is not as highly educated as it is economically prosperous; its members are still socially parochial, not yet having been exposed to foreign or cosmopolitan values.[46] They probably will be new Internet users and an "accessible mass" for the regime.

However, capturing the heart of the new middle class in China will be an even more daunting task than in Singapore. The main distinction between Singapore and China is probably not their respective sizes, but the quality and aptitude of their governments. The PAP regime is clean, while the CCP regime is yet to bridle widespread corruption. Upon gaining national independence, the PAP regime in Singapore drastically raised the pay scale for government officials (the carrot), formed an anticorruption commission (the stick), and ever since has practiced meritocracy (the ruler) all along. The CCP regime has been wielding the stick to punish corrupt elite, but has yet to fully adhere to meritocracy. Given the growing income disparity in China's society, chronic fiscal imbalance, and widespread layoffs in the state sector, the CCP regime probably is not in a position to overhaul the compensation scheme for its officials any time soon.[47] The government remains a formidable player

---

[46] David S. G. Goodman, "The New Middle Class," in *The Paradox of China's Post-Mao Reforms,* ed. Merle Goldman and Roderick MacFarquhar (Cambridge, MA: Harvard University Press, 1999), 241–261, especially 259.

[47] Former premier Zhu Rongji raised the pay scale for the civil service three times, but the wage gap between the government sector and the private sector remains

in the market place, possesses immense regulatory power, and is barely under the oversight of its own disciplinary board. A free press and independent judiciary are yet to be permitted. And, corruption is a problem that the CCP regime must live with for the foreseeable future.

In addition to corrupt politics, the continued closure of the political market in China places the CCP regime in an indefensible position in public discourse. The political market in Singapore is biased toward the PAP, but at least it is partially open. Electoral competition in some districts has been real and intense; elections have never been rigged or cancelled; and the public can cast protest votes against the PAP, albeit not dislodge it from power. In China, aside from village elections, all other electoral competitions are more apparent than real. Finally, the leadership in the CCP regime is yet to oblige itself to practice political persuasion in the public sphere. As Daniel Lynch meticulously demonstrates, continual market reform has steadily eroded the propaganda machine and thought control architecture that were constructed in the Maoist era.[48] And yet, the post-Mao leaderships and their entourages did and still give hortatory speeches from the podium of the Great Hall of the People, unwilling and unable to become interlocutors in the emerging, market-driven public sphere, which includes cyberspace. The SARS epidemics in 2003 prompted the CCP leadership to allow information flow and individuals to visit Web sites to "hear" the voice of the alarmed public, leading one to hope for the emergence of "Internet democracy."[49] As the epidemic subsided, control over information

---

wide. Keen to tread a populist line, Secretary General of the Chinese Communist Party Hu Jingtao and Premier Wen Jiabao are yet to launch their plan to rationalize the bureaucracy while boosting its morale.

[48] Daniel Lynch, *After the Propaganda State* (Stanford, CA: Stanford University Press, 1999).

[49] Shaw Dau-sheng, "Zhongguo de minzhu zhi neng zai Zhongguo de gaige shijian zhong fazhan: Xilong hulianwang shi de minzhu" [Chinese democracy can only develop through Chinese reform and practice: Part ten on "Internet democracy"], www.chinaelections.com, October 22, 2003.

was again tightened.[50] The Internet remains a listening post for the government, rather than a place where the leaders and cadres care to have discourse with the public.

CONCLUSION

Pursuing information technology has led China to become a leading player in the age of the information revolution. In barely a decade, China has emerged as a key manufacturer of high-tech products and the most coveted market for information technology sectors. Information technology, however, is a double-edged sword, empowering the economy, but potentially undermining authoritarian political control. China's leadership hopes to eat the cake and have it, too. Gate-keeping and screening information flow, imposing random surveillance, and applying stiff punishments for offenders might deter users from accessing or disseminating subversive materials. However, while nurturing a culture of self-censorship among most users, the control mechanism is ineffective in curbing devoted dissidents. Moreover, given the prohibitive administrative costs they incur, current mechanisms to control the information that reaches China's citizens may not be sustainable in the long run. By 2002, Internet users outnumbered CCP members, and mobile phone users outnumbered fixed-line phone users. At some point, the "audit rate" may drop to a level at which deterrence can no longer work. If the government cannot monitor and sanitize cyberspace, then it will need to manage this social space, by explaining its policies and defending its views. The authoritarian leaders in Beijing may have to prepare for that challenge, if they are unwilling or unable to do away with information technology.

---

[50] "China Tightens Its Rules on Internet Address Managers," Reuters, November 22, 2003.

Chapter 6

The Future of SOEs: From Shortage Economics to "Enron–omics"?

Xiaobo Hu

Despite China's success in economic development, economic reform has always been a challenge to the Chinese government. In the late 1970s and the early 1980s, the Chinese government first looked to Eastern Europe for more efficient socialist managerial systems, but later the socialist systems in Eastern Europe collapsed. It then looked to the Japanese development model, but later the Japanese economy slid into a decade-long recession. More recently, China looked to South Korea for insights on economic development models, but the South Korean model raised more questions than anyone could answer after the 1997 Asian financial crisis. Finally, as China modernized its enterprise system and looked to the United States for models, the sudden collapse of Enron proved to teach China's economic planners a timely lesson.

Enron Corporation was formed in July 1985, when Texas-based Houston Natural Gas merged with InterNorth, a Nebraska-based

---

Note: The author gratefully acknowledges the research assistance of Nicole Cariri.

natural gas company. In the 1990s, Enron introduced a number of revolutionary changes to energy trading. It started to tailor electricity and natural gas contracts to reflect the cost of delivery to a specific destination by creating a nationwide energy-trading network. However, as 2002 began, Enron found itself at the center of one of corporate America's biggest scandals. In less than a year, it had gone from one of the most innovative companies of the late twentieth century to a synonym for corruption and mismanagement.

At its peak, Enron controlled more than 25 percent of the "over the counter" energy-trading market. Much of its balance sheet, however, did not make sense to analysts. Enron shuffled many of its debt obligations into offshore partnerships and it reported inaccurately high trading revenues. In October 2001 when the United States Securities and Exchange Commission had begun an inquiry into Enron and its partnerships, Enron's Chairman and CEO, Kenneth Lay, started to call government officials, including the Federal Reserve chairman, the treasury secretary, and the commerce secretary. In early December, Enron, which a year before had been touted as the seventh largest company in the United States, filed for Chapter 11 bankruptcy protection. A month later, Kenneth Lay resigned, and the White House announced that the Department of Justice had begun a criminal investigation of Enron.

The lessons that have been learned since December 2001 when Enron declared bankruptcy are multifaceted. They are important not only for Americans, but also for the people in China who have strived continuously in their attempts to clarify their economic relationships in the market. The essential features of the Enron problem include flawed corporate governance, collusion between auditors and the audited, the role of the government in the long chain of oversight, as well as the collective action problem of shareholders. A more important question for the Chinese government, as well as for Chinese scholars, is how China should and will handle those problems that were observed in Enron and three other American companies[1] in the summer of 2002, which mirror the problems of

---

[1] These troubled companies included Sunbeam, WorldCom, and Adelphia.

The Future of SOEs: From Shortage Economics to "Enron–omics"? 167

many Chinese state-owned enterprises and worry analysts about the future of China's economy.

The Enron-like problems in China and the United States share similarities but also have their differences. Cases in both countries have involved flawed corporate practices and collusion between auditors — the government in the China case — and the audited. The Chinese-style Enron problems have resulted from decentralization policies, reforms of the state-owned enterprises (SOEs), and the rise of a new economic sector where bureaucrats and entrepreneurs collude.

In an attempt to provide a sound understanding of the problems in the relationship between the state and business in China, this chapter aims at drawing lessons from the Enron collapse in two areas: State corporatism and business partnership. It focuses on the relationship between political power and economic power. All these problems together may be referred to as "Enron-omics." Government oversight and protection are at the roots of Enron-omics in China. If China's new administration under the fourth generation of leadership cannot tackle such problems in a timely fashion, the entire Chinese economy will face grave challenges in the post-Jiang era.

In the following pages, this chapter first outlines the process of economic transition in China, which has provided structural opportunities for the emergence of Enron-type problems. Such structure was produced as a by-product of various decentralization reform programs in the 1980s. These programs created a local state corporatism by separating components of property rights and placing them into the hands of different people. Then, the chapter explores the development of township and village enterprises (TVEs) and the tertiary sector, which helped to produce the human capital that could lead the Chinese enterprises toward the Enron-like problems. Discussion of TVEs and the tertiary sector illustrates business collusion between the government and the enterprises. Finally, the chapter examines the 1997 round of the reform of the state-owned enterprises and collective enterprises, where the insiders obtained the privatized goods. The insiders (i.e., former directors, managers, and bureaucrats) were transformed into an elite bureaucratic-entrepreneurial class that embodies powerful influence over state policy-making as well as market operations.

A DECENTRALIZED STRUCTURE

Chinese economic reform started with decentralization programs in the late 1970s. The decentralization reforms significantly transformed the state ownership system and separated the three major components of property rights — user rights, extractor rights, and seller rights — and placed them into the hands of different players.[2] This separation of property rights created various types of principal-agent problems, but more importantly, it created an economic structure where local state corporatism could flourish.[3]

At least three types of decentralization programs were implemented, to different degrees, by the Chinese leadership more than twenty years ago when China started its ongoing economic reform. The first type of decentralization was the delegation of decision-making authority — the user rights — formerly in the hands of the Chinese Communist Party (CCP) secretaries, to government administrators and enterprise managers; this was the so-called "separation of the party and government administration" (*dang zheng fenjia*). This decentralization involved restraining the power of party secretaries on all governmental levels, especially their power over day-to-day economic planning and management, and providing more freedom to bureaucrats and managers. Despite a serious setback in 1989, the government made obvious advances in taking the authority to manage the economy away from the party and placing it into the hands of its technocrats. Although there has been a clear decline

---

[2] User rights allow agents to use assets without necessarily claiming ownership; extractor rights are rights to returns from the assets; and seller rights are rights to transfer the assets. For a full discussion, see Xiaobo Hu, *Problems in China's Transitional Economy: Property Rights and Transitional Models* (Singapore: Singapore University Press, 1998).

[3] See, for example, Jean C. Oi, "The Evolution of Local State Corporatism," in *Zouping in Transition: The Process of Reform in Rural North China*, ed. Andrew Walder (Cambridge, MA: Harvard University Press, 1998), 35–61.

of the party's administrative power and a clear increase in the power of the technocrats, the separation has yet to be completed.

The second type of decentralization was the delegation of decision-making authority, formerly residing at a central point (e.g., the State Council, central commissions, and ministries) to local government administrations and local departments; this was the so-called "straightening-out of the relationship between the central and local government" (*lishun zhongyang yu difang guanxi*). This type of administrative decentralization included tax-retention schemes, departmental contract responsibility systems, the transfer of enterprises to local governments, and the provision of more freedom to local governments to manage their local economies. As some scholars have pointed out, Chinese leaders have played to the provinces or other local entities.[4] Other scholars also pointed out that local state corporatism emerged as a result of these first two decentralization programs.[5] We will return to this last point shortly.

The third type of decentralization was the delegation of decision-making authority from the state all the way down to individual enterprises; this was the so-called "separation of government administration and enterprise management" (*zheng qi fenjia*). This belongs to the category of liberalization, which started to be implemented on a large scale only in the late 1990s.

Decentralization in the first decade of post-Mao reform was quite limited. The reform involved primarily an administrative decentralization, the second type of decentralization, rather than a straightforward liberalization, not to mention privatization, which

---

[4] See, for example, Susan Shirk, "'Playing to the Provinces': Deng Xiaoping's Political Strategy of Economic Reform," *Studies of Comparative Communism* 23, nos. 3–4 (Autumn 1990): 227–258.

[5] See, for example, Jean C. Oi, "Fiscal Reform and the Economic Foundations of Local State Corporatism," *World Politics* 45, no. 1 (October 1992): 99–126, and Nan Lin, "Local Market Socialism: Local Corporatism in Action in Rural China," *Theory and Society* 24, no. 2 (June 1995): 301–354. See also, Jonathan Unger and Anita Chan, "Corporatism and the East Asia Model," *Australian Journal of Chinese Affairs* 33 (January 1995): 29–54.

started on a large scale only in the late 1990s. Administrative decentralization delegated decision-making authority to lower levels of government office — rather than to the market, which would result in liberalization, or to individuals, which would result in privatization. Indeed, through this administrative decentralization of user rights, more power was gained by local governments than by individual enterprises. It was this limitation in China's decentralization that gave local governments considerable power over local enterprises and the local economy.

Decentralization has separated user rights from those of the owner — the state — and delegated them to local governments. It has created state corporatism, Chinese style. In such corporatism, Chinese local governments are a major partner in local business. Frequently, local governments "treat enterprises within their administrative purview as one component of a larger corporate whole."[6] Local governments have been actively involved in designing policies that facilitate economic development within the region and help local companies to compete with others from different regions. Sometimes, local officials "act as the equivalent of a board of directors ... [or] more directly as the chief executive officers."[7]

When it is formed, it is difficult for local state corporatism to be broken down. In a decentralized structure, the local governments have an inherent interest in generating revenue from the local economy. As a major business partner, local governments can acquire a larger share of the revenue than otherwise would be the case, and insert more control over the revenue that is generated. In turn, enterprises are interested in the economic and political backing of local governments or government officials.[8] This is not uncommon for businesses in a transitional economy, where rules are expected to change frequently and enforcement of the set rules is difficult.

---

[6] Jean C. Oi, "The Role of the Local State in China's Transitional Economy," *China Quarterly* 144 (December 1995): 1132.
[7] Ibid.
[8] David D. Li, "A Theory of Ambiguous Property Rights in Transition Economies: The Case of the Chinese Non-State Sector," *Journal of Comparative Economics* 23, no. 1 (August 1996): 1–19.

China's new structure has been labeled "federalism, Chinese style," in which local governments are pitched against each other in protecting and promoting their own regional economies.[9] Chinese federalism results from decentralization of authority, a market-oriented approach, and an open economy, whereby local governments provide economic protection for local businesses. It is through such local protectionism that local government and local business collude. Ironically, Chinese political forces and economic forces started to collude at the very beginning, when the two were about to be transformed separately.

Decentralization of authority and an opened economy provided a structural opportunity for local state corporatism to emerge and proliferate, which in turn provided a base for large-scale Enron-like problems. Therefore, Enron-omics may have emerged in China long before the beginning of the twenty-first century. In such an economy, business decisions are not based on market factors, but on political and personal considerations. In the long run, local state corporatism breeds inefficiency even in an open economy.

NEW HUMAN CAPITAL

Following the implementation of a decentralized structure, new economic development has helped to produce the human capital that has led Chinese enterprises to Enron-like problems. Such human resources have formed an important part of the emerging "bureaupreneurial class."[10] This is a group of people who are found in both public and private sectors.[11] Many of them are government officials and entrepreneurs at the same time.

---

[9] Gabriella Montinola, Yingyi Qian, and Barry R. Weingast, "Federalism, Chinese Style: The Political Basis for Economic Success in China," *World Politics* 48, no. 1 (October 1995): 50–81.

[10] This term is borrowed from, Xiaobo Lu, "Booty Socialism, Bureau-preneurs, and the State in Transition: Organization Corruption in China," *Comparative Politics* 32, no. 3 (April 2000): 273–294.

[11] David J. Lynch, "Emerging Middle Class Reshaping China," *USA Today*, November 12, 2002, 13A–14A.

New economic development has transformed China's traditionally centrally-planned economy into a mixed economy in which a variety of ownership types coexist. However, it is in the tertiary sector,[12] where the economy has achieved the most rapid development, that more human capital has been intensively produced to run the business engine that has driven the economy into Enron-type problems.

Before the state started to promote rapid development of the tertiary sector in the early 1990s, township and village enterprises in rural China were the primary machines that produced a hybrid class of governmental officials and entrepreneurs. Township and village officials were actively involved in collective enterprises under their jurisdiction. The township governments and village communities were regarded as *de facto* owners, and they provided initial capital and hired the managers. An enterprise's activities were not included in any state plan or placed under any form of state control. Therefore, the reward system was determined by the community officials and managers themselves, within a very flexible accounting system. There were not many restrictions nor was there guidance on how the budget should be spent. In effect, officials and managers had the *de facto* right to extract income from the collective enterprises. Thus, they became both politically and economically powerful insiders in local business.

In the 1980s when privatization was still a taboo in China, property rights became fragmented because of the separate transformation of their different components. In property rights transformation, the extractor rights became informal, that is, the property owner's right to economic returns was exercised by the "user" of the property without formal transfer.[13] In other words, the manager — the

---

[12] Traditionally, the tertiary sector referred to any industry or service other than agriculture, mining, manufacturing, energy, or construction. However, the Chinese State Statistics Bureau redefined the three economic sectors along a similar line: agriculture, industry, and service. See "China Redefines Three Economic Sectors," *Luoyang Daily*, May 23, 2003.

[13] Xiaobo Hu, "The State and the Private Sector in a New Property Rights System," in *China after Jiang*, ed. Gang Lin and Xiaobo Hu (Stanford, CA: Stanford University Press, 2003), 69–89.

user — extracted economic returns from operating the state-owned enterprise without necessary formal endorsement.

In effect, the exercise of the informal extractor rights meant law-breaking or corruption. Such exercises thrived in a rather grey area of the Chinese economy.[14] The systems that induced such operations were all legal, but the operations themselves were not legally protected. This paradox, according to David Li, compelled managers in China to include a third party to share the dividends in order to reduce the transaction costs for their enterprises.[15]

During the 1980s and the 1990s when socialist public ownership continued to dominate the economy, the "third party" obviously included primarily governmental officials. These officials participated in daily business operations of local enterprises. They acted as the equivalent of boards of directors. Sometimes, they even performed the functions of a chief executive officer. The officials formulated policies to accommodate the interests of the enterprises that opened their doors to the officials, bent central policies in favor of these enterprises, reduced red tape, protected the enterprises from competition, and rescued them when they ran into financial troubles. These officials, of course, also accumulated economic power and personal wealth. Officials thus became insiders of local business.

While most parts of the economy took cautious steps to "grope the rocks while crossing the river," rapid expansion of the tertiary sector out of the state plan opened up new frontiers that linked the government officials and enterprise managers in a variety of ventures. The tertiary sector had been extremely suppressed during Maoist times. After the post-Mao economic reform started, individuals rushed to try their entrepreneurial skills in the newly opened market, but they lacked experience and capital. Consequently, the government offered necessary initial capital as well as a safety net that protected mostly officials from business liability or failure.

---

[14] Guoqiang Tian, "Property Rights and the Nature of Chinese Collective Enterprises," *Journal of Comparative Economics* 28, no. 2 (June 2000): 247–268.

[15] Li, "A Theory of Ambiguous Property Rights in Transition Economies," 1–19.

In the late 1980s, typically every Chinese work unit could use state properties — land, capital, and infrastructure — to set up trading companies and other businesses in the tertiary sector. In many cases, the state-owned work unit even provided some cash to start the business operation. The head of the new business was usually a government official working in the unit. These companies were not directly supported by state finance, hence, they were not included in the state plan or placed under state control. Managers of the new businesses could act as the *de facto* owner and extract additional income in forms of bonuses, commissions, or dividends. Further, the bureaucrats-turned-entrepreneurs were allowed to return to their previous positions if the new business was not successful in the market. This was a very important safety net for these government officials.

For the government, development of the tertiary sector could resolve such problems as the surplus labor force, lack of services, shortage of capital, and low productivity. From a political perspective, by means of this developmental policy, the government could gain support and loyalty from the targeted population because the tertiary sector transferred extractor rights to powerful individuals and created informal extractor rights for those who had influence over policy-making or policy implementation.

The directives issued by the CCP Central Committee and the State Council in the early summer of 1992 and at the Fourteenth Party Congress convened later that year further extended the benefits of informal extractor rights to more governmental officials. For instance, middle-ranking officials in China everywhere were allowed to participate in or run their own businesses. Later on, tax reform adopted in 1994 could be regarded as a legal outlet for money laundering that involved gains through the exercise of informal extractor rights. A typical practice in this area was that gray earnings were legalized after their taxes were paid through a nonstate business account.[16] Thus, an economically powerful class became consolidated.

---

[16] See Chen Jian, *Loss of Chinese Property* (Beijing: China Urban Press, 1998), 154. See also, "China's Underground Wealth: Money Laundering Reaches 200 Billion *Yuan* Every Year," *Xiamen Daily*, April 3, 2003, http://www.zaobao.com/special/newspapers/2003/04/xmdaily030403.html (accessed April 4, 2003).

The development of rural collective enterprises and the tertiary sector in the late 1980s and early 1990s indeed transferred the extractor rights to individuals — bureaucrats and managers — without formal recognition. The state tolerated officials' corrupt abuse of the extractor rights to state assets, resulting in asset-stripping of the state-owned enterprises, hence, transferring informally the extractor rights to certain groups of individuals and creating a new bureaupreneurial class in China.[17] This class consists of bureaucrats, bureaucrats-turned-entrepreneurs, and entrepreneurs who have tight relationships with government officials. This class embodies influence over both government policy-making and market operations.

In sum, there are two modes of entry into the bureaupreneurial class. First, government officials and SOE managers use state assets to open a new business outside the state plan. Many of them become bureaucrats-turned-entrepreneurs. Second, governmental officials are approached by existing enterprises and included in their boards of directors or similar functions. Some in this second group remain in their governmental posts. Thus, a decentralized, market-oriented economy provided a structural opportunity for local state corporatism. The rapid development of a new economic sector, either through rural collective enterprises or in the tertiary sector, accumulated human capital ready for business collusion between the state and the enterprises.

ANOTHER ROUND OF SOE REFORM

"When you cannot fix it, discard it" — that sounds like the working philosophy of the Chinese government. When it could not solve the problems of inefficiency in the state-owned enterprises, the state transferred the resultant budget deficit to the state banks by requiring them to continue the bad loans (*daizhang, huaizhang,*

---

[17] Angang Hu, *China: Fighting against Corruption* [in Chinese] (Hangzhou: Zhejiang People's Publishing House, 2001), and Andrew Wedeman, "Corruption and Politics," in *China Review, 1996*, ed. Maurice Brosseau, Suzanne Pepper, and Tsang Shu-ki (Hong Kong: Chinese University Press, 1996).

sizhang).[18] However, when the state banks could not continue the bad loans without going bankrupt, the state began looking for other "victims" through shareholding, mergers, and sales. This has been the process of economic problem-solving in China in the eyes of some Chinese economists. However, through privatization, shareholding, mergers, bankruptcies, and sales, the state has transferred some of the property rights over state assets to the bureaupreneurial class, creating Chinese "Enrons" and Enron-like problems in the Chinese market economy.

Transformation of different components of property rights has taken place at different times in China's economic transition. Decentralization reform transferred user rights to local governmental officials who were in charge of local enterprises, while development of TVEs and the tertiary sector later transferred the extractor rights to a new hybrid class of bureaucrats and entrepreneurs. Transformation of the seller rights did not really start until 1997, when the government launched a new round of economic reform in an attempt to renovate and retain the large state-owned enterprises and to privatize the smaller ones (*zhuada fangxiao*).

A new round of the SOE reform was initiated at the Fifth Session of the Eighth National People's Congress and the Fifteenth Party Congress, both convened in 1997. It aimed at improving the state sector and "letting go" of those state-owned enterprises that could not be revitalized — especially medium- to small-sized enterprises. A wave of mergers swept across the country in 1997, with mergers of some three thousand large enterprises and reorganization of some 15.5 billion *yuan* in state assets. In addition, more state-owned enterprises and collective-owned township and village enterprises were sold to the nonstate sectors.[19] As a result, although the state decided to give up medium- to small-size SOEs, the 1997 round of SOE reform provided another opportunity for the formation of Enron-type enterprises and the operation of Enron-type business relationships with the state.

---

[18] X.L. Ding, "Systemic Irregularity and Spontaneous Property Transformation in the Chinese Financial System," *China Quarterly*, no. 163 (September 2000): 655–676.

[19] For a detailed discussion, see Xiaobo Hu, "Transforming the Property Rights," in *Transition towards Post-Deng China*, ed. Xiaobo Hu and Gang Lin (Singapore: Singapore University Press, 2001), 15–40.

The 1997 reform was obviously an insider transformation, since the majority of the medium- to small-size state-owned enterprises and township and village collective enterprises were sold to their previous directors or managers, or to former bureaucrats. During the transformation, previous executives — the *de facto* rights-holders — were in the best position to obtain, exercise, and keep the newly-created rights to themselves. Workers were not among this privileged group, nor were the peasants. Further, in the late 1980s and the first half of the 1990s, those who controlled the allocation of the state assets were the ones who could enjoy the state property rights: they were *de facto* user rights-holders and extractor rights-holders. By the time of the 1997 reform, they had accumulated enough capital to purchase an entire SOE or the controlling shares of the SOE. Those "who were in the right place at the right time" could also enjoy opportunities presented to them during the SOE reform. If they did not have enough funds for purchase, they worked out measures to secure their (*de facto*) ownership, such measures as "lay-away," similar to the lay-away plan in American department stores. After all, many buyers were chief officers in governmental bureaus and state-owned enterprises.

Take the example of an industrial district in Shenyang, Liaoning Province, in northern China. The municipal district of Huanggu had sold forty-one state-owned or collective enterprises within its jurisdiction by the summer of 2000. Seventy-one percent was sold to their own directors, formerly the *de facto* rights-holders. Take another example of a rural town Changjing, in Jiangsu Province in southern China. Changjing had transformed 191 collective enterprises by summer of 2002. Except for eight enterprises that have been discontinued, almost all the rest of the enterprises are now in the hands of their former directors or managers, in one form or another. The transformation of the enterprises took a variety of forms, which included shareholding, leasing, lay-away, and internal transfers.[20]

The examples of Huanggu and Changjing reveal typical beneficiaries of the 1997 transformation. In a 2000 study of Chinese collective

---

[20] For a detailed discussion, see Xiaobo Hu, "Transformation of Property Rights in China: The Institutional Origins," Entrepreneurial Leadership Working Paper Series, no. 02-101, Arthur M. Spiro Center for Entrepreneurial Leadership, Clemson University, 2002.

enterprises, Guoqiang Tian affirmed that the administrative bureaucrats held special resources that gave them a comparative advantage in transitional economies.[21] If one traces the path of transformation back to the beginning of the reform, a pattern of path dependency is unveiled of how insiders have continued to do well in the Chinese transformation of property rights. Indeed, after the 1980s, decentralization programs transferred the economic decision power to the local governments and produced local state corporatism and rapid development of TVEs. Also, the tertiary sector created a bureaupreneurial class, which later became the beneficiary of insider transformation. Economic reforms in the 1980s and 1990s, such as contracting, responsibility, and dual-track systems, gave members of the bureaupreneurial class the chance to experience risk-taking, to explore market mechanisms, and to accumulate private capital. When the time arrived, they were the chosen up-front beneficiaries of forming private properties out of state assets.

In this round of economic reform in China, bureaucrats and business executives proceed to redistribute "social valuables" in their favor and to exclude other people from sharing them. What observers saw in the cases of Huanggu and Changjing was not unique, but typical practice regarding the insider's benefits. Typically, the supervising agency of the state or collective enterprise has actively engaged in identifying "proper" potential buyers of the enterprise. Not surprisingly, the agency has admitted that incumbent directors or managers are its first preference. In this sense, China's economic transformation also has been a process of transferring the state's rights and assets to a certain group of people, the former bureaucrats and state managers. This process has produced a business and managerial class of former governmental bureaucrats and managers of the state-owned and collective enterprises. Many of the business leaders are old acquaintances from the government's bureaus. Again, this new class embodies powerful influence over state policy-making and market operations.

---

[21] Guoqiang Tian, "Property Rights and the Nature of Chinese Collective Enterprises," *Journal of Comparative Economics* 28 (June 2000): 247–268.

Insider transformation continues to tie the state and business together, yet in market collusion. The state has not become an impartial referee, nor has it represented the interests of the entire economy, nor has it acted as an important counter-balance between big businesses and the poor and powerless. Equally dangerous is that business and economic decisions may not be made based on market factors, but rather on political and personal considerations. Indeed, many CEOs are shielded from accountability for wrongful business decisions.

FROM SHORTAGE ECONOMICS TO "ENRON-OMICS" IN CHINA

SOEs were created by the centrally-planned economy. They represented an extreme form of state corporatism and business collusion between the government and the corporations. Corruption cases involving government officials in China exemplify the Enron problem,[22] including the investigation of Liu Jinbao, president of the Bank of China Hong Kong Branch, and premier Shanghai tycoon, Zhou Zhengyi, chairman and CEO of Nongkai Conglomerate.[23] However, current economic reforms in China face a danger of transforming the old Shortage Economics into Enron-omics in the future.

During the period of central planning, SOEs were managed by government officials and produced an economy of shortage.[24] In

---

[22] See, for example, Weng Chengzhong, *Xin Guangchang Xianxin Ji* [New official corruption cases] (Hong Kong: Popular Culture, 1990). See also, Ding Zijiang, "From Corruption to Capital Flight: The Loss of Chinese State Assets," *Modern China Studies*, no. 1 (2000): 84–105, and Guilhem Fabre, "Separation of Power, Corruption and Criminalization: China in a Comparative Perspective," *Modern China Studies*, no. 4 (2002): 45–64.

[23] "Zhou Zhengyi Case Exposes Twenty Officials," *Xinming Daily*, June 6, 2003, http://www.zaobao.com/special/newspapers/2003/06/xmrb060603.html (accessed June 6, 2003).

[24] Janos Kornai, *Economics of Shortage* (New York: North-Holland Publishing, 1980), and Christine Wong, "The Economics of Shortage and Problems of Reform in Chinese Industry," *Journal of Comparative Economics* 10 (December 1986): 363–387.

Shortage Economics, due to soft budget constraints and the political incentives to meet state production targets, the more that SOEs produced, the more serious was the shortage that the economy experienced. Since the SOEs' budget constraints were "soft" and they could not go bankrupt, SOE officials overfulfilled the state targets in order to earn personal career advances. Overproduction was a serious drain on scarce resources, inflated production demands, and lowered the quality of China's products. All this resulted in shortage of production inputs as well as high-quality outputs. Shortage Economics created a vicious circle.

Post-Mao economic reforms have introduced competition for high-quality products and linked managerial responsibility to market performance. At the same time, however, these reforms have tied the state and business together in a new way. The state has not privatized all its enterprises; perhaps it will not do so. A newly-emerged hybrid class of bureaucrats and entrepreneurs discussed above carries out the close ties between the state and business. Such state-business ties have led to mounting corruption and devastating asset-striping of the state, currently serious problems in Chinese Enron-omics. According to a study in China, SOE corruption had caused a loss of state assets worth 1.2 trillion yuan by 1998, during the post-Mao economic reforms. In addition, SOEs spend 100 billion yuan of state funds on meals and entertainment and the state loses another 100 billion yuan in tax evasions every year.[25]

The SOEs have lost most of their value in transformation, regardless of whether the transformation has been in the form of a merger, incorporation, or sale. Such losses have resulted from official oversight in some cases and collaboration in others. Although some shares of the SOEs have been allocated to the workers, the workers cannot engage in collective action to increase their shares because independent workers' unions that represent workers' interests are

---

[25] Chen Jian, *Loss of Chinese Proprety* (Beijing: China Urban Press, 1998).

not permitted. Workers are basically not well-organized, nor are their interests well-represented.[26]

Chinese Enrons are different from their American counterparts in significant respects, and have been formed in three different ways. First, some Chinese Enrons have been formed by SOEs or other state agencies, for instance, in the tertiary sector, as discussed above. Second, some Chinese Enrons are non-SOEs but they have recruited current or former government officials to serve as board members or executive officers. Last but not least, some of these troubled organizations are SOEs and enterprises in which the state holds a considerable amount of stock. No matter how the Chinese Enrons have been formed, they are all well-connected in a complicated web, whereby these enterprises can expect favoritism, protection, and preferential treatment.

Enron-omics is different from state corporatism as well. State corporatism gives the state a prominent position in the economy, whereas Enron-omics does not prescribe state dominance. Enron-omics does not focus on the development of the entire economy, nor does it support a developmental state for which some East Asian countries are noted. Enron-omics is crony capitalism in which enterprises abuse state protection and promotion. It favors the big businesses that are involved. In Enron-omics, business takes the initiative and command rather than the state.

When Chinese leader Jiang Zemin stepped down as party boss at the Sixteenth Party Congress, he emphasized the importance of China's continual economic growth. Jiang's "Three Represents" might have been aimed at consolidating the basis for continued communist rule rather than at elevating the economy to a higher level of development. By including the "Three Represents" into its new constitution, the Chinese Communist Party could legitimately recruit its former class enemies — the capitalists. The collusion between China's political

---

[26] See also, Philip P. Pan, "In China, Labor Unions Offer Little Protection," *International Herald Tribune*, October 16, 2002, http://www.iht.com/cgi-bin/generic.cgi?template=articleprint.tmplh&ArticleId=73982 (accessed October 16, 2002).

power and economic power proceeds with a "bright future for the power holder," yet creates concerns. One article called the Sixteenth Party Congress "China's Congress of Crony Capitalists."[27] Bao Tong, former close adviser to the ousted liberal reformer, Premier Zhao Ziyang, who died in January 2005, wrote an article of extended analysis of Jiang's "Three Represents" and post-Jiang development. According to Bao Tong, Jiang's "Three Represents," in effect, were intended only for "the rich, the corrupt, and the powerful."[28] Jiang was criticized for building crony capitalism in China, another name for Enron-omics. In such an economy, business decisions are not based on market factors, but political and personal considerations. In a long run, Enron-omics becomes counterproductive even in an open economy. Crony capitalism washed away the forty-year accumulation of national wealth within a couple of months in Indonesia and some other Southeast Asian newly industrialized countries (NICs) at the end of the 1990s. Such collapse of economies should be very alarming to the new Chinese leadership; it provides evidence that China's fourth generation of leadership cannot afford to ignore the potential dangers of Enron-like problems in China, especially when the Chinese market system has not yet reached maturity and rule of law has not been entirely implemented.

It is very interesting that Bao Tong criticized Jiang's new direction for China as too liberal or right-wing elitist, when he was an advocate of neoauthoritarianism (i.e., he was a right-wing liberal on China's then political spectrum) under former Premier Zhao Ziyang.[29] But the difference between neoauthoritarianism and the "Three Represents" might be similar to that between state corporatism and Enron-omics.

---

[27] Joseph Kahn, "China's Congress of Crony Capitalists," *New York Times*, November 10, 2002.

[28] Bao Tong, in an untitled manuscript that was disseminated via www.wenxuecity.com in November 2002. This view was later expressed by Bao Tong in an interview, "Bao Tong on Wen Jiabao: An Interview" (in Chinese), *Jinri Pinglun*, December 22, 2003, http://news.wenxuecity.com/BBSView.php?SubID=news&MsgID=7511, November 2002.

[29] Xu Yufang, "The Fading of Jiang's 'Three Represents,'" *Asia Times*, November 6, 2002, http://www.atimes.com/atimes/printN.html (accessed November 6, 2002), and Joseph Kahn, "China's Communist Party Opens Its Doors to Capitalists," *New York Times*, November 4, 2002.

When Jiang Zemin replaced Zhao Ziyang in the wake of the Tiananmen demonstration in 1989, the former was considered to be very conservative. Therefore, the more serious question might be: How will the post-Sixteenth Party Congress leadership build its power basis and power legitimacy? Will it be on Enron-type enterprises, or on a "state corporatism" that favors powerful insider companies?

It still might be too early to tell about the new government's policy since Chinese President Hu Jintao and Premier Wen Jiabao have not been in power for very long by Chinese standards, and much of the early period of their new administration was dedicated to the critical problem of SARS. However, during the initial days of the post-Jiang era, the rhetoric of the "Three Represents" died down quickly.[30] Indeed, Hu delivered his first important speech in Xibaipo in early December 2002, calling for more attention to the poor, seemingly trying to revitalize the revolutionary tradition of fighting with and for the poor. "With a deft series of public gestures meant to identify him with old-time Communist virtues of self-sacrifice and devotion to the downtrodden," Hu tried to create an image for himself as a champion of China's forgotten poor.[31] Then, Wen issued a new management regulation concerning state assets in an effort to minimize graft by managers in SOEs and in enterprises in which the state holds stock.[32] The regulation, entitled Provisional Regulation of Supervision and Management over State Assets in Enterprises, aims to take control over the powerful executive officers of SOEs and other enterprises that involve state assets. Nevertheless, in Chinese politics, there is no reason to expect linear progress in achieving the goals that are emphasized by China's fourth generation of leaders, even if they continue to maintain these goals as their policy priorities.

---

[30] See Xu, "The Fading of Jiang's 'Three Represents.'"
[31] Erik Eckholm, "China's New Leader Works to Set Himself Apart," *New York Times*, January 12, 2003, A8; see also, *Lianhe Wanbao*, December 9, 2002, http://www.zaobao.com/special/newspapers/2002/12/lhwb091202z.html (accessed June 8, 2003).
[32] "New Round of SOE Reform Just Started," *Economic Information*, June 5, 2003, http://www.zaobao.com/special/newspapers/2003/06/homeway050603.html (accessed June 5, 2003).

Chapter 7

The Evolution of Elections in China

Amy E. Gadsden

The legendary origins of Chinese grass-roots elections are in Guozuo Village, a poor agricultural village in China's southwest Guangxi Province. It was there in 1980 that village elders decided to elect leaders from their ranks to put an end to the lawlessness that plagued the area following the collapse of production brigades in the late 1970s. Under the elected committee's guidance, disputes were resolved, theft and misappropriation of resources diminished, and a basic level of governance was resumed. Provincial officials urged neighboring villages in the remote region to follow Guozuo's example by electing committees to run village affairs with similar positive results. These officials reported this successful political experiment to their higher-ups and it eventually caught the attention of senior leader, Peng Zhen, who at the time was overseeing revisions to China's constitution as head of the National People's Congress. He dispatched deputies to Guangxi Province to investigate the report. Impressed by what they saw, the deputies returned to Beijing and recommended to Peng that the 1982 constitution designate the village committee as the unit of government at the village level. In the years that followed, debate ensued over how these basic units of government (which are below the lowest formal units of the state) should be formed, and in 1987 an experimental law allowing for the direct elections of village committees was passed.

Little attention was paid to this experimental election law until after the Tiananmen "Incident" in 1989. In the aftermath of the crackdown, several Chinese bureaucrats who had expressed sympathy for the students were demoted to the Ministry of Civil Affairs (MCA), which is the government agency responsible for local-level government in urban and rural areas. Events in 1989 had demonstrated that China's leaders would not tolerate overt demands for rapid democratization. However, it was not clear how they might respond to a slower, step-by-step process to build democracy at the grass-roots level. The 1987 Organic Law on Villagers' Committees, which allowed for direct elections to determine the committees, provided the opportunity to introduce direct, transparent, competitive elections in China. In the early 1990s, the MCA began efforts to introduce and strengthen direct elections at the village level.

VILLAGE ELECTIONS: THE FIRST DECADE

After a few trial elections, it became clear to MCA officials that they faced a technical challenge as much as a political one in trying to introduce grass-roots democracy in China. Simply put, organizing an election, even for a village of only several hundred people, was not easy. Communist China had little experience with direct, open elections. Communist Party elections were pro forma affairs with predetermined candidates, signed ballots, and compulsory voting. Civil Affairs officials realized that old habits might die hard. They began to develop and test appropriate technical procedures that would ensure a democratic process.

This was harder than it seemed. Township- and county-level cadres were reluctant to give up their control over village government (and enterprises). Moreover, even when resistance was not an issue, profound lack of familiarity with basic democratic principles resulted in honest, but significant mistakes that compromised the integrity of the election.

Secret ballot voting (*mimi tou piao*) was a primary goal for the Civil Affairs election organizers. The initial response to the MCA's push for secret ballots was to have voters cast their ballots anonymously (*wuming tou piao*). But Civil Affairs officials wanted to introduce higher standards for democratic elections and urged the use of private voting booths. Voters could not vote freely if they had to mark their ballots in front of local officials, even if they were anonymous. Election officials could immediately notice villagers who picked up a pen to write an unofficial candidate's name on the ballot. Thus, the MCA officials would not accept anonymous ballots cast in the presence of election officials as secret ballots.

Opponents to secret-ballot voting challenged that erecting polling booths in each village for elections held only once every three years would be expensive. Advocates of democratic elections set out to prove otherwise. In a meeting with foreign advisers from the International Republican Institute (IRI) and the Ford Foundation, two nongovernmental organizations (NGOs) that committed themselves early to helping Civil Affairs officials develop election procedures, two participants responded to these complaints about the expense of secret-ballot voting by grabbing a string, two nails, and a bed sheet and jerry-rigging a polling booth in the corner of the conference room. This cheap, makeshift private voting booth made it impossible to argue cost as an excuse for not allowing villagers to mark their ballots in secret.

But lack of experience was a detriment to conducting elections even when resistance was absent. In the first poster commissioned by the Civil Affairs office to promote civic education, the secret polling booth was shown as three-sided and open at the top and on the fourth side to allow voters to mark their ballots. The booth rested on four poles, which were secured at the bottom by four 2×4s. Village officials, determined to adhere to correct procedures, constructed the voting booths as they saw them in the poster. The fourth 2×4, however, did not allow voters to stand inside the booth to mark their ballots, forcing them to lean into the booth awkwardly. New posters, designed several years later, corrected the problem, but the incident confirmed to MCA officials that lack of experience was as much an obstacle to their efforts to institute elections as resistance from entrenched officials.

In addition to secret-ballot voting, MCA officials and a growing cadre of Chinese election specialists advocated other processes that would ensure direct and competitive elections. They spoke animatedly about the *haixuan*, or sea election, which was an open candidate selection process pioneered by Lishu County in Jilin Province, and the *houxuan jianmian*, or candidate meeting, which was a way to introduce aspects of campaigning, a very sensitive political activity in China. These terms and others (such as *xuanju guancha*, or election monitoring, and *liang piaozhi*, or two-ballot system, which describes simultaneous elections for village and party leaders) became part of the vocabulary of Chinese elections. By the end of the 1990s, Chinese officials had developed a tested set of procedures that ensured open nomination, competitive and direct selection of candidates, secret balloting, and transparent vote counting, if implemented properly.

In addition to developing an election process, Civil Affairs officials achieved two additional goals in the first decade of implementing village elections. The first was training a large corps of officials who could implement elections correctly. China has approximately 700,000 villages. If each village were to have at least one official trained in running an election, that would require a minimum of 700,000 villagers. The numbers, as with everything else in China, were staggering. Nevertheless, the MCA made training local officials a priority of their work. With significant contributions from foreign NGOs and development agencies, Chinese election officials conducted multiday training seminars from province to province, often finishing the session with a mock election (*moni xuanju*) that allowed local officials to select a leader from their own ranks. In addition, they drafted multiple handbooks and guidebooks for leaders at different levels that were distributed by the thousands. Civil Affairs officials also took advantage of China's vast publications and media networks and relied on magazines such as *Xiangzhen Luntan* [Town and Townships Tribune] to spread the word about grass-roots democracy and how it worked.

The Evolution of Elections in China 189

Besides training thousands of local officials on how to hold elections, Chinese election activists also secured broad support for elections both at home and abroad. In the early 1990s, following the events at Tiananmen, the idea of promoting electoral reform at the village level was a very sensitive topic to party authorities. To overcome this resistance, MCA officials began to popularize stories about the successes of directly-elected committees. When a village in Sichuan made the decision not to join with other local villages when they banded together to riot against a proposed tax to build roads, the decision was attributed to the community's elected village committee. There also were anecdotes about villagers electing young entrepreneurs who turned moribund local enterprises into prosperous collectives, generating prosperity in the rural hinterland. Direct elections at the village level were the key to rural stability and development, election officials argued. Thus, China's leaders might see the obvious benefits of their implementation.

Domestic support was vital, but MCA officials also garnered international support for the effort. Civil Affairs officials welcomed cooperation from foreign NGOs, which helped to generate interest in China's democracy experiment in international capitals around the world. At the same time, foreign media outlets reported news about the elections with realistic but genuine enthusiasm, welcoming them as an important first step, while acknowledging that democracy in China was still a long way off. In the wake of the 1989 Tiananmen catastrophe, positive political stories in China were rare. However, China watchers saw limited but significant progress for political reform in the experiments with direct balloting in remote villages.

With positive internal and media reports, foreign and Chinese leaders began to acknowledge village elections as a promising political development. President Jimmy Carter became an ardent supporter of village democracy, observing elections, making speeches, raising the topic with Chinese leaders, and committing the resources of the Carter Center to helping Chinese officials to conduct training and implement other election development projects. In 1998, during the first post-Tiananmen U.S. presidential visit to China, President

Bill Clinton expressed support for China's nascent electoral reform efforts in a meeting with villagers near Xi'an.

Chinese leaders also praised grass-roots political reform. Premier Zhu Rongji spoke positively about village elections in two separate press conferences. Political reformers warmly received Zhu's response, "the sooner, the better," when he had been asked by a reporter when direct elections should be raised to higher levels of government.[1] In his first visit to the United States in May 2002, China's current President, Hu Jintao, also pointed to village elections as proof that China was executing political liberalization.

Indeed, within a decade after Tiananmen, village elections comfortably occupied a place on the very short list of positive steps that China had taken toward political reform. The elections were far from perfect, and astute observers of village politics rightfully pointed out that the village Communist Party branch and township and county government organs often wielded tremendous power over the elections and the committees once elected. Nevertheless, foreign leaders praised these experiments in democracy and urged China to go further. Chinese leaders pointed to village elections as evidence of democratization to defend against criticism that political reform had stagnated after 1989. From the perspective of election supporters in China, the high-level domestic and international support that grass-roots-level reforms had received meant that it would be difficult for China's leaders to order a retreat from village democracy.

After a decade of concerted effort to entrench direct elections at the village level, Chinese election activists had set the standard for democratic election procedures in China, trained thousands of officials on how to implement them, and garnered senior-level domestic and international support for their efforts. In 1998, the experimental election law was revised and passed as a permanent law. This was a victory for election activists, securing important institutional and legal backing for grass-roots democracy. Although

---

[1] For a transcript that includes the remark, see http://www.chinaembassy.org.au/eng/jmhz/t46188.htm.

elections were far from perfect or implemented nationwide, and even as broader political reform efforts stalled or were rolled back, the concept of democracy at the village level seemed more or less secure. The question was where should elections go (or be allowed to go) from there?

TO THE TOWNSHIP

In 1995, Minister of Civil Affairs Doje Cering described village elections as a democracy training class for 800 million farmers that would "install...the democracy concept in every one's [sic] mind."[2] This statement gave rise to speculation that village elections were the first step in a vertical progression of elections from the village level to the township, county, provincial, and even national levels. Such evolutionary democratization had taken place in South Korea and Taiwan, and many observers saw this course as the logical development of electoral democracy in China.

In 1998, a direct election for a township magistrate was held in Buyun, Sichuan Province. The official response to this election was mixed: China's *Legal Daily* provided information about the experiment, but declared it unconstitutional on the grounds that China's constitution states that township leaders must be elected by the local people's congress. Still, the election results were allowed to stand. Election proponents took this as a positive sign and hoped to maneuver within the boundaries of political possibility to introduce contested elections in townships in the "step-by-step, demonstrate the benefits of elections" way that they had done in villages.

In August 2001, however, President Jiang Zemin issued a circular banning further experimentation with township elections. This step seriously slowed but did not cease experimentation at the township level. In September 2003, the party secretary in the township of Pingba in Sichuan Province tried to organize a direct election for township magistrate with the help of well-known Beijing-based

---

[2] "Civil Affairs Minister Affirms Village Autonomy," in Foreign Broadcast Information Service (FBIS) CHI-95-223, November 20, 1995, 29.

election specialist, Li Fan. On the day before the scheduled election, county officials placed the election organizer under house arrest and stripped him of his job and party membership. Chongqing City Communist Party members (after hearing reports from their county-level underlings) traveled to Beijing to report Li's role in the political experiment, trumping up charges against him by accusing him of being a member of Falun Gong and trying to overthrow the Communist Party.[3] Li was harassed by State Security agents and his Web site was temporarily shut down.

The ban on direct elections for township leaders has prompted election activists to pursue a different tack to promote electoral reform beyond the village level. The National People's Congress (NPC) is working with foreign election specialists to develop new election procedures for township people's congresses. The constitution does not permit the direct election of township magistrates, but it does call for the direct election of township people's congress deputies, whose primary responsibility to date has been to rubber stamp the elections for township head. If the elections for local deputies are more competitive, election supporters reason that might result in a more competitive vote for township leader within the congress. Another way around the ban involves holding a preliminary election in which residents cast their ballots for township leader and then holding a second election in which the deputies to a people's congress cast their ballots in accordance with popular will. In January 2004, *China Daily* reported on one such "election through public competition" in Jintan City, Jiangsu Province, where the successful candidate (of 59, total) received support from 540,000 local residents and 229 of the 233 people's congress deputies.[4]

National leaders have pointedly withheld public support for expanding elections vertically to the township. In December 2003, Premier Wen Jiabao made clear in public remarks that the "education

---

[3] John Pomfret, "Taking on the Party in Rural China, Reformer Risks Livelihood for Direct Elections," *Washington Post*, September 27, 2003, A14.
[4] Liu Li, "Mayor Elected by People's Congress," *China Daily*, January 11, 2004, http://www1.chinadaily.com.cn/en/doc/2004-01/11/content_297860.htm.

level" of Chinese was not high enough for elections beyond the village level.[5] China's leaders are aware that sanctioning township elections would be taken as a sign that they are interested in pursuing broad democratic reform, including at the national level. So far, they are not prepared to take such a step.

Election advocates in China, however, as seen above, continue to pursue experimentation at the township level by tweaking methods of candidate selection and making polling procedures more transparent. Jiang's ban and the lack of express leadership support has made it difficult to pursue township and other higher-level elections, but not impossible. Clearly, there are some within the leadership who, while not interested in embracing township elections, have decided to let isolated experiments, such as the ones in Pingba and Jintan, unfold. These elections create fertile ground for broader electoral reform, if Chinese leaders open the door to the possibility.

TO THE CITIES: URBAN COMMITTEE ELECTIONS

At the same time that some election specialists are pushing elections at the township level, others see revitalizing elections in urban areas as the next step in China's democratization. From a bureaucratic perspective, a shift to urban direct elections is a smoother next step than township elections, since the Ministry of Civil Affairs, which spearheaded the village election movement, is also responsible for overseeing urban local governance. Township elections, as noted above, come under the management of the people's congresses and thus the election specialists of the Ministry of Civil Affairs are not directly involved in their development.

The village committee's urban counterpart, known as the *shequ weyuanhui*, or community committee, is also technically a directly-elected body (many communities do not bother with elections and the committees are appointed bodies). Unlike village

---

[5] "Wen: Too Soon for China Democracy," *Associated Press*, December 10, 2003, http://edition.cnn.com/2003/WORLD/asiapcf/east/12/10/china.wen.rights.ap/ (accessed December 19, 2003).

committees, however, which are designated as autonomous units of government and have control over local resources, urban committees exist within a web of urban governmental organizations and have little real authority. Skeptics argue that election reform in urban areas amounts to nothing more than "Voting 101" for city-dwellers. However, advocates of urban electoral reform contend that higher-level officials increasingly will look to the committees to manage public safety, waste removal, and other basic government services. The committees also are poised to become an important link between residents and local government, placing them in the position to be advocates of the interests of urban residents and, some speculate, even overseers of local public officials. If urban committees were truly to emerge as civilian oversight bodies, then elections for committee members might become a fundamental expression of local democracy and popular participation in government. For now, urban committee elections have not generated the same kind of buzz that township election experiments have as the possible next step for democracy in China.

TO THE PARTY: INTRAPARTY DEMOCRACY

While President Hu Jintao has studiously avoided expressing any overt support for election reform in townships or cities, he has tentatively encouraged greater "intraparty democracy" (*dangnei minzhu*). Intraparty democracy has come to mean several things: increasing transparency within the party, evolving checks and balances among party organs, and diminishing cronyism in the selection of party representatives. Concerning the latter, most observers assume that progress in this area will be marked by allowing party cadres to elect their representatives to high-level party meetings and congresses through some sort of competitive process. Yet, experimentation in Sichuan Province with the regular convening of local party congresses to supervise general party activity (and not just convening the congresses to select delegates to a higher level) has also been labeled a sign of greater party democracy.[6] New measures to increase checks and balances between the Politburo, the Central Committee, the party Congress (which elects the Central Committee every five years), and the party's antigraft watchdog, the Central Commission for Disciplinary Inspection (CCDI), are further signs of reform within the party.[7]

If intraparty democracy is to be a hallmark of the Hu regime, it seems likely this will mean increased use of fair(er), competitive elections to select party representatives. But intraparty democracy is certainly not interparty democracy. Indeed, party elections, which may be the next step in the progression of elections in China, would likely have the effect of strengthening the party's hold on power, thus undermining democratic reform.

TO THE PEOPLE: BEYOND GOVERNMENT ELECTIONS

In addition to the more obvious vertical progression of elections (to the township level) and horizontal progression of elections (to the party and to urban areas), there is a third possible next step for elections in China. Elections are being used with limited but increasing frequency in places such as factories and schools, where officials are deploying the procedures developed in the village in the service of selecting shop leaders (to serve on closely-supervised worker committees) and campus presidents (again, closely-supervised). These elections are not widespread, but they do suggest that the concept of elections is spreading beyond the governmental arena.

---

[6] See, for example, Willy Wo-lap Lam, "China: Breaking with the Past?" July 23, 2003, http://edition.cnn.com/2003/WORLD/asiapcf/east/07/21/willy.column/index.html.

[7] Willy Wo-lap Lam, "China Toys with De-Jiangification," September 24, 2003, http://edition.cnn.com/2003/WORLD/asiapcf/east/09/22/willy.column/index.html.

TAKING OFF THE TRAINING WHEELS: WILL CHINA MOVE TOWARD DEMOCRATIC ELECTIONS?

Just as Minister of Civil Affairs Doje Cering suggested in the mid-1990s, elections have become a kind of democracy training class, not only for China's hundreds of millions of villagers, but also increasingly for township residents, urban-dwellers, students, and factory workers. The catch is that the majority of these elections are precisely that, a training class and not the real thing. Chinese elections—even in many cases those at the village level — are exercises in democracy, closely supervised to ensure that independent candidates are not on the ballot and that opposition candidates do not win.

This was illustrated in December 2003, when Beijing residents went to the polls to elect 4,403 representatives to the city's eighteen people's congresses. One could find banners in every part of the city urging residents to vote in the elections, and the polling places were well-organized. But secret polling booths, while offered, were optional and most voters cast their ballots in the view of onlookers. If a voter wanted to write in a candidate, he or she instantly stood out. Candidates reportedly made greater efforts to meet voters prior to election day than in previous elections, but such activities fell far short of constituting a campaign that one would see in an open polity. While one independently-nominated candidate, Xu Zhiyong, a professor from Beijing's Haidian district, won election to the local people's congress, other independent candidates faced numerous challenges to the placement of their names on the ballot. Xu was the exception; otherwise, the Chinese government was able to keep prominent independent candidates, such as Shu Kexin, a real estate developer, from appearing on the ballot.[8] In sum, the Beijing elections demonstrate that the emphasis remains on superficial electoral procedures, not on meaningful democratic substance. A sound technical process is a good start, but the challenge now for election advocates in China is to find ways to move beyond process and into content.

---

[8] Hamish McDonald, "Vote Independent, If You Can Find Their Name on the Ballot," *Sydney Morning Herald,* December 13, 2003, http://www.smh.com.au/articles/2003/12/12/1071125654352.html.

It is difficult to predict what the next step may be for elections in China. With ongoing experimentation in townships and cities across the country, it seems clear that election activists are intent on sustaining momentum for additional reform. At the same time, the use of elections beyond government shows that a new election mentality is slowly taking root in China. When Ministry of Civil Affairs officials first began urging the leadership to accept elections at the village level in the early 1990s, they had to combat the perception held by many in China that elections caused chaos. China's leaders had fomented the view that too many people participating in the political process would be disruptive and destabilizing. Now, with public protests by farmers and workers showing no signs of abating, some in China are coming to realize that elections are a means of increasing, not decreasing, stability. Townships and small cities in China's hinterland are embracing elections as a means of giving people some way to vent their frustrations with local leaders. Elections are coming to be seen as an approach to minimize corruption and abuse of power and to make local leaders more responsive to the concerns of the electorate. If elections continue to be seen as a means of increasing stability and local government effectiveness, that will help to ensure their proliferation. Of course, questions of meaningful democratic content (e.g., how candidates are selected) will continue to dog at the heels of the development of elections in China.

One new factor possibly influencing the future of elections in China is the regime's growing interest in playing a positive role on the international stage. China's "new diplomacy" received considerable attention in 2003, with many praising China's responsible foreign policy and the U.S. Secretary of State's claiming that the relationship between the United States and China was stronger than it ever had been.[9] As China moves further into the twenty-first

---

[9] For a discussion of China's new diplomacy, see Evan S. Madeiros and M. Taylor Fravel, "China's New Diplomacy," *Foreign Affairs* 82, no. 6 (November–December 2003): 22–35. In "A Strategy of Partnerships," former Secretary of State Colin Powell wrote, "Today … U.S. relations with China are the best they have been since President Richard Nixon first visited Beijing more than 30 years ago." See *Foreign Affairs* 83, no. 1 (January–February 2004): 32.

century, it seems determined to assume the great-power status it has long sought and long been denied. But China's ability to command respect on the international stage is constrained by its political system. There are no other great powers that are not democracies. Even medium- and small-size powers are able to advance their international position by burnishing their democratic credentials. China recognizes this, giving its quiet, but firm support to the democratization of Iraq and Afghanistan. But as it votes in favor of democracy in other countries as part of the United Nations club, it denies democracy at home and in Hong Kong. Therefore, it may become increasingly difficult for China's leaders to support democracy abroad, while avoiding it at home.

China's new diplomacy is a new factor in the more than decade-old story of electoral reform in the People's Republic of China, and it is unclear what role it may play (if any) in shaping elections there. For now, the next steps for electoral reform remain to expand direct elections beyond the village level and to allow true competitors to secure places on the ballot and to campaign fairly for positions in local government. This may be asking too much of the Chinese Communist Party, which is intent on holding on to power. If that is the case, then elections in China are likely to be continued, but the criticism that they are more like training classes than free and fair elections will persist.

Chapter

8

What Does Buyun Township Mean in the Context of China's Political Reform?

Yawei Liu

On the last day of 1998, Buyun Township conducted a direct election to select a township magistrate. It caused a whirlwind in China and overseas. In China, many scholars and officials declared that Buyun's significance to China's political reform was what Xiaogang Village was to China's economic reform.[1] The *New York Times* even

---

[1] See Ri Yueming, "Buyun xuanju: yici you yiyi de minzhu changshi" [The Buyun election: A significant attempt on democracy], in *Zhongguo Gaige* [China Reform], no. 1 (2002), in *Buyun Zhixuan* [Direct elections in Buyun], ed. Zhang Jinming and Ma Shengkang (Xi'an: Northwest University Press, 2002), 293–298. The decision by the twenty farmers in Xiaogang Village, Fengyang County, Anhui Province, in December 1978 to divide the land of the Production Brigade among themselves triggered one of the most significant reforms in recent Chinese history. Deng Xiaoping would later call it the second revolution in China. Back then, these farmers were risking their lives to introduce this system of household responsibility. In the secret document that bore the signatures and fingerprints of the twenty farmers, they declared that, if the government disavowed their act, they were willing to be jailed or executed. Their only request was to have fellow farmers take care of their children until they were eighteen years old. See Xu Yong, *Baochan Daohu Chenfulu* [The rise and fall of the household responsibility system] (Zhuhai: Zhuhai Press, 1998), 251.

carried an editorial, calling Buyun a visionary town in a politically arcane country.[2] A correspondent from the *Washington Post* went to Buyun but was stopped by the local police. A *Los Angeles Times* journalist managed to get to the marketplace of Buyun. He was reported to authorities by the vigilant peasants and was detained for a few hours by the township government.[3]

While the story was chased by Westerners and spawned speculation about possible introduction of choice in the selection of officials at the township level, the election was quickly determined to be unconstitutional by the authorities in China. A television documentary on the Buyun election was banned and an NPC official was disciplined for making unauthorized positive comments on the Buyun experiment.[4] This attempt to freeze experiments of expansion of grass-roots democracy was not totally successful. In the wake of the Buyun election, Chinese election and Communist Party officials experimented with new methods of nomination and selection of township magistrates in two other towns, Zhuoli in Linyi, Shanxi, and Dapeng in Shenzhen, Guangdong.[5]

---

[2] *New York Times*, January 26, 1999.

[3] Conversations with the reporters and Chinese who worked with these reporters in China, January through June 1999. The *Washington Post* article on the Buyun election appeared on February 26, 1999.

[4] The unconstitutionality of the election was first mentioned in Zha Qingjiu, "Minzhu buneng chaoyue falu" [Democracy cannot overstep the law], *Fazhi Ribao* [Legal Daily], January 15, 1999. On February 26, the Chinese Central Television (CCTV) Channel II broadcast an extended news report praising the Buyun election, in a program dealing with rural affairs called *Golden Lands*. The announcer commented that the Buyun election was "another step forward in the process of deepening rural reform" and that there was "no need to analyze who first brought up the idea." A senior official who has worked to promote democracy in the countryside told the *Washington Post* correspondent that the broadcast of the Buyun election by CCTV was an indication of the Chinese leaders' endorsement of this act. See *Washington Post*, February 26, 1999.

[5] For the Linyi and Dapeng experiments, see Shi Weimin, *Gongxuan yu zhixuan* [Public elections and direct elections] (Beijing: China Press of Social Sciences, 1999), 350–383 and 411–427.

The top leaders, who were sternly dismissive about an earlier request for trial direct elections of township magistrates, did not seem to be impressed or encouraged by these promising experiments. They remained silent. However, many election officials mistook the silence as tacit approval. They began to plot for new experiments at the next round of township elections. In July 2001, these officials were shocked to receive Circular No. 12 from the Party Central Committee that stipulated: No experiment similar to that in Buyun was to be allowed in the new round of township elections.[6]

The officials who orchestrated the first Buyun election did not ignore this warning, but felt they could not let the peasants down. It was going to be very hard to convince the peasants that the 1998 method of selecting their township magistrate was not good. Local officials assessed the risks and went ahead with another experimental election at the end of 2001, with minor procedural changes. To avoid political trouble and possible retribution, the officials did not invite the media to observe the new experiment. Not until well after the event did the details of the new round of elections begin to emerge.[7]

This chapter retells the stories of two elections in 1998 and 2001 in Buyun, to investigate the motivations for the bold and original changes to the former method of selecting leadership, to find out what happened after the first experiment, and more importantly, to examine what both elections meant to China's overall political reform. The chapter seeks to answer the question (given the fact that the first election openly violated both the letter and spirit, and

---

[6] For the text of Circular No. 2, see General Office, Standing Committee, the National People's Congress, *Xianxiang renda huanjie xuanju gongzuo ziliao huibian* [Collection of working documents on the term-change elections of county-township people's congress elections] (Beijing: China Democracy and Law Press, 2001), 3–7. In 2000, the China Elections Project at the Carter Center and the Duke China Election Research Group were invited by provincial leaders to design new township magistrate election procedures for the new round of elections. Circular No. 12 ended the cooperation.

[7] For the 2001 election, see Zhang and Ma, *Direct Elections in Buyun*, 107–240.

the second election only followed the letter but not the spirit, of the current Chinese law governing such elections): Should this type of illegal activity be encouraged or frozen? In other words, in the context of one party dominating the political landscape, and with specific electoral procedures on paper, what is the best and most effective way for China to undertake political reform?

BUYUN TOWNSHIP AND ITS FIRST ELECTION

Buyun is a small township with a population of 16,421. It has ten villager committees and one neighborhood committee. Its people engage in farming, and have an annual average income of 1,636 *yuan*. In 1998, 4,675 of its residents joined the army of migrant laborers working in various parts of China. Buyun is one of thirty-four townships and towns under the jurisdiction of Shizhong District, Suining City, Sichuan Province.[8] Suining is sandwiched between two better-known metropolitan cities in China, Chengdu and Chongqing. The party and the government officials in Suining and the Shizhong District are open-minded and reform-oriented. Indeed, they had pushed for and designed the first election. They were undaunted by Circular No. 12 and went ahead with the second election; but they were resourceful enough to avoid career-threatening moves.

In late June 1998, district officials orchestrated the first public election for a township magistrate in China in Baoshi Town. Baoshi Town has a population of 35,000. Its ex-magistrate was relieved of his position due to financial misconduct. When it was time to elect a new magistrate, the district party committee decided to try something new. Having reviewed the past effort to reform the personnel system, they had decided that the most effective method to correct past problems was to initiate choice, to let the public become involved in the selection process, and to give more people the chance to run for public office. With endorsement from the organization departments of both the municipal and provincial party committees, the district proceeded with a public election of the magistrate. This decision triggered an

---

[8] Ibid., 2.

avalanche in Baoshi. There were sixty-seven residents who registered to run for the position of magistrate. After political and cultural tests, interviews, and reviews conducted by the district departments of organization, six were selected to participate in the final run for the position.

June 22, 1998, was election day. A meeting was held to evaluate the candidates and determine who among them would be the final two on the official ballot. This meeting, indeed, was a limited primary, which was attended by selected deputies of the town people's congress, deputies to the municipal and district people's congresses who had residence in Baoshi, officials from the villages, the town government and the district government, as well as retired officials in the town. After a Q & A session, the electors cast ballots and the result was announced immediately. Members of the standing committee of the district people's congress promptly reviewed the qualifications of the top two vote-getters and submitted their names to the Baoshi Town People's Congress for its selection of the new magistrate. Shortly after noon, Xiang Daoquan, a twenty-nine-year-old town party official, was elected overwhelmingly by the deputies as the new magistrate.

The initial success of a public election received endorsement from the municipal and provincial leaders. Both the print and television media in Sichuan and other provinces publicized the story, comparing the district to Xiaogang Village in terms of initiating a far-reaching reform. The district leaders were encouraged and became bolder. They conducted thirteen public elections in the next several months to select leading township officials, including a secretary of a township party committee. Farmers in the district embraced the public elections, but also complained that they had made little difference in actually picking their leaders. Members of the district leadership agreed with the farmers that public election did not break away from the old tradition of "the party presenting candidates and deputies circling names."[9]

---

[9] For details of the Baoshi experiment, see Shi Weimin, *Gongxuan yu zhixuan* [Public elections and direct elections] (Beijing: China Social Science Press, 2000), 384–392. Also see *Nanfang Zhoumo* [Southern Weekend], January 15, 1999.

On November 4, 1998, the district made the decision to conduct a direct election of the township magistrate. Anticipating consequences, the committee prepared an elaborate defense of its decision to launch a direct election. The first argument was that it was mandated by China's constitution, because the constitution makes it clear that all political power belongs to the people. Second, at the Fifteenth National Party Congress, Jiang Zemin had called on the party to perfect electoral methods for grass-roots governments and self-governing organizations. The final argument was that reform could not take place without breakthroughs. Commenting on the motivation for taking this political risk, a district official said: "To expand grass-roots democratization, direct election of township magistrates would be introduced sooner or later. If it were successful, we could create a model that others might follow. If it ended in failure, it could be a lesson from which others could learn."

Buyun was picked from three top choices. First, there was popular demand for a direct election there. Second, because it was a relatively small township, it would be easy to manage an election. Third, there was no discernible clan influence. Last but not least, it would be easy to keep the election a secret, since Buyun is the most distant township from the city.[10]

Following an intensive publicity campaign, with 2,896 letters sent to eligible voters who were not in Buyun and promotion of the direct election through wall posters and broadcast messages, district officials established a joint election district steering committee to handle the nomination process, supervise the campaign, administer the election, and mediate any possible disputes.

The steering committee subsequently decided not to use the *haixuan* (sea selection) method, an individual nomination method that has become popular in villager committee elections throughout China. Instead, the committee gave itself the authority to nominate

---

[10] See Zhang and Ma, *Direct Elections in Buyun*, 3–106; *Southern Weekend*, January 15, 1999; Shi, *Public Elections and Direct Elections*, 384–392; *Huasheng yuebao* [Voice of China Monthly], April 1999; and Erik Eckholm, "Without Beijing Nod, Town Has Election," *New York Times*, January 26, 1999, A3.

final candidates after a primary that would be attended by a selective group of voters. Political parties and other mass organizations also could nominate candidates. Their candidates would enter the final stage of the election automatically. Individuals could nominate themselves or others, but to become a formal candidate required thirty signatures of endorsement. A limited primary, similar to the one used in other public elections, would be used to winnow the number of candidates.

Political campaigning was an alien concept in Chinese politics, but to ensure that the voters were informed and could make their own choices, final candidates had to be permitted to reach out to the people. The steering committee scheduled a ten-day campaign period, December 20–29, with thirteen open debates, one in each of the ten villages, one before the township neighborhood committee, and two in the township market. Campaigning would be organized by the steering committee and accompanied by election officials. No candidate was allowed to campaign on his or her own, make empty, unrealistic promises, engage in deception, or lodge personal attacks.

There were fifteen initial candidates who came from very diverse social and political backgrounds. They included middle school teacher Zhou Xingyi, village committee chair Cai Yunhui, Tan Pan and Yang Xiaobin, a couple who owned a meat processing factory, and Liu Fengbing, a female elementary school teacher. The most impressive group, known as the "township cadre corps," had three heavyweights: Liu Shiguo, current chair of the presidium of the Buyun People's Congress, Zou Kun, deputy party secretary of Buyun, and Zou Rong, director of the Buyun Comprehensive Management Office. There was speculation that this group would overwhelm other candidates in the primary because its members had name recognition and management experience.

The steering committee organized the limited primary on December 15 to determine the final two candidates. The public interest was so high that the police set up a cordon to keep order. All fifteen candidates were allowed to give a twenty-minute speech and had ten minutes to answer questions from township officials, village leaders, village small group leaders, and three villager representatives from each village, totaling 162 persons. This elite group then cast ballots to determine the final two candidates. The result was quite a shock even to the electors themselves. The so-called township cadre corps was wiped out. Zhou Xingyi received seventy-five votes. Village chair Cai Yunhui received fifty-eight votes, barely beating Liu Fengbing, who had fifty-seven votes.

Tan Xiaoqiu, the Buyun party committee's nominee, was placed into the final election automatically. Tan once had served in the Army and had a junior college education. He was deputy party secretary before the election. Within the party, he was in line to become the next magistrate in Buyun. He did not like having to go through the process of being "elected," and he did not believe that this agonizing uncertainty should be part of his promotion. Moreover, he had a reputation for spending public money on dining and drinking. Worse, he was not a native son of Buyun. He looked sleek in his leather jacket, and during open debates, he was slow and often read from notes.

Initially, the open debates were characterized by angry complaints regarding everything that had impacted Buyun's life, including an exorbitant hog tax, lack of roads, excessive fee collection, environmental pollution, increased taxation for education, tough family planning procedures, and cadre corruption. The candidates had to endure the voters who took advantage of this chance to show their discontent. In the latter half of the campaign, the attention of the voters shifted to whom, among the three candidates, was most qualified and could bail Buyun out of poverty.

Zhou Xingyi was forty-one years old. Although not a party member, as a chemistry teacher at the local middle school, he had more than 2,000 students all over Buyun. He was the first to announce his candidacy. Unfortunately, the other two candidates quickly eclipsed Zhou because he failed on many occasions to answer questions related to agriculture and income-generating strategies. He was also mistakenly associated with the increased tuition that had embittered many Buyun residents. Zhou was aware that his performance had already eliminated his chance of winning, but he would not quit. He told his friends and supporters that this race would be carved into history. "Even if I have my legs broken I will persist to the end with crutches."

Cai Yunhui was thirty-eight and had been chair of a village committee for ten years. But he was not a typical villager committee chair. He was practical but not reticent. He was much more eloquent than Tan Xiaoqiu and his ambition knew no bounds. He believed that he was more capable than Tan. From day two of the campaign, he seized every opportunity to express himself through monopolizing the microphone. Besides oratory skills and enormous experience in agriculture, Cai also had an edge that Tan would never be able to enjoy — he was a native son. Cai was the most common family name in Buyun, that of nine thousand residents. When farmers were airing their anger during the initial stage of the campaign, Tan Xiaoqiu was the unanimous target and Cai gained momentum. Slowly, Cai's limited knowledge of things beyond agriculture and his inability to convince the voters that he had a feasible plan to deliver prosperity to Buyun undercut his popularity. When Tan boasted his connections, Cai made a fatal mistake: He invoked Mao Zedong's doctrine of self-reliance, a doctrine no one believed could solve Buyun's lack of resources.

Tan Xiaoqiu, at the age of forty, did not have the eloquence required by a hotly-contested political race, but he did have a blueprint for Buyun: to stabilize the average annual grain output at four hundred kilograms per capita, to raise the annual per capita income from 600 RMB ($73) to 800 RMB ($97), and to secure an annual increase of 8 percent in the township's revenue. He vowed that, if elected, he would turn Buyun into a township of relative prosperity by 2001 when his term ended. His note-reading delivery was irritating, but one of his promises caught the attention of the voters. During one of the open debates, he proclaimed that he would never build his performance on the burden and complaints of the voters. "If there is a conflict between my position and your interest, trust me, I will choose you instead of my *Guanmao* [official job]." Tan slowly overcame his introversion and began to enjoy the power of words. At a meeting with voters, he made an even more passionate appeal: "The weather is cold, but my blood is boiling. Thank you for giving me a chance to use my blood, sweat, and tears to help."

Tan had another advantage in the race. He had worked in Buyun for many years. He knew the Buyun government inside out and had many friends and connections, an advantage to which he made frequent references during the campaign. He was rumored to have a brain trust that was plotting campaign strategies and drafting speeches for him. Furthermore, ordinary Buyun farmers believed Tan was trustworthy because the party endorsed him.

With Zhou Xingyi sidelined, Tan and Cai "fought" hard with each other. On the last day of the open debates, tempers flared for the first time. Cai appealed to the voters about his roots in Buyun. He said he grew up drinking Buyun water and eating Buyun rice. Tan jumped up and angrily accused Cai of soliciting votes through nativism. A few minutes into the shouting match, a member of the steering committee had to call a time-out.

On December 29, the last day of campaigning, Tan gathered his supporters and friends and visited all ten villages with a big entourage of flatbed trucks and motorcycles. Zhou Xingyi rode on the scooter of one of his relatives and visited three villages. Cai Yunhui did not have access to a motorized vehicle and decided to try something else. He gathered all the students at the village elementary school and asked them to work on their parents.

December 31 was election day, and 6,236 voters cast votes in eleven polling stations in the township in rain. Many voters had to walk more than three miles to cast their ballots. Among the eligible voters, 5,113 either did not come back from other places to cast their votes or abstained from voting. The turnout rate was 54.19 percent. All election workers at one polling station had tearful eyes when Ms. Wang, at the age of more than a hundred, came to cast her ballot, riding on the back of one of her grandsons.

All eleven polling stations were outfitted for secret ballots — a measure adopted by the steering committee at the last minute. Photographs were placed on the ballots to enable Buyun's large population of illiterate persons to recognize for whom they were voting. The ballots were printed in such a way that the name of each candidate would appear at the top of one-third of the ballots.

The one suggestion the local officials refused to implement was to allow monitors chosen by each candidate to observe the vote.

Around 5:00 P.M., Buyun's public address system announced the election result: Tan Xiaoqiu had received 3,130 votes (50.19 percent), Cai Xunhui had received 1,995, and Zhou Xingyi, 1,013. At first blush, it was not a close race because the gap between the top two vote-getters was quite large. However, a rule made it a very close call. One had to receive more than 50 percent of the votes to win. Had Tan received twelve fewer votes, he would have had to campaign against Cai in a run-off election.

On January 4, 1999, the Fourteenth People's Congress of Buyun Township passed a resolution, recognizing the electoral procedure and the election of the magistrate as valid and legal. Tan took his oath and became the first magistrate directly elected by voters in China.[11]

RESPONSES TO THE FIRST ELECTION

To the organizers of this unprecedented election, this was an exhilarating and enriching experience. One of the planners of this secret experiment said that this was not just an election; it was a great

---

[11] In addition to the sources cited in note 10, also see Shou Zi, "Yige keai de sishengzi" [A lovely bastard], in *Zawen bao* [Daily of Essays], February 23, 1999; Shui Zhuzong, "Buyun zhixuan xiangzhang ji" [The story of the directly elected township magistrate in Buyun], *Sichuan dangde jianshe* [The Journal of the Sichuan Communist Party], no. 3 (1999), in Zhang and Ma, *Direct Elections in Buyun*, 275–276; *Yazhou Zhoukan* [Asia Weekly], February 8–14, 1999; *Lianhe zaobao* [United Morning Daily], April 11, 1999; Melinda Liu, "Real Chinese Democracy," *Newsweek* (Atlantic Edition), February 8, 1999, 34; Renee Schoof (Associated Press), "A 10-Village Election Comes Out on Top: County-Level Vote Gets Enthusiastic Reception in Remote Part of Southwestern China," *Boston Globe*, January 26, 1999; Michael Laris and John Pomfret, "Ssshhh! This Is a Secret Election: Chinese Quietly Test Democratic Waters," *Washington Post*, January 27, 1999, A15; and Michael Laris, "China Praises Sichuan Election: Television Report Calls Vote Key Step Toward Rural Reform," *Washington Post*, February 27, 1999, A17.

learning process as well as an intensive and expansive opinion survey. For example, the district officials were never aware that their constituents resented so deeply the hog tax. In answering voters' questions, the candidates explained the current government policies and reduced the confusion about them. The election led to an unprecedented direct contact with the ordinary farmers and made it possible for the officials to listen to their complaints of burden and their voices of hope. "It [the election] has moved the party much closer to the people," the officials maintained. They had no regret and would very much like to do it all over again. After all, they were "obeying the will of the people."[12]

If township and district officials in Suining, who stood to lose many of their privileges in elections, were so supportive of this poll, it is easy to imagine how voters responded to it. Cai Jingfeng, a ticket-taker on the Buyun–Suining bus, described the election as wonderful because "[t]he masses knew. It's not like in the past, when the masses didn't know." She complained that the township was cheating the ordinary people by imposing taxes. "Raising pigs is a lot of trouble for the farmers. The officials forcibly demand the money. If you don't give the money, the pig is led away, and the grain is taken from the house. It's just that harsh, that tyrannical."[13]

An old farmer told an Associated Press reporter that Tan Xiaoqiu had a good record, would not cheat people, and had "the spirit to get things done. What the people wanted was to select their own officials."[14] A fairly cosmopolitan and young Buyun resident, who had worked as a security guard in Guangzhou, told reporters that "open and democratic [election] is much better.... If transparency is not good," said he, "how can you improve your conditions?" A seventy-year-old farmer made this comment on his choosing Tan Xiaoqiu as the magistrate and on past practices: "We know him because he used to work here. We have seen how he works. He has

---

[12] *Southern Weekend*, January 15, 1999, in Zhang and Ma, *Direct Elections in Buyun*, 254–264.
[13] *Washington Post*, January 27, 1999
[14] *Boston Globe*, January 26, 1999.

influence. In the past, higher levels of government sent people here. We had no other way. We had to accept it."[15]

Many voters praised the election as unprecedented and otherwise exceptional. One farmer said that, in the past, villagers did not know what a new magistrate looked like, let alone were they able to know about his work plan. Another voter remarked that, whoever the magistrate was, this time people knew what he was going to do. The election "has reduced the distance between him and us. We can monitor him."[16]

What a scholar at the Sichuan Academy of Social Science said might reflect the thinking of leaders in Suining and provincial government: The Buyun election was a good and positive development. Democracy was not a capitalist monopoly. It had been a flag of socialism since its birth. "There are areas in the Buyun election that can be improved and should be studied but the election itself is a precious step forward.... There will be no political reform if we dare not to be creative in our thinking."[17]

The official response to the Buyun election was mixed and had such fluidity to it that outside observers could not really be certain where China's top leaders stood on this issue. The first salvo came from the *Legal Daily* on January 15, 1999. In an editorial entitled "Democracy Cannot Surpass Law," the author, Zha Qingjiu, charged that the Buyun election violated China's constitution and declared that it was incorrect to regard the election as an example that the Chinese people were capable of building socialist democracy with Chinese characteristics. However, Zha stopped here and began to caution that "we cannot be too critical of the Buyun election" because the election demonstrated sharp democratic awareness of the people and this awareness should be protected by all means. He also made the unabashed claim that the Buyun election showed that "democracy is not a patented product from the West."

---

[15] Jennifer Lin, "Chinese Voters Push Envelope, Villagers Allowed to Hold Direct Election," *San Jose Mercury*, January 26, 1999, 13A.
[16] *Voice of China Monthly*, April 1999.
[17] *Asia Weekly*, February 8–14, 1999.

Zha's argument was very interesting in other ways. Democracy could not surpass law, he wrote, because China had just undertaken the great cause of the rule of law. Second, the problem with China's democracy was not that there were no direct elections, but that the people never took the direct elections at the township and county levels seriously. Therefore, the best approach to democratization was not to seek new paths, but to (1) conduct people's congress elections at all levels, according to the law; (2) strictly prevent any attempt to take these elections as a formality; and (3) prohibit any violation or deprivation of the voters' democratic rights. In the end, Cha wrote that the constitution and the laws were not permanent, but also that the people should not engage in such activities until the constitution and the laws were amended.[18]

What is intriguing is that the *Legal Daily* seemed to have reversed itself on January 23, 1999. In a short commentary on current affairs on the second page of the paper, there appeared the following passage:

> Significant changes often take places in the countryside quietly. History has remembered Xiaogang Village that started the household responsibility system twenty years ago. By the same token, history will also remember Buyun Town for its effort to promote direct election of township magistrates. Xiaogang Village is the prelude of China's economic reform. Will Buyun become a landmark of China's political reform?[19]

Most officials who talked with Western journalists seemed to embrace the Buyun election. A longtime observer of political reform in Beijing told a *Washington Post* correspondent, "Did the elections exceed the rules? Maybe. But if there are no breakthroughs, there is no reform. Everybody recognizes that in China." According to a senior Chinese official who had been involved from the outset in the country's tentative experiment with democratization, the election in Buyun was "the high-point of ten years of democratic development."

---

[18] *Fazhi ribao* [Legal Daily], January 15, 1999. For a complete translation of the *Legal Daily* editorial, see *BBC Summary of World Broadcasts*, February 5, 1999.
[19] Ibid., January 23, 1999.

A high-ranking party official said he did not think that the Buyun election would be overturned or its participants arrested: "This is reform within the system; the opposition party was outside the system. It is not the same."[20]

China Daily, the only English-language newspaper in China, joined the fray on February 3 with the publication of an article by Lu Jingxian. Two-thirds of Lu's article praised the implementation of the Organic Law of the Villager Committees and described how villager committee elections had fundamentally changed the political and economic dynamics in China's vast countryside. Toward the end of the article, Lu turned his attention to Buyun in the same approach as Zha's editorial:

> With an increasing appreciation by farmers of the openness of direct elections, the city of Suining in Sichuan Province launched a trial direct election of a township head in Buyun. As people are excited by democratic progress in rural areas, few seem to have noticed the fact that Buyun's election ran against the law, which stipulates that the authority to elect and remove the head of a township is held by the people's congress at the township level....It should be acknowledged that the current rural electoral system of the country is quite complete and gives a full guarantee for farmers' democratic rights. The question is how to ensure strict implementation of the law. Of course, we should not put too much blame on this election, instead, democratic awareness of local farmers should be protected and encouraged to accelerate the democratic reform of the country.[21]

A scholar in Beijing who observed the Buyun election said corrupt officials and abusive local officials around the country were sparking protests. "Is shooting between people good or are elections better?" he asked. "To reduce tension, you have to find a good method. Democracy is a way to deal with practical problems in the countryside."[22]

When asked about the constitutionality of the Buyun election, Chen Sixi, an official from China's National People's Congress (NPC), which supervises all Chinese elections above the village

---

[20] *Washington Post*, January 27, 1999.
[21] *China Daily*, February 3, 1999.
[22] *Washington Post*, January 27, 1999.

level, said, "Although it has some areas that do not completely coincide with the current law, it does seem to coincide with the spirit of the regulations." The Buyun election "brought up a new question for discussion" in law-makers' efforts to "adapt to the common people's demands for democracy."[23]

Liu Ji, former Vice President of the Chinese Academy of Social Sciences (CASS) and a very close friend of then President Jiang Zemin, was also believed to be in favor of the Buyun election. "Everything is worth a trial," was his comment on the Buyun election.[24] Li Fan, Director of the Institute of China and the World, a nongovernmental think tank based in Beijing, told an interviewer from Singapore that the Buyun election had ramifications in three areas: (1) it would reduce the tension between the farmers and the government; (2) it would provide effective means to curtail corruption in the countryside and cleanse it of official corruption; and (3) it would knock open the door to China's political reform. All these, according to Li Fan, would help the ruling Chinese Communist Party (CCP) to deal with the excruciating challenge of losing its mandate and legitimacy.[25]

On February 26, Chinese Central Television (CCTV) broadcast an extended news report, praising the Buyun election in a program called *Golden Lands*, which dealt with rural affairs. The announcer commented that the Buyun election "is another step forward in the process of deepening rural reform" and that there was no need to analyze who first brought up the idea. A senior official, who had worked to promote democracy in the countryside, told the *Washington Post* correspondent that the broadcast of the Buyun election by CCTV was an indication of the Chinese leaders' endorsement of this act.[26]

Perhaps this was too optimistic an estimate. According to a report in Singapore's *United Morning Daily*, the decision of the Central Government in response to the Buyun election was "to criticize but

---

[23] Ibid.
[24] *United Morning Daily*, April 11, 1999.
[25] Ibid.
[26] *Washington Post*, February 27, 1999.

not to overturn." While Tan Xiaoqiu still served Buyun as its elected magistrate, the planned rerun of the Buyun election on CCTV was abruptly cancelled. The Sichuan People's Congress adopted a four-point decision on the Buyun election, which was approved by the NPC. The four decisions were as follows: (1) to declare that the election in Buyun was unconstitutional; (2) to announce that the election violated the organizational procedure of the party because there was no request made to the appropriate provincial leaders for approval; (3) since the newly elected magistrate was the candidate endorsed by the district organization department, to recognize the election result; and (4) to make clear that any secret experiment of this nature should be strictly prohibited in the future. In other words, direct election was still a taboo and the likelihood was slim that one would see any attempt at this kind of election in the near future.[27]

THE SECOND BUYUN ELECTION

As reported by officials from the Shizhong District, significant changes took place in Buyun as the result of the remarkable direct election in 1998. Following the inauguration, Tan Xiaoqiu focused on delivering on the promises he had made concerning matters he had told the voters he would fix: building a road, improving the marketplace, repairing the irrigation system, modernizing telecommunication equipment, reducing peasants' burden, strengthening fiscal transparency, and preventing corruption. The residents were generally satisfied with Tan's leadership and the new responsiveness of the township government.[28]

As another election approached in 2001, district officials were concerned. They were required to observe Circular No. 12 and carry out the next election according to established procedures — but

---

[27] *United Morning Post*, April 11, 1999, and *Asia Weekly*, February 8–14, 1999.
[28] Tan Xiaoqiu, "Nuoyan jiushi zhaiwu" [Promises are debt], *Zhongguo gaige* [China Reform], no. 1 (2002), in Zhang and Ma, *Direct Elections in Buyun*, 287–292, and Sha Lin, "Buyun zhixuan xiangzhang sannian ji" [What happened in the three years after directly electing the township magistrate], *Fenghuang zhoukan* [Phoenix Weekly], no. 12 (2002), in Zhang and Ma, *Direct Elections in Buyun*, 299–309.

they decided to consult the voters first. The district organization department and people's congress sent many teams to investigate and test public response. Buyun residents were unanimous in supporting a direct election. Officials faced an awkward dilemma: They would break the law if they obeyed the will of the people; they would break the hearts of the people if they observed the law. They left no stone unturned in exploring a way out, looking for a middle point that could meet both demands. The solution they found was to have all eligible voters determine the final candidate for the township magistrate and then send the single popularly "nominated" candidate to the township people's congress for the final election.[29]

Most of the electoral procedures were the same as in the first election — open and free declaration of candidacy, examination of eligibility, determination of final candidates by the joint election steering committee, and popular election. Where the two elections differed in procedures were also quite significant: The 20 yuan registration fee was dropped; the number of required endorsements of a candidate dropped from thirty to ten; the candidate nominated by the party no longer had the privilege to move directly into the second stage; the joint steering committee was expanded to include twenty ordinary peasants; the process of determining the final candidates by the joint steering committee was broadcast live by the township cable television and public radio; the two final candidates were allowed to post two monitors selected by them at each polling station (both declined to do so); and in order to help illiterate voters to cast ballots, pictures of the two final candidates were printed on the ballots. (In the first Buyun election, pictures were posted at the polling sites, not on the ballots.)[30]

---

[29] *Phoenix Weekly*, no. 12 (2002), in Zhang and Ma, *Direct Elections in Buyun*, 299–309, and Tang Jianguang, "Zhixuan xiangzhang xuren" [Reelection of the township magistrate who was directly elected], *Xinwen Zhoukan* [China Newsweek], no. 20 (2002), in Zhang and Ma, *Direct Elections in Buyun*, 310–321.

[30] For the details of the procedures of the second election, see "Xuanmin gongkai zhixuan di shisan jie xiang renmin zhengfu xiangzhang houxuanren shishi banfa" [The measures for the election of candidates for the township magistrate of the 13th township government], in Zhang and Ma, *Direct Elections in Buyun*, 109–114.

What Does Buyun Township Mean in the Context of China's Political Reform? 217

A total of twelve candidates registered to run for the magistrate position. When the election began, one candidate decided to quit and one was transferred out of Buyun, leaving ten candidates to battle for the single position of final candidate. They first drew in a lottery to determine who would speak first to the joint steering committee of 165. After each of the ten candidates made his or her campaign speech, members of the steering committee cast ballots to choose the two preliminary candidates. The top two vote-getters were the incumbent, Tan Xiaoqiu, who received 122 votes, and Tan Zhibin, a staff member at the township land bureau, who received 59.[31]

These two candidates either made speeches together or debated each other at eight rallies that were organized by the joint steering committee, trying to get their message across to the villages. Like the first election, questions asked by the voters at the rallies all focused on the issues of how to improve the living conditions in the township and to reduce the tax burden. For example, the two questions from Precinct No. 1 were: (1) If elected township magistrate, can you bring natural gas to the township residents as needed by 2002? and, (2) If elected township magistrate, what can you do to improve the environment and clean up the river? Questions from Precinct No. 5 were on the illegal hog tax imposed by the local government and how candidates would address not collecting fees from those in Buyun who were living and working outside the township. The question from Precinct No. 12 concerned what candidates would do to get the township government out of debt.[32]

The election was held on December 31, 2001. Of the 10,910 eligible voters, 4,940 cast ballots. Tan Xiaoqiu received 2,615 votes and Tan Zhibin 2,088. Tan Xiaoqiu became the single final candidate for the position of Buyun magistrate by a small margin of 527.[33] The Buyun Township Party Committee reported the result of popular nomination of township candidate to the Shizhong District Party

---

[31] See Zhang and Ma, *Direct Elections in Buyun*, 136–138.
[32] Ibid., 139–351.
[33] Ibid., 168.

Table 8.1: Buyun Elections, 1998 and 2001

Comparison	1998	2001
Nature of the elections	Directly electing township magistrate	Directly nominating township magistrate candidate
No. of candidates	15	12
No. of candidates facing the steering committee	15	10
Formal candidates	3	2
Party nomination timing	After the primary	After popular nomination
No. of campaign rallies	13	8
No. of voters casting ballots	6,236: 54.95%	4,940: 45.2%
No. of votes received by Tan Xiaoqiu	3,130: 50.9%	2,615: 52.91%

Committee on the same day.[34] Eighteen days later, on January 18, the Organization Bureau of the District Party Committee approved the candidacy of Tan Xiaoqiu.[35] On January 25, 2002, the township people's congress was convened. Fifty-one deputies cast ballots and Tan Xiaoqiu received fifty, winning reelection to the magistrate office.[36] Before the symbolic voting by the people's deputies of the Buyun Township People's Congress, Tan Xiaoqiu delivered a passionate speech on his performance and achievements in the past three years and outlined what he would do in the next three years. According to Tan, by the end of 2001, under his leadership, there was a 4.8 million RMB GDP growth in Buyun (from 77 million to 82 million RMB) and the average per capita income was at 1,910 RMB, an amazing growth rate of 16 percent.[37] Tan also vowed in the next three years, he was determined to raise the GDP growth to 86 million RMB and the per capital income to 2,160 RMB.[38]

---

[34] Ibid., 169.
[35] Ibid., 170.
[36] Ibid., 188.
[37] Ibid., 171–192. The average per capita income in 1998 was 1,636 RMB.
[38] Ibid.

THE GOOD, THE BAD, AND THE UGLY IN THE TWO BUYUN ELECTIONS

Compared to township-wide elections witnessed by this author and other researchers, both Buyun elections were conducted remarkably well, with a good set of rules laid out by the joint election steering committee. They were largely free and fair, making it possible for voters to choose in a secret manner. There were some procedural deficiencies, particularly in the first election. These shortcomings, if overlooked, could cause serious problems in future elections, especially if elections were to take place at higher levels and involve more voters.[39]

Nomination

The initial public notice announcing the direct election had a restriction on the age and level of education of any candidate attempting to run for the position. The right to be nominated was given only to those who were between twenty-five and forty-five years of age, and had at least a high school education or its equivalent. There was an immediate reaction among the potential candidates in Buyun to these restrictions and the steering committee quickly removed the article on maximum age of forty-five — but the education restriction was not lifted. To make an election a truly free and fair one, it is necessary to ensure that no potential candidate is eliminated by age

---

[39] For scholarly studies of the two Buyun elections, see Tian Xiaohong, "Cong buyun de xiangzhang zhijie xuanju kan zhongguo zhengzhi gaige de quxiang [How does the direct election of the township magistrate in Buyun inform us about China's political reform?], in Zhang and Ma, *Direct Elections in Buyun*, 322–339, and Zou Shubin, Huang Weiping, and Liu Jianguang, "Shenzhen shi dapeng zhen yu Sichuan sheng buyun xiang liangci xiangzhenzhang xuanju gaige mingyun zhi bijiao' [The comparison of the fate of the electoral reform of township/town magistrates in Dapeng Town, Shenzhen City, and Buyun Township, Sichuan Province], in *Dangdai zhongguo yanjiu* [Modern China Studies], no. 1 (2003); see http://www.chinayj.net/StubArticle.asp?issue=030110&total=80.

(particularly old age) or educational requirements.[40] However, making the eligibility transparent and equal was a huge step, and Buyun certainly did a good job in this regard.

To allow candidates of the party and other organizations an automatic entry into the final round might have been necessary in the trial stage to calm the party's fear of losing control of the process. However, if this practice is continued, it will eventually give organizational candidates an insurmountable edge and lead to party domination. The resources of individual candidates are already thin by all means, and this method, if perpetuated, will add an extra burden on their shoulders. More than a decade of villager committee elections has already rendered a dear lesson to both the voters and organizers that organizational nomination only creates a fertile ground for unequal and unfair elections. This is why the amended Organic Law of Villager Committees has barred any organizational nomination. During the second election, the party subjected its nomination to popular approval. If Tan Xiaoqiu had failed to receive most of the votes, the party certainly would not have nominated him to the People's Congress. This was a step forward.

Determination of Final Candidates

The primary system adopted by the Buyun Election Steering Committee was also problematic because only 162 "electors" determined the fate of the initial candidates. The majority of these electors all had leadership roles either at the township or village level, thus they harbored a bias and subjectivity that was hard for them to overcome. While the Buyun primary did not show any clear pattern of manipulation by the powers, with all five township officials' being stripped of their candidacy, this method of primary could be easily used to give the government's favored candidates an advantage. Recognizing the fact that it is hard to organize ordinary voters to cast ballots twice — both in a primary and a general election — it might

---

[40] Tian Xiaohong, interview by author, Chengdu, Sichuan, August 2002.

have been better to pick the electors from a larger pool of voters and to guarantee maximum participation from the ordinary voters. Although one of the chief organizers of the first election wrote that twenty ordinary peasants were added to the joint steering committee the second time around, the total number was only three more in the second election than in the first. One improvement during the second election was that it was mandatory for all electors to cast their ballots in a secret polling booth.[41]

Campaigning

A township magistrate election involves a much larger group of voters than a villager committee election, and campaigning, therefore, becomes crucial in helping the voters to be familiar with the candidates and to make an informed choice. Buyun, with a population of sixteen thousand, is not a typical township in China. The average population of a Chinese township is about forty thousand. To get a message to such a large group of voters in the countryside is no easy task.

The organizers of the Buyun election understood the importance of campaigning. During the first election, they entertained the idea of allowing candidates to set up their own campaign committees and to raise necessary funds to conduct the campaign. For reasons unknown, they abandoned this approach but did stipulate that all final candidates should agree to a campaign arrangement. All three candidates had observed this arrangement. However, it seemed that Tan Xiaoqiu had access to more resources and the support of an unofficial campaign committee. Before there are opposition parties and detailed regulations governing campaign activities, it is better for a neutral organization such as the joint steering committee to supervise the campaign. Allowing candidates to raise their own funds will subject an election to undue influence from several sources in the

---

[41] Ma Shengkang, "Buyun xiang liangci xiangzhang xuanju de gaikuang, bijiao he sikao" [Context, comparison and thoughts on the two elections of township magistrate in Buyun], in Zhang and Ma, *Direct Elections in Buyun*, 241–251.

countryside, particularly the entrepreneurs. Observers have already seen many cases of wealthy businessmen who have tried to buy their way into township and county people's congresses in the recent rounds of elections. However, to ensure a fair campaign, it is necessary for the government to give an equal number of resources to the final candidates in terms of printing campaign posters, using available closed-circuit radio or television systems, and providing transportation. It was speculated by some observers of the second election that Tan used his leverage to influence the members of the joint steering committee. The margin of the electoral-college vote and the popular vote was certainly indicative of the existence of this undue influence on the elite members of the township.[42]

Registration of Voters and Verification of Voter Identification

China has a very good registration system in place, but among all the elections that members of the Carter Center have observed, there seems to be a tendency to neglect the verification of voter identification. Rarely have observers seen election workers checking for voter identification against a master registration list and marking identification to prevent multiple voting. Multiple voting is unlikely in elections at the village level, but it is certainly very likely at the township level because voters do not know each other. Observers have not seen any report on what mechanism, if any, the Buyun steering committee had installed to ensure verification of voter identification and to prevent multiple voting in both elections. Another problem of voter registration in Buyun as well as in China is that it is conducted by the government. The voters do not have to register themselves. Many reform minded election officials in China feel it is better to introduce a system to have the voters register themselves and use the number of registered voters as the basis of calculating if the candidates have won the majority of the votes. At the present, in

---

[42] Li Fan, interview by author, Beijing, March 2002.

most places in China, all elections seem to use a roster of eligible voters prepared from the roll of the *hukou* system (household registration). One consequence of this method is that it is almost impossible to get the majority of the eligible voters to cast ballots on the election day. As a result, proxy voting is used very extensively (see next section). The Buyun design was good as the voter roster did not include those "eligible" voters that were living outside Buyun at the time of the election. It would be better if the election officials could make voting a right, not a privilege, and require voters to register themselves before they can vote.

Roving Boxes and Proxies

Another glaring problem in the Buyun elections was the large number of eligible voters who were not in Buyun at the time of the election. It almost derailed the elections because, according to the electoral laws, an election is invalid if less than 50 percent of the eligible voters cast votes. The second Buyun election was illegal in a strict sense, because less than 50 percent of the eligible voters were present on election day. Buyun did not allow proxies or roving ballots boxes, two of the most serious problems in Chinese elections. However, if the Chinese National People's Congress does not drop the minimum 50 percent turnout requirement, it will be highly desirable to find a way to make it possible for eligible voters who cannot be at the site of an election to cast their votes.

Monitoring

During the first election, both losers complained that most of the election workers who marked the ballots for the large number of illiterate voters were village leaders and could have influenced the voters' choice one way or the other. They hoped that independent monitors would assume this responsibility in the future.[43] Their complaints certainly pointed out an important aspect of an election

---

[43] Li Fan, interview by author, Beijing, January 1999.

that can easily become a source of tension and even instability. Not only is it necessary to have independent election workers to attend to the electoral procedures, but also it is necessary for the candidates to pick their own poll watchers to monitor the election. With an effective monitoring system in place, winners win convincingly and losers more likely lose in the spirit of good will. A monitoring system was introduced during the second election, but both candidates chose not to use it. However, the implementation of a monitoring system in the second election showed how fast district officials learned from past lessons.

THE BUYUN ELECTIONS AND CHINA'S POLITICAL REFORM

When asked why they undertook such a daring endeavor in the wake of the first Buyun election, officials from the Shizhong District answered that they were following the letter and spirit of Jiang Zeming's speech at the Fifteenth National Congress of the CCP. At the Sixteenth Party's Congress, Jiang went even further. He emphasized that reform of the political system was the self-perfection and development of the socialist political system and declared that China must insist on and perfect the democratic system and enrich democratic means, orderly expand political participation by the citizens, and see to it that the people practice democratic elections, democratic decision-making, democratic management, and democratic supervision. He called on the party to standardize, institutionalize, and systemize democratic politics.

While these remarks can be perceived as a clarion call for political reform and expansion of grass-roots democracy, they are also very vague. Jiang and his successors have created a space wide enough to implement low-level political reform. It is now up to open-minded officials to introduce procedures to fill that space. This is where the Buyun elections are the most relevant and significant.

The Buyun elections underscore the necessity to push for deeper political reform at a faster pace. Moving the election from the village level to the township level was a quantum leap. Villages are self-contained autonomous units but townships have many responsibilities, including building roads, collecting taxes, running schools and hospitals, disbursing funds from the Central Government, and overseeing land leases. The past decade of villager committee elections, indeed, has proven to be a training seminar for a vast number of voters, and has sharpened the desire of the farmers to seek higher and deeper levels of participation in governance in the countryside. The leaders have definitely felt the popular begging for greater participation in governance and some decided to make a positive response to this demand. The tension between the government and the farmers has clearly increased in recent years and official corruption has aggravated this tension. The leaders have gradually realized that, to reduce the tension, restore the party's legitimacy, and install accountability, it is necessary to try something drastically different and that a form of direct election seems to be the best option.

The success of the Buyun elections is a powerful rebuke of the claim that Chinese farmers are too uneducated and entrenched in feudalistic thinking to exercise their democratic rights in a sensible and rational manner. The voters in Buyun began their political exercise with an excessive flow of emotions, but calmed down relatively quickly. They asked meaningful questions and made their choices in a very careful and calculated way. They understood what was at stake and made their decisions accordingly. The election process also calmed the fear held by many Chinese officials and scholars that other social forces in the countryside, particularly clans and religions, would obstruct or derail the democratic process.

The fact that Tan Xiaoqiu, the party's choice for Buyun's magistrate, was elected twice, should serve as a strong tranquilizer to the Communist Party and reduce its concern that matters will get out of control in a direct election. The party still has strength in the countryside and that strength will grow even deeper if the party chooses to allow its candidates to face the voters directly and to convince the people that they are better equipped to serve the public. Any delay in implementing direct elections at the township level will only jeopardize the party's legitimacy in the countryside and may accelerate its downfall.

The most significant meaning of the two Buyun elections lies first in the introduction of a series of well-designed procedures governing every aspect of the contested elections, and second, in the speedy adjustment to the criticism of having conducted illegal elections. Shizhong District officials introduced measures that contravened current Chinese laws governing elections, but these procedures, as was argued by NPC officials, conformed to the spirit of the law. The first election, indeed, was unconstitutional. Once the officials realized the adopted procedures had placed them in an indefensible and precarious position, they quickly changed their posture and retreated. The procedures of the second election generally complied with the Chinese laws, but were in violation of the nomination procedures for township magistrates, stipulated by the *Organic Law of Local Governments and People's Congresses at All Levels*. Local officials felt that this small infraction would not jeopardize their careers.

Buyun may be a harbinger of many new experiments that focus on introducing new procedures and implementing existing procedures forcefully. In September 2002, Yangji Town in Jinshan County, Hubei, conducted what was called by some correspondents a "rock-shattering" and "heaven-collapsing" experiment in selecting the town party secretary, magistrate, and deputy magistrates. While the experiment was laudable, the procedures were way behind what Shizhong officials had introduced and implemented in the two Buyun elections. The fact that this experiment was encouraged by the party organization chief, Zeng Qinghong, might have signaled that, what was begun by Buyun, could become the norm during township-level official elections.[44]

---

[44] For the Yang Ji experiment, see Xu Yong and He Xuefeng, *Yangji Shiyan* [The Yangji experiment] (Xi'an: Northwest University Press, 2004). As for Zeng Qinghong's involvement, it was a widely-circulating rumor that could not be confirmed. In March 2004, the National People's Congress amended the constitution and the term of the township government was changed from three years to five years. The third election that was supposed to take place in Buyun in December 2004 did not take place. It will probably be held in 2006.

The Buyun elections are a natural development of villager self-governance pushed by the Chinese leaders more than a decade ago. To a certain extent, such political liberalization is inevitable. The elections definitely will have the so-called "*Xiaogang* effect." In the Chinese dictionary of reform and opening up, Xiaogang means two things: it is an inevitable choice on the part of ordinary citizens of the republic; and when citizens and their immediate leaders make a decision to take an enormous risk in pursuing a seemingly taboo goal, the high-level leaders must respond; otherwise, they will lose their mandate.[45] The essence of China's remarkable reform of the past two decades was motivated by Deng Xiaoping's advocacy of the principle that practice is the only standard by which one can discern truth. The Buyun election is a tested and proven truth that people want to directly elect their leaders. Buyun is an insignificant pinpoint on a Chinese map. However, it is enormous on China's map of political reform. It is no less important than Zunyi, or Yan'an, or Xiaogang.

---

[45] See Xu, *Baocan Dahu Chenfulu*, 251.

Part III

Chapter 9

China and the WTO: Evolving Agendas of Economic Openness, Domestic Reform, and International Status, and Challenges of the Post-Accession Era

Jacques deLisle

When the People's Republic of China (PRC) entered the World Trade Organization (WTO) at the end of 2001, it marked the completion of a decade-and-a-half quest to join the central institution of the international trading regime and the principal formal organ of the international economic order. Begun in the Deng Xiaoping era, Beijing's bid to accede to the General Agreement on Tariffs and Trade (GATT) finally succeeded near the end of the Jiang Zemin years. Charting China's course as a member of the WTO and participant in the broader WTO-centered regime falls primarily to the PRC's fourth-generation leadership, headed by Hu Jintao.

At a general level, China's long march to WTO membership and beyond has pursued consistent, interrelated goals. WTO accession has been an important element in the overall economic and related political agenda of the reform era. As the four-character slogan that has guided the People's Republic for the last quarter-century put it, "reform and opening [to the outside world]" have been overarching goals that have driven more specific initiatives.

Opening to the outside world has meant first and foremost greater integration with the international economy, through trade (especially exports) and inbound investment (and the technology and management expertise that accompany predominantly project-based investment). Reform has meant primarily market-oriented economic change, including dismantling of planning, diversification of ownership, development of stock markets and other capitalist-style financial institutions, and the like. Throughout China's reform era, GATT/WTO entry has demanded and promised to advance these agendas.

Joining the WTO was also an important element in Beijing's broader drive to become a full, "normal" member of the major institutions of the global economy and the international order more generally. China's earlier acceptance into organizations such as the World Bank, the International Monetary Fund, the Asian Development Bank, and the Asia-Pacific Economic Cooperation organization — and a host of noneconomic multilateral institutions as well — were smaller steps along the same road.

Not least because "reform" and "opening" have been interdependent elements of economic policy and because legal rules and the institutions that make them are significant factors in the international order that the PRC has sought to join, China's agenda also has entailed a turn to law. Specifically, this has included the development of laws governing the domestic economy and external economic relations that are compatible with international standards and norms. Engagement with the key institutions that make international economic rules and pursuing domestic legal conformity to international standards, thus, have been goals for China's post-Mao leaders. In this respect, too, membership in the World Trade Organization (with all of the general WTO requirements and the specific terms of China's accession protocol) is an important milestone in reform-era China's pursuit of markets, modernization, and normalization.

At a more specific level, the motivations driving China's pursuit of membership in the WTO, and participation in the international economic legal and institutional order more broadly, have evolved over the course of Beijing's long campaign to join the GATT/WTO and the first years of its membership. Such shifts reflect changes in China's international circumstances (including the costs and benefits of GATT/WTO participation) and changes in what Chinese leaders, institutions and constituencies have seen as the demands, opportunities, and risks of reform and openness (including those accompanying GATT/WTO accession).

While periodizations — especially gross ones — ill fit complex reality, the developments under consideration here can be divided into three periods that more or less parallel generally recognized phases in reform-era Chinese politics. The third phase, the beginning of which roughly coincided with the advent of the PRC's fourth-generation leadership, includes the initial years of China's membership and full engagement in the WTO. Many of the issues of this period are distinctly post-accession, including implementation of obligations imposed by WTO rules and China's protocol of accession, coping with the domestic challenges spawned in part by WTO-related and WTO-conforming reforms, and shaping China's relationship to an evolving WTO regime.

China's approach to these matters has continued to reflect experiences and trends from two earlier phases. The first period began before the official pursuit of WTO membership in the middle 1980s and, like so much else in China's internal politics and international relations, came to a halt in the aftermath of June 4, 1989. The second period roughly coincided with the second wave of reform that began around 1992 and continued through the endgame of negotiating China's entry into the WTO.

An understanding of the third phase's issues and their emergence from developments during the first and second phases cautions against simplistic readings of the early record and near-term prospects for Beijing's post-accession engagement with the WTO and broader international economic regimes. To demand and expect rapid compliance and coherence, or to perceive and denounce indifference and opportunism are both likely off the mark. China's behavior and the issues of the early post-accession period, considered in light of earlier developments, suggest that Beijing's long-standing and powerful motives for accession and acceptance persist, but that several recent or emergent factors may foretell rising tension and declining accommodation in China's approach to the WTO and related issues.

SECURING MFN, FINDING DEVELOPMENT PARTNERS, BUILDING DOMESTIC REFORM COALITIONS, AND SEEKING INTERNATIONAL ACCEPTANCE: THE QUEST FOR GATT CONTRACTING PARTY STATUS IN THE 1980S

During the initial years of China's quest to join the GATT, the broad agenda of opening, reform, and seeking "normal" status entailed four principal aims that were closely entwined with one another and with basic policies of the post-Mao era and their perceived legal requisites.[1]

First, China sought secure access to product export markets, especially in the industrialized world. For much of this period, it seemed as if the politics of U.S.-PRC economic relations was all about most favored nation (MFN) trade privileges.[2] While that

---

[1] For accounts of China's pursuit of GATT membership and integration in international economic regimes during this era, see Margaret M. Pearson, "China's Integration into the International Trade and Investment Regime," in *China Joins the World: Progress and Prospects*, ed. Elizabeth Economy and Michael Oksenberg (New York: Council on Foreign Relations Press, 1999), 161–170 (primarily emphasizing considerations associated with the first and second aims discussed here); Yang Guohua and Cheng Jin, "The Process of China's Accession to the WTO," *Journal of International Economic Law* (2001): 297–328; Raj Bhala, "Enter the Dragon: An Essay on China's WTO Accession Saga," *American University International Law Review* 15 (2000): 1479–1481; Harold K. Jacobson and Michel Oksenberg, *China's Participation in the IMF, World Bank and GATT: Toward a Global Economic Order* (Ann Arbor: University of Michigan Press, 1991); and Susan L. Shirk, *How China Opened Its Door* (Washington: Brookings Institution, 1994).
[2] James R. Lilley and Wendell L. Willkie II, *Beyond MFN: Trade with China and American Interests* (Washington: AEI, 1994).

would be, of course, an oversimplification, MFN did loom very large. To a significant degree, and especially in the first decade or more of the reform era that began in the late 1970s, the architects of Chinese policy sought to emulate many of the features of the then-still-triumphant East Asian model of export-led development. The model had the obvious attractions of promising high-speed growth, rapid industrialization, and no immediate need for political democratization — an appealing combination for the increasingly market-friendly but residually Leninist (or at least authoritarian) leadership after the Mao years, and an at-least tolerable arrangement across the spectrum of leaders from Peng Zhen to Chen Yun to Deng Xiaoping and heirs apparent, such as Hu Yaobang and Zhao Ziyang.[3]

Export-led development, of course, required reliable access to foreign markets, especially those of the advanced industrialized economies where purchasing power and economic complementarities with China could allow China to capitalize on its comparative advantage in light industrial or consumer goods and, thus, offer an engine to drive China's growth. One difficulty was that the PRC could not count — or at least could not be sure that it could count — on secure access to those markets. It faced a number of legal-political obstacles, which took their starkest form in the world's largest economy. Many long-standing restrictions that the United States imposed on trade with "Communist China" began to fall only after mutual recognition by the two governments and the establishment of diplomatic ties in 1979. Although China's trade prospects with many other developed countries had faced less severe constraints, the newness of China's export-oriented development strategy meant that any such ties were still in their infancy and could seem precarious.

---

[3] On these issues, see generally Jacques deLisle, "Chasing the God of Wealth while Evading the Goddess of Democracy: Development, Democracy and Law in Reform-Era China," in *Development and Democracy*, ed. Sunder Ramaswamy and Jeffrey W. Cason (Lebanon, NH: University Press of New England, 2003), 252–293; Joseph Fewsmith, *Dilemmas of Reform in China* (Armonk, NY: M.E. Sharpe, 1994); Harry Harding, *China's Second Revolution: Reform After Mao* (Washington: Brookings, 1987); and Nicholas R. Lardy, *Foreign Trade and Economic Reform in China, 1978–1990* (New York: Cambridge University Press, 1992).

The PRC's enjoyment of the nondiscriminatory trade rules and other benefits accompanying MFN status with the United States remained contingent on a presidential waiver of the strictures of the Jackson-Vanik amendment to the Trade Act (which denied the low-tariff trading privileges to nonmarket economy countries that, like China, restricted free emigration), and nonapplication of other provisions targeting countries engaged in various human rights abuses.[4] Absent the annual waiver and congressional acquiescence, China's exports to the United States would face the high duties imposed under official tariff schedules imposing often-ruinous rates that constituted the baselines from which many rounds of GATT talks had negotiated down the barriers facing exports from countries that enjoyed MFN. The process famously made China's MFN status an object of annual wrangling in Washington over China's human rights record.

For many years following normalization, the broader politics of American foreign policy also animated the application of these laws and assured recurrent controversy over Chinese practices. The human rights themes introduced by the Carter administration lingered in the early days. The revived anticommunism of the Reagan years followed. During the first Bush administration, the insecurity that annual MFN review produced for China's export-led strategy reached its highest point when Congress nearly overrode the president's veto of congressional action that would have rejected the president's waiver and stripped China of MFN status in the aftermath of the Chinese regime's crackdown on the democracy movement of 1989.[5] But Chinese concern (or at least expressions of concern that cannot be dismissed lightly) predated the closely-fought struggle at the end of the 1980s. To be sure, PRC complaints sounded most heavily the notes of United States human rights reviews' intrusion on Chinese sovereignty, but there was more than a little economic worry behind such comments

---

[4] Section 402 of the 1974 Trade Act, 19 U.S.C. § 2432 (Jackson-Vanik); see also, 22 U.S.C. § 2370 (foreign assistance and human rights in China and other communist countries).

[5] David M. Lampton, "America's China Policy in the Age of the Finance Minister: Clinton Ends Linkage," *China Quarterly*, no. 139 (September 1994): 597–621. See also, Lilley and Willkie, *Beyond MFN*.

from a regime that increasingly staked its mandate to rule on the twin pillars of economic performance and international respect.[6]

The legal-political threats to China's access to American markets extended beyond human rights issues to politically potent pressures for protectionism. The United States had influential constituencies that would not welcome the torrent of exports from China that Chinese accession to the GATT might portend. Given China's comparative advantage in labor-intensive light manufacturing (including textiles and low-end consumer electronics), the sheer size of China's economy (even in the early days of reform), and the continuing deep involvement of the state in China's economy, the prospect of U.S. measures to restrict Chinese exports — some of them underpinned by charges of dumping, state subsidies, or other forms of unfair competition — were something Chinese policy makers could easily expect and soon came to encounter in proceedings against Chinese enterprises under American trade laws.[7] While such complaints rarely resulted in formal remedies, they were a plausible source of insecurity and likely a hard-to-guage one for a PRC regime that had notoriously little understanding of American law and domestic politics. The same problems, although of a less serious, immediate and politicized nature, confronted China with respect to other trading partners as well.

For China, there was an obvious solution: the PRC should enter GATT. That would confer MFN and other trade-related rights (including ones related to nontariff barriers, safeguards, and standards for antidumping and countervailing duties) in relations with all other parties to the regime, including the developed economies that comprised China's major markets. Although the PRC secured

---

[6] See, for example, Fu Xuezhe, "Constraints on 'Human Rights Without Boundaries,'" *Renmin Ribao*, November 18, 1991, in BBC Summary of World Broadcasts, November 12, 1991, and "Chinese Statement Criticizes Adoption of UN Resolution," Xinhua, September 2, 1989, in BBC Summary of World Broadcasts, September 4, 1989.

[7] See, for example, *ICC Industries, Inc. v. United States*, 632 F. Supp. 36 (Court of International Trade 1986), and *China National Arts and Crafts Import and Export, Corp. v. United States*, 771 F. Supp. 407 (1991).

GATT observer status in the early 1980s and initiated a bid for full membership in 1986, GATT accession remained clearly beyond reach until the closing years of the first decade of the reform era. The gulf between Chinese institutions and practices and GATT norms was too vast. Opposition from the world's leading trading states was too strong. And support within the Chinese leadership and party and state institutions was too new and limited.

Facing these circumstances, early reform-era PRC leaders pursued a second-best strategy that included reforming Chinese economic laws and related policies to make them conform more closely to what key GATT parties and GATT norms demanded. This promised to reduce foreign criticism and risks of trade restrictions and to satisfy preconditions for eventual GATT accession. Moves that served this strategy included laws and policies that began to lower tariffs, dismantle the planning system in trade and in the economy more generally, weaken (through decentralization and competition) the monopoly held by central state trading companies, build a more arm's-length relationship between the state and the then-still-dominant state-owned enterprises, and create greater transparency in economic regulation.

Pursuing reliable access to rich country markets was not solely a matter of a reform-era decision that China should emulate the export-led and market-oriented pattern of its successful and culturally similar neighbors. (Indeed, it was clear that China was simply too big — and too poor — to become the next Korea or Taiwan.) The quest for secure export opportunities also served other ends. One was consistent with traditional socialist approaches: export to generate the foreign exchange needed to import capital goods and technology that were essential to the Four Modernizations (particularly the second and third — industry and science and technology).

Here, the early years of the post-Mao era had taught a bitter lesson that the leadership of the Deng Xiaoping era was determined not to repeat. During the brief Hua Guofeng interregnum, the PRC had launched a "Great Leap Outward." Massive commitments to import technology and equipment to spur speedy development were made without laying a sufficient foundation in exports. Much of the foreign exchange to pay for the committed imports and projects was to come from raw material exports — a policy that led to a law governing foreign investment in extractive industries, and particularly off-shore oil, emerging as one of the post-Mao years' first important laws governing external economic relations. The "gigantism" of Hua's ten-year plan exceeded what was likely supportable. And the approach had serious political vulnerabilities as well, given its resemblance to postcolonial or neocolonial development patterns, its resonance with nationalist critiques from the Mao era (which derided those who would sell — and sell out — China to foreigners), and the taint it acquired after a disaster on an oil rig in the Bohai Gulf became a symbol of rashness and incompetence that Dengist reformers used against Hua and the so-called "petroleum faction."[8]

Access to export markets — with the still-elusive prospect of GATT accession as its ultimate guarantee — also was important in advancing a more radically reformist end, one that constituted a second principal aim during the first decade of China's reforms and quest for full acceptance in the international trading regime. The MFN treatment that GATT members were bound to accord one another was something China could use to draw in foreign investors as partners in economic development.

Transfers of capital, technology, and managerial know-how that China's developmental strategy required could be best accomplished through a greatly expanded foreign investment presence in the Chinese economy. This meant foreign investment of a particular sort — active, project-based investment rather than passive, share-purchasing investment. Thus, the end of the 1970s and much of the 1980s were marked by the development of a legal infrastructure for project-focused foreign investment that foreign capitalists could find tolerable, with little development of structures for portfolio investment. The equity joint-venture framework emerged in skeletal form in 1979, with detailed implementing regulations in 1984, and

---

[8] On this period and these developments, see A. Doak Barnett, *China's Economy in Global Perspective* (Washington: Brookings, 1981), chaps. 1–2; Richard Baum, ed., *China's Four Modernizations* (Boulder, CO: Westview, 1980); and Richard Baum, *Burying Mao* (Princeton, NJ: Princeton University Press, 1994), chaps. 1–2.

remained the PRC-favored form, in part because its requirement of a Chinese and a foreign partner promised more effective transfers of know-how and skill and its initial demand that the Chinese partner own the majority stake seemed to promise to further those same ends. Throughout the decade, the rules became more tolerant of foreign ownership and control, with the more flexible cooperative joint-venture form being allowed to outpace the initially rigid equity joint-venture. By 1986, wholly foreign-owned enterprises were given their own legal framework, offering the prospect of drawing in more capital and technology albeit at some cost in Chinese control and, perhaps, transfer of managerial skills. To encourage investment further, Chinese authorities moved to create dispute resolution institutions in which foreign investors placed some confidence.[9]

The link between this quest for active foreign investors as partners in the development and transformation of the Chinese economy, on the one hand, and GATT-like access to foreign markets, on the other hand, was straightforward: Foreign investors came to China in the early days of the reform era largely to lower production costs for goods to be sold mostly in their traditional, richer country markets. Low per capita income in the PRC meant that for many foreign investors the China market at most brimmed with distant potential.

In addition, numerous PRC laws and policies limited and discouraged local sales by foreign-invested enterprises, requiring them to focus on customers abroad. Aspiring foreign investors had to submit detailed project proposals and, especially in the early years, faced difficulties when they could not promise to generate enough foreign exchange to cover their foreign currency expenses (including repatriation of profits) or when they sought to sell largely in Chinese markets. Although these restrictions gradually eased during the first decade of reform, the *renminbi* remained not fully convertible in the

---

[9] For overviews of these developments, see Li Mei Qin, "Attracting Foreign Investment into the PRC," *Singapore Journal of International and Comparative Law* 4 (2000): 159ff, and Pitman B. Potter, "Foreign Investment Law in the People's Republic of China: Dilemmas of State Control," *China Quarterly*, no. 141 (March 1995): 155ff.

current account, and enterprises with foreign exchange deficits often had to rely on relatively inefficient and badly fragmented "swap markets" that emerged to allow ventures with extra convertible currency (which initial reforms had allowed foreign exchange-generating firms to retain) to sell it, at a premium. Despite the broad trend toward liberalization of rules governing the foreign presence in the Chinese economy, the focus on selling abroad and importing means for rapid modernization persisted through the first ten or more years of the reform era. Tellingly, a central foreign investment policy document of the period — the Twenty-two Articles of 1986 — emphasized that foreign investment projects were to be favored if they promoted exports or introduced advanced technology.

The regional dimension of foreign investment and trade policies and laws worked in tandem with these sectoral features. The most foreigner-friendly rules were established initially in the coastal enclave Special Economic Zones, established in 1979 near Hong Kong, Macao, Taiwan, and the ancestral homes of much of the Chinese diaspora. Proximity to export infrastructure and markets and ease of access to external capital and management were principal strengths of those sites. In the middle 1980s, a similar legal and policy regime was extended to fourteen coastal cities and then to other coastal regions, most of which had attributes similar to the SEZs' and had established foundations in industrial sectors in which China could be internationally competitive.

In various proportions for different leaders and constituencies, these measures reflected the outward-oriented developmental vision that dominated the period, fears of foreign exchange shortages (which grew severe amid a technology and capital import boom in the early-middle 1980s), worries about the "spiritually polluting" effect of a large foreign presence in China's newly decontrolled society (colorfully described as a problem of "flies" coming in through the "open door") and imperatives to protect vulnerable, long-sheltered domestic enterprises from devastating foreign competition. While the concerns contributed to an "enclave effect" and gradualism in early reforms, the broader policy of openness vastly expanded foreign companies' presence in China and domestic enterprises' opportunities for foreign trade. Such developments transformed China's economy (particularly in eastern cities) and, in turn, altered its politics.

This was much to the chagrin of more conservative elements within the broad coalition of the post-Mao reformist leadership, but it famously became a central feature of the policies of more radical reformers. And it defined a third principal aim in the quest for GATT membership: building support and pressure for the domestic legal and economic reforms, including those that GATT accession would demand.

This strategy, most strongly associated with Premier and later Party General Secretary Zhao Ziyang among the top leadership, relied upon the new "open door" as an entry point for market-oriented norms and laws, as part of a broader strategy of having the economy "outgrow the plan."[10] This, in turn, was to help create political coalitions favoring further, more radical and more development-promoting reforms. With foreign markets open to Chinese exports, some of the most dynamic and internationally competitive enterprises in China's economy found new possibilities for growth and increased incentives to become more efficient and to play by the market rules that constituted the first principles of the GATT-centered international trading order. These developments made an important economic sector (primarily, the internationally competitive light and consumer goods industry) more market-oriented and more influential (because of its increased share in the national economy and its disproportionately large contribution to generating politically valued foreign exchange). To the considerable extent that these enterprises also competed in the domestic market, or at least had linkages to the domestic market (primarily to suppliers of inputs), reformers could expect that these firms would spread a benevolent contagion of markets and support for markets and openness. Decentralization and liberalization of rights to engage in

---

[10] Principal accounts of this policy strategy and the politics of its success include Barry Naughton, *Growing out of the Plan* (New York: Cambridge University Press, 1996); Shirk, *How China Opened Its Door* (especially chaps. 4–5); and Susan L. Shirk, *The Political Logic of Economic Reform in China* (Berkeley, CA: University of California Press, 1993).

foreign trade further expanded the range of entities with a direct stake in China's international economic engagement and openness.

To the extent that foreign-invested enterprises remained concentrated in the export sector, foreign investment nonetheless still furthered the more radically reformist agenda by adding greater scale and intensity to China's export-oriented enterprises. Because foreign-invested enterprises were presumptively more market-oriented at their inception, they could be expected "pound for pound" to provide a greater push in the same direction than did purely Chinese enterprises that competed in global markets. To the extent that foreign-invested enterprises were increasingly allowed to compete with domestic producers in Chinese markets, opening to foreign investment added an additional front in elite reformers' battle to strengthen forces for market-oriented change. A limited liberalization of restrictions on imports was part of the story as well, with low-cost or high-quality foreign goods a promising source of competitive pressures to improve the efficiency and quality of domestic producers serving the same Chinese markets, particularly as increasingly affluent consumers grew more demanding.

In pursuing this agenda of markets and economic liberalization, Zhao and other promoters of rapid reform could play the GATT card: If China hoped to join the GATT (a goal that China very publicly committed itself to pursuing with the launching of its formal bid for accession in 1986), it would have to bring its economic policies and legal order more nearly into line with GATT norms, which included limits on discrimination between foreign and domestic firms, reduction in tariffs and other trade barriers, less opaque regulation, fair and neutral application of laws, and a more nearly market-conforming economic order. The decision to seek these direct and collateral benefits of GATT accession — and to run the correlative economic and political risks — appears, not surprisingly, to have been a highly centralized one.[11] While such a major foreign policy decision ordinarily might be so made, the intimate connection between GATT membership and the domestic reform agenda

---

[11] See Shirk, *How China Opened Its Door*, 73ff.

made the stakes higher still, and also raised the prospect of crippling opposition if powerful interests in the broader party and state participated to the extent that they often did in significant policy choices.

Because Chinese politics remained authoritarian and bureaucratic, even as it moved ever farther from its Maoist and Leninist past, however, the Zhao-era strategy could not be merely a matter of shifting top leaders' preferences and building economic-sector constituencies for market-oriented, internationally open, generally GATT-conforming reforms. Success still depended in part on support from key institutional actors.[12] Because early reforms had decentralized political power, especially over economic affairs, provincial-level party and government organs were major participants, as were still-powerful ministry-level central bodies. The policy and legal initiatives promoting exports, foreign investment, GATT-conforming rules, and the pursuit of GATT membership attracted the backing of some of these key institutional actors and made them politically stronger. Because the rapid growth in export-oriented industry and foreign investment was heavily concentrated along the coast and especially in the southeast, those provinces became increasingly influential (given their outsized contributions to China's economy, economic growth rate, sectoral transformation, and foreign exchange earnings) and strongly supported the agenda of reform, opening, and international economic integration. Some policies and practices also made local authorities'

---

[12] On the features of Chinese bureaucratic politics described here generally, see Kenneth G. Lieberthal and David M. Lampton, eds., *Bureaucracy, Politics and Decision Making in Post-Mao China* (Berkeley, CA: University of California Press, 1992); Kenneth G. Lieberthal, *Governing China* (New York: W.W. Norton, 1995), chaps. 6–7; Elizabeth J. Perry and Christine Wong, eds., *The Political Economy of Reform in Post-Mao China* (Cambridge, MA: Harvard University Press, 1985); Shirk, *The Political Logic of Economic Reform in China*; and David Bachman, "Implementing Chinese Tax Policy," in *Policy-Implementation in Post-Mao China*, ed. David M. Lampton (Berkeley, CA: University of California Press, 1987), 119–153. In the GATT accession context, see Shirk, *How China Opened Its Door*; and Jacobson and Oksenberg, *China's Participation in the IMF, World Bank and GATT*, 89ff.

stake in this agenda tangible and direct, in the form of tax revenues, retained foreign exchange, and the prosperity of enterprises that had become closely linked to the local state.

Similarly, at the central level, vested interests in and strong support for the same agenda emerged from favored new institutions and from old departments with newly important and newly expanded responsibilities — most notably the Ministry of Foreign Economic Relations and Trade (MOFERT, later renamed the Ministry of Foreign Trade and Economic Cooperation, or MOFTEC, which oversaw China's trade relations and foreign investment and which would see its power further enhanced by GATT accession as the department in charge of China's dealings with GATT and China's expanded external economic relations more generally), the State Economic Commission (which became the patron of market- and export-oriented enterprises and rival to the more conservative and once-dominant State Planning Commission), and the State Commission on Restructuring and its similarly named party counterpart (which the Zhao-era reformist leadership created out of whole cloth to serve as incubators for reformist policies and as reformist bureaucratic power bases).

Additional factors further defanged the central bureaucratic and provincial organs and the sectoral and regional constituencies that were faring less well, or that stood to lose, under the changes that reformers hoped to advance in conjunction with their pursuit of GATT accession. The foreign trade-related reforms that were in place or immediately in the pipeline remained relatively modest and not terribly threatening to key Chinese interests through much of the 1980s. Complying with GATT rules was not likely to demand fundamental change in China's domestic economic and legal orders, certainly not when compared to what the WTO regime would require after 1994, and especially if China entered the GATT with the special privileges accorded to developing countries (as was widely expected in the 1980s). In addition, reformist leaders could and did make concessions and side-payments, going slow on price reform, allowing particularistic negotiations of tax rates, and maintaining state investment in vulnerable enterprises.

A fourth aspect of GATT's appeal to China during the first decade of reform had less to do with economics and more to do with broader foreign policy imperatives. After relative exclusion from the international order during the Mao years, and especially after the foreign policy radicalism and extreme isolation of the Cultural Revolution era and the weakness it produced, the leadership in Beijing sought China's acceptance as a normal power. Membership in the major institutions of the international legal and economic orders was a symbol, or even a prerequisite, of attaining such status. The achievement of these goals was increasingly important for domestic legitimacy too, as the 1980s brought a turn to nationalism, along with economic performance, as a pillar of support for a regime that had eschewed revolution and greatly diluted socialism.[13]

In this aspect, joining GATT was one part of the broad return to engagement with the world that had its origins in securing the Chinese seat at the United Nations years before the reform era began, proceeded through the long process of winning nearly universal international recognition of the PRC as the government of China, and included the pursuit of membership in the full range of new and old functional and regional international organizations. Among international economic institutions, GATT was clearly the big prize. Only by joining the most important of the major organs of the international economic order could China aspire, as a large and rapidly rising trading and political power, to influence and status commensurate with its self-image and aspirations. To pursue that end, it appeared worthwhile making the concessions necessary to play by largely Western and developed country-created rules, especially in the view of more reformist elements in the PRC that saw such changes as desirable for other purposes.

---

[13] On these developments, see generally, Economy and Oksenberg, eds., *China Joins the World*, especially chaps. 5–6; David M. Lampton, ed., *The Making of Chinese Foreign and Security Policy in the Era of Reform* (Stanford, CA: Stanford University Press, 2001), especially chaps. 7, 11; and Jacques deLisle, "China's Approach to International Law: A Historical Perspective," *American Society of International Law Proceedings* 94 (2000): 267–268, 273–275.

The sometimes uneasy mix of economic and nationalist aspects of China's interest in GATT during the 1980s was evident in the negotiation of membership for postreversion Hong Kong, which became a separate party to GATT in 1986. While prompt action on Hong Kong clearly was important to the economic interests of reform-era China, China's concerns with sovereignty and status required a delicate and complicated formula of official PRC support for the future Special Administrative Region's entry — well in advance of China's own accession — as an independent customs territory that was (or at least soon would be) under PRC sovereignty, rather than the obvious and simple path of joining under London's sponsorship as a British colonial territory. Taiwan posed related, but far simpler, issues. For Beijing, it was imperative to prevent Taiwan's joining before China, even if exercising this *de facto* veto delayed or increased the price of the PRC's entry.

By the later 1980s, the PRC's pursuit of GATT membership seemed to be nicely on track, and to entail only relatively limited additional costs for China. A decade of reforms in China and the GATT's rather modest requirements (especially for developing economies) and intrusions on sovereign autonomy yielded a seemingly bridgeable gap between Chinese policies and practices and GATT rules. Such an optimistic scenario seemed still more plausible with the formation of a GATT Working Group on China's accession. Entry by decade's end was widely expected. This relatively rosy picture darkened dramatically near the turn of the decade, to be followed by the reemergence of a transformed version of the same basic agenda.

LIBERALIZING TRADE, EXPANDING THE FOREIGN ECONOMIC PRESENCE, DEEPENING DOMESTIC REFORM, AND RACING FOR A ROLE IN A MORE ROBUST INTERNATIONAL ECONOMIC REGIME: THE PURSUIT OF GATT/WTO MEMBERSHIP IN THE 1990S

The violent suppression of the student-led democracy movement in June 1989 brought an abrupt end to the first phase of China's quest to join GATT, as well as a striking setback for the agenda of economic opening, domestic reform, and "normal" international status more generally. All of the four aims that characterized and drove the pursuit of GATT during the 1980s were damaged or imperiled.

China's MFN trading privileges with the United States faced pressures unprecedented in the postnormalization period. MFN in 1989 survived by the margin of a handful of votes in the Senate that prevented an override of President Bush's veto of congressional action rejecting the president's decision to renew China's privileges. The 1989 renewal came at the cost of a stinging executive order that allowed Chinese students in the United States to avoid returning home and expanded asylum for PRC nationals claiming to flee or face political persecution in China. The annual cycle of MFN approval and attendant human rights review coincided uncomfortably each year thereafter with the approaching anniversary of June 4, 1989. In 1992, candidate Clinton criticized his incumbent rival for being too soft on Beijing's human rights record. In Clinton's first year in office, the post-Tiananmen vulnerability of MFN privileges seemed to persist, receiving new emphasis in a 1993 executive order formally linking future renewal of MFN to Beijing's human rights performance and improvement in several specific areas.[14] Under pressure from critics of China's human rights record and constituencies that faced harm from increases in Chinese exports, the U.S. administration insisted throughout much of the 1990s that any WTO accession deal be "commercially viable" or "commercially meaningful."[15]

At the same time, foreign investors became warier about their roles as partners in Chinese developmental strategies. Doubts borne of their sometimes sobering and frustrating business experiences in

---

[14] See Lampton, "America's China Policy in the Age of the Finance Minister"; "Policy Implementation with Respect to Nationals of the People's Republic of China," Executive Order No. 12711, 55 *Federal Register* 13,897 (April 11, 1990); and "Conditions for Renewal of Most-Favored-Nation Status for the People's Republic of China in 1994," Executive Order No. 12850, 58 *Federal Register* 31,327 (May 28, 1993).

[15] See, for example, "China and the World Trade Organization," U.S. Department of State Bureau of Public Affairs Fact Sheet, June 3, 1997, http://www.state.gov/www/regions/eap/fs-china_and_wto_970603.html.

the 1980s were compounded by a heightened post-Tiananmen sense of political risk from the Chinese regime and fears of backlash by home-country investors, developed country consumers, and the United States and other foreign governments against Chinese-made products and China-investing corporations.[16]

Most strikingly, a severe reversal befell China's reformist coalition and constituencies that had pushed hardest for GATT accession and broadly GATT-conforming changes to Chinese laws, policies, and practices. Major changes at the top included the fall of Zhao Ziyang and his supporters, Deng's retrenchment from his earlier embrace of reform, and a resurgence of political and economic "conservatives" such as Premier Li Peng. Among key organizations came shifts in the power of relatively proreform and relatively antireform organizations, including the decline or demise of special "system reform" bodies, and heightened criticism of the hotbeds of sedition in many, mostly coastal, cities and party and state authorities that had allowed them to develop. At the same time came the rise in influence of more tradition-minded bureaucratic actors and, on some accounts, the military, as well as inland provincial organs and leaders associated with more conservative policy approaches. Especially from the ascendant critics of radical reform, expressions of concern grew about the economic costs to China of GATT/WTO obligations. And these would resonate strongly amid the economic pain inflicted by austerity programs that would follow overheating in the decade's early years.[17]

More broadly, the rising tide of international acceptance of China as a normal state and full participant in global regimes and the international order receded as well. In the aftermath of the military crackdown on the Tiananmen movement and amid the

---

[16] See generally, Diane F. Orentlicher and Timothy A. Gelatt, "Public Law, Private Actors: The Impact of Human Rights on Business Investors in China," *Northwestern Journal of International Law and Business* (Fall 1993): 66–124.

[17] On these developments, see Baum, *Burying Mao*, especially chaps. 12–13, and Joseph Fewsmith, *China Since Tiananmen* (New York: Cambridge University Press, 2001), especially chaps. 1–4.

government's prosecution and persecution of the movement's leaders and United Nations human rights bodies' consideration of measures to censure the PRC, there was no hope of gathering the necessary international support for China's bid to join any significant institution. And GATT was a particularly hard sell, given that allowing China's accession in the relatively near term would require extensive concessions from the demands of the trading regime's generally liberal rules, and would do so at a time when the PRC was not only in international ill-odor but also seemed newly unwilling to institute reforms that would be needed to approach conformity with GATT requirements.

Despite these inauspicious beginnings, and additional setbacks along the way, the 1990s brought a new and ultimately successful push by China to join the GATT/WTO. Developments during this period reflected a four-fold set of motives that evolved from related imperatives of the 1980s and that fit within the enduring broader agenda of reform, openness, and international acceptance and participation.

First, the PRC pursued an expanded and accelerated program of liberalizing its own trade regime. Secure access to developed country markets for Chinese goods made such reforms both more promising and more pressing. By the early 1990s, it became clear that China's trading privileges were not at risk. Once MFN relations with the United States survived the attempt to override Bush's veto in 1989, the moment of greatest danger had passed. Clinton's 1993 executive order specifically and tightly linking MFN and human rights quickly proved an empty threat as the administration back-pedaled, making implausible certifications of China's progress to justify renewal of privileges in 1994, and scrapping the pretense of enhanced linkage from 1994 on.

At the end of the decade, the only remaining question was when the United States would grant the PRC permanent normal trading relations (PNTR, with NTR being the successor term to MFN). PNTR legislation did prove contentious, facing opposition from labor unions, industries vulnerable to imports from China, critics (both left and right) of China's human rights record, their allies on Capitol Hill, and other congressional opponents of the Clinton administration's terms for dropping American opposition to China's entering the WTO. The scandals that had dogged the administration — including especially those stemming from allegations of espionage and illegal campaign contributions involving PRC parties and interests — made "pro-China" legislation still more difficult.

The White House's fear of legislative defeat was such that it rejected the package of concessions Premier Zhu Rongji brought to Washington in April 1999 to close the deal on United States support for China's WTO entry. Although this rebuff of China's offer and the leaking of its purported contents caused Zhu considerable political difficulty (especially in light of the American bombing of the PRC embassy in Belgrade the following month), it did little to change the ultimate outcome and nothing to imperil the *de facto* normal trading relations that China had long enjoyed. Opposition to PNTR legislation was a rear-guard action, focusing on the statutory changes that were considered necessary for the United States to fulfill the international legal obligations it would have to China as a fellow WTO member.[18] Following on a November 1999 agreement between the U.S. and China that differed little from the deal Zhu had presented in April, the legislation passed relatively easily in May 2000. The legislation passed not least because the PNTR bill enjoyed the strong support of major United States businesses that had become partners in China's development as product-exporting foreign investors and importers of Chinese goods during the first two decades of reform, as well as from agricultural, manufacturing, and service

---

[18] Retaining regular human rights review as a condition of NTR was widely thought to be inconsistent with the WTO's NTR requirement. If PNTR legislation had not been passed and China then joined the WTO, the United States would have had to argue that nonuse of Jackson-Vanik and similar measures was enough to meet NTR obligations, or the U.S. would have had to invoke the nonapplication provision of the WTO to deny China WTO-based rights in its relations with the U.S., which would allow China to do the same in its relations with the U.S.

sector interests that foresaw gains from the enhanced market access that implementation of China's WTO commitments would provide.[19]

If American denial of MFN/NTR status seemed far-fetched throughout the 1990s (which it did), the prospect that other major trading countries would strip China of market access was even less likely. United States laws and American politics had been unique among major powers in the threat (albeit quite modest) that they posed to China's ability to export. Few states had Jackson-Vanik-like statutes, and most states had repaired relations with the PRC more quickly in the post-Tiananmen period.

Nonetheless, joining the WTO still promised China significant benefits in securing stable and favorable access to export markets. Membership would make NTR a matter of international legal right enforceable through the WTO's unprecedented robust institutions for dispute resolution, not a privilege bestowed or withdrawn at the discretion of individual states. Moreover, WTO rules and dispute resolution processes would apply to other trade-impeding measures that other states commonly applied or threatened to apply, often with the effect of eliciting Chinese concessions. Prominent among these were duties levied to off-set export sales at allegedly below normal value or below cost (which led to the PRC being a top target of antidumping claims in the United States during the 1990s), intellectual property rights-related sanctions (which Washington threatened

---

[19] For accounts of these developments, see Joseph Fewsmith, "China and the WTO: The Politics Behind the Agreement," *NBR Analysis* 10, no. 5, Essay 2 (1999); Margaret M. Pearson, "The Case of China's Accession to GATT/WTO," in Lampton, ed., *The Making of Chinese Foreign and Security Policy in the Era of Reform*, 337–370; Zong Hairen, *Zhu Rongji in 1999* (Mirror Books, 2000); Supachai Panitchpakdi and Mark L. Clifford, *China and the WTO: Changing China, Changing World Trade* (Singapore: John Wiley & Sons, 2002), 69–99; Bhala, "Enter the Dragon," 1482ff; Jeffrey L. Gertler, "Negotiating China's Protocol of Accession," in *China and the Long March to Global Trade*, ed. Sylvia Ostry, Alan S. Alexandroff, and Rafael Gomez (New York: Routledge, 2002); 22–29; and Alan S. Alexandroff, "Concluding China's Accession to the WTO: The U.S. Congress and Permanent Most Favored Nations Status for China," *UCLA Journal of International Law and Foreign Affairs* 3 (Summer 1998): 23–42.

to impose to induce China to agree to a series of "Memoranda of Understanding" promising enhanced legal protections and enforcement measures), and trade barriers to protect importing states' industries from surging Chinese exports (which are "safeguard measures" that many states' laws and GATT rules permit to a limited extent). Membership also promised China an institutionalized role in shaping and interpreting the definitions of "normal" trading relations, dumping, permissible safeguards, and adequate intellectual property protection in the international trade regime.

With openness of key foreign markets thus assured as a practical matter and anticipated as a legal right, the PRC set about dismantling many remaining restrictions on foreign trade. These moves broadened and deepened China's pursuit of the trade-linked strategy for development begun in the late 1970s, and also helped to satisfy some of the preconditions of WTO accession and some of the core obligations that would accompany WTO membership. Many remaining elements of planning in the foreign trade sector were progressively dismantled. Export licenses and quotas were reduced. State-owned trading companies and other firms increasingly were allowed to compete with one another. More and more enterprises were granted "foreign trade rights" — the legal authority to conduct international trade for their own account and, later, for other entities too. Liberal, market-promoting changes were not confined to the export side. Competition among trading companies and the extension of foreign trade rights included imports as well. Tariffs were lowered, implementing high-profile pledges made by Jiang Zemin himself. Nontariff barriers such as quotas and licensing systems were scaled back. With the severe foreign exchange crunches of the 1980s receding into memory, a vast and rapidly growing swath of export industries in place (by the early 1990s, including burgeoning township and village enterprises as well as a reinvigorated foreign-invested sector), and the drive to join GATT (and, later, the WTO) heating up, confidence and a sense of urgency combined to make the prospect of increased imports relatively palatable, even under a strategy that still emphasized exports. Many of these reforms culminated and were embodied in the 1994 Foreign Trade law (the first such statute of the reform era) and other regulations, which were drafted with an eye to advancing China's GATT/WTO bid.[20] Notably, foreign trade legal reforms included commitments to MFN and to a trade law regime that was uniform throughout the country.

Other complementary changes fell outside core trade law and policy but similarly served to enhance China's conformity to GATT norms and to advance China's membership bid. For example, changes in foreign exchange regulation made the renminbi fully convertible at generally market-conforming fixed rates in the current account (but not the capital account) by mid-decade. And changes to foreign investment laws and approval processes made export-oriented ventures in the PRC attractive to a broader range of foreign investors by encouraging or permitting them to enter additional sectors and allowing them to take smaller equity stakes.[21] Tellingly, when Deng Xiaoping undertook his last major intervention in the policy process, he began with a visit to the Special Economic Zones, which had been the incubator of China's export-led strategy for growth at the beginning of the reform era. In this famed 1992 "southern tour," Deng declared the SEZs good and invoked them to support a sweeping reinvigoration and extension of the era's basic policy line.

As this suggests, liberalization of China's foreign trade regime contributed to a second aim in China's 1990s pursuit of GATT/WTO membership and a broader agenda of openness, reform, and

---

[20] For an analysis of China's 1994 Foreign Trade Law and its conformity to GATT, see Bing Ling, "China's New Foreign Trade Law: Analysis and Implications for China's GATT Bid," *John Marshall Law Review* 28 (Spring 1995): 495–538; for a parallel analysis of the 1997 antidumping and countervailing duty regulations, see Jianming Shen, "A Critical Analysis of China's First Regulation of Foreign Dumping and Subsidies and Its Consistency with WTO Agreements," *Berkeley Journal of International Law* 15 (1997): 295–320; see also Nicholas R. Lardy, *Integrating China into the Global Economy* (Washington: Brookings, 2002), 22–62 (describing pre-WTO accession reforms to China's trade regime).

[21] On currency convertibility and controls and the connection of reforming them with China's GATT bid, see Chris Brown, "China's GATT Bid: Why All the Fuss about Currency Controls?" *Pacific Rim Law and Policy Journal* 3 (June 1994): 57–102.

normalcy: encouraging quantitative and qualitative expansion of foreign partners' roles in China's development. The former emphasis on foreign-invested enterprises' being export-oriented and meeting foreign exchange targets faded rapidly. Under new "foreign investment catalogues" in the middle 1990s and related reforms, rules that once channeled foreign capital narrowly gave way to expanded lists of sectors in which foreign investment was "encouraged" or "permitted." Remaining protectionist measures mostly sought to shield infant and some excess-capacity industries (as well as national security-sensitive areas).[22] Undertaken in response to foreign pressures and in conjunction with China's joining the major relevant conventions and organizations, substantial revisions to intellectual property laws and (to a lesser extent) enforcement mechanisms also addressed issues that were of major concern to foreign investors and that were key obstacles to Beijing's WTO bid.

The geographic enclave character of foreign-investment-friendly zones faded as SEZ-like arrangements and decentralized foreign-investment rule-making authority spread beyond the initial four zones and fourteen coastal cities to a large swath of eastern China, and then to border regions and then inland with the "go West" policies and the Ninth Five Year Plan of the late 1990s. Foreign investment vehicles became more varied and more flexible (and project approvals more forthcoming) as well.[23] Amendments to framework laws and regulations made the equity joint-venture form more flexible in terms of ownership shares, management rights, and mandated duration. The always-more-pliable cooperative joint-venture vehicle became still more accommodating as well, with implementing rules supplementing the basic statute that had finally been adopted in the late 1980s. The foreign equity stake required for an enterprise

---

[22] See, for example, State Council, *Catalogue for Guidance of Foreign Investment* (June 20, 1995) and State Council, *Catalogue for Guidance of Foreign Investment (First Revision)* (December 29, 1997).

[23] See generally Li, "Attracting Foreign Investment into the PRC"; Potter, "Foreign Investment Law in the PRC"; and Anyuan Yuan, "Practical Problems of Complying with China's Company Law and Laws for Foreign-Invested Enterprises," *Northwestern Journal of International Law and Business* 20 (Spring 2002): 475–508.

to qualify for the privileges accompanying "foreign-invested enterprise" status was lowered, ultimately falling to 25 percent.

During the decade's early and middle years, enterprise and corporations law developed (including the passage of the framework Company Law), providing a more unified structure that helped to create a more uniform legal landscape for "foreign" and "domestic" enterprises. This established an alternative that was attractive to some classes of foreign investors (although not all, given the special privileges that some categories of foreign-invested enterprises enjoyed) and that was in keeping with WTO norms of national treatment and nondiscrimination. Closely bound up with the Company Law's "corporatization" effort was the development of equities markets, starting in Shanghai and the Shenzhen SEZ in the early 1990s. This was designed in part to tap additional pools of foreign capital for China's development, and specifically for the relatively large, converted state enterprises that dominated the ranks of listed firms.[24] The exchanges offered so-called "B-shares" to foreign investors seeking a more modest or diversified investment role than the traditional joint-venture offered. This experiment was soon supplemented by moves to seek foreign capital abroad, through H-share (Hong Kong) and N-share (New York) listings and bond issues in foreign financial markets as well. The unfortunately (in English) acronymed Foreign Invested Company Limited by Shares joined the repertoire of investment forms. And Chinese regulators began to tolerate acquisitions of majority ownership or even full ownership of share-issuing companies through foreigners' purchases of stock (including "legal person" or even "state" shares that

---

[24] On these developments, see Fang Liufang, "China's Corporatization Experiment," *Duke Journal of Comparative and International Law* 5 (Spring 1995): 149–269; Robert Art and Minkang Gu, "China Incorporated: The First Corporation Law of the People's Republic of China," *Yale Journal of International Law* 20 (Summer 1995): 273–308; Minkang Gu and Robert Art, "Securitization of State Ownership: Chinese Securities Law," *Michigan Journal of International Law* 18 (Fall 1996): 115–139; and Jiangyu Wang, "Dancing with Wolves: Regulation and Deregulation of Foreign Investment in China's Stock Market," *Asian-Pacific Law and Policy Journal* 5 (June 2004): 1–30.

were, in theory, not to be traded). Here, too, the direction of legal reform was toward level playing fields and national treatment, in accordance with and sometimes in pursuit of WTO-consistent principles, international standards, and possible conditions of China's accession.

All of this reflected and contributed to a significant change in the reform-era conception of what it meant for foreign investors to be partners in China's development. In the late Deng and post-Deng years, it was much less important that foreign capital generate export earnings or directly transfer advanced technology (or avoid threatening weaker Chinese enterprises or keep out "unhealthy" ideas). In what might be called the Jiang-Zhu view of the world, foreigners performed important functions as partners in China's development in many other ways as well, in part simply by being there. Soaring levels of foreign investment made China the largest destination for project-based foreign capital (and a near-peer of the United States in overall inflows). Such investment was concentrated in the economy's most dynamic sectors, and was vital to fulfilling the regime's promise to provide development and prosperity. Increased investment from abroad helped sustain high growth rates long after early gains from dismantling the planning apparatus had been reaped, and again in the wake of the investment and broader economic downturns associated with Tiananmen and the Asian financial crisis. Notably, the perceived need to reinvigorate foreign investment has been identified as a significant prod to the Chinese leadership's increased zeal in pursuing WTO accession near the end of the decade.[25]

In the logic of the Jiang-Zhu approach, transfers of foreign technology and know-how were relatively likely to take care of themselves, even in the absence of the formal requirements that laws and project approvals formerly imposed. Linkages into the local economy, the movement of personnel among foreign-invested enterprises and ordinary Chinese firms, demonstration effects of foreign firms' behavior in domestic or export markets, pressure from foreign

---

[25] Lardy, *Integrating China into the Global Economy*, 11–19; see also, Panitchpakdi and Clifford, *China and the WTO*, 145ff.

shareholders who demanded performance from Chinese companies, and the like, were increasingly accepted or counted upon as important mechanisms for foreign contributions to advancing the market-orientation and the market-competitiveness of Chinese industry. The increasingly liberal and nondiscriminatory character of the legal and policy environment — which advanced China's WTO bid and which could be "sold" politically in part because it helped to advance that bid — encouraged the development of such foreign roles in China's economy.

As this expanded foreign role and broadened conception of foreigners' desirable presence in China's economy suggest, the agenda of reform, opening, and normalcy in the 1990s included a third element: substantial deepening of market-oriented economic reform, in which the prospect and the imperative of GATT/WTO entry could provide political pressure, and build supportive coalitions, for changes that would entail significant cost, risk, and opposition from still-powerful interests. Changes in the composition and attitudes of the top elite were a significant part of the story. Prominent among these were Deng Xiaoping's renewed embrace and relaunching of reform in 1992, the passing of the premiership from Li Peng to Zhu Rongji, Zhu's reported conversion to the idea that the core goal of state-owned enterprise reform would be advanced by the commitments that WTO accession would entail, and what many saw as Jiang's growing concern with crafting a legacy that would include both fundamental extensions of market reform and accession to the WTO.

Institutional-bureaucratic politics continued to play a major role as well, but the battleground had shifted as provincial and ministerial protectors of state control, residual socialism, and relative autarchy had weakened considerably.[26] Although many of the

---

[26] On the elite and bureaucratic politics of these developments, see Shirk, *How China Opened Its Door*; Fewsmith, "The Political and Social Implications of China's Accession to the WTO," *Current History*; Yong Wang, "Why China Went for WTO," *China Business Review* (July–August 1999); Yong Wang, "China's Domestic WTO Debate," *China Business Review* (January–February 2000): 54–62; and Pearson, "The Case of China's Accession to GATT/WTO," 346–363.

specialized proreform institutions of the Zhao years had proved to be hothouse flowers, many mainstream established institutions of the central economic bureaucracy had become substantially more reformist. The attitudes and clout of the foreign trade and investment departments and the ministries and commissions associated with the most market-oriented elements of the economy had developed in tandem with the growth of China's trade, inbound capital, and nonplanned, nonstate-owned economy. At the same time, the positions of more old-line ministries had become more market-friendly and internationalization-supporting as their sectors shrank and the enterprises in those sectors (including those directly under ministerial supervision or control) adapted to more open and market–based environments. Moreover, restructurings of the ministries and commissions under the State Council — most strikingly in 1998 — seemed designed to advance and consolidate this shifting balance. The State Planning Commission morphed into the State Development and Planning Commission. Much economic regulatory oversight authority was transferred to the relatively reformist State Economic and Trade Commission from traditional industrial and planning ministries.

At the provincial level, a broadly similar pattern held. The long-booming, internationally open and market-friendly coastal provinces continued to outpace the hinterland in economic growth and, in turn, political clout. At the same time, the portion of China covered by "special" open and market-oriented rules, and the areas benefiting from rapid development, had expanded greatly since the 1980s, with the Pudong special zone in Shanghai being the most glittering newcomer in the 1990s. And the attitude from the economic backwaters increasingly shifted, amid envy and desperation, from resisting further reform and openness to trying to jump on the bandwagon.

As this suggests, social and economic constituencies that favored reform, markets, and international engagement grew in influence. Many tens of millions of mostly coastal urbanites saw their living standards rise dramatically during the 1990s. They became stakeholders in the second wave of reform and openness, as did the enterprises and institutions in which they worked. Foreign-invested enterprises — most involving Chinese partners — were at the vanguard of these developments and were especially strong in the export sector. Many of these firms were highly competitive in international markets, even without the benefit of state support. Especially during the first half of the decade, the rise of township and village enterprises — often entangled with the local state but operating in markets — similarly brought prosperity and reasons to support reform to a significant swath of rural (or formerly rural) areas that had benefited from the earliest reform policies but fared relatively poorly in the intervening years. Perhaps most strikingly, a stratum of entrepreneurs — some grown fabulously wealthy — were declared politically correct. In his most celebrated slogan and self-proclaimed contribution to the canon of Chinese communist thought, Jiang Zemin promulgated, late in his tenure, the "Three Represents" which included this new business class among the key elements that the party should include and protect.[27]

While the political context and the political leadership thus supported extending and deepening reform and openness, success was not going to come easily. Opponents, losers, and potential losers had not been rendered impotent. The next items on the reformist agenda promised to be more widely and more deeply costly and disruptive, at least in the short run, as they deprived vulnerable sectors of state support and protection from market and international competition. Moreover, some of the tools used to build support and erode opposition during earlier phases were becoming less viable.[28] Side-payments and subsidies to losers, and ostensibly "test point" special privileges finely differentiated by region or sector for winners and potential winners were not consistent with new central goals of nationwide and economy-wide reforms to the enterprise

---

[27] See generally Barry Naughton, "China's Macroeconomy in Transition," *China Quarterly*, no. 144 (December 1995): 1083–1104; Jean C. Oi, "Two Decades of Rural Reform in China," *China Quarterly*, no. 144 (December 1995): 1132–1149; and Bruce J. Dickson, *Red Capitalists in China* (New York: Cambridge University Press, 2003).

[28] See Shirk, *How China Opened its Door*, chap. 7; Nicholas R. Lardy, *China's Unfinished Economic Revolution* (Washington, DC: Brookings, 1998); and Wang Shaoguang, "China's 1994 Fiscal Reform: An Initial Assessment," *Asian Survey* 37 (1997): 801–817.

system. They were also in tension and sometimes in conflict with the uniformity of trade-affecting regulatory structures that the WTO regime presumed and demanded. And they cut against the partial recentralization of power that the top leadership sought in order to overcome the inefficiency, corruption, foot-dragging, and state revenue hemorrhaging that earlier decentralizing reforms had wrought. Of course, limited reprises of older methods occurred. Examples included the extension of "special zone" structures to selected inland areas, the adoption of "industrial policy" measures to protect or nurture "pillar industries," the continuation of commercially unviable "policy lending" by state-owned banks to floundering state-owned enterprises, repeated postponements of a new and tougher bankruptcy system, and negotiations to ameliorate the impact of fiscally centralizing tax reforms on provincial government revenues.

The Jiang-Zhu leadership turned to an unprecedented degree to the long-standing but now-earnest quest for GATT/WTO membership as a means to push forward more radical changes. Crucial items on the agenda of domestic economic reform in the middle and late 1990s were legal and policy reforms that could be portrayed as closely linked to China's bid for accession to the WTO. The reasoning was simple and politically powerful: WTO membership was desirable for reasons that could appeal to many, including those who otherwise had doubts about the speed and pace of domestic reforms. WTO accession would require major changes, whether as a precondition for China's entry or as a pledge concerning China's postaccession policies. The obligations that would attend WTO membership (by virtue of the regime's general rules and the specific undertakings in China's accession protocol) would have to be taken seriously, not only because the WTO enforcement mechanisms (unlike their GATT predecessors) would have real teeth, but also because China's reputation and credibility in living up to its international commitments would be at stake. On the other hand, failing to make or to pledge to make key reforms would mean ongoing exclusion from the WTO, which would cast a shadow over China's status as a normal and great power.

Pegging key domestic economic reforms that the Jiang-Zhu leadership sought to WTO requirements and norms was relatively easy.[29] The former included extensive (though partial) privatization of state-owned enterprises, which was a centerpiece of the Fifteenth Party Congress "line" and Jiang's slogan of "grasping the large and letting go the small" among state enterprises. Supplementing ownership reform were major market-consistent changes to contract law and other economic laws, and moves to strengthen institutional capacity for resolving commercial disputes. Also near the top of the agenda were commercializing and market-oriented reforms to a banking system plagued by bad debt in the form of the massive "policy loans" that financial institutions had to make to insolvent and inadequately reformed state enterprises. Other priorities included building a "modern" (that is, market-regarding) enterprise system. In part, this meant extending the disciplining and reform-promoting effects of competition, including foreign and foreign-invested competition, to still broader sectors of the Chinese economy, including potentially sensitive and vulnerable sectors such as telecommunications, financial services, and heavy industry.

---

[29] It was a staple of analysts' accounts as well. See, for example, Harry G. Broadman, "A Litmus Test for China's Accession to the WTO: Reform of Its State-Owned Enterprises," in Ostry, Alexandroff, and Gomez, eds. *China and the Long March to Global Trade*, 47–64; Fewsmith, "The Political and Social Implications of China's Accession to the WTO" (linking pursuit of WTO accession to perceived need to address economic crisis in the state-owned enterprise sector); Daniel H. Rosen, "China and the World Trade Organization: An Economic Balance Sheet," *International Economic Policy Briefs*, no. 99–96 (Institute for International Economics, June 1999): (arguing that WTO accession concessions reflected effort by Zhu and others to use WTO commitments to shift China to a strategy of "competition-based growth"); Lardy, *Integrating China into the World Economy*, 20ff. (WTO entry to promote domestic reforms and fuel growth); Panitchpakdi and Clifford, *China and the WTO*, 32ff, 140ff (similar); and Julia Ya Qin, "WTO Regulation of Subsidies to State-Owned Enterprises (SOEs) — a Critical Appraisal of the China Accession Protocol," *Journal of International Economic Law* 7 (December 2004): 863–919 (assessing WTO and China's accession protocol provisions that mandate significant reform in the state-SOE relationship and describing SOE reform as a key aspect of WTO accession).

Recentralizing, strengthening, and standardizing the state's revenue-raising system constituted core aims as well. And efforts to combat the patchwork of local protectionist regulations and practices, and pervasive problems of corruption and undisciplined policy non-implementation at provincial and lower levels became a primary focus, particularly during Zhu's final years in office.

Each of these economic reform aims (and others as well) resonated with WTO principles and rules, such as the presumption of a market economy, prohibition of state subsidies as unfair competition, requirements of nationally uniform, fully transparent and fairly applied laws governing or having significant effects on trade, and national treatment and nondiscrimination requirements and liberalization imperatives that mandate relatively equal state treatment for foreign and domestic producers and products. Some of the items high on the Chinese leadership's agenda also paralleled specific demands — for market access, legal protection of foreigners' economic rights, greater rule of law and so on — pressed by the United States, the European Union, and others who held the keys to China's entry into the WTO.

The possibility of forging links between extensive and expansive reforms and the pursuit of WTO membership during the 1990s was greater than had been the case with GATT in the 1980s, for several reasons. Negotiation over terms of the PRC's accession had reached a stage where specific preconditions were on the table. More fundamentally (and as the foregoing suggests), the reach of the WTO-centered international regime was far broader in the 1990s than its predecessor had been in the 1980s when agriculture, services, trade-related investment measures, and intellectual property had remained largely beyond GATT's purview and when the institutional mechanisms for enforcing conformity with GATT requirements were far weaker. Moreover, by the later 1990s, it had become clear that the PRC would enter the WTO under terms granting only very limited and temporary relief from obligations to undertake the domestic legal, policy, and institutional reforms that the WTO regime and China's protocol of accession would demand.

Advocates of reform had to construct these political connections largely in the still-relatively-secretive process for making major policy changes in China. Still, their efforts broke through into the public and semipublic debate often enough to suggest that such political linkages were pervasive, important, and contested. Some establishment commentators and advisers were frank on the subject, and officials sometimes were as well, openly articulating a relationship between WTO accession and economic, legal, and administrative reform at home.[30]

Perhaps the most striking indications came from Zhu Rongji's trip to Washington.[31] The apparent one-sidedness and attendant risks of his April 1999 offer made a good deal more sense if the leadership's aims included using WTO accession as a lever for WTO-conforming domestic reforms that were seen as indispensable in their own right. True, the prospects for closing the deal looked strong in early 1999, given the progress recently made in bilateral negotiations, the generally good state of relations between Washington and Beijing, and the American administration's apparent desire to get China into the WTO before the end of Clinton's tenure. But it was also clear that Zhu had to offer an expansive package of concessions. Pledges of extensive opening to foreign trade, investment, and competition, commitments to difficult legal and institutional changes, and tolerance for a large dose of American (and therefore other trading partners') protectionism were on offer in return for relatively few accommodations to permit China to depart from full-fledged WTO requirements — and far less than the developing country preferential treatment that China had sought in the 1980s and early 1990s, or the temporary "transitional economy"

---

[30] See, for example, Gao Shangquan, "Speeding Up the Reform and Liberalization Process to Meet the New Challenges for China's Post-WTO Accession," *International Lawyer* 24 (Spring 2000): 355–359; Cao Jianming, "WTO and the Rule of Law in China," *Temple International and Comparative Law Journal* 16 (Fall 2002): 379–390; Long Yongtu, head of China's WTO delegation declared that WTO "negotiations are not solely for accession to the WTO" but "more importantly ... accession will facilitate China's reform and opening up." See http://www.wto.org/english/news_e/news01_e/china_longstat_jul01_e.htm.

[31] See Fewsmith, "China and the WTO: The Politics Behind the Agreement"; Pearson, "The Case of China's Accession to GATT/WTO"; Zong, *Zhu Rongji in 1999*; and other sources cited at the beginning of this section.

concessions enjoyed by former Soviet Bloc states when they joined the WTO. Zhu's offer — and the connections it underscored between the WTO and relatively radical reform at home — entailed considerable political risk, given a context that included: the pain that fulfilling those promises predictably would inflict on significant Chinese actors and interests; the heightened critiques in China of increasing international openness in the wake of the Asian financial crisis (which some argued China had weathered relatively easily because its economy was more closed than that of its neighbors); the expanding reach of foreign companies and capital (which some construed as "selling the country"); and resentment toward the United States and others for having progressively "raised the bar" to the PRC's accession (by making ever more intrusive demands for domestic reform and preventing China from becoming a founding member of the WTO).

Zhu also faced the seemingly low probability but high-stakes risk that his offer would be rejected (which it was), and the seemingly still-lower probability but still-higher-stakes risks that its contents would be leaked (which they were) or, worse yet, that what was leaked would either report even more concessions than Zhu offered (which plausible accounts assert was the case) or would accurately reflect proposals that went beyond what Zhu had been authorized to deliver (which is less likely but has not been definitively ruled out). The United States' bombing of the PRC's embassy in Belgrade soon made matters worse. And Zhu — and the Jiang-Zhu leadership's WTO-related strategy — soon found itself under attack from those who drew the line at (or short of) the terms the premier had actually or reportedly taken to the United States, who construed the American rebuff as an insult to China and a setback to China's quest for international status (which was supposed to be advanced, not damaged, by the pursuit of WTO accession), or who simply seized upon the opportunity to press long-standing opposition to the reformist policy lines associated with Zhu and Jiang.

As these last points imply, there was also a fourth, noneconomic dimension to China's pursuit of membership in the international economic order's central institution during the 1990s. Indeed, this aspect of the drive for membership had become more compelling and urgent. Communist or socialist ideology had grown even more hollowed-out during the post-Tiananmen decade. Continued high growth rates and the economic performance-based legitimacy that they underpinned seemed to be at risk. The deregulatory gains of early reforms had been largely exhausted. The Asian financial crisis and a series of austerity programs designed to combat inflation threatened to bring the Chinese economy back down to earth. The retrenchment of the overexpanded TVE sector and the much-delayed painful restructuring of state-owned enterprises and many industries threatened to create a new and discontented group of reform "losers." In this atmosphere, nationalism and international status became by default a potentially more important underpinning of the regime's claim to authority, and one that accession to the WTO could help and that exclusion from the WTO surely could hurt.

The birth of the WTO in the mid-1990s increased the salience of such international status concerns, as China first pursued entry in time to be a founding member. Once that proved beyond reach, it became important for China to remove the aberration of nonmembership, which was more embarrassing and galling than exclusion from the less important and less institutionalized pre-WTO GATT regime. The 1999 Seattle ministerial meeting — expected, incorrectly, to be a significant step in the WTO's early growth — became another sought, and missed, target for accession.

The prospect and pursuit of WTO membership also was bound up with the PRC's broader desire for standing as a great power that was entitled to, and enjoyed, influence in the major regimes and institutions that shaped the rules of the international order. China's newly pivotal role in the post-Cold War United Nations Security Council was one aspect, happily achieved from Beijing's viewpoint. Chinese membership in the international economic regime's nearest equivalent — the WTO — was part of the same agenda, one that stressed China's right and desire to be at the table, and the wrongfulness of excluding so important a nation with so formidable an economy. While a role in making the rules could, of course, redound to China's material benefit, that is not all there was to the story. The tone of Chinese comments goes far beyond such tangible economic considerations and cannot be dismissed as disingenuous given China's long-nursed wounds from being treated as less than an equal by the "club" of powerful and rich states.[32]

The nationalist dimension of China's 1990s race to join the WTO drew additional impetus from what Beijing saw as another legacy of its former maltreatment by the world community. One product of an "unequal treaty" — Hong Kong — had already entered the WTO, under the embarrassing cosponsorship of the colonial power that had occupied what Beijing regarded as inalienable Chinese territory. Another legacy of an unequal treaty and civil war — Taiwan — had undertaken reforms that made it a credible candidate for WTO membership. With Taiwan having formally applied to join GATT at the beginning of the 1990s and with a Taiwan WTO accession working group functioning in parallel to the one for the PRC, Taiwan's exclusion became increasingly clearly attributable only to political pressure that China exerted on WTO members — a situation that was hardly conducive to China's pursuit of an image of being a cooperative member of the international community and candidate for WTO accession.[33]

---

[32] See, for example, "A Major Decision for Promoting China's Open Door Policy," *Qiu Shi*, in BBC Summary of World Broadcasts, February 16, 2000 (stating that China, when it gets into the WTO, will behave in a way that "will show to the rest of the world that it is a responsible major power"); Joseph Fewsmith, "The Impact of WTO/PNTR on Chinese Politics," *NBR Analysis* 11, no. 2 (2000); Tang Xiaobing, "China's Economic System and Its New Role in the World Economy," in *China in the World Trading System*, ed. Frederick M. Abbott (Cambridge, MA: Kluwer Law International, 1998), 53–61 (both indicating Chinese bristling at the prospect of continued accession delays as an insulting or unfair effort to keep China down or out).

[33] For legal analyses of the PRC's political "veto" of Taiwan's accession to GATT/WTO, see, for example, Lori Fisler Damrosch, "GATT Membership in a Changing World Order: Taiwan, China and the Former Soviet Republics," *Columbia Business Law Review* (1992): 33ff.; Jacques deLisle, "The Chinese Puzzle of Taiwan's Status," *Orbis* 44, no. 1 (2000): 35ff.

IMPLEMENTATION AND ACCESS, OPENNESS AND PROTECTIONISM, DOMESTIC BACKLASH AND MISSION CREEP, AND DEFINING CHINA'S (AND TAIWAN'S) ROLES: WTO MEMBERSHIP AND ITS DISCONTENTS IN THE 2000S

Although the 1990s, like the 1980s, ended badly for China's quest to join the principal institution of the international economic regime, the setback proved short-lived. The Clinton administration quickly reversed course, accepted a package that differed little from what Zhu had proposed in 1999, declared support for China's accession, and won passage of PNTR legislation in 2000. Although negotiations over specific terms continued between China and the U.S., the EU, and others through much of the following year, and although frictions over Taiwan and a collision between a Chinese military jet and an American EP-3 reconnaissance plane strained relations between Beijing and Washington, the last steps in China's accession proceeded relatively smoothly.

With China's entry into the WTO at the end of 2001, the basic imperatives behind China's quest for membership during the 1990s seemed likely to remain operative for a long time, and to augur relatively high degrees of continuity and compliance. First, access to foreign markets remained important and had received a newly firm international legal foundation. Relatively sanguine assessments foresaw WTO accession adding one percent or more to China's growth rate, at least after an initial adjustment period. WTO privileges and related developments (such as the phasing out of the Multi-Fiber Agreement) promised a much greater boon to some export-intensive sectors. Beijing thus appeared to have strong reasons not to violate WTO rules or to shirk implementation of commitments. Serious or pervasive violations could drive trading partners to initiate proceedings before the WTO's impressively effective dispute resolution process, and possibly to win judgments authorizing the aggrieved parties to retaliate in ways that would hurt Chinese exports. Second, the WTO's extensions of the GATT regime beyond trade in goods to services, investment, and intellectual property, and many of the specific undertakings in the PRC's accession protocol (including those concerning telecoms, local currency banking, insurance and other financial services, and the automobile industry) promised a further expansion of foreigners' roles in China's economic development. Moreover, the Asian financial crisis had dimmed the luster in China of Korean- or Japanese-style industrial policy and its relatively illiberal approaches to sectoral opening.[34]

Third, as the Jiang-era leadership appears to have intended, China's WTO obligations drew unprecedented tight connections between China's compliant participation in the international trade regime and implementation of market-oriented and playing field-leveling laws and policies at home. Fourth, with the PRC having at last claimed the prize of WTO membership, Beijing still had good reasons not to taint its newly won status with roguish or regime-rejecting behavior that would alienate or embarrass the governments that in the end had championed China's accession. More broadly, China's proclaimed self-image, accepted by some but not all observers, was that the PRC honored its treaty obligations.[35] On a benign reading, Beijing's pursuit of an ASEAN-China Free Trade

---

[34] For a sanguine view of many of these issues, see Lardy, *Integrating China into the Global Economy*, 111–133, 150ff. For a less rosy but still positive assessment, see Elena Ianchovichina and Will Martin, "Trade Policy Reform and China's WTO Accession," in *China and the World Trading System*, ed. Deborah Z. Cass, Brett G. Williams, and George Barker (New York: Cambridge University Press, 2003), 93–114. See also Ian Dickson, "China's Interest in the World Trade Organization's Deregulation of International Textiles Trade," in Cass, Williams, and Barker, *China and the World Trading System*, 175–201.

[35] For examples of expectations that China would be a status quo, regime-conforming member of the WTO, see Frederick M. Abbott, "Reflection Paper on China in the World Trading System," in *China in the World Trading System*, ed. Frederick M. Abbott, 1–43; Yang and Cheng, *The Process of China's Accession to the WTO*; Margaret M. Pearson, "China's Track Record in the Global Economy," *China Business Review* (January/February 2000) chinabusinessreview.com. For more critical views of China's approach to international legal obligations, see, for example, James V. Feinerman, "Chinese Participation in the International Legal Order: Rogue Elephant or Team Player?" *China Quarterly*, no. 141 (March 1995): 186–210.

Area by 2010 was (with the exception of its exclusion of Taiwan) an extension and deepening of China's engagement with and support for open, market-oriented international economic regimes, particularly with its neighbors.[36]

The orderly transition at the top of the Chinese polity that formally began at the Sixteenth Party Congress in late 2002, and that installed a president and party general secretary who had received Deng's imprimatur, a premier with strong reformist credentials, and several other top leaders who were acolytes or allies of Jiang, heralded no major change in these imperatives, or in the Chinese regime's broad commitment to market-oriented reform, economic openness, and international normalcy. Moreover, many observers saw the transition as incomplete and expected Jiang's personal influence to persist. Also, a new leadership facing significant policy challenges at home and high expectations and scrutiny abroad, had good reason not to get off on the wrong foot with its foreign economic partners.[37] Nonetheless, WTO membership has its burdens and difficult consequences. Joining the WTO constituted enough of a fault line that it predictably marked the beginning of a distinct phase in China's engagement with the international economic regime and its principal institution. The near-coincidence of WTO entry with leadership transition enhanced the prospect of some discontinuity. China's fourth-generation leadership inherited at its inauguration the significant task of

---

[36] For a balanced account that includes this reading, see Qingjiang Kong, "China's WTO Accession and the ASEAN-China Free Trade Area: The Perspective of a Chinese Lawyer," *Journal of International Economic Law* 7 (December 2004): 839–886. See also, Alice Ba's chapter, "*China-ASEAN Relations: The Significance of an ASEAN-China Free Trade Area*," in this volume.

[37] On the new leadership, see Andrew J. Nathan and Bruce Gilley, *China's New Rulers: The Secret Files* (New York: New York Review of Books, 2002); Joseph Fewsmith's chapter, "Political Succession: Changing Guards and Changing Rules," in this volume; and Szue-Chin Philip Hsu, "China's Domestic Politics and U.S.-Taiwan-China Relations: An Assessment in the Aftermath of the CCP's 16th National Congress," *American Foreign Policy Interests*, no. 25 (2003).

formulating China's approach to the distinctive challenges of the post-accession era.

Although evidence from the initial postaccession years is necessarily inconclusive, China's behavior as a WTO member and under the post-Jiang leadership suggests that changing circumstances and shifting goals could bring significant and increasing friction. Each principal area of emerging or potential conflict is a descendant of the evolving quadripartite aims that characterized China's long quest to join the GATT/WTO. First, China's WTO membership meant that other states' willingness and, indeed, obligation to create a regulatory and policy environment favorable for China's still-export-dependent growth strategy became more closely tied, legally and politically, to China's providing access to its own markets for foreign goods, services, and investors. In assuming general obligations of membership and in its accession agreement, China promised much, partly because doing so served domestic reformers' ends, partly because the United States and other gatekeepers to the WTO demanded it. This may yield a study in the maxim, "Be careful what you wish for because you may get it."

China has routinely touted its extensive measures to comply with its WTO obligations, and even Beijing's harshest critics must concede significant effort and accomplishment. Thousands of laws and regulations governing trade and other matters covered by WTO rules and China's accession protocol were revised in the run-up to accession and its aftermath. A new Foreign Trade Law, adopted in 2004, and related measures have dropped former restrictions on enterprises' rights to engage in foreign trade and pledged compliance with such WTO obligations as uniformity and transparency of trade regulation, most favored nation, and national treatment principles. Tariffs have been lowered, in some areas sharply. Licensing and some other nontariff barriers have been further reduced or removed. Rights to seek judicial review under the Administrative Litigation Law were extended plenarily to trade and intellectual property cases. China also undertook to eliminate problematic direct export subsidies, remove many other trade-affecting subsidies for entities other than state-owned enterprises, and require state-owned enterprises to behave in a more commercial manner.³⁸

In 2002, a new foreign investment "catalogue," and legislation underlying it, further liberalized sectoral restrictions and reduced lingering emphases on export promotion and technology transfer to comply with WTO Trade-Related Investment Measures (TRIMs) requirements. Amendments to laws and regulations and approval processes governing the principal vehicles for foreign investment redressed export performance, foreign exchange balancing, and local sourcing provisions and other matters at odds with WTO norms. New regulations provided improved and clearer legal foundations for foreign firms' acquisition of existing Chinese companies and assets.³⁹ To redress a chronic deterrent to foreign investment

---

³⁸ See Mark O'Neill, "China Begins Legal Race to Change," *South China Morning Post*, November 30, 2001 (quoting PRC account of revisions of laws and regulations); Foreign Trade Law of the People's Republic of China (2004); Provisions of the Supreme People's Court on Certain Questions Concerning the Hearing and Handling of International Trade Administrative Cases (2002); and "Chinese Official Interviewed on New Foreign Trade Law," *Renmin Ribao* Web site, in BBC Worldwide Monitoring (April 14, 2004).

³⁹ Guideline Catalogue of Foreign Investment Industries (approved by the State Council, 2002); State Council of the PRC, Regulations on Foreign Investment Guidelines (2002); Anyuan Yuan, "China's Entry into the WTO: Impact on China's Regulating Regime of Foreign Direct Investment," *International Lawyer* 35 (Spring 2001): 195–218 (assessing TRIMs and GATS obligations' implications in requiring changes in China's separate, fragmented, and restrictive legal regime regulating foreign investment); Use of Foreign Investment to Reorganize State-owned Enterprises, Tentative Provisions (State Economic and Trade Commission, the Ministry of Finance, State Administration for Industry and Commerce and State Administration of Foreign Exchange, 2003); Acquisition of Domestic Enterprises by Foreign Investors, Tentative Provisions (Ministry of Foreign Trade and Economic Cooperation, State Administration of Taxation, State Administration for Industry and Commerce and State Administration of Foreign Exchange, 2003); and Michael Moser, "Traditional Barriers are Starting to Fall Away: Legislation is Making it Easier for Foreigners to Make Direct Purchases of the Equity Assets of Domestic Chinese Companies," *Financial Times*, September 24, 2003.

and to address China's Trade Related Intellectual Property (TRIPs) obligations, additional measures — albeit of disputed and limited efficacy — have been taken to enhance protections, including adding intellectual property articles to the Foreign Trade Law and amending intellectual property laws, creating and strengthening specialized intellectual property chambers in people's courts, enhancing criminal penalties for intellectual property rights violations, and emphasizing administrative enforcement efforts by the State Administration of Industry and Commerce, the Customs Ministry, and others. China also has made meaningful moves to fulfill WTO accession-related pledges to liberalize foreign firms' and investors' access to service sectors, including local currency banking, insurance, legal services, telecommunications, distribution, and retail. Even some potential reforms that foreign investors have disliked — such as removing or threatening to remove favorable tax treatment and special zone-specific privileges — are consistent with WTO obligations and arguably advance WTO ideals of national treatment and nationwide uniformity.[40]

More broadly, the endorsement of entrepreneurship in the party charter and state constitution, and the elevation of private property to a status nearly equal to that of other forms of property were post-accession moves that signaled a highly visible — and, thus, difficult to abandon — reaffirmation and extension of an ideological commitment to the market economy principles that are core to the WTO regime. There was a parallel renewal of the rhetorical embrace of rule of law norms. More substantively, extensive programs focused on building judicial competence generally, providing WTO education for judges and officials, and steering disputes with WTO relevance to higher-level courts (where competence and honesty

---

[40] See the government and industry group reports on China's implementation performance cited later in this section. See also, Wu Jing, "WTO Accession — Judiciary Faces Challenges," *Renmin Ribao* Web site, in BBC Worldwide Monitoring (February 17, 2002); "Foreign-Invested Firms to Keep Preferential Treatment — For Now," *China Online* (May 10, 2002).

are generally higher) or specialized chambers (such as those for intellectual property).[41]

Still, along with undisputed accomplishments have come highly publicized shortcomings. Foreign governments' and industry groups' criticism of China's implementation of its strongly liberalizing and WTO regime-conforming pledges has quickly become a defining feature of the PRC's interaction with the formal global trade and trade-related order. Principal concrete complaints during the first three years included claims that: enforcement actions, civil and criminal penalties, and formal legal protection (most famously in the rejection of patent protection for Viagra) for intellectual property rights remained inadequate; value added tax rebates discriminated against imported semiconductors; instances of subsidies and dumping persisted; measures to open the distribution sector to foreign companies lagged; tariff rate quotas for bulk agricultural products were allocated in commercially unviable quantities and through opaque processes; and procedural, public health, and scientific standards were abused to exclude agricultural imports. More broadly, outside critics raised objections to burdensome and byzantine bureaucratic processes for securing needed licenses or approvals for imports or investment projects and service-sector businesses, inadequate transparency in rule-making and law-making processes, and weak implementation and enforcement of new WTO-conforming rules, especially in courts and at local levels. Surveys of American

---

[41] On judicial capacity building efforts related to and following WTO accession, see Veron Mei-Ying Hung, "China's WTO Commitment on Independent Judicial Review: Impact on Legal and Political Reform," *American Journal of Comparative Law* 52 (Winter 2004): 77–132, and Wu, "WTO Accession — Judiciary Faces Challenges." On efforts to promote the rule of law or rule by law generally, see, for example, Jacques deLisle, "Chasing the God of Wealth while Evading the Goddess of Democracy"; Jacques deLisle, "Lex Americana?: United States Legal Assistance, American Legal Models and Legal Change in the Post-Communist World and Beyond," *University of Pennsylvania Journal of International Economic Law* 20 (1999): 179–308; and Randall Peerenboom, *China's Long March toward the Rule of Law* (Cambridge, UK: Cambridge University Press, 2002).

businesses gave China middling grades for effort and accomplishment in implementing WTO obligations.[42]

Other critiques have ranged wider still, to matters involving less allegedly clear violations of duties or actions with less direct (though potentially no less important) implications for trade in goods and services. Following on complaints from American manufacturers shortly after China's accession, the Bush administration began in 2004 to press China to revalue the renminbi, blaming part of the cavernous United States trade deficit with the PRC on what Washington regarded as Beijing's market-flouting and surplus-seeking handling of the exchange rate. China's industrial policy and state banks' low-interest and low-repayment-rate loans to state-owned enterprises raised issues of impermissible subsidies and disguised trade barriers. And some have argued that continuing vagueness and nontransparency of Chinese laws, failure to undertake more extensive reforms in primarily domestic-focused laws, and continuing

---

[42] For examples of these criticisms, charges, and assessments, see United States Trade Representative, *2004 Report to Congress on China's WTO Compliance* (December 11, 2004); United States Trade Representative, *2003 Report to Congress on China's WTO Compliance* (December 11, 2003); United States Trade Representative, *2002 Report to Congress on China's WTO Compliance* (December 11, 2002); United States General Accounting Office, *World Trade Organization: U.S. Companies' Views on China's Implementation of Its Commitments* [GAO-04-508] (GAO March 2004); U.S.-China Business Council, *China's WTO Implementation: An Assessment of China's Third Year of WTO Membership* (September 7, 2004); U.S.-China Business Council, *China's WTO Implementation: An Assessment of China's Second Year of WTO Membership* (September 10, 2003); "Statement of William Primosch, Director, International Business Policy, National Association of Manufacturers," *Is China Playing by the Rules? Free Trade, Fair Trade, and WTO Compliance* (Congressional-Executive Commission on China, September 24, 2003); Myron A. Brilliant and Jeremie Waterman, *China's WTO Implementation: A Three-Year Assessment* (U.S. Chamber of Commerce, September 2004); U.S.-China Security Review Commission, *The National Security Implications of the Economic Relationship Between the United States and China* (July 2002), chap. 3; and William B. Abnett, "China and Compliance with World Trade Organization Commitments: The First Six Months," *NBR Special Report No. 3* (November 2002).

weaknesses of China's judiciary and the rule of law make fulfillment of WTO obligations infeasible.[43]

The targets of such criticism, and the tensions such criticism produces in China's relations with other WTO members, are likely to expand in the near future. In 2005 and shortly thereafter, many additional obligations — some of them among the most painful or difficult for China to implement — will come fully on line. Examples include: the removal of import quotas in the automobile sector, substantial increases in the range and scope of permitted foreign investment in the telecommunications sector, removal of geographic restrictions and establishment of "national treatment" — that is, equality with domestic Chinese counterparts — in regulations governing local currency banking, lifting of geographic restrictions on foreign-invested insurers, and elimination of some remaining restrictions on foreign participation in the distribution and retail sectors. Uncertainty over whether to attack certain practices as violations are likely to decline as experience accumulates, more extensive assessments of PRC actions occur, and special transitional arrangements expire. The transitional review mechanism that will apply to China for several more years will assure continued close and institutionalized scrutiny. Whether attributable primarily to poor implementation of WTO obligations or other factors, disappointment of foreign

---

[43] Brian Bremner, "A Slow Boat to Yuan Devaluation," *Business Week*, February 15, 2005. The currency peg and state-owned industry subsidy issues were raised in some of the government and industry reports cited above. On the transparency issue, see Sylvia Ostry, "The WTO: Post Seattle and Chinese Accession," in *China and the Long March to Global Trade,* ed. Ostry, Alexandroff, and Gomez, 9–21 (discussing transparency and legality issues), and Sylvia Ostry, "China and the WTO: The Transparency Issue," *UCLA Journal of International Law and Foreign Affairs* 3 (Summer 1998): 1–18. See also, Bhala, "Enter the Dragon," 1519ff (noting areas of early controversies over interpretation of commitments). For the most sweeping critiques concerning laws and institutions, see the discussions of explanations for problematic implementation and "mission creep" later in this chapter.

producers' likely inflated expectations of sharply increased exports to the PRC can be expected to sharpen charges of PRC noncompliance.[44] The same is likely true with respect to foreign investment in manufacturing and services.[45]

Such loud and growing objections to the PRC's implementation failures could unravel what some observers discern as other members' willingness to hold off on bringing formal complaints against China, in part out of concern that the WTO's dispute resolution process become overwhelmed. Three years after China's entry, no complaints against China had reached the WTO's dispute resolution body. The United States had taken initial steps in one instance — concerning value added tax rebates that favored domestic semiconductor manufacturers — but the matter was settled at a relatively early stage. Even the extraordinary unilateral mechanisms — such as the special product-specific safeguards that China's accession protocol permits its trading partners to use to protect against surges of PRC exports — have been rarely used during the first years of China's WTO membership. Such actions are far less than what

---

[44] Mark W. Frazier, "Coming to Terms with the 'WTO Effect' on U.S.-China Trade and China's Economic Growth," *NBR Briefing* (September 1999): (foreseeing a decline in tariff cut-driven and perhaps rapid Chinese economic expansion-based growth in U.S. exports to China); see also Lardy, *Integrating China into the Global Economy*, 22–62 (arguing that China had greatly liberalized its trade before accession, resulting in relatively low import barriers, especially by developing country standards).

[45] For examples of assessments that presented relatively rosy pictures to foreign business audiences on the prospects for vastly expanded roles (and that resonated with cautious Chinese parties' worries about "selling" the country), see *China/WTO: Shaping the Future* (Hong Kong: Asia Law & Practice, 2000); *China After the WTO: What You Need to Know* (New York: Practicing Law Institute, 2001). For a favorable Chinese commentary on assessments that WTO accession would reaccelerate foreign investment and contribute to a greatly expanded role, see Zhao Jinping, "Ten Major Trends in China's Foreign Capital Utilization," *Liaowang* in World News Connection (May 19, 2003).

aggrieved parties credibly could have brought if one credits critics' accounts of China's behavior.[46]

The widespread declarations of significant shortcomings in China's implementation have been attributed to diverse causes, including critics' exaggeration of the extent or the impact of Chinese noncompliance, China's persistently mercantilist approach to foreign economic relations, and the Chinese government's shortage of legal-institutional resources or lack of political will to make changes that face resistance from powerful local authorities in China's decentralized reform-era polity and that will impose great hardship on significant economic sectors, large state enterprises, and many millions of Chinese workers and farmers.[47] Most of these considerations provide reasons to slow or evade promised changes — many of them

---

[46] See generally, Mark W. Frazier and Peter M. Hansen, "China's Accession to the WTO: A Candid Appraisal from U.S. Industry," *NBR Briefing* (1999) (U.S. corporate executives predicting dangerously high levels of PRC-related WTO disputes); Sylvia Ostry, "WTO Membership for China: To Be and Not to Be — Is that the Answer?" in *China and the World Trading System*, ed. Cass, Williams, and Barker, 31–39; see also, Christopher Duncan, "Out of Conformity: China's Capacity to Implement World Trade Organization Dispute Settlement Body Decisions After Accession," *American University International Law Review* 18 (2002): 399–505, and Greg Mastel, "China and the World Trade Organization: Moving Forward Without Sliding Backward," *Law and Policy in International Business* 31 (Spring 2000): 981–997.

[47] See, for example, Donald C. Clarke, "China's Legal System and the WTO: Prospects for Compliance," *Washington University Global Studies Law Review* 2 (Winter 2003): 97–118 (stressing institutional incapacity, including weak courts, political decentralization, and opaque laws, and noting arguments of lack of will); Duncan, "Out of Conformity" (noting weakness and generality of laws, lack of clarity of administrative allocation of enforcement authority, corruption); Mastel, "China and the World Trade Organization" (discussing China's poor implementation of, and possible lack of will to implement, pre-WTO international trade agreements); Ravi P. Kewalram, "WTO Dispute Settlement and Subnational Entities in China," in *China and the World Trading System*, ed. Cass, Williams, and Barker, 413–420 (discussing localism as a factor and the difficulty for China under WTO doctrine of asserting a "federalism" defense); Hung, "China's WTO Commitment on Independent Judicial Review" (concerning judicial weaknesses as a likely source of WTO compliance problems); and Kong Qingjiang, *China and the World Trade Organization: A Legal Perspective* (Singapore: World Scientific Press, 2002), chap. 11 (similar).

seemingly primarily for foreigners' benefit — that would force enterprises entangled with the local state out of business, cause massive layoffs at state-owned enterprises, close intellectual property rights-violating factories, make farm products uncompetitive, and so on.

In such circumstances, it requires no leap of the imagination to foresee China relying less on claims that foreign criticisms are exaggerated, or that the PRC is doing as much as it can and is making impressive progress, given problems of limited legal resources, local resistance, and other political constraints. An increasingly assertive pushback against the painful demands of WTO membership, foreign companies, and governments is conceivable. This prospect, signs of which are immanent in postaccession developments, constitutes a second major element of China's engagement with the WTO in the 2000s, one that manifests increased ambivalence about foreigners' roles in China's development, whether as Chinese enterprises' partners or as their competitors, and whether as producers of imports or as investors in local production entities.

Of course, many of the obligations that China has implemented and other major changes surrounding the PRC's joining the WTO have continued and extended the project of permitting foreigners an ever larger and less constrained role in China's economy. But these, equally plainly, coexist with evidence and allegations of noncompliant PRC policies and actions that impede foreign access to investment opportunities (often formally classed as "trade in services"), as well as access to product markets. To the extent such failures of implementation are willful, they indicate skepticism in policy-making and policy-implementing circles about the desirability of the expanded foreign presence that WTO-mandated changes and related reforms would encourage. Some observers and critics discern significant and growing resort in postaccession China to various forms of "sneaky protectionism" that appear to reflect and serve such agendas. Among the examples cited by foreign industry groups and their governments are: arbitrary and high capitalization requirements for foreign-owned and foreign-invested companies in newly opened service sectors; perennial weaknesses in protecting the intellectual property — and other legal rights — of international firms with production or research facilities in China; technical and other standards that require costly adaptations to produce and sell in China; abuse of discretionary and nontransparent foreign investment licensing and approval processes; and failures to address local officials' disregard for central directives and WTO and other legal obligations. Other complaints have pointed to postaccession regulations governing construction, engineering, information industries, and postal services as eroding access that foreign investors previously had enjoyed.[48]

Chinese sources have become publicly much less tolerant of the special treatment that reform-era laws and policies have long extended to foreigners.[49] Also, even from the ranks of those who have supported and participated in China's long opening to foreign trade and investment have come rising calls to imitate means that other WTO members have developed — such as strong antidumping laws, safeguard measures against import surges, currency restrictions to protect against balance of payments problems, and the many sectoral restrictions on foreign participation that the General Agreement on Trade in Services, China's accession protocol and the WTO regime as a whole tolerate — to protect domestic industries from the perils of the increasingly liberal international regime that comes with WTO membership.[50]

---

[48] See the business group and government reports cited above.

[49] "Foreign-Invested Firms to Keep Preferential Treatment — For Now"; "Tax Breaks for Foreign Firms to be Eliminated," *China Online*, November 15, 2001.

[50] Deborah Z. Cass, "China and the Constitutionalization of International Trade Law," in *China and the World Trading System*, ed. Cass, Williams, and Barker, 46 (describing pledges to make use of such means); Yang and Cheng, "The Process of China's Accession to the WTO," 18ff (noting possible use of such means and reasons to do so); Wei Huo, "Introduction and Critical Analysis of Anti-Dumping Regime and Practice in China Pending Entry of WTO," *International Lawyer* 36 (Spring 2002): 197–214 (describing importance to China and commitment of Chinese officials to using antidumping measures to protect Chinese interests); Lihu Chen and Yun Gu, "China's Safeguard Measures under the New WTO Framework," *Fordham International Law Journal* 25 (June 2002): 1169–1186; "Trade Remedy Measures Safeguard Chinese Industry," *Xinhua* , July 29, 2004; "Chinese Economists Warn of Risks of Foreign Acquisitions," *Asia Pulse* , October 24, 2003; "The Prospect of a Powerful Trading Nation," *Business Daily Update*, January 11, 2005; and "Long Yongtu Says Anti-Dumping Cases Should be Calmly Treated," *Xinhua*, December 26, 2002.

Such pushback or foot-dragging derives additional impetus and legitimacy from a widespread sense that China's membership deal demanded extraordinary liberalization from the PRC while permitting extensive protectionism by its trading partners. China, after all, had had to forego the "special and differential" privileges that typically give developing countries preferential market access and greater latitude for protectionism than general WTO terms permit. Kept out of the WTO longer than many post-Soviet states, China has also been unable to take advantage of the exceptions to some WTO market disciplines that were available to postsocialist "transitional economies" during the first several years following the organization's founding. Phase-in periods for PRC commitments are generally short, with few exceeding five years. And concessions on subsidies to state-owned enterprises and agriculture are expansive. On the other hand, other WTO members will be allowed for twelve years to impose safeguards against Chinese exports where they threaten merely "material injury" (rather than the usual GATT standard "serious injury") to domestic producers, and to impose special safeguards against Chinese textile exports until 2008. WTO members enjoyed even more extended privileges to use the "nonmarket economy" method — a standard significantly less favorable to exporting states than the usual exporting state home market price — to discern dumping and impose offsetting duties. And, almost immediately upon China's accession, industry groups (including textiles and steel) in the United States and elsewhere sewed consternation among Chinese industry groups and officials by trying to invoke these protections and other WTO mechanisms, albeit on a limited scale, and traditional WTO-permitted mechanisms (such as antidumping remedies).[51]

---

[51] On these issues, see Qin, "WTO Regulation of Subsidies to State-Owned Enterprises" (extensive account of Chinese concessions, judging them to be too harsh and one-sided to be optimally effective in promoting reform and compliance); Michael Schroeder and Phillip Day, "U.S. Manufacturers Target China for Trade Sanctions," *Wall Street Journal*, September 8, 2003; "Backlash over American Textile Appeal," *China Daily*, August 21, 2003; "The Prospect of a Powerful Trading Nation"; "Long Yongtu Says Anti-Dumping Cases Should be Calmly Treated."

Beyond such relatively clearly trade and investment-related developments, the first notable rhetorical shift from the Jiang era was the Hu Jintao-Wen Jiabao leadership's emphasis on the need to address the problems of those whom the boom borne of economic reform and openness had left behind. In the early days of the fourth-generation leadership, and especially in the wake of the SARS crisis, official and mainstream discussions began to emphasize the need to consider human development and social development as well as the long-dominant goal of economic development. A substantial shift of policy in that direction would accord greater weight to considerations that do not so strongly favor expansive roles for foreigners, whose presence in the Chinese economy has been, of course, far more strongly associated with rapid and unequal growth than with addressing inequality and noneconomic measures of well-being.

In a more dramatic, although more remote, scenario, the costs and consequences that flow from — or might be blamed on — WTO membership could feed a more severe backlash against WTO obligations and the agenda of openness and reform with which they are politically and practically intertwined. A coalition of the unwilling and the wounded could emerge to slow or reverse the reformist momentum that the quest for WTO accession had helped foster in the 1980s and 1990s, and that WTO entry has been expected to accelerate. This possibility constitutes a third, potentially disjunctive feature of postaccession China's engagement with the WTO.

The prospect should not be exaggerated. Many developments during the 2000s and under the fourth-generation leadership point to continuity and extension of reform generally and pursuit of WTO-conforming domestic reforms specifically. Many of the moves to implement specific obligations entailed further steps in domestic reform. Beyond those, examples of such changes include implementation of a unified Contract Law that mandates more uniform, more market-friendly and broadly capitalist-style rules for economic and commercial dealings, replacing prior laws that were more fragmented and that reflected heavier vestiges of the planning era. Much the same can be said of new laws for enterprise bankruptcy and property rights that have been high on the legislative agenda during the early and middle 2000s. Examples of similar-in-spirit changes to formal institutions include the major reshuffling in 2003 of entities under the State Council, which formally eliminated the State Planning and Development Commission and the State Economic and Trade Commission (as well as MOFTEC) and created a new National Reform and Development Commission and a vast Ministry of Commerce (which subsumed the former MOFTEC and much of the SETC). In practice, efforts and progress continued in building courts and other legal institutions. These and other moves marked the creation or strengthening of entities with professional roles and stakes in continuing reform, openness, WTO compliance, and so on. Restructuring or partially privatizing enterprises moved forward as well. Among the remaining traditional state-owned enterprises, corporatization continued. As expected, a quarter century of reforms had produced some significant internationally competitive firms and sectors that saw benefits in the WTO regime. Chinese industry associations offered highly visible (if not necessarily spontaneous) critiques of foreign firms' protectionist calls targeting Chinese steel and clothing exports. And Chinese enterprises in newly opened service sectors rushed to establish joint ventures with strong foreign partners.

At the elite level, while the fourth-generation leadership began to stake out some distinctive ideological positions, nothing signaled a major departure from existing basic policy lines in economic reform. The "Three Represents" received endorsement from Hu and recognition in party charter and state constitutional amendments in 2002 and 2004.

Still, a prognosis that foresees retrenchment in reform, openness, and cooperation is hardly a matter of groundless speculation. Significant social groups that have lost out under reform and initial rounds of WTO-mandated changes, or are at risk as such reforms and implementation continue, have become more restive. Recent years have brought more numerous and, for the authorities, increasingly disconcerting mass protests — sometimes large and occasionally violent ones. Prominent in the ranks of the discontented are workers whom state firms have laid off or left unpaid. So too is the vast "floating population" of rural-to-urban migrants who have pursued often-marginal jobs in thriving coastal cities and who live at the margins of regulation and protection by local authorities. Also included are farmers whose land-use rights or money have been taken by local authorities who collaborate — often corruptly — with developers, or who face severe shortages of revenue needed for government functions. Such problems could grow more serious as WTO-implementing and related reforms proceed, throwing troubled state-owned enterprises and other economically weak domestic firms into greater competition with foreign and foreign-invested firms, forcing sharp structural adjustments in industries ranging from automobiles to financial services, sustaining or increasing the rate of capital inflows that go disproportionately to developed areas along China's littoral, and opening vulnerable agricultural sectors to the challenges of cheap imports.[52]

Constituencies with reasons to resist or worry about WTO-related changes and other reforms continue to retain and develop institutional patrons and allies. Weakened but not gone are traditional opponents of more radical reform and openness in older line industrial and planning bureaucracies and in northeastern and inland regions that continue to straggle economically and face some of the most severe readjustment costs imposed by new waves of reform and WTO implementation. In addition, other central organs, such as the Ministry of Finance and the Ministry of the Information Industry (MII), have had to grapple with the prospect that the major entities in their sectors — the state-owned banks and affiliated institutions and the big state-linked telecommunications companies — face the need to make drastic and rapid adjustment if WTO pledges

---

[52] On these issues, see Edward Friedman's chapter *"Jiang Zemin's Successors and China's Growing Rich-Poor Gap,"* in this volume. See also Dorothy J. Solinger, *Contesting Citizenship in Urban China* (Berkeley, CA: University of California Press, 1999), and Elizabeth J. Perry, *Challenging the Mandate of Heaven: Social Protest and State Power in China* (New York: M.E. Sharpe, 2002).

are fully implemented. The MII, in particular, has faced charges of protectionism and suspicion that it was using the pretext of political sensitivity to resist openness and foreign participation in areas that it regulates.[53] At the subprovincial level, local governments have had ample reason to protect local industries from threats unleashed by WTO compliance or other reforms. Under the mercantilist logic of local protectionism, this extended even to competitive firms. That such phenomena have been significant and widespread is reflected in the continuing refrain from foreign observers and Chinese leaders concerning the evils of local protectionism and the need to recentralize authority to implement WTO obligations and other reforms effectively.[54]

Although biography and rhetoric do not reliably predict policy, they have suggested to observers in China and abroad that Hu Jintao and other fourth-generation leaders differ, at least marginally, from their predecessors in their solicitude for interests and issues that cut against full WTO implementation and some aspects of deepening reform. Much has been made of Hu's extensive

---

[53] On telecommunications and Internet regulation and MII during this period, see Kong, *China and the World Trade Organization*, chaps. 10–12, and T.J. Cheng's chapter, "Information Technology in China: A Double-Edged Sword," in this volume. On the financial sector, see Lardy, *China's Unfinished Economic Revolution*, and John D. Langlois, Jr., "Pressures on China from the Asian Financial Crisis," in *China and the Long March to Global Trade*, ed. Ostry, Alexandroff and Gomez, 99–118.

[54] See, for example, Shirk, *How China Opened its Door*, chap. 7 (concerning the need for recentralization); Bruce Gilley, *Model Rebels: The Rise and Fall of China's Richest Village* (Berkeley, CA: University of California Press, 2001) (providing a vivid case study of local government-business fusion and disregard for central directives); and Stanley Lubman, *Bird in a Cage: Legal Reform in China After Mao* (Stanford, CA: Stanford University Press, 2000), 260–269 (describing local protectionism and its effects on courts and legal remedies). See also, the government and business groups' reports concerning China's implementation of WTO obligations, cited above, which often refer to local protectionism as a significant problem in WTO implementation. Additionally, see Clarke, "China's Legal System and the WTO: Prospects for Compliance."

experience in China's more backward areas, in contrast to Jiang Zemin's Shanghai-dominated résumé. And Hu and Wen have engaged the ideas of noneconomic dimensions of development, and have spoken of the importance of addressing the suffering of those who have not fared well under reform. The handling of the SARS episode brought their relatively populist style and, perhaps, substance to the fore. For now, there is room for disagreement over whether these are true exercises of leadership in service of a deep-seated agenda, or attempts at co-optation or preemption, or the epiphenomena of intra-elite struggle. But they do point to more acceptance of a critique of the adverse side effects of reform and negative consequences of WTO-compliant changes.[55]

"Mission creep" in the WTO regime could enhance the prospects of a backlash in China against the WTO and the broader package of reforms associated with it. Forces inside and, especially, outside the WTO have pressed to expand its mandate to include a wide range of trade-affecting factors. Foremost among these are environmental and human rights issues, in part (but only in part) because abuse of labor rights and lax pollution controls can create at least short-term production cost advantages. The United States had pressed, but ultimately dropped, efforts to include concessions on labor rights in China's accession deal. Human rights, of course, long has been an issue in U.S.-China trade relations, and legislation accompanying PNTR sought to sustain some vestige of the linkage despite the demise of annual MFN review. Beijing had been vocal, at the Seattle meeting in 1999 and elsewhere, in opposing expansion of the WTO's reach to include such matters. Given China's poor and widely criticized record on these issues, the PRC would be a loser if the trade regime shifted to permit higher trade barriers to goods

---

[55] For assessments of these questions of elite agendas and related issues, see Joseph Fewsmith's chapter in this volume and Nathan and Gilley, *China's New Rulers*. On the implications of the SARS episode, see Jacques deLisle, "SARS and the Pathologies of Globalization and Transition in Greater China," *Orbis* 47, no. 4 (2003): 587ff.

produced in countries with ill-treated and underpaid workers or toxin-spewing factories.⁵⁶

More fundamentally, the PRC's deeply entrenched position is to resist international enforcement of human rights and environmental and many other international legal norms as impermissible intrusions on the targeted nation's sovereignty. That has been the PRC's loud and clear position on human rights, only partially relaxed with China's softening its stance in the 1990s. It has sometimes been China's position on environmental questions as well, though this view more often surfaces as a corollary to the principle that China has a sovereign right (and duty) to pursue economic development, which implies a degree of intransigence toward externally imposed, potentially growth-restricting environmental obligations. This "strong sovereignty" view has been at the core of China's approach to a wide range of international law and international relations issues for a very long time. As such, it will not be lightly abandoned. Increased conflict between that political imperative and China's cooperative and conformist approach to the WTO could be far more damaging to the latter.

Moreover, official supporters and academic commentators in the United States and elsewhere have envisioned a far more radical form of "mission creep" or "contagion," asserting that implementation of China's WTO obligations will cause — or require — fundamental alterations in China's polity. The rule of law, a basic redefinition of the party's role, extensive political liberalization, and even democracy

---

⁵⁶ On these issues, see Panitchpakdi and Clifford, *China and the WTO*, 201–206; Roda Mushkat, "Potential Impacts of China's WTO Accession on Its Approach to the Trade-Environment Balancing Act," *Chinese Journal of International Law* 2 (2003): 227–264; Alice E.S. Tay and Hamish Redd, "China: Trade, Law and Human Rights," in *China and the World Trading System,* ed. Cass, Williams, and Barker, 156–172. See also, WTO Consultative Board, *The Future of the WTO: Addressing Institutional Challenges in the New Millennium* (Geneva: WTO, January 17, 2005), chap. 3 (criticizing invocation of sovereignty as a red herring for protectionism and arguing that positive effects of international cooperation to establish harmonized and liberal trade-related laws outweigh negative impact on states' latitude for domestic policy choices).

are among the changes cited.[57] If Chinese leaders see WTO compliance and related reform exerting major pressure in such directions, the risk of backlash will escalate.

Despite the unwelcome pressures and costs that membership has imposed or threatened, entering the WTO has secured for China a significant symbol of status as a normal member of the community of states. Accession thus brought a signal success in the fourth, noneconomic dimension that has in various forms characterized Beijing's marathon pursuit of GATT/WTO accession. But China's assumption of membership in the organization also has sharpened the question of how — and how "normally" — the rising great power will participate in the operation and development of the still young but singularly potent international organization. China's early postaccession behavior suggested a disinclination to do much more than grapple with its own compliance issues and play a secondary role in pursuing violations by fellow members. Examples of the former include numerous official and semi-official statements highlighting China's compliance successes and implementation efforts, and expressions of determination to address remaining problems that bear on WTO obligations, including local protectionism, shortcomings in the rule of law, and so on.[58] Examples of the latter include the PRC's taking a

---

[57] For accounts of the prospect of such changes being used to "sell" U.S. constituencies and leaders on China's accession, see, for example, *Beginning the Journey: China, the U.S. and the WTO: Report from the U.S. Council on Foreign Relations Independent Task Force on China* (2001), and U.S.-China Economic and Security Review Commission, *The National Security Implications of the Economic Relationship Between the United States and China* (July 2002), chap. 3. For academic assessments, see, for example, Pitman Potter, "The Legal Implications of China's Accession to the WTO," *China Quarterly*, no. 167 (September 2001): 592–609 (arguing that WTO compliance implies a thoroughgoing transformation of China's laws and legal system, including matters of constitutional law, property, contracts, and other matters), and Donald C. Clarke, "GATT Membership for China?" *University of Puget Sound Law Review* 17 (Spring 1994): 517–531 (asserting broad "rule of law" and "open society"—as well as "market economy"—premises of the GATT system).
[58] "China Begins Race to Legal Change," and "A Major Decision for Promoting China's Open Door Policy." See also, Kong, *China and the World Trade Organization*, chaps. 3–4. Many of the critiques of China's implementation cited

backseat in the dispute over the Bush administration's measures to protect American steel producers, despite economic interests China shared with the more vocal EU and Japan.[59]

In its first few years as a WTO member, China undertook no major initiatives in shaping WTO rules and their interpretation. Whether quietly learning the ways of the WTO, or lacking strong guidance from Beijing, or operating under instructions not to provoke other members to increase scrutiny and criticism of the PRC's implementation record, China's delegation kept a relatively low profile for such an important trading state. The PRC's reformist agenda seemed not to go beyond the tepid solidarity with poorer states that China had long displayed in international organizations. At the WTO's Cancún meeting and more generally, the PRC notably did not side strongly with developing countries' agendas of seeking concessions on intellectual property rights (especially those that primarily benefited developed country-based pharmaceutical firms), reduction in developed countries' protectionism in agriculture, and increased tolerance for developing countries' measures to protect agriculture and to promote development at the expense of liberal trading principles.

China was less quiet and accepting of the status quo on another perennial issue: Taiwan.[60] Beijing's concern with rising

---

earlier in this section also concede that sincere, if not yet effective, efforts have been made in many areas. And foreign programs to increase China's compliance and implementation capacities implicitly agree. See, for example, "Testimony of Under Secretary of Commerce for International Trade Grant D. Aldonas," *WTO: Will China Keep Its Promises? Can It?* (Congressional-Executive Commission on China, June 6, 2002); "Statement of Loren Yager, Director International Affairs and Trade," *World Trade Organization: Ensuring China's Compliance Requires a Sustained and Multifaceted Approach* [GAO-04-172T] (General Accounting Office, October 30, 2003); see also, deLisle, "Lex Americana?"

[59] "China Condemns U.S. Steel Tariffs," *China Daily*, March 7, 2002, and "China Joins WTO Case Against U.S. Steel Tariffs," *New China News Agency*, in BBC Monitoring International Reports (June 25, 2002).

[60] On these issues generally, see Nancy Bernkopf Tucker, "The Taiwan Factor in the Vote on PNTR for China and Its WTO Accession," *NBR Analysis* 11, no. 2, Essay 1 (2000); Kong, *China and the World Trade Organization*, chap. 5.

pro-independence sentiment and rhetoric from Taiwan at the end of the 1990s and in the early 2000s, and Taiwan's entry into the WTO immediately after the PRC produced new strains in the "nationalist" or "status" dimension of China's interactions with the WTO. On one hand, the two sides' comembership in the WTO offers rich and obvious opportunities for Beijing to pursue one of its core strategies for advancing reunification. It is, of course, widely recognized that the large and growing asymmetrical interdependence in cross-Strait economic relations can give Beijing leverage (whether directly with the Republic of China government or indirectly through politically powerful Taiwanese business interests that rely on mainland markets and investments) to check Taiwan's drift toward more formal independence or to induce an outcome acceptable to the PRC. With both sides members, WTO rules legally deprive Taipei of some means for limiting economic integration. Taiwan's nontariff barriers to some Chinese exports and ban on direct transportation links are among the laws and policies vulnerable to possible WTO challenges.

On the other hand, comembership in the WTO also offers a beleaguered (or beleaguered-feeling) Taiwan opportunities for political gain. While the WTO is not a states-member-only organization (a feature that was indispensable to Beijing's acquiescence in Taiwan's accession), comembership does put the PRC and Taiwan on a formally equal footing in a primarily states-member institution that is surpassed (if at all) in importance and visibility only by the United Nations. Beijing has been acutely aware of this and has sought to avoid situations that imply equality and thereby undermine its insistence that Taiwan does not enjoy the international status and legal personality that would legitimate other countries' objections to PRC pressure on Taiwan to reunify. Beijing made clear its determination to avoid having PRC-Taiwan cases reach the WTO's dispute resolution mechanism, which indisputably performs a function of adjudication among juridical equals. China has denounced Taiwanese efforts to invoke — as an equal party and, implicitly, superior complier — the transitional review mechanism process to address shortcomings in China's trade-related laws and policies. The PRC has also refused bilateral talks with Taiwan in

WTO contexts and required that meetings be held outside official WTO space. As it has done in other international organizations, Beijing has pressed the WTO to eschew language that symbolizes or implies state-like status, insisting that Taiwan be referred to as the "Independent Customs Territory of Taiwan, Penghu, Kinmen and Mazu" (rather than "Taiwan"), that the head of Taiwan's delegation be called "representative" (instead of "ambassador"), and that its presence in Geneva be labeled "office of the permanent representative" (rather than the "permanent mission").[61]

Beijing's proposal for an ASEAN-China Free Trade Area excluding Taiwan provides a WTO-permitted, trade-centered institutional means for eroding Taiwan's regional standing and support. Less plausibly, the PRC floated the idea of a cross-Strait free trade area, which would take bilateral disputes initially outside the WTO framework.[62] Such gambits need not lead to significant problems in China's engagement with the WTO, but they could. To the extent that they are seen as primarily politically motivated, they may make Chinese behavior seem less "normal" and accommodating within the WTO framework. More broadly, to the extent that comembership in the WTO leads to situations in which Beijing's adherence to WTO obligations comes into conflict with its Taiwan agenda, the former may well be sacrificed to the latter.

Finally, despite China's generally "regime-taking" stance on matters other than Taiwan, Beijing might become less status quo-oriented

---

[61] "Taiwan Seen to be Reaping Benefits of Joining World Trade Organization," *Taiwan News*, September 9, 2003; "FM Spokeswoman Urges Taipei to Rectify Error in WTO Representatives' Title," *Xinhua News Agency*, May 27, 2003; see also, "Taiwan Joins International Law Advisory Body," *Central News Agency* (Taiwan), May 6, 2004 (describing controversy in Taiwan about whether Taiwan had agreed to participate in the body advising WTO on legal matters under the name "Chinese Taipei"), and "Mainland Toughens Attitude Against Taiwan's TRM Questions at WTO," *Central News Agency* (Taiwan), November 5, 2004.

[62] Chloe Lai, "Macau and Taiwan 'Needed in Cepa Deal,'" *South China Morning Post*, July 30, 2003 (including statement by deputy director of the PRC State Council's Taiwan Affairs Office and report by the China National Institute of the World Trade Organization).

in its approach to the WTO and the international economic regimes of which the WTO increasingly forms the centerpiece. As China's clout and confidence grow, and if China becomes sufficiently discontented with some WTO norms and rules, Beijing may become more of a "regime-challenger" or try to become a "regime-shaper." Some hints of what such developments might look like and how they might emerge may be visible already. China's urgent push to become a WTO founding member in the mid-1990s and to join before the Seattle ministerial conference in part reflected a desire to be a full participant in developments that would define the rapidly developing regime. Around the time of China's accession, officials and spokesmen put down clear markers, publicly asserting that China was now in a position to play a significant role in the evolution of the international trade regime.[63] Even Beijing's rather indifferent engagement with the attempt to forge and strengthen a developing country bloc at Cancún could portend a more robust similar effort in the future. The PRC's importance as a trading and economic power and the WTO's institutional structure give Beijing significant and diverse capacities for influence, whether through exercising something approaching a veto in the WTO's consensus-based procedure, or siding with other developing countries, or more loosely helping to off-set the influence of the major industrialized states, or bringing or defending claims before the dispute resolution

---

[63] "Opening Wider to Outside World with WTO Entry as Opportunity," *Renmin Ribao*, December 11, 2001 (recapitulating this and other stated goals and opportunities of WTO entry, on occasion of the date of the PRC's accession); Christian Wade, "China Looks for Large WTO Role," *United Press International*, March 14, 2002 (quoting Foreign Trade Minister Shi Guangsheng's statement that, "Now China can participate in making the rules...reflect[ing] our own interests"); see also, Supachai Panitchpakdi, "Putting the Doha Development Agenda Back on Track: Why it Matters to China," *WTO and China: 2003 Beijing International Forum* (WTO Director General describing influence in making international trading rules as a key motivation for China's joining the WTO and expressing hope that China would use that role to strengthen and liberalize the global regime).

China and the WTO 291

body, or having PRC nationals serve as judges on trial and appellate panels in the WTO.[64]

Concerns old and new provide possible foci for attempts to exercise such influence. Beijing has long openly expressed resentment toward a GATT-centered international economic regime created primarily by developed Western states primarily for their benefit and with significant costs to other states' (including China's) interests and autonomy.[65] On matters ranging from intellectual property protection, to expanding the WTO's reach over environmental and labor rights, to permitting WTO bodies to entertain complaints over behavior that does not violate WTO rules, the PRC may press positions at odds with those of industrialized powers and their allies within the WTO.

Outside the WTO, China has moved to cast itself as an Asian regional leader, including on matters that overlap with the WTO's jurisdiction. During and after the Asian financial crisis, Beijing emphasized its commitment to being a paragon of stability and responsibility, pledged to maintain its currency peg despite the risks this posed for China and its still significantly export-dependent growth strategy, and despite the challenges that the crisis posed and revealed for China's own financial sector.[66] On the eve of WTO accession, Beijing pressed for a ten-year effort to create an ASEAN-China Free Trade Area (ACFTA) — a bolder move than any proposed

---

[64] Panitchpakdi and Clifford, *China and the WTO*, 190–193; Cass, Williams, and Barker, eds., *China and the World Trading System* (several essays predicting various aspect of significant Chinese impact on WTO), and "China Urges Group of 77 to Advance Interests of Developing Nations," *Xinhua*, September 25, 2003 (quoting statement of Foreign Minister Li Zhaoxing concerning agenda in WTO and other organizations).

[65] For discussions of these issues, see, for example, Pearson, "China's Integration into the International Trade and Investment Regime," 182–183; Potter, "Foreign Investment Laws in the People's Republic of China: Dilemmas of State Control"; and Jacques deLisle, "Politics, Law and Resentment on China Coast," *Foreign Policy Research Institute E-Note* (July 2001).

[66] "Central Bank Governor Rules Out RMB Devaluation," *Xinhua News Agency*, March 11, 1999; "With WTO Deal, Zhu Re-Issues No Devaluation Vow," *China Online*, November 30, 1999; and Langlois, "Pressures on China from the Asian Financial Crisis."

by Japan or any other regional or global power. Even assuming such an arrangement would be designed and implemented to satisfy the WTO's demanding provisions governing FTAs and thus prohibit any PRC-favored illiberalism, the ACFTA still would take out of the WTO's immediate purview a vast and growing swath of international trade. As analysts and some Chinese official and semi-official sources have noted, an ASEAN-China FTA would reflect and enhance China's clout as a regional economic and political power and would give Beijing an opportunity — absent in the WTO — to shape the rules for a major trading regime in ways that are more to its liking and, perhaps, to rely upon fellow ACFTA members to provide greater support for China's (or a Chinese-led ACFTA's) agenda in the WTO.[67]

Any major changes in China's engagement with the WTO and broader related regimes remain somewhat speculative and likely remote. But some are plausible enough and sufficiently consistent with the aims that China pursued in the twenty years before accession to suggest the real possibility that a third, postaccession phase may differ significantly from the second and first. This should not be a shocking proposition. After all, securing the long-sought prize of WTO membership necessarily altered China's relationship with the organization and international economic regimes, and membership came on the eve of China's leadership transition and amid domestic challenges and international developments that raised new doubts about the desirability and necessity of further extension of past policy lines and full adherence to the WTO's painful and possibly expanding requirements.

---

[67] On these issues, see Kong, "China's WTO Accession and the ASEAN-China Free Trade Area," and Alice Ba's chapter in this volume. On issues of the WTO regime's role in Asia and in China-East Asia relations generally and the impact of the Asian financial crisis, see Panitchpakdi and Clifford, *China's and the WTO*, 101–137.

Chapter

10

China's Accession into the WTO and China's Financial Markets

K. Thomas Liaw

The World Trade Organization (WTO) is an organization that formalizes trade agreements among 142 member countries. The goal of the WTO is to create a favorable environment to help producers of goods and services, exporters, and importers conduct their business.[1] The benefits of membership in the WTO include a relaxation of trade barriers among member countries, an established forum for trade disputes, increased economic growth for member countries, increased income levels, and a more efficient economy.

China was a founding member of the WTO's predecessor, the General Agreement on Tariffs and Trade, or GATT. After China's revolution, its former ruling party dropped China's membership in GATT and China's new government did not take any action to rectify this situation. China realized that, as it developed a market-based

---

[1] Will Ianchovichina and Emilio Fukase, "Assessing the Implications of Merchandise Trade: Liberalization in China's Accession to WTO," mimeo, July 2000.

economy, increasing world trade and globalization needed to be embraced in order for its economy to flourish.

It took fifteen years for China to become a full-fledged member of the international trading system. This entailed resolving trade disputes with member countries as well as implementing major changes in tariffs, trade restrictions, laws, and state ownership in industry. With WTO membership, China will reap the long-term benefits of increased development through foreign investment, increase its competitive position as an exporter to industrialized countries, increase employment, and enjoy more consumer choices at home. Now, China is required to implement reforms. Many observers believe the post-Jiang leaders, after the Sixteenth Party Congress, are likely to continue President Jiang's approach of a cautious and slow process of opening.

This chapter is organized as follows: The next section describes the process leading toward the WTO accession. The third section examines WTO-related regulatory changes in the banking, securities, and insurance businesses. Section four discusses the implications of these regulatory changes on the financial services industry. Finally, section five provides a concluding summary.

CHINA PROGRESSES TOWARD ACCESSION

China applied to become a member of the General Agreement on Tariff and Trade on July 11, 1986, and in November, the GATT started the process of negotiations. As a result, China presented a memorandum on its foreign trade policy to the GATT. In March 1987, the GATT conducted meetings to settle problems regarding China's bid to renew its membership status. By May 1989, seven meetings had been concluded.

During this period, the GATT's contracting parties, including Japan, the European Community (EC), Australia, New Zealand, and Canada supported China's accession. The process was going smoothly, even though China had not agreed to any major changes in its trade policy to meet GATT requirements.

Yet, all the goodwill GATT members showed toward China up to June 1989 was lost after the Tiananmen Square "Incident." China's suppression of the democratic movement at home derailed the accession process, as most contracting parties became nonsupportive toward China's accession. Not only was the negotiation progress interrupted but also a more critical approach was taken by the United States toward the control China's state had over its own economy. The United States made greater demands for economic reform as a condition for China's rejoining the GATT. As a result, China began to align its policy with GATT requirements.

By 1991, China's relationship with the United States had soured over disputes on China's handling of Intellectual Property Rights (IPR), China's Most-Favored-Nation (MFN) status in the United States, human rights violations in the mainland, and Beijing's military technology transfers to third-world countries. This created difficulties for China as it sought renewal of its favorable MFN treatment by the United States. As a result, China changed its tactics and started to negotiate with smaller countries. By 1991, China had won the support of Belgium, Brazil, and Argentina, and soon had won over more important contracting parties, such as Germany, Australia, and Britain. Bolstered by this new momentum of support, China was able to gain the support of other countries.

The period from 1989 to 1992 marked two important themes: building a coalition of support outside the United States, and internal policy changes to conform to GATT principles. During this period, China offered several significant concessions, including (1) amendment of Sino-foreign investment law in December 1989; (2) publication of trade policies in December 1991; and (3) the establishment of a research institute to study international trade rules and to help the country rejoin the GATT.

As the GATT evolved into the WTO (by 1995), China had the opportunity to gain a founding member status. Yet, China's contentious relationship and trade imbalance with the United States continued to hamper its quest for accession. After more than a year and a half of inactivity on China's part, it resumed negotiations with the GATT in February 1992.

Negotiations continued until December 1994, as both the United States and other member countries demanded concessions from

China in many areas. The primary focus of negotiations during 1992–1993 was on tariff reduction. In 1994, the emphasis shifted to other areas, such as intellectual property rights and market access by service sectors.

China's desire to become a founding member led to many concessions on its part including (1) concessions on human rights issues; (2) concessions covering sensitive areas, such as the automobile industry; and (3) extension of copyright protection.

With many major concessions addressed, the European Union (EU), Japan, and Australia supported China's admission into the GATT by the first half of 1994. To win the support of the United States, China offered concessions on a list of products that no longer needed import licensing and named fifty import categories whose tariffs were to be reduced. By 1993, the United States had focused on nontariff trade barriers and other trade-related issues. Progress slowed, and by the middle of 1993, a new trade dispute had resulted due to China's textile import quotas and exchange rate manipulation.

After its bid for founding member status failed, China suspended formal negotiations. Both the United States and China came to loggerheads as neither was ready to back off of its position. The United States was upset over China's inaction on U.S. copyright issues and the growing trade deficit with China. The beginning of 1995 was the breaking point, as talks on copyrights fell through; a trade war broke out between the two countries.

Other areas of dispute soon erupted, including China's aggression toward Taiwan and continued disputes over developing country status, which drew opposition from the American commercial and agricultural sectors. With regard to developing country status, the United States considered China to be a developed country due to its vast economic size and fast economic growth. Yet, China viewed this designation negatively and believed it would result in economic instability. Formal bilateral negotiations were stalled. The EU attempted to restart negotiations on China's behalf; it recognized China's developing country status and pushed for a transition period that would gradually change China's status to a full member. This approach received a lukewarm reception from the United States.

In 1996, the WTO's larger contracting parties, such as the EU, Canada, and Japan, resumed formal negotiations with China and sought to accelerate China's accession. The EU "transition period" approach for China received widespread support among WTO members and China. The questions were which areas would be phased in, how long would they last, and which areas were to be immediately opened? The EU now focused its negotiations on addressing these issues. It sought better terms on market access, subsidies, and tariffs. Access to the automobile sector was the most significant issue, as the EU demanded drastic cuts in Chinese auto-tariffs and greater transparency of China's long-term policies in the auto industry. During this time (1996), the relations between the United States and China soured even further as a result of the intellectual property rights disputes. In March, the United States slapped three million dollars worth of preliminary sanctions against Chinese exports due to China's failure to protect U.S. intellectual property rights. In June, China and the United States reached an agreement over intellectual property rights. Yet, other areas of American concern needed to be addressed, such as agricultural issues and the trade deficit. This led the United States to push for increased access to China's markets.

In 1997, China made a series of offers to WTO members and carried out many negotiations with member countries. The new offers covered tariff reduction, in which China reduced the average tariff rate from 23 percent to 17 percent by October 1997. Regulations on distribution and production for foreign companies in China also were addressed. China promised to open the wholesale and retail sectors to foreign investment and to grant rights to all enterprises in China to import or export after a short transition period.

During 1997, the United States Congress took a tough stance on a variety of issues with China and proposed several stringent sanctions. Congress wanted sanctions to include (1) a ban on prison-labor products; (2) a ban on travel to the United States by Chinese officials who engaged in religious persecution or who forced women to have abortions as a means of population control; (3) addition of American human rights monitors in Beijing; (4) a ban on American trade with companies controlled by the Chinese military; and (5) denial of below-market-rate international loans to China.

In 1998, negotiations centered on China's liberalization of the agricultural and services sectors. Adding to WTO members' arguments was the fact that China had increased its share of exports over its Asian neighbors' as a result of the 1997 Asian financial crisis. Members maintained that China's increased fortunes allowed it to increase its share of Western countries' imports drastically. As a result, China offered to reduce tariffs to 10.8 percent by 2005 and to eliminate import restrictions on 385 types of commodities over the next ten years. Additionally, China provided concessions concerning the telecommunications and services sectors, including banks and insurance markets.

In 1999, China focused its attention on negotiations with the United States. China offered tariff cuts on beef and wheat. The United States had several additional concerns: accusations that Chinese were stealing nuclear secrets from the United States, a rising trade deficit with China, and apprehensions raised by both the U.S. steel and information technology industries.

To further complicate issues, a NATO bomb hit China's embassy in Belgrade during the conflict in Bosnia. To curb internal dissent over the incident, China suspended negotiations with the United States. As this issue faded, China resumed negotiations with the United States. By November 1999, the United States and China were in accord and a bilateral agreement was signed. In the same month, another bilateral agreement was signed by China and Canada.

In January 2000, China and the EU held bilateral talks on several outstanding issues, including market access, tariffs, investment, and industrial goods. Other important issues still needed to be addressed, including market access for telecom and insurance companies. In February, China and India signed a bilateral agreement, which increased the trade volume between them. By May, China had agreed to concessions pushed by the EU, which resulted in the signing of a bilateral agreement. China made a commitment to lift restrictions on the insurance business, which would include allowing foreign operators to sell the same products as their Chinese competitors. Restrictions on location of foreign insurers were relaxed — previously overseas insurers were permitted only in the cities of Shanghai and Guangzhou. Also, foreign partners in Chinese life insurance joint ventures would be permitted to exercise "effective management control," for they could choose their Chinese partners and secure a legal guarantee of freedom from any regulatory interference in private contracts on a fifty-fifty equity basis. Additionally, in May 2000, China signed a bilateral agreement with Australia, after reaching an agreement to liberalize access to one thousand product categories across agricultural and manufacturing exports and to key service sectors.

In September 2000, China and Switzerland reached a bilateral agreement. This left only Mexican-Chinese negotiations as the last remaining obstacle before the WTO accepted China as a member. In September 2001, China and Mexico wrapped up bilateral negotiations. China made concessions to extend current countervailing duties on 1,300 Chinese products in textiles, garments, footwear, and toys for six years. It also permitted an antidumping measure, which allowed Mexico to maintain the import duties after a six-year period if it discovered dumping. The eighteenth meeting of the WTO China working group finalized legal documents on the country's accession; China was formally approved as a member at WTO's November Doha meeting.[2]

REGULATORY CHANGES IN THE FINANCIAL SERVICES INDUSTRY

China made a variety of commitments to the WTO for membership. In the financial services sector, similar to other sectors, China was required to take steps to implement deregulatory measures in order to ensure compliance with WTO accession agreements. This section first outlines those relevant changes and then discusses the specific

---

[2] WTO Press, "WTO Ministerial Conference Approves China's Accession," Press no. 252, November 10, 2001.

steps that have been taken in the banking, finance, and insurance industries.

The regulatory changes cover both tariff and nontariff measures. In the tariff area, deregulation was intended to reduce the average tariff level from 22.1 percent to 17 percent within six years after accession:

- Tariffs on automobiles would decline from 80–100 percent to 25 percent,
- Tariffs on autoparts would drop from 30 percent to 10 percent,
- Tariffs on wood would be lowered from 12–18 percent to 5 percent,
- Tariffs on paper would decline from 15 percent to 5 to 7.5 percent,
- Tariffs on semiconductors, computers, computer equipment, telecommunications equipment, and other information technology products would drop from an average level of 13.3 percent to zero,
- Tariffs on 70 percent of chemical products would be lowered from 35 percent to 5.5–6.5 percent, and
- Tariffs on agricultural products would decline from an average of 31.5 percent to 14.5 percent.

In nontariff areas, the intent was to eliminate nontariff barriers within six years after accession. More specifically, import quotas would grow from the current level at a 15 percent annual rate until elimination. Another major focus was to open the service sectors to foreign direct investments:

- *Telecommunications:* China would allow up to 49 percent investment by foreign telecom providers from the date of accession, increasing to 50 percent two years after accession. Foreign companies would be allowed to invest in Chinese Internet content providers.
- *Banking:* Foreign banks were to be able to conduct local currency business with Chinese enterprises two years after accession. Foreign banks could conduct local currency business with

Chinese individuals five years from accession, and have the same rights as Chinese banks within the various geographic areas. Branching would be permitted. Since accession, foreign financial institutions have been able to provide auto-financing.

- *Insurance:* Foreign companies could own up to 50 percent of Chinese life insurance firms.
- *Securities:* Foreign companies would be allowed to own 33 percent of fund management companies in China, increasing to 49 percent three years after accession. Foreign companies are allowed to own 33 percent of securities companies that engage in underwriting in China. Foreign minority joint ventures can underwrite domestic securities issues and underwrite and trade in foreign currency denominated securities, both debt and equity.
- *Audio-visual:* China agreed to import forty foreign films after accession, rising to fifty films in three years. China allows 49 percent foreign participation in joint ventures involved in distribution for videos and sound recordings.
- *Travel and tourism:* China would allow unrestricted access to the hotel market, with ability to establish wholly-owned businesses within three years. Foreign travel operators can provide the full range of travel agency services.
- *Trade and distribution:* China agreed to grant trading (importing and exporting) and distribution rights on industrial goods, the right to import and export directly without Chinese middlemen, and the right to market through distribution, wholesale and retail, after-sale service, repair, maintenance, transport — the entire range of distribution-related services.
- *Professional services:* For a range of professional services, including legal, accountancy, taxation, management consultancy, architecture, engineering, urban planning, medical and dental, and computer-related services, China agreed to permit foreign majority control, except for practicing Chinese law. For accountancy, China agreed to eliminate a mandatory localization requirement and would allow unrestricted access to its market to professionals licensed as CPAs in China. Further, China agreed to

apply national treatment in issuing CPA licenses and to follow transparent procedures.

Banking

In the banking field, China committed to "phase in" the loosening of domestic banking regulations with regard to foreign banking institutions. It ultimately hopes to strengthen its banking system by encouraging limited equity investment in domestic banks and educating its workforce in modern banking practices.[3]

China's commercial banking industry currently consists of four large state-owned commercial banks (SOCBs) that have enjoyed dominant market shares in loans and deposits. The quality of the financial assets of these four banks is poor, with an estimated average proportion of nonperforming loans (NPLs) between 40 and 50 percent in the early 2000s. Although a program is in place to remove the stock of old bad debt from these four banks' balance sheets by transferring it to asset management companies, the likelihood of the state retaining majority ownership of these banks for the foreseeable future is high. Furthermore, the government sets interest rates centrally and banks have little leeway in pricing risk.

The mid-term solution requires China to develop strong financial institutions that will not be hurt unduly by foreign competition and to develop an interbank market to facilitate the liberalization of interest rates. China has made major commitments to reform its banking industry with respect to foreign banks. Over time, foreign banks gradually will be given permission to accept deposits and extend credits. The geographic coverage of their banking operations will extend from Shanghai and Guangzhou to other cities in China. Five years after China's accession, the geographical restrictions will be lifted.

---

[3] John P. Bonin and Huang Yiping, "Foreign Entry into Chinese Banking: Does WTO Membership Threaten Domestic Banks?" in World Economy 25, no. 8 (2002): 1077–1093.

Insurance

China's major concessions in the deregulation of its insurance industry include:

- *Geographic limitations:* China permitted foreign property and casualty insurers to insure large-scale risks nationwide, immediately upon accession to WTO, and pledged to eliminate all geographic limitations within three years.
- *Scope:* China agreed to expand the scope of activities for foreign insurers to include group, health, and pension lines of insurance, which represent about 85 percent of total premiums, phased in over five years.
- *Prudential criteria:* China consented to award licenses solely on the basis of prudential criteria, with no economic needs test or quantitative limits on the number of licenses issued.
- *Investment:* China agreed to allow 50 percent ownership for life insurance. Life insurers can choose their own joint venture partners. For nonlife, China pledged to allow branching or 51 per cent ownership on accession, and to form wholly-owned subsidiaries within two years.
- *Effective management control:* This was negotiated for foreign insurers in life insurance joint ventures, through choice of partner, and a legal guarantee of freedom from any regulatory interference in private contracts on a fifty-fifty equity basis.
- *Licenses:* China made a commitment to immediately give seven new licenses to European insurers, in both the life and nonlife sectors. Furthermore, two EU firms would be permitted to establish operations in two new cities.
- *Property and casualty:* In this sector, the state-owned People's Insurance Co. of China (PICC) holds some 80 percent of the market. Although geographic restrictions on foreign insurers were lifted once the PRC joined the WTO, the business opportunity for foreign insurers is likely to be limited simply because of a small market size. In China, as in most countries, the greatest volume of nonlife insurance that is written is auto

insurance. However, the stock of autos is small, PICC is entrenched in the state-owned sector, and there are many competitors.

- *Life:* PRC demographics, shrinking state subsidies for social services (such as medical care), and rising incomes virtually guarantee huge market potential in life insurance and increasingly in pension and health insurance as well. Life insurance premiums now account for about 60 percent of total insurance premiums, a level similar to that of developed countries, and have been growing at triple-digit rates in recent years. Chinese firms, particularly state-owned China Life, dominate the market. Yet, the experiences in Shanghai and Guangzhou of American International Assurance Co., Ltd., a life insurance operation of the American International Group, Inc. (AIG), show that foreign companies with innovative selling methods and products can achieve high growth rates and market shares.

China's life insurers, like its banks, need foreign capital and expertise. Beijing's pragmatic approach to dealing with these needs has been to grant case-by-case approvals of foreign investment in Chinese life companies and new life insurance joint ventures. In October 2001, for example, Beijing-based Taikang Life Insurance won approval to sell up to 20 percent of its equity to foreigners. It was the second such "experimental-basis" approval. The fifty-fifty joint venture was between Sun Life Assurance of Canada and China Everbright Group.

Deregulation has granted life insurers a broader scope to offer flexible investment-type products in addition to the fixed-rate, savings-type products that dominate the market today. In this area, foreign firms have a competitive advantage. As Chinese financial-market deregulation continues, foreign investors can expect life insurance companies to begin providing active asset management, for example, for pension funds. The need to learn from foreigners will drive cooperation and has resulted in the establishment of joint-venture asset-management companies, with foreigners restricted to minority positions.

Securities

Making certain that its capital markets continue to facilitate a steady flow of private investment into reforming state and nonstate enterprises is among China's highest priorities. Upgrading the capabilities and professionalism of China's domestic securities industry is part of this process, as is nurturing an institutional investment industry.[4]

The domestic securities industry is consolidating. To survive in a more competitive and open marketplace, securities firms must expand their capital bases. Given the high profitability of the domestic securities business, leading firms will have no trouble raising capital. Better companies will likely raise equity from private placements and, in some cases, through initial public offerings in the domestic market or by listing overseas.

Chinese authorities have taken steps to allow foreign money managers to set up operations in China. The purpose is to leverage their expertise to build an investment management industry. The China Securities Regulatory Commission's policy now focuses on increasing the number, professionalism, and performance of Chinese securities investment funds. The listed closed-end mutual funds have contributed to an increasing share of trading volumes on China's two exchanges.

Chinese authorities will also encourage foreign securities firms to take minority equity stakes in existing or new fund-management companies offering new funds. Foreign firms will do well. In return for their contributions of expertise, foreign investors will gain experience in the domestic A-share market, which will be open to the joint-venture funds.

Apart from developing listed mutual funds, China needs and wants to expand and professionalize its asset-management institutions. Institutional managers, now generally securities firms and trust companies, take money from institutional investors, principally state-owned enterprises and listed domestic companies.

---

[4] Linklaters & Alliance, "Links to China: China's Accession to the WTO – Securities," *Legal Research Note* (February 2002): 1–8.

Regulators should begin to allow life insurance companies to develop professional asset-management departments or subsidiaries. In recent years, China has taken steps to promote the establishment of specialized asset-management and investment-advisory companies that can accept and manage client funds. There may also be a change in the current regulations, which prohibit the social-security trust, housing, and other funds from investing in the stock market. Some of these funds should eventually go to asset managers.

Qualified foreign financial institutions have been given opportunities to participate in this sector. Since what the Chinese want most is foreign business know-how and capital, foreign participation will be limited to joint-venture arrangements. While foreign firms are keen to gain experience in the domestic market, Chinese partners are interested in learning about foreign firms' offshore capabilities, with an eye toward developing such activities themselves.

IMPLICATIONS FOR THE FINANCIAL INDUSTRY

As China phases out its restrictions on foreign entities and sells off its state-owned enterprises, the influx of business and financial services to support these industries will grow.[5] WTO accession is a catalyst to push China's economic restructuring and movement toward its aim of establishing a socialist market economic structure.

Yet, some sectors are plagued by concerns about the potentially disastrous implications that the liberalization process could have on the Chinese banking system. China's domestic banks are burdened with huge nonperforming loans (NPLs), inadequate regulatory and credit-control systems, and insufficient capital on which to operate, resulting in very low profitability. Undoubtedly there will be major changes in this sector; either China's banks will push for joint ventures to increase their banking sophistication or weaker banks will be acquired or liquidated. Restrictions on banking that have limited

---

[5] Stephen M. Harner, "Financial Services and WTO: Opportunities Knock," *China Business Review* 27, no. 2 (March/April 2000): 10.

competition in the industry have been lifted gradually. The market practice will have to move toward risk-based pricing.[6]

In the securities business, China's stock market has been one of the better performers in recent years. However, the continued development of the stock market will be difficult unless China takes steps to improve corporate governance, transparency, performance-based compensation, and a legal system that protects investor interests. Furthermore, the current practice of "rationing" initial public offerings must stop. Whether a company is able to go public should not be based on the company's political connections, but on future profitability.

Before accession, it was anticipated that the change in the fixed-income market would be most dramatic after China's entry into the WTO. As in most developing countries, China's focus has been on the stock market. The fixed-income market is underdeveloped. The size of the bond market is relatively insignificant, and the markets are very thin with poor liquidity. This has created two significant problems. First, corporations rely on the stock market and house banks for financing. Second, credit risk is not monitored by investors, which has contributed to the severity of the financial market crises in emerging markets. The entrance of foreign securities firms will introduce the fixed-income culture. The development of the fixed-income market is essential; it provides capital to corporations and it requires credit analysis. Rating agencies will assess the financial status of the instrument and/or the issuer.

The mutual fund business and insurance are changing as well. In the past, these were closed-end mutual funds only. The Chinese government allowed the establishment of open-end mutual funds in May 2001. So far, there are only a few open-end mutual funds in China. Many well-known asset managers from the United States and other countries have applied for licenses to operate in the open-end mutual fund business. In insurance, both domestic (such as People's Insurance Company of China) and foreign insurers (such as AIG)

---

[6] "Chinese Banks Urged to Prepare for Post-WTO Competition," *People's Daily*, May 10, 2001.

will eventually offer life, health, property/casualty, and financial insurance.

In summary, in the financial industry, an improved foreign investment environment will facilitate the inflow of foreign capital, technology, and management expertise. Leaders in the financial industry will help to develop a depth of products to manage risk, raise capital, float debt, and provide insurance. The success of the regulatory changes will critically depend on how China implements them.

CONCLUSION

China traveled a long road in its bid to become a WTO member and share equal footing on trade issues with most of the world. In the near term, China will experience the normal growing pains associated with such a transition. For example, the lifting of import quotas on a variety of industries is placing a strain on domestic producers who are not used to competition. In the short run, this has led to unemployment and a shift in employment demographics. Yet, the reduction/ elimination of tariffs for Chinese goods is boosting trade and increasing industry within China.

Free trade, such as that espoused by the WTO, is already having an impact. China's financial markets are becoming more competitive, providing funding to corporations with solid business plans, and promising future profitability. In addition, the new environment also provides various asset classes for investors to save for retirement or other objectives. A fair and free financial market provides efficient channels for money to flow from those with savings to those who need additional funds to invest in profitable projects. Sustainable economic growth depends on it.

In spite of the enormous potential, China has been a very difficult country in which to do business. That was the experience of foreign firms operating in China during Jiang Zemin's era. This has not improved much following the Sixteenth Party Congress. There is a strong sensation within the Chinese government that the market share of the Chinese enterprises should be protected in order to give them more time to prepare for international competition. The WTO agreement is being implemented over time. During the implementation process, the major concern many observers have is that the Chinese government may create new and different obstacles for foreign participants. This will cause further complexity in doing business in China, making it harder and more frustrating than some investors may have previously expected.

Chapter

11

China-ASEAN Relations: The Significance of an ASEAN-China Free Trade Area

Alice D. Ba

On the eve of China's Sixteenth Party Congress in November 2002, China and the Association of Southeast Asian Nations (ASEAN) concluded a landmark framework agreement committing states to the creation of an ASEAN-China Free Trade Area (ACFTA) by 2010 for China and ASEAN's original five members[1] plus Brunei, and by 2015 for ASEAN's newest members.[2] Though important uncertainties remain, the ASEAN-China Free Trade Area has the potential not only to transform East Asia's economic and political landscape but also to play a powerful role in the larger world economy. If realized, the China-initiated ACFTA would create the world's largest free trade area, with a combined gross domestic product of about U.S.$2 trillion, a combined marketplace of approximately 1.7 billion consumers, and

---

Note: The author thanks George Cheng, Tun-jen Cheng, Jacques deLisle, and Bruce Dickson for their helpful comments on an earlier draft of this chapter.

[1] Indonesia, Malaysia, Singapore, Thailand, and the Philippines.

[2] Vietnam, Cambodia, Laos, and Myanmar.

a total international trade of around U.S.$1.23 trillion.³ At the very least, the agreement represents a diplomatic coup for China, which has carefully cultivated its relations with ASEAN states, especially since 1997.

Given the wariness, tensions, and hostility that have characterized past relations, the framework agreement signed in November 2002 is an indicator of China's improving relations with ASEAN since the late 1980s. This chapter begins by situating the ACFTA and its Framework Agreement on Economic Cooperation in the context of China's steadily improving relations with ASEAN during the 1990s, and identifies 1997 as an important turning point. In addition to illuminating the immediate economic and political considerations that directly gave rise to the proposal, the chapter also explores the agreement's strategic significance for China. The chapter concludes with a discussion of some of the potential implications of the ACFTA for East Asia's nascent regionalism.

UNCERTAIN GLOBAL AND REGIONAL RELATIONS

The ending of the Cold War and related uncertainties about the commitment of the United States to East and Southeast Asia generated countless articles on regional security, especially regarding the challenge, if not the threat, posed to ASEAN by an ascendant China. China's military modernization program and its new assertiveness in the South China Sea were particular preoccupations in Southeast Asia. Those same uncertainties, however, also created new opportunities and incentives for China and ASEAN to expand and improve their relations economically and politically. For ASEAN, positive engagement of China became a matter of necessity — the possibility of United States military retrenchment meant that good relations with China were imperative, while harder-line United States-Asia

---

[3] ASEAN-China Expert Group on Economic Cooperation, *Forging Closer ASEAN-China Relations in the Twenty-First Century*, prepared for ASEAN by the ASEAN-China Expert Group on Economic Cooperation, 2001, www.aseansec.org.

trade policies heightened the attractiveness of China as a potential market for ASEAN goods. The result was a concerted policy of engagement that included expanded bilateral trade and political interactions and, most significantly, an expanded regional multilateralism that included arrangements such as the ASEAN Regional Forum (ARF), an unprecedented regional security dialogue in East Asia.

For China, too, developments in the early 1990s created new reasons to work with ASEAN. As early as 1989, China had identified good relations with Southeast Asia as an important interest; however, that interest initially was the product of a more general foreign policy reorientation.[4] Specifically, the largely Western reaction to Chinese officials' 1989 crackdown at Tiananmen Square renewed concerns about the growing influence of the outside world on China politically, economically, and culturally. A decade after reorienting its foreign relations to support market reforms at home, China found itself in 1989 more exposed to the world and the influence of Western ideas, as well as increasingly more dependent on others for growth and stability. Thus, it was more vulnerable to international criticism and isolation. While economic sanctions were short-lived, they were nevertheless troubling to a country for which autonomy had long been an important foreign policy value. The year 1989 began an important period of strategic reevaluation in Chinese foreign policy, resulting in more focused attention to the cultivation of relations with its neighbors all along its borders, including Southeast Asia. As Quansheng Zhao wrote, "[F]or Deng the very threat of international isolation was sufficient to inspire a rapid improvement in China's relations with its Southeast Asian neighbors."[5]

---

[4] Samuel S. Kim, "Peking's Foreign Policy in the Shadows of Tiananmen," *Issues and Studies* 27, no. 1 (January 1991): 39–69.

[5] See Quansheng Zhao, "Chinese Foreign Policy in the Post-Cold War Era," *World Affairs* 159, no. 3 (Winter 1997): 122–124. See also, Lowell Dittmer, "China's Search for Its Place in the World," in *Contemporary Chinese Politics in Historical Perspective,* ed. Brantly Womack (Cambridge, UK: Cambridge University Press, 1991), 245–246.

Other developments in the early 1990s also heightened China's sense of insecurity, especially *vis-à-vis* the United States. In the unipolar post-Cold War order, the Gulf War, especially, with its dramatic display of American technology and hardware, lent to Beijing's ongoing strategic reevaluation mostly by calling attention to China's military limitations.[6] Later, China's failed bid for the Olympics, its difficulties involved in gaining World Trade Organization (WTO) membership, as well as the new legitimacy of humanitarian interventions illustrated China's outsider status. These developments confirmed Beijing's need to be on good terms with its neighbors.

Even so, at first, Southeast Asia did not seem a particular priority in China's new "all-directional" or "omnidirectional"[7] good neighbor policy. In fact, many of China's actions during the first part of the 1990s were widely considered more "negative" and confrontational than they were "positive" and reassuring. Also, China, like ASEAN, remained wary and uncertain about the future of relations. For a decade, China and ASEAN had enjoyed a tacit alliance of sorts, premised on their common opposition to Vietnam's occupation of Cambodia. The end of that conflict, as well as the end of the Cold War, left China-ASEAN relations without clear common ground. Moreover, the problems of their past relations seemed to make competition and confrontation a more likely possibility. China was especially wary of arrangements such as the ARF, given the uncertainties that characterized its relations with both ASEAN and the United States. Leaders in Beijing suspected these arrangements to be ways for smaller powers to "gang up on China," as well as avenues for the United States to dominate and dictate the regional agenda.[8] They

---

[6] See, for example, You Ji, *The Armed Forces of China* (New York: I.B. Tauris, 1999), especially chap. 1.

[7] James Hsiung, "China's Omnidirectional Diplomacy," *Asian Survey* 35, no. 6 (1995): 573–586.

[8] See Jing-dong Yuan, "Regional Institutions and Cooperative Security: Chinese Approaches and Policies," *Korean Journal of Defense Analysis* 12, no. 1 (Autumn 2001): 263, and Michael Swaine and Ashley Tellis, *Interpreting China's Grand Strategy* (Santa Monica: Rand Corporation, 2000), 136.

also harbored concerns that such arrangements might be used to force China's concessions on contentious territorial issues such as Taiwan and the South China Sea.

By the late 1990s, however, there was evidence of improvement in China's views toward ASEAN. China's and ASEAN states' expanded economic and political interactions provided opportunities for their mutual discovery of some common interests on trade, human rights, and the form and content of regional processes, such as Asia-Pacific Economic Cooperation (APEC). This is not to say that concerns had completely disappeared, but only to note that positive interactions over the first part of the 1990s helped to set the stage for better relations. These exchanges also contributed to more positive views toward regional multilateralism, in general, so that by 1997, China had become an active participant in both formal ("Track 1") and informal ("Track 2") processes.

By 1997, there were notable signs of China's heightened attention to ASEAN. In fact, in Jiang Zemin's words, 1997 marked the "beginning of a new stage of development in Chinese-ASEAN relations," involving more active participation, enhanced mutual trust, and strengthened cooperation.[9] China's changing views of ASEAN also corresponded with a generally more confident, less reactive foreign policy from Beijing. In Southeast Asia, signs of this new confidence and new approach to foreign policy could be found in China's more proactive efforts to engage the ASEAN states toward softening China's image in Southeast Asia. Most notable was the articulation of a "new security concept" which aimed to present a kinder, gentler China to its Southeast Asian neighbors. First advanced by China's then-foreign minister Qian Qichen at a 1997 meeting of the ASEAN Regional Forum, the new security concept would be given further articulation in a July 1998 defense white paper, *China's National Defense*, as well as by other Chinese officials, including Hu Jintao. That concept set forth an understanding

---

[9] "Chinese President Jiang's Speech at Informal China-ASEAN Summit," *Xinhua*, December 16, 1997.

of security that eschewed the power politics of the Cold War. Instead, it championed security based upon "equality, dialogue, trust and cooperation"; security would be enhanced through dialogue and consultation, not competition and confrontation.[10] The 1997–1999 financial crisis would provide additional opportunities to China to display its new diplomacy. In addition to underscoring the importance of economic growth and cooperation contained in the new security concept, it would set the stage for China's ACFTA initiative.

Indeed, the 1997–1999 financial crisis played an especially important role in shifting the emphasis of China-ASEAN relations away from the political-security concerns that had defined relations during the first part of the 1990s. While the crisis also provided opportunities for China to demonstrate its "good neighbor" credentials, the crisis additionally heightened concerns in ASEAN about Southeast Asia's ability to compete with China for trade and, increasingly, investment. Some ASEAN economies had already begun to feel competition from China in the early 1990s; however, the financial crisis greatly intensified ASEAN concerns. Moreover, other developments — Indonesia's political instability, ASEAN's weak collective response to the crisis, problems in Cambodia, the environmental haze caused by fires in Kalimantan — only reinforced a growing image of Southeast Asia as unstable and in disarray. Indeed, overnight it seemed, ASEAN had been transformed from being "miracle economies" into "problem economies" in the eyes of investors and the international community.

By contrast, China, whose economy was less open and thus more insulated, had been left relatively untouched by the 1997–1999 crisis. While the economic possibilities associated with China's huge population and its economic reforms had already generated much international (including ASEAN) interest in the China market, Southeast Asia's troubles seemed to accentuate China's advantages

---

[10] Carlyle A. Thayer, "China's 'New Security Concept' and ASEAN," *Comparative Connections* (Third Quarter, 2000), http://www.csis.org/pacfor/cc/003Qchina_asean.html.

and thus intensify ASEAN's concerns about Southeast Asia's economic recovery and long-term ability to compete economically. The financial crisis also served to underscore structural asymmetries that characterized the China-ASEAN relationship. While ASEAN had found such asymmetries worrisome before, the crisis, by revealing the problems of ASEAN growth strategies and regional organization, diminished ASEAN's economic and political leverage over regional developments and heightened a sense of vulnerability.

However, the 1997–1999 financial crisis also offered opportunities for China to demonstrate its commitment to relations and even its potential for regional leadership. Some high-profile gestures, along with China's continued attention to the region since the crisis, helped to mitigate some of ASEAN's postcrisis fears about China's growing economic presence. At the very least, China was able to benefit from the general ASEAN unhappiness toward related American and international responses to the financial crisis in East and Southeast Asia. Not only was the United States closely associated with the problematic IMF conditions imposed on East Asian economies, but also it was widely perceived as benefiting from East Asia's financial problems.[11] More than any other event during the last few years, the financial crisis drew attention to the fact that there were important areas of "divergence" from the United States and that ASEAN's "convergence" with Western neoliberal models could not be assumed.[12] The perception that ASEAN needs to develop

---

[11] See, for example, Douglass Webber, "Two Funerals and a Wedding? The Ups and Downs of Regionalism in East Asia and the Asia-Pacific after the Asian Crisis," *Pacific Review* 14, no. 3 (2001): 339–372. Webber discusses how ASEAN states felt "let down," even "betrayed," by the way that the United States responded to the financial crisis in Asia.

[12] See, especially, Richard Higgott and Nicola Phillips, "Challenging Triumphalism and Convergence: The Limits of Global Liberalization in Asia and Latin America," *Review of International Studies* 26 (2000): 359–379. See also, Alice D. Ba, "Contested Spaces: The Politics of Regional and Global Governance in Southeast Asia," in *Coherence and Contestation,* ed. Alice D. Ba and Matthew J. Hoffmann (London: Routledge, forthcoming).

alternative relationships that can offset ASEAN's dependency and vulnerability and to give it greater voice over issues of concern helped to heighten interest in cultivating relations with China.

Moreover, China's readiness to assist ASEAN economies through both the IMF and bilateral supplementary packages stood in marked contrast to the United States and Japan, both of which were perceived as doing too little.[13] Most "laudable,"[14] China kept its promise not to devalue its currency, despite what some saw to be important interests to do so.[15] Even if its decision not to devalue the *renminbi* was motivated primarily by self-interested domestic concerns, the action nevertheless helped generate important good will in ASEAN, whose economies felt besieged economically and from all levels of politics. Indeed, among the United States, Japan, and China, China was the only one to emerge from the crisis with an improved image among ASEAN members.[16]

CHINA'S PROPOSAL

Both the progress made in relations and heightened ASEAN concerns about competing against a growing Chinese economy, as well

---

[13] In Japan's case, this perception may be somewhat unfair given its significant contributions to various IMF packages, its proposed Asian Monetary Fund, and the Miyazawa Initiative. It is possible that Japan's image suffered in part because expectations of Japan began much higher.

[14] See comments of Mahathir Mohamed in "Sino-Malaysian Forum Held on Economic Recovery," *Xinhua,* August 21, 1999; Kamarul Yunus, "KL Given Approval to Establish Consulate in Shanghai," *Business Times* (Malaysia), August 19, 1999, 18. See also Michael Richardson, "Japan's Lack of Leadership Pushes ASEAN toward Cooperation with China," *International Herald Tribune*, April 17, 1998, http://www.iht.com/IHT/MR/98/mr041798.html.

[15] For example, the fact that devaluation of ASEAN currencies made ASEAN products more competitive (cheaper) against China's would have given China an important incentive to also devalue.

[16] Vatikiotis, for example, points to how Thai officials "contrasted the hurtful shrug-off from Washington with Beijing's warmth and sympathy." Michael Vatikiotis, "Catching the Dragon's Tail: China and Southeast Asia in the 21st Century," *Contemporary Southeast Asia* 25, no. 1 (2003): 69–70.

as China's still-relevant strategic concerns, provide the important context for the China-initiated framework on economic cooperation, which would include a proposed ASEAN-China Free Trade Area. First placed on the table by Chinese premier Zhu Rongji in November 2000, the proposed ACFTA was initially greeted by ASEAN states with both surprise and hesitation. This section outlines some of the driving concerns that led to China's initial proposal in 2000, before discussing the economics and politics associated with the 2002 agreement.

In addition to China's more commonly discussed political-security interests in Southeast Asia, there are also some economic interests (most with security implications) that likely had bearing. For one, Beijing may have had concerns about possible competition from ASEAN's own free trade area (AFTA). While ASEAN's individual economies may have difficulty competing against China's huge market, an ASEAN market of 500 million, though considerably smaller than China's, could make ASEAN competitive enough to inject greater competition into the relationship. For China, the ACFTA may be one way to preempt "vicious competition from occurring."[17]

Also important, China shares with ASEAN many concerns about the global economy. These interests figure prominently not just in China's and ASEAN's evolving relations, but also in the changing East Asian political economy, in general. Their shared concerns include regionalist trading arrangements in Europe and North America, Western protectionism, vulnerabilities to economic globalization forces, the WTO's (in)sensitivity to the concerns of developing economies, and diversification of their trade and investment dependencies. In this vein, each has identified the other as a potential partner that can help it to better navigate a fast-changing global economy. Long Yongtu, China's chief WTO negotiator and vice minister of foreign trade and economic cooperation, for example, emphasized China's and ASEAN's shared interests when he argued

---

[17] Cao Yunhua, "Sino-ASEAN Ties to Improve Greatly," *China Daily,* January 5, 2002.

that the ACFTA could offer to both China and ASEAN occasion to "better take advantage of each other's strengths, explore new development opportunities, and jointly defend risks arising from economic globalization."[18]

Both ASEAN and China have drawn special attention to the continued economic integration of the European Union and North America (through the North American Free Trade Agreement), and to efforts to develop a Free Trade of the Americas, as strong motivations for the ACFTA. Not only could an ASEAN-China Free Trade Area offer some insurance against negative trends in the global economy, including protectionism in Western advanced economies and the persistent threat of an American backlash against Asian goods,[19] but also the agreement could help to develop alternative markets so as to mitigate dependence on the United States. Through the ACFTA, parties also hope to gain greater negotiating clout and leverage vis-à-vis other groupings in global fora, such as the WTO. Again quoting Long, "If all other countries are engaging in regional economic integration, why not China and ASEAN? If we don't get together to have a free trade area like they have, we will be victims of trade protectionism and economic trade blocks and will not become the victors."[20] The "dramatic growth in the number of regional trading arrangements," especially over the 1990s, is also explicitly cited in support of the ACFTA in the report of the ASEAN-China Expert Group and by country representatives.[21]

Nevertheless, even taking into account the expected economic benefits listed above, China's concessions to ASEAN and the fact that, on balance, China's benefits from the agreement (in the short term at least) are considerably less than ASEAN's suggest that

---

[18] "China Says FTA with ASEAN Needed to Fight Western Trade Blocs," *Japan Economic Newswire*, April 29, 2002, *Lexis-Nexis Academic: World News*, online, July 3, 2003. See also Cao, "Sino-ASEAN Ties to Improve Greatly."

[19] As discussed, ASEAN (along with Japan) bore much of the brunt of the backlash from the United States in the early 1990s. Today, it is the United States' trade deficit with China that is receiving the most attention.

[20] "China Says FTA with ASEAN Needed to Fight Western Trade Blocs."

[21] *Forging Closer ASEAN-China Relations in the Twenty-First Century*, 8.

political motivations are the stronger driving force behind China's free trade proposal. By one calculation, China's welfare benefit from the ACFTA will be U.S.$1.787 billion, compared to collective ASEAN's U.S. $2.986 billion.[22]

In short, the ACFTA is about more than economics; it also "has great strategic meaning to China."[23] Initiating the ACFTA serves Beijing's interests in a number of ways: (1) it helps to reassure an anxious ASEAN, which stabilizes its regional neighborhood, serving Beijing's interests at home, as well as abroad; (2) good relations with ASEAN enhance China's legitimacy and influence with respect to regional developments; relatedly, (3) initiating the ACFTA demonstrates China's leadership potential and credentials; and lastly (4) the ACFTA can help to mitigate what both China and ASEAN worry is an overdependence on any one economy. For China, especially, there is great concern about becoming too dependent on the economy of the United States, in particular. Autonomy will continue to be an important value in China's foreign policy. Thus, it might be argued that the intensification of the Sino-ASEAN trade relationship, as well as the development of the Asian regional economy more broadly, will take on additional import if China is not to be a "mere appendage to the West."[24]

Another of China's more important, though less direct, political considerations is domestic. Increasingly, the legitimacy of the Chinese Communist Party rests on its ability to maintain economic growth and domestic stability. This requires a stable and peaceful

---

[22] Suthiphand Chirathivat and Sothitorn Mallikamas, "ASEAN-China FTA: Potential Outcome for Participating Countries," paper presented at the International Conference on Southeast Asia and China: Global Changes and Regional Challenges, National Sun Yat-sen University, Taiwan, March 4–6, 2004.

[23] Shi Yinhong, professor at China's School of International Studies, Renmin University, quoted in Mark Clifford, "How Asia Can Learn to the Live with China," *Business Week,* March 28, 2002, *Lexis-Nexis Academic: World News,* online, August 1, 2004.

[24] Joseph Fewsmith, "The Political and Social Implications of China's Accession to the WTO," *China Quarterly* 167 (September 2001): 573.

regional environment. While China's economy escaped the 1997–1999 crisis relatively unharmed, the likelihood of a similar crisis spilling over into China will only grow as it continues to move toward a more comprehensive liberalization of its economy and financial markets. Therefore, it is in China's interest that ASEAN economies remain stable.

It is also worth noting that, despite the sometimes hyperbolic optimism expressed about China's economy, China's leadership is acutely aware that the reform process is fragile and comes with a number of significant challenges, not the least of which is the challenge of maintaining political stability. From Chinese assessments, any number of things (social, economic, political, and/or international) has the potential to derail reforms and growth. Certainly, it remains a good question whether China's leadership will be able to manage all the socioeconomic dislocations and likely political consequences that come with the harder stage of reforms. Well known are China's fragile financial system, pervasive corruption, and lack of transparency in the system as a whole, which may discourage future investment and growth and encourage broad diversification of investment on the part of foreign investors.[25]

At the very least, China's leaders believe that "China's modernization construction [will be] a long process,"[26] and that if China is to be able to focus on these significant domestic challenges, it has strong interest in a stable and friendly regional environment (nonnegotiable items include Taiwan). In this sense, as an expression of commitment to the ASEAN relationship, the ACFTA can be seen as supporting that objective. There are also those in China who see the FTA agreement with ASEAN as a way to intensify development and growth in China's southern and western provinces, where much of China's minority populations live and where development has often

---

[25] See, for example, Nicholas Lardy, *Integrating China into the Global Economy* (Washington, DC: Brookings, 2002); "China, Japan, and Asia: Between Integration and Rivalries," *Societe Generale France: Monthly Economic Report, Janet Matthews Information System, Quest Economics Database*, September 17, 2002.

[26] "Hong Kong Paper Hails Premier's Southeast Asia Trip, Stepped up Diplomacy," *BBC Summary of World Broadcasts*, December 7, 1999.

fallen behind compared to China's thriving eastern seaboard. Regional socio-economic disparities are considered to be one of China's more serious sources of political instability.[27]

Perhaps most of all, the ACFTA supports China's interest in a stable periphery — although it is important to note that this interest applies to all of China's borders, not just to Southeast Asia. This interest is most notably illustrated by China's initiation of the "Shanghai Five" with its Central Asian neighbors, which would become the Shanghai Cooperation Organization (SCO). (The SCO's original five members — China, Russia, Kazakhstan, Kyrgyzstan, and Tajikistan — first met in 1996.) The SCO also points to China's new thinking about regionalism and security.

In Southeast Asia, as in Central Asia, China has sought a stable and friendly regional environment that will both mitigate external influences in the region and allow Beijing to concentrate on more pressing domestic concerns. Neither China's domestic nor international interests are served by a fearful and suspicious ASEAN. China's wants a friendly, and at the very least, neutral ASEAN, which is important not only for the domestic reasons cited above, but also because of the uncertainties that remain in China's relations with the United States. Incidents such as the bombing of the Chinese embassy in Belgrade in 1999 by American-led NATO forces likely added to China's insecurities about the United States, which, in turn, underscored the importance of a friendly neighborhood. According to Sheng Lijun of the Institute of Southeast Asian Studies, for example, the bombing of the Chinese embassy "pushed discussion [about a regional FTA] from ... academic circles to [the] high policymaking level," which led to Beijing's 2000 decision to "strengthen cooperation" with ASEAN, which then led to Zhu Rongji's proposal.[28]

Consequently, China has responded to ASEAN's increasingly public concerns about China's growing economic presence with

---

[27] See, for example, "Southwest China Anticipates Free Trade with ASEAN," *Xinhua,* September 9, 2002.
[28] Sheng Lijun, "China-ASEAN Free Trade Area," ISEAS Working Paper, International Politics and Security Series, no. 1 (2003).

measures designed to reassure and to keep relations moving in positive directions. In fact, although most ASEAN economies recovered from the crisis better than many had expected, it is clear that time has not eased ASEAN's economic concerns about China. Popular characterizations of China as a growing "economic threat" suggest that concerns about China have become quite acute in most countries. Such characterizations are also worrisome given Beijing's strategic interest in a friendly neighborhood.

Beijing's ASEAN diplomacy and recent statements suggest that China's leaders are very cognizant of ASEAN's concerns about China's growing economic and political influence. High-profile diplomatic visits, including a number of visits by Hu Jintao, have served to impress upon ASEAN members China's continued commitment to good relations despite new economic challenges and political circumstances. The visits by Hu Jintao, in the months leading up to China's expected transfer of power at the Sixteenth Party Congress, had the additional purpose of reassuring ASEAN about China's new leadership. As for the ACFTA, it directly responds to ASEAN's concerns about trade and investment, as well as about China, in general, by emphasizing ASEAN members' and China's interdependence and the mutual benefits that can come from their closer economic association.

The ACFTA can also be seen as an example of China's "new security concept" and, relatedly, of its attempt to ensure that its growth will take place without incident, that is, to ensure what Chinese scholars have called China's "peaceful ascendancy."[29] As one Beijing-based research organization explained, "peaceful ascendancy" means that "China aims to grow and advance without upsetting existing orders." It also means "trying to rise

---

[29] "Peaceful ascendancy" has been attributed to Ruan Zongzee, deputy director of the Beijing-based China Institute for International Studies. See Bruce Klingner, "Peaceful Rising Seeks to Allay 'China Threat,'" *Asia Times Online*, March 12, 2004.

in a way that benefits our neighbors."[30] Put another way, China seeks to grow and advance in ways that will not spark new competitive pressures or spirals of insecurity. This is especially important in Southeast Asia, where fears of China could convince some states to reintroduce a stronger American presence and/or negatively affect China's aspirations to regional leadership. In this sense, the ACFTA is also an exercise in preemption, whereby China seeks to preempt attempts by third parties to exploit ASEAN's concerns about China.

ASEAN'S CONCERNS

As suggested, there was much uncertainty in ASEAN about how best to respond to China's proposal. It is worth noting that it took two years of study and negotiation between the time the proposal was introduced and when it was finally signed. A few concerns can be considered particularly important in explaining ASEAN's delayed response: (1) continued uneasiness about China's influence and uncertainty about its long-term intentions; (2) concern about how the agreement would affect ASEAN's newer members; (3) disquiet among some ASEAN members about domestic industries and Chinese competition in domestic markets; and (4) the unexpectedness of China's proposal. Differences among members also complicated ASEAN's ability to respond to China's proposal.

Concerns about, and from, ASEAN's newest members — Vietnam, Laos, Myanmar, and Cambodia — were among the top reasons for ASEAN's uncertainty about how to respond to China's proposal.[31] As lesser developed economies, these states are anxious about what lowered tariff barriers, as required by the FTA, might mean for them. They have been especially troubled by the possibility

---

[30] Quoted in Yoichi Funabashi, "China is Preparing a 'Peaceful Ascendance,'" *International Herald Tribune* December 30, 2003.

[31] While there may be other intra-ASEAN differences regarding China, the most important consideration concerns the newest members. See, for example, "China, Indonesia 'The Big Issues for S'pore and KL,'" *Straits Times* (Singapore), April 20, 2002.

that their individual markets will be "swamped by Chinese goods that are cheaper and of better quality."[32] Meanwhile, the original ASEAN members plus Brunei have been concerned that, unless special attention is paid to newer members, ASEAN will be increasingly undermined by a growing "development gap" between old and new members.

Also of note were concerns about how the agreement would affect domestic industries. After all, the ACFTA called on market access to work both ways. Reciprocity requires ASEAN states to open their economies to Chinese goods and products, too. On this issue, Malaysia, the Philippines, and Indonesia proved most concerned, especially about how the agreement would affect agriculture, electronics, light machinery, and textiles. Worries that the agreement would flood ASEAN with cheap Chinese products prompted domestic industries in Indonesia and the Philippines, for example, to vigorously lobby for their governments to negotiate greater flexibilities in the implementation of identified tariff cuts. In Malaysia's case, a desire to protect its national car industry (the Proton), which long was a pet project of (former) Prime Minister Mahathir, meant its support for the ACFTA was weaker than expected given Mahathir's rhetoric of East Asian cooperation. Malaysia's reluctance to liberalize its automobile sector has also been a source of contention in Malaysia's relations with other ASEAN states, especially Thailand, and has been a stumbling block in the creation of an ASEAN Free Trade Area, as well as the ACFTA.

Also of concern were ASEAN uncertainties about China itself. Singapore trade minister George Yeo, for example, made the comment in early 2002 that ASEAN members had originally found China's proposed free trade area "quite a shocking proposition."[33] Yeo suggested that the proposal, in its timing and its detail, took

---

[32] Sarasin Viraphol, executive vice president of Thai MNC, the Charoen Pokphand Group, quoted in "Export Boon for S-E Asia," *Straits Times*, April 29, 2002.
[33] "China's Free-Trade Proposal Shocked ASEAN," *Agence France Presse*, March 15, 2002.

ASEAN members by surprise. The concessions China seemed willing to offer were also unexpected, given what many viewed to be the "heavy price" it had already made to gain entrance into the World Trade Organization.[34] Perhaps especially because China's economic interests in forging an FTA with ASEAN were unclear, there were questions from the beginning in ASEAN about what China hoped to gain from the FTA and what the political implications of such an agreement would be. China's offerings may have raised some suspicions in ASEAN about possible ulterior motives. At the very least, as one Malaysian trade official put it, there continues to be some "apprehensiveness" in ASEAN about the agreement because of the historical and material asymmetries that are part of the Sino-ASEAN relationship.[35]

During the two years that it took to study and negotiate the framework agreement, economic developments and continued economic trends heightened ASEAN's economic insecurities at the same time that they seemed to make cooperation with China more persuasive (or more inevitable). In 2000 and 2001, ASEAN concerns coalesced around China's impending admission to the World Trade Organization. Still recovering from the Asian financial crisis, ASEAN states saw themselves losing more jobs, trade, and investment to China. In the all important United States market, for example, China's share expanded from one percent in 1987 to 9 percent in 2002, moreover at a time when East Asia's overall share of the American market had dropped 14 percent (from 38 percent to 24 percent). Even Singapore (which had suffered its worst economic downturn since 1965, losing over 42,000 jobs between 1997 and 2002 in a population of 4.5 million[36]) felt the pressure from China, a

---

[34] Comments of Barry Desker in a conversation with the author at the Institute of Defense and Strategic Studies, August 2002. See also Nicholas Lardy, *Integrating China into the Global Economy* (Washington, DC: Brookings, 2002).

[35] Confidential interview with author, Kuala Lumpur, Malaysia, August 2002.

[36] Jane Perlez, "China to Replace US as Economic Power in Asia," *New York Times,* June 28, 2002.

subject that was made a prominent theme of Prime Minister Goh Chok Tong's 2002 and 2003 National Day Rally speeches.[37]

Most of ASEAN's attention and concern, however, was (and continues to be) focused on China's ability to attract foreign direct investment away from ASEAN economies — a far from idle worry, judging from investment patterns over the last ten years. As discussed above, China is perceived to have benefited from ASEAN's loss of investor confidence since the Asian financial crisis. This was, for example, the conclusion of the ASEAN-China Expert Group on Economic Cooperation, which was created to study China's proposal. That group subsequently reported that the financial crisis "significantly changed the economic environment of ASEAN for FDI flows." According to its report, FDI inflows to ASEAN dropped from U.S.$32.5 billion in 1997 to U.S.$13.8 billion in 2000, a reduction of over 50 percent.[38] While overall FDI inflows to China declined during this period as well, the impact was considerably less (at most only 11 percent),[39] and more significantly, China appeared to be seizing the lion's share of FDI bound for East Asia. According to one frequently cited estimate in Southeast Asia, between 1995 and 2000, China received nearly 40 percent of the FDI inflows into Asia.[40] Although it is unclear how much of the FDI in China is *new* investment as opposed to *diverted* investment from ASEAN, there is a widespread perception that China's growth is increasingly at ASEAN's expense.

ASEAN's concerns have been underscored by a number of high-profile plant closings in Southeast Asia and relocations of production facilities to China, especially on the part of Japanese manufacturers.

---

[37] For the texts of Goh's 2002 and 2003 speeches, see http://www.gov.sg/nd/ND02.htm, and http://www.gov.sg/nd/ND03.htm.
[38] ASEAN also experienced a decline in its percentage of FDI flows to all developing countries, dropping from 17.4 percent to 5.8 percent during the same period. See *Forging Closer ASEAN-China Relations in the Twenty-First Century*, 22.
[39] Ibid.
[40] See, for example, "S'pore's FTAs help ASEAN, Not Hinder," *Business Times* (Singapore), August 15, 2002; see also, Erik Eckholm, "Asia Worries about Growth of China's Economic Power," *New York Times*, November 24, 2002, A10.

This trend was detailed in a July 2002 article by the *Nihon Keizai Shimbun*.[41] Although many of these closings in Southeast Asia may be the result of downsizing, and despite efforts by Tokyo officials to downplay their significance, others confirm ASEAN's worst fears. For example, Tetsuya Matsuoka, the secretary general of the Japanese Chamber of Commerce and Industry of the Philippines (JCCIP), observed, "I think from now on, no newcomers will come to [the] Philippines [from Japan]. If they [Japanese companies] would go out of Japan, they will go to China because China is a big market."[42] UNCTAD's 2002 *World Investment Report* similarly concluded that China has emerged as "the leading destination by far" in terms of investment by Japanese manufacturing transnational corporations, and the top recipient of all inbound foreign investment to developing Asia and, indeed, the developing world.[43]

In short, ASEAN members perceive the economic challenges from China to be in both trade and investment. Not only have ASEAN economies been concerned that China will divert important foreign investment away from them, but also they have been fearful that they will be unable to compete against cheaper Chinese goods,

---

[41] For example, Dell, NEC, and Minolta. The *Nihon Keizai Shimbun* report pointed to a growing trend by which "Japanese manufacturers with operations in Southeast Asia are increasingly shutting down their factories and moving production to China." See, among other writings on the topic, Jane Perlez, "China Races to Replace U.S. as Economic Power in Asia," *New York Times*, June 28, 2002, 1; "Japanese Firms Saying Hello China, Sayonara Southeast Asia," *Deutsche Press-Agentur*, August 14, 2002, *Lexis-Nexis Academic: World News*, online, August 1, 2004; and "China Defends 'Win-Win' Surge in Japanese Investment," *Deutsche Press-Agentur*, August 14, 2002, *Lexis-Nexis Academic: World News*, online, August 1, 2004.

[42] "Japan Inc. 'Hollowing Out' in Southeast Asia?" *Deutsche Presse-Agentur*, August 14, 2002. See also, Michael Dwyer, "Will China Crush Asia?" *Australian Financial Review*, June 15, 2002, which addresses a report issued by ING Barrings, entitled "What if China is the World's Lowest-Cost Producer of Everything?"

[43] According to JETRO, 99 percent of Japanese transnational corporations already invested in ASEAN said that they did not intend to relocate their operations, although this did not preclude their expanding operations in China. UNCTAD, *Trade and Development Report, 2002* (New York: United Nations, 2002), 44–57.

especially in critical third markets. This is especially true of ASEAN's lesser developed economies which more directly compete against China currently; however, many ASEAN nations expect that China will soon compete in high technology and high-skilled areas as well, areas in which ASEAN's more developed economies, Malaysia and Singapore, have been competitive.[44] In fact, some analyses, including the report by UNCTAD, argue that it may be Southeast Asia's more developed economies that will be most adversely affected by the combined effects of contracting demand from industrialized economies, on the one hand, and price competition from newer, emerging economies such as China's, on the other.[45] A related concern is that, as China catches up and becomes more competitive in the industrial sector, ASEAN economies will be relegated to the role of low-end suppliers of resource products for China's economy.[46]

RESPONDING TO ASEAN'S CONCERNS

All of the above concerns factored into ASEAN's initial hesitation about the ACFTA proposal. At the same time, most ASEAN members also recognized that China represented and offered important economic opportunities. Additionally, many saw the proposal, and by extension, closer economic relations with China, to be, in the words of the ASEAN Expert Group on Economic Cooperation, "a natural response to regional and global developments during the course of the past decade."[47] In 2001 and 2002, the prospect — and then reality — of an economic downturn in the United States offered

---

[44] Singapore, anticipating the inroads China will make in electronics, already has designated biotechnology as the "next pillar" of its manufacturing growth. See ibid., 57–58.

[45] UNCTAD, *Trade and Development Report, 2002*, ix. Malaysia has similarly lost about sixteen thousand jobs in the electronics sector, including managerial and engineering jobs, in Penang alone between 2001 and 2002. See Eckholm, "Asia Worries about Growth of China's Economic Power," A10.

[46] Eckholm, "Asia Worries about Growth of China's Economic Power."

[47] "Forging Closer ASEAN-China Economic Relations in the Twenty-First Century," 4, 6, 7.

further evidence of ASEAN's precarious position in the global economy, a view that grew stronger after the 1997–1999 crisis. According to UNCTAD, Singapore, Malaysia, and Thailand, for example, all saw their exports to the American market contract by 5 percent as a result of the 2001 economic downturn in the United States.[48] ASEAN's vulnerability to the vicissitudes of the economy, not to mention politics, of the United States further lent to China's economic appeal as an alternative motor of Southeast Asian growth. On the ACFTA, William Choong of Singapore's *Straits Times* expressed it well: "At a time when the world's three biggest economic locomotives are losing steam, many export-oriented economies in Asia are eyeing the spending power of China's 1.3 billion populace for their economic salvation."[49]

Relatedly, although most ASEAN-China trade remains relatively low compared to their trade with the United States,[50] there has been important growth in trade of about 15–20 percent over the last ten years.[51] Potentially even more significant is that China's trade with the ASEAN-4 economies (Thailand, Malaysia, Indonesia, and the Philippines) grew faster than those four nations' combined trade with the United States since 1986.[52] While Chinese and ASEAN economies today may be best characterized as competitive, it is also expected that there will be growing complementarities as China's

---

[48] UNCTAD, *Trade and Development Report, 2002.*
[49] William Choong, "China Can Fuel Demand for Asian Exports," *Straits Times*, December 18, 2001.
[50] In 2001, for example, ASEAN's total trade with the United States (U.S.$108.4 billion) exceeded that with China (U.S.$55.4 billion) by almost two times. See the ASEAN Web site, www.aseansec.org.
[51] Between 1995 and 2002, for example, Sino-ASEAN trade increased at about 15 percent a year. Lee Kim Chew, "Slow and Not So Easy ASEAN Talks with China," *Straits Times*, October 9, 2002. Mari Pangestu and Sudarshan Gooptu, "New Regionalism: Options for China and East Asia (chap. 3)," in *East Asia Integrates: A Trade Policy for Shared Growth*, ed. Kathie Krumm and Homi Kharas (Washington, DC: World Bank, 2003), 94–95.
[52] Jan P. Voon and Ren Yue, "China-ASEAN Export Rivlary in the US Market," *Journal of Asia Pacific Economy* 8, no. 2 (2003): 157–179.

economy becomes more developed and complex, and as China's population acquires more affluence. In particular, many members of ASEAN expect that Chinese demand for commodities and primary products from ASEAN will increase over time. Chinese tourism is also expected to increasingly benefit ASEAN as China's population grows wealthier. The ACFTA can be interpreted as responding to these anticipated complementarities.[53] The ASEAN Expert Group on Economic Cooperation expects the ACFTA, when fully realized, to increase ASEAN's exports to China by 48 percent.[54]

The ACFTA is also expected to have a positive effect on foreign investment. As Singapore's Ministry of Trade and Industry explains, the ACFTA means that investors can invest and locate in ASEAN member states to serve the Chinese market.[55] It is also anticipated that Chinese investment abroad will increase correspondingly with China's economic growth. ASEAN hopes that the ACFTA will help make ASEAN an attractive first destination and "priority market" for Chinese investment abroad.[56]

Further, China's willingness to engage and respond to ASEAN's concerns has been especially notable. China, for example, accommodated ASEAN members on some of their most important concerns. This included offering early and "WTO-plus" liberalization on ASEAN exports to China, giving ASEAN economies a "head start" in seizing market opportunities in China and developing an alternative market for ASEAN goods. Explained Malaysian Deputy International Trade and Industry Minister Kerk Choo Ting, for example, "The FTA would allow for ASEAN to make early inroads into the China market through preferential import duties."[57]

China also offered a number of additional "sweeteners" to demonstrate its commitment to the relationship. Specifically, China

---

[53] Again see, "Forging Closer ASEAN-China Relations in the Twenty-First Century."
[54] Loh Hui Yin, "AFTA Will Ensure Better Fit with China," *Business Times*, April 16, 2002.
[55] See Singapore Ministry of Trade and Industry Web site, http://www.mti.gov.sg/public/FTA/frm_FTA_Default.asp?sid=143.
[56] "Forging Closer ASEAN-China Economic Relations in the Twenty-First Century," 2.
[57] "China Says FTA with ASEAN Needed to Fight Western Trade Blocs."

agreed to include an "early harvest" provision that would cover 130 agricultural[58] and manufacturing products. China's agreement to the partial liberalization of its agricultural sector over three years (no tariffs by 2005) is considered especially significant, given the importance of agriculture to ASEAN economies. Equally important, the early harvest program would begin immediately. The rest of the agreement would then come into effect in stages beginning in 2005. In addition, China agreed to lift tariff and nontariff barriers on ASEAN palm oil, a major export of Indonesia and especially Malaysia, whose palm oil makes up 80 percent of China's total annual purchase.[59] As part of the framework agreement signed in November 2001, China and ASEAN also negotiated an additional early harvest program for their service sector in early 2003.

Regarding concerns about ASEAN's newest members, China proved again to be responsive. Under the framework agreement, China agreed to extend WTO privileges and concessions on agriculture to lesser-developed economies, such as Cambodia and Vietnam, which are not yet WTO members. It also agreed to a delayed time frame for ASEAN's lesser-developed economies, whereby newer ASEAN members will receive "special and differential treatment and flexibility in implementation" by having five extra years (by 2015) to comply with the agreement.[60] In this way, newer members may take advantage of the early entrance into the China market before they have to open their own markets to Chinese competition. In addition, China has agreed to write off the debts owed to it by ASEAN's four newest members.[61]

---

[58] Products covered under the early harvest package include about six hundred selected agricultural products under the categories: live animals, meat, fish, dairy products, other animal products, live trees, vegetables, fruits, and nuts.
[59] Carol Murugiah, "Council: Promote Palm Oil Aggressively," *Business Times* (Malaysia), December 19, 2003, 4.
[60] ASEAN Secretariat Press Release: "ASEAN-China Free Trade Area Negotiations to Start Next Year," October 30, 2002, ASEAN Web site, http://www.aseansec.org.
[61] "Vietnamese PM Cites New Challenges Facing ASEAN at Summit in Phnom Penh," *VNA News Agency*, via *BBC Worldwide Monitoring*, November 5, 2002.

In general, China has continued to take great care to emphasize themes of cooperation and interdependence over themes of competition and dependence as a way to address the ASEAN states' concerns about China and the implications of the proposed ACFTA. As Hu Jintao put it during his April 2002 visit to Malaysia, "China's development would be impossible without Asia and Asia's prosperity without China."[62] In trying to persuade ASEAN states that there are benefits of closer economic relations with China, Beijing's representatives also called attention to increasing trade linkages and opportunities, as well as to growing Chinese demand for ASEAN products, arguing that ASEAN is uniquely situated to benefit from China's rise and growth. As Vice Minister Long has observed, the ASEAN-China FTA, along with ASEAN's "specific geographic and resource advantages" will mean that "ASEAN will be one of the first selected targets to which China's enterprises implement [their] 'going global' strategy."[63] By reframing the economics of their relations in more positive-sum, "win-win" terms, China hopes to convince ASEAN to view China not as a negative force, or "a growth spoiler," that pulls the rest of Asia down, but instead as a "positive force," or "a growth driver," even a needed "ballast" that can steady East Asia in the face of turbulent global forces.[64]

In the accommodations China has made, the ACFTA can be considered one of China's more significant gestures toward ASEAN. Again, because the Asian financial crisis diminished ASEAN members' attractiveness as economic and trade partners and their influence over

---

[62] Cheah Chor Sooi, "We Are Good Partners," *New Straits Times* (Malaysia), April 25, 2002, 1.

[63] "China to Import US$1.4 TLN from 2001-2005," *Bernama* (Malaysia), August 29, 2002, *Lexis-Nexis Academic: World News*, online, August 1, 2004.

[64] "China-ASEAN Free Trade Area Economically Important, Says Editor," *Malaysia Economic News*, May 6, 2002; "China to Open Up 1.5 Trillion Dollars Trade Market in Five Years," *Agence France Presse*, April 24, 2002. See also statement of Zhu Rongji at the close of the ASEAN-China meeting: "Nearly a year after China's entry into the WTO, facts have shown that economic growth in China has not come about at the expense of the development of others. On the contrary, it has become an important pillar and stimulus to the East Asian economy as a whole." Philip P. Pan, "China Signs Accords with ASEAN Group on Disputed Territory, Free Trade," *Washington Post*, November 5, 2002, A17.

regional developments, it was certainly possible that China might refocus some of its diplomatic energy toward other relationships. The fact that China did not downgrade, but, in fact, upgraded ASEAN in its priorities, despite different postcrisis circumstances, has not been lost on ASEAN, especially given the perceived neglect by other major powers. Consequently, although ASEAN states may have been initially uncertain how to interpret China's FTA proposal and may still harbor concerns about Chinese influence, George Yeo explains that the decision was made to take China's proposal at face value, as "a friendly gesture" aimed at assuring ASEAN that China intended to be a "long-term friend."[65]

Still, this is not to say that all concerns have been addressed. Individual ASEAN economies continue to have different concerns that have complicated both regional and bilateral negotiations with China. Those apprehensions, for example, led to a modification of the original multilateral approach of the framework agreement's early harvest program to allow for bilateral negotiations between China and each of the ASEAN states (to prevent "free riding").[66] What happened in the Philippines in the first months of 2003 is illustrative of the domestic interests brought to bear on negotiations, but also of how fears of being left behind, combined with peer pressure effects, have nevertheless pushed the process forward. In March 2003, for example, Philippine concerns about domestic industries being able to compete led a cabinet-level committee to say that the Philippines would not participate in the ACFTA's early harvest program, a decision that was reversed in May due to concerns that it would be left behind as others proceeded forward.[67]

---

[65] "China's Free Trade Proposal Shocked ASEAN," *Agence France Press*, March 15, 2002.

[66] See Jiang Yu Wang, "A China-ASEAN Free Trade Area," paper presented at the international conference on Southeast Asia and China: Global Changes and Regional Challenges, Kaoshiung, Taiwan, March 4–6, 2004.

[67] See Gil C. Cabacungan, Jr., "RP Not Joining ASEAN-China Early Harvest Program," *Philippine Daily Inquirer*, March 7, 2003, 8, and "RP Joining China-ASEAN Deal After All," *Manila Standard*, May 9, 2003, *Lexis-Nexis Academic: World News*, online, July 3, 2003.

Finally, ASEAN's decision to accept the agreement also reflects a growing sense of inevitability about closer economic relations with China. Alongside acknowledgment of the potentially great economic opportunities represented by closer ties to China is a sense of resignation. Among many members of ASEAN, there remains hope that Western and Asian investors will want to diversify their investments in Southeast Asia as a way to hedge against something going wrong economically or politically on the mainland. Governments in Taiwan and Japan have both voiced arguments in favor of diversification (mostly for their own security reasons), although their efforts have done little to stem the flow of investment from both countries into China. Meanwhile, some ASEAN economies have explicitly tried to portray themselves as safer, more predictable investment options than China, as illustrated, for example, when the Severe Acute Respiratory Syndrome (SARS) epidemic first broke out in China in 2003.

Even so, there is the sense among ASEAN economies that, individually and collectively, they will not be able to compete against the combined lure of China's domestic market and cheaper (and increasingly skilled) labor force, and that time is unlikely to make matters easier. As Singapore's environment minister noted, "In Singapore, we believe that China will be both factory of the world as well as a market for the world."[68] Moreover, over time, China is expected to become an even more formidable competitor. Consequently, there is the sense that the only real option for ASEAN members is to work with China in the hopes of tapping into its growth and injecting new dynamism into their own economies by association. As National University of Singapore Professor Toh Mun Heng remarked, "[H]owling and growling will not stop the wheel from turning. Take the bull by the horns and unseen opportunities may turn

---

[68] "ASEAN Can Benefit from China," *Straits Times,* April 16, 2002, *Lexis-Nexis Academic: World News*, online, August 1, 2004.

up."[69] Because most members of ASEAN view China's economic growth as virtually inevitable — a train that cannot be stopped — the ACFTA has been viewed as a ticket to ride on China's growth as much as a move to avoid being left behind (or run over).[70]

FTA FEVER?

ASEAN states have not been the only ones concerned about China's growing influence in the region. In particular, China's proposal exerted competitive pressures on Japan and the United States to offer FTA proposals of their own. While these other FTAs also have held the potential of side-lining China-ASEAN relations and/or pushing regional developments in directions that China may not have originally desired, China's FTA proposal has compared favorably against the other two and seems to have helped bolster its desire to be seen as a "responsible big nation" in the region."[71]

China's proposal has been especially detrimental to Japan. As Robert Sutter has discussed, there are those who anticipate "an intensified rivalry for leadership in Asia" between China and Japan especially,[72] and signs of tension along these lines are already in evidence. In Japan, especially, China's proposed ACFTA "was widely seen as an attempt by Beijing to try to usurp the leadership role in Southeast Asia which has traditionally been played by Tokyo."[73] Not surprisingly, Japan offered its own proposal soon after China and

---

[69] Kao Chen, "Will the Dragon Hollow Out?" *Straits Times*, September 15, 2002, H12, H13.
[70] Ibid.
[71] Anonymous Chinese scholar, quoted in Anatoneta Bezlova, "Southeast Asia Trip: A Test for Hu," *Inter Press Service*, April 24, 2002.
[72] Robert Sutter, "China and Japan: Trouble Ahead?" *Washington Quarterly* (Autumn 2002): 37.
[73] "China's Hu Jintao Urges Talks with ASEAN on Fee-Trade Zone," *South China Morning Post*, April 27, 2002, 7.

ASEAN announced their intent to pursue the ACFTA.[74] Japan's "Comprehensive Economic Partnership (CER)" involved a ten-year process of building a "broad-based economic partnership covering not only liberalization of trade and investment, but also trade and investment promotion and facilitation."[75]

Significantly, Japan's foreign ministry identified a Japan-China FTA as a lesser priority, behind ASEAN, Korea, and Mexico, which were identified as near-term priorities. According to the "MOFA [Ministry of Foreign Affairs] strategy," Japan would pull ASEAN and South Korea into an "umbrella" economic partnership before concluding an FTA with China, and well ahead of the ACFTA's target date.

In its bid for regional leadership, however, Japan has been hindered by domestic constraints and especially by its own ambivalence toward playing a leadership role in Southeast Asia. Although Japan's heightened attention to ASEAN is certainly welcomed there, Japan's efforts are also often seen as reactive and falling short of expectations. Consequently, Japan has found its leadership potential and credibility diminished in Southeast Asia, which the weakness of its FTA proposal did little to help. Not only do many Southeast Asian leaders view Japan's proposal as a transparent effort to counter China's influence, but also they regard Japan's initiative as lacking the substance and details of China's.[76] Even in the case of the bilateral FTA it concluded with Singapore in January 2002 — which

---

[74] Singapore's *Business Times*, for example, commented: "The overriding impression given by Japan's decision to pursue bilateral accords selectively is that it is trying to steal a march on China in its diplomacy towards Southeast Asia." "Japan's Regional Grand Design," *Business Times*, October 22, 2002, *Lexis-Nexis Academic: World News*, online, August 1, 2004.

[75] Hardev Kaur, "Japan, Playing Catch Up With China," *New Straits Times*, November 6, 2002, 2.

[76] Philippine President Arroyo, for example, said that Japan's proposals "are not as well developed or as well defined as China's." Greg Sheridan, "Tokyo Trade Foggy in Arroyo's Vision," *Weekend Australian*, April 27, 2002, 17. As one indicator of the contrasts between the two FTA initiatives, Japan's remains only a declaration and is only five pages, including two pages of signatures, compared to the ASEAN-China agreement which is fourteen pages, not including the eighteen pages of appendices.

provides the model for FTAs with other ASEAN economies — Japan still refused to liberalize its agricultural sector, which has long been an area of contention between Japan and ASEAN states. The perceived triviality of Japan's refusal to liberalize goldfish imports in an agreement with a country such as Singapore that exports very few agricultural products, only underscored growing questions about Japanese leadership.[77]

Of the major economies with significant interests in East Asia, the United States has been the last to catch "FTA fever" in Asia. On the sidelines of the October 2002 APEC meeting in Los Cabos, Mexico, the American counterproposal to ASEAN came in the form of the "Enterprise for ASEAN Initiative (EAI)," which, according to President George Bush, aimed to "create a network of bilateral and regional liberalization, and help APEC reach...free and open trade and investment in [the] Asia-Pacific region."[78] A White House Fact Sheet explains, "The EAI offers the prospect of bilateral FTAs between the US and ASEAN countries that are committed to economic reforms and openness."[79] As illustrated by Malaysia's reversal on the acceptability of bilateral FTAs and Philippines' President Gloria Macapagal Arroyo's urgings to her ASEAN colleagues to consider the EAI seriously,[80] there is little doubt that ASEAN states are keen to develop an FTA with the United States, which remains a primary, if not the most important, trade partner for ASEAN states.

Certainly, as an expression of renewed American economic interest in the region, the EAI has been most welcomed in Southeast

---

[77] Said U.S. trade representative Robert Zoellick, for example, "Japan goes around saying it wants to do free-trade agreements but it wants to leave out agriculture. That's not really a free-trade agreement." "In China's Shadow, Japan to Court ASEAN on Trade," *Reuters*, November 22, 2002.

[78] "Bush Announces Trade Initiative for ASEAN," *Japan Economic Newswire*, October 27, 2002.

[79] See EAI Fact Sheet, http://www.state.gov/p/eap/rls/14700.htm.

[80] "Philippines to Seek ASEAN Support for US Trade, Investment Proposals," *Philippine Star*, November 2, 2002, *Lexis-Nexis Academic: World News*, online, August 1, 2004.

Asia. Nevertheless, how substantive that expression is can still be questioned. The EAI calls for no new measures or commitments on the part of the United States. The EAI also comes with conditions that are not part of ASEAN's agreements with China or Japan. Specifically, the EAI requires potential FTA partners to be (1) members of the WTO, and (2) to have concluded a Trade and Investment Framework Agreement (TIFA) with the United States. Currently, Indonesia, the Philippines, Thailand, Singapore, and more recently Brunei have concluded such TIFAs, which create "a Joint Council to expand and liberalize trade and investment, including ... such areas as intellectual property, information and communications technology, biotechnology policy, tourism ... and capacity building."[81] As of April 2004, the only successfully negotiated bilateral FTA was the United States-Singapore FTA, which came into effect in 2004; however, the United States and Thailand were in the process of negotiations. Of particular importance, ASEAN's newest members must wait for WTO membership before they can begin to negotiate an FTA with the United States.

Will the EAI have any effect on the ACFTA? Mainly, the EAI could slow down the ACFTA if only because the United States is, for the moment, the most important trade relationship for most ASEAN economies. Also, ASEAN simply does not have the necessary resources and knowledgeable personnel to devote to both free trade agreements at the same time.[82]

In sum, of the three FTA offerings, China's stands out for being the most substantive and most directly responsive to ASEAN concerns. It is also the only one offered to ASEAN as a collective from the start. This is significant in that China's proposal is now being interpreted by some analysts as more supportive of ASEAN as a

---

[81] Office of the United States Trade Representative, "Press Release: United States and Brunei Sign Bilateral TIFA," December 16, 2002.
[82] Confidential interview with Malaysian trade ministry official, MITI, Kuala Lumpur, Malaysia, August 2002. See also comments of outgoing ASEAN Secretary-General Rodolfo Severino, quoted in Frank Ching, "Observer," *South China Morning Post*, October 26, 2002, 14.

Table 11.1: Major Powers' FTA Proposals with ASEAN

Proposed FTA's with ASEAN	China	Japan	United States
	Framework Agreement on Comprehensive Economic Cooperation between ASEAN and the PRC: ASEAN-China Free Trade Agreement (ACFTA)	Comprehensive Economic Partnership (CEP)	Enterprise for ASEAN Initiative (EAI)
Eligible Participants	All ASEAN members	All ASEAN members	All ASEAN members that meet preconditions below
Type of Framework	The framework agreement is with ASEAN as a collective, although the Early Harvest Program was negotiated bilaterally.	The 2003 framework agreement between Japan and collective ASEAN will be based on bilateral agreements between Japan and selected ASEAN countries, with a common set of rules of origin. The agreement between Japan and Singapore is cited as the model.	Agreements are with individual ASEAN members, on a bilateral basis. The free trade agreement between the United States and Singapore is to provide the model.
Preconditions	None	None	Signers must: (1) be WTO members, and (2) have signed a Trade and Investment Framework Agreement (TIFA) with the United States.
Time Frame	Framework agreement commits parties to have completed negotiations on nonearly harvest tariff lines by June 30, 2004. ACFTA to be in effect by 2010 for Indonesia, Malaysia, the Philippines, Thailand, and Singapore. ACFTA to be in effect by 2015 for Cambodia, Laos, Vietnam, Myanmar.	2012 for the ASEAN Six 2017 for ASEAN's four newest members	There is no collective timeframe. FTAs will come into effect as individual members successfully negotiate their FTAs with the United States.

(*continued*)

Table 11.1: (Continued)

Key Elements, New and Special Terms of Trade	Early Harvest Program involving liberalization of manufacturing and especially agricultural products (over six hundred tariff lines). Tariffs to be eliminated over three years, beginning no later than January 1, 2004. Special consideration for newer ASEAN members (Cambodia, Laos, Myanmar, and Vietnam). Update: Regarding the Early Harvest Program, Singapore and Brunei put the EH program into effect immediately. Thailand's EH came into effect in October 2003. Malaysia implemented the EH in January 2004; the Philippines completed EH negotiations, sealed by a memorandum of understanding, in April 2005, despite some significant domestic opposition to the program. Indonesia has also agreed to the EH program. The first phase of ASEAN's and China's FTA in goods went into effect in July 2005. Though ASEAN states still mostly view the EH as friendly initiative from China, concerns about competition from Chinese agriculture have heightened in some ASEAN countries.	Covers both trade and investment but the current declaration significantly lacks detail. Particular point of contention: Japan's reluctance to open its agricultural sector. Update: ASEAN and Japan held a first round of talks about the possibility of an ASEAN-Japan FTA in April 2005. As of August 2005, Japan had concluded basic economic partnership agreements with Singapore, the Philippines, and Malaysia; however, a number of differences remained to be addressed. Japan has been in negotiations with Thailand since February 2004, but differences over a variety of items (including steel, agriculture, automobiles and auto parts, and investment and services) have hindered their ability to conclude a basic accord. Japan and Indonesia agreed in June 2005 to begin bilateral talks by July 2005.	The EAI resembles the Enterprise for Americas Initiative. While the EAI may suggest renewed attention to ASEAN, the EAI subtantively does not appear to offer collective ASEAN much that was not already on the table. The initiative is also unclear in some of its details, including timeframe. Developments suggest that details will be negotiated on a bilateral basis. Update: As of August 2005, only Singapore had signed an accord with the U.S. under the EAI. Thailand, Malaysia, Brunei, the Philippines, and Indonesia had signed TIFA's with the United States. Of these countries, only Thailand was in the process of negotiating an FTA with the United States. The fourth round of meetings was held in July 2005.

group than other proposals. The bilateral approach adopted by the United States and Japan,[83] although certainly welcomed, is viewed as more problematic because it may leave behind ASEAN's lesser-developed members and, thus, widen the previously discussed developmental gap between old and new members. The bilateral approach is also seen as more divisive of ASEAN, in general. According to the *Yomiuri Shimbun,* for example, ASEAN rejected Japan's original draft of the joint declaration on the CEP precisely because it overly stressed bilateral ties versus Japan's relationship to ASEAN as a group.[84] While China's framework agreement with ASEAN also involves bilateral negotiations, China's attention to ASEAN as a group has been a welcome shot in the arm in that China's proposal has served to renew outside, post-Asian financial crisis interest in ASEAN. Argues Sheng Lijun of Singapore's Institute of Southeast Asian Studies, for example, "China's ... FTA that takes ASEAN as one single identity [as opposed to dividing it] ... is exactly what ASEAN needs at this critical moment of its survival crisis."[85]

AN EAST ASIAN FTA?

Consistent with ASEAN states' "long tradition of striking a strategic balance in economic and political ties," the renewed attention to Southeast Asia by other states was most welcomed by ASEAN states, which have had concerns about the asymmetry of their relations

---

[83] It appears that Japan's response may have been complicated by bureaucratic differences between the Ministry of Foreign Affairs and the Ministry of Economy, Trade, and Industry, with the former preferring the bilateral approach and the latter originally pursuing a group approach to ASEAN. See "Japan's Regional Grand Design," *Business Times*, October 22, 2002; and Junichi Fukazawa and Tohimano Ishli, "China's ASEAN Strategy Outmaneuvers Japan," *Daily Yomiuri*, November 6, 2002, *Lexis-Nexis Academic: World News*, online, August 1, 2004.
[84] Junichi Fukazawa and Tohimano Ishli, "China's ASEAN Strategy Outmaneuvers Japan," *Daily Yomiuri*, November 6, 2002.
[85] Marwaan Macan-Markar, "ASEAN to Profit From Free Trade Pact With China," *Inter Press Service*, October 18, 2002.

with China. As for the long-term significance of these various FTAs, some see the flurry of FTA activity as exerting pressure toward the creation of an East Asian FTA. While it is true that, in the short-term, the many bilateral FTAs — each with different rules and different scope — could complicate regionalization processes in the context of common rules for the entire East Asia region, the inefficiency of current bilateral arrangements and the material and technological limitations of ASEAN states, especially regarding the implementation of all these different rules and regulations, could exert additional pressure to create one common East Asian framework.[86]

Both ASEAN and China have had mixed reactions to a common East Asian framework due to political concerns. If ASEAN could position itself as a "hub" of a network of bilateral FTAs or at the center of a more explicitly East Asian arrangement (in the same way that it did in the ARF, for example), ASEAN states envision that "East Asia" as a bloc could give the organization new relevance at a time when world attention has focused more on Northeast Asia's prospects than on those of Southeast Asia. However, ASEAN states also fear what East Asian arrangements would mean for ASEAN's organizational relevance and leverage. This is why some in ASEAN have argued that there should be greater attention given to the AFTA before other arrangements.

On China's side, its concerns have focused mainly on Japan. Its rejection of Tokyo's proposed Asian Monetary Fund at the height of the Asian financial crisis stemmed mostly from its distrust of Japan (especially since there had been no consultation with Beijing). Also, if, as some argue, China's recent policies have aimed to "preempt" other bids for regional leadership, then its enthusiasm for an East Asian arrangement may be limited. On the other hand, others have argued that an East Asian economic group has been China's goal all

---

[86] Interestingly, in November 2003, Singapore, which has been the most active in pursuing bilateral FTAs, said that the ACFTA must have priority, and that until the ACFTA was finalized, it would not even begin to negotiate a bilateral FTA with China. "Asean-China FTA is Singapore's Top Priority," Trade News Headlines, *Importers.Com*, November 2003, http://www.importers.com.

along. By this argument, China may view the ACFTA as a stepping stone to building an East Asian free trade area. According to Zhang Yunlong, one of the five Chinese members of the China-ASEAN Expert Group who studied the merits of the ACFTA, "China will not just stop at this [ACFTA] arrangement. Its larger interest lies in EAFTA [East Asian Free Trade Area]."[87] Zhang goes on to explain, "China believes that East Asian regional cooperation and integration could help to create a stable and cooperative environment, which is crucial for realizing its ambitious modernization dream."[88] Reflective of ASEAN's influence, Zhang also sees East Asian processes as important for long-term confidence building. As he envisions it, "East Asia needs political and security cooperation" in the interest of building trust but political circumstances mean that the cooperative environment must be developed "cautiously and gradually."[89] However, until East Asian states feel more comfortable with one another, they may have to settle for a more "pragmatic approach," pragmatic meaning different kinds of arrangements, bilateral and multilateral, intraregional and interregional, and in areas where progress is possible.[90]

CONCLUSION

The developments described above point to deeper systemic changes ongoing in East Asia, which today provide the important context for China's and ASEAN's framework agreement on economic cooperation. As the discussion above reveals, the East Asian regional system has been in flux, especially since the end of the Cold War, and both China and ASEAN have pursued closer relations as a way to stabilize their regional environment and to bolster their negotiating power vis-à-vis more industrialized economies such as

---

[87] Zhang Yunling, "East Asian Regionalism and China." *Issues & Studies* (June 2002): 213–223.
[88] Ibid., 223.
[89] Zhang Yunling, "East Asian Cooperation and Integration: Where to Go?" 2002, http://www.iapscass.cn/English/Publications/showcontent.asp?id=67.
[90] Zhang, "East Asian Regionalism and China," 220.

the United States. To be clear, American military and economic power make relations with the United States the most important relationship for both China and ASEAN; thus, good relations with the United States will remain a priority for both. However, because both China and ASEAN also have important concerns about their relationships with the United States, they will continue to cultivate their regional relations.

Given that perceived American retrenchment and inattention to Southeast Asia played an important catalytic role in recent developments in China-ASEAN relations, it is possible that renewed American attention to East and Southeast Asia, especially since September 2001, could also redirect some regional developments and trends. At the same time, while the United States has been more attentive to Asia in the security realm, trade and economics remain a primary point of grievance and divergence on the part of the ASEAN states. Also, as China grows, it is likely to become an even more important driver of the regional, if not global, economy. Further, China's willingness to respond directly to ASEAN's economic concerns and to focus on trade and investment has contrasted well against what many in ASEAN see to be Washington's single-minded focus on security and now terrorism. Especially given its limitations, the EAI, as welcomed as it is, is unlikely to change ASEAN's sense of economic insecurity or its perceived need to develop closer economic relations with China. Most of all, ASEAN members' "instinctive reflex…to seek a strategic balance in their economic and political ties"[91] is also never far from the surface, meaning that ASEAN is likely to continue doing what it always has done — which is to work with all interested powers toward achieving a balanced constellation of interests and influence, where no one power dominates.

As for China, it remains deeply concerned about possible confrontation with the United States. Despite the improvements in relations since the 2001 terrorist attacks on New York and the Pentagon, relations remain clouded by suspicion and distrust.

---

[91] Vatikiotis, "Catching the Dragon's Tail."

Consequently, China has continued to assure ASEAN of its benign intentions and value as a partner in ensuring a friendly regional environment. For example, the ACFTA proposal has been followed by significant initiatives and overtures — including China's becoming the first non-ASEAN country to sign ASEAN's Treaty of Amity and Cooperation (TAC); pledges to increase Chinese investment in Southeast Asia; and a "Joint Declaration on Strategic Partnership for Peace and Prosperity," China's first such partnership with a regional organization.[92] Also, China's interest continues to lie in a stronger, as opposed to weaker, ASEAN.

Most importantly, in the short to medium term, China's main preoccupation will be domestic, which means good relations with everyone — ASEAN, as well as Japan and the United States. As a senior Chinese foreign ministry official has observed, "The next 20 years are critical to China. We will either take off or run into bottlenecks. We will be dealing with the most fundamental reforms. So we need this period of stability and regional prosperity very badly."[93]

As discussed above, China does not wish to feed American or regional impressions of a China that is bent on regional hegemony. Again, China's primary and overriding goals have to do with consolidating its economic growth and ensuring political stability, both of which require peaceful relations with all countries and especially a stable regional neighborhood. The current objective of Chinese leaders is less to dominate than it is to persuade ASEAN (and also the United States) that there is little to fear from Chinese power and that China can play the role of a responsible leader. Thus, as Thai journalist Kavi Chongkittavorn has observed, "China has been very concerned to tread fairly softly as its power grows."[94]

---

[92] Lyall Brackon, "China-Southeast Asia Relations," *Comparative Connections* 5, no. 4 (2003), http://www.csis.org/pacfor/cc/0304Qchina_asean.html.

[93] John Pomfret, "China Embraces More Moderate Foreign Policy," *Washington Post*, October 24, 2002, A23.

[94] Vatikiotis, "Catching the Dragon's Tail."

Finally, what is the significance of the ACFTA for an East Asian group? In light of ASEAN's concerns about being dominated by any one power, it seems likely that the ACFTA will be supplemented by separate ASEAN and China FTAs with Japan and Korea, if not eventually subsumed under an East Asian free trade area agreement. An East Asian FTA, however, is likely to remain a long-term goal, as it is unclear that all thirteen East Asian states are in agreement about its desirability.[95] While there appears to be a general consensus about the value of an East Asian grouping in the long term, a number of voices have expressed the view that East Asia is not yet ready for an East Asian free trade arrangement. Singapore's trade minister, for example, has stated a preference for ASEAN to maintain separate trade talks with the three Northeast Asian economies.[96] In its November 2002 report, the East Asian Study Group continued to support its previous recommendation that East Asian states consider the formation of an East Asian FTA but now considered its establishment a "long term goal, taking into account the variety of differences in developmental stages and the varied interests of the countries in the region."[97] Even former Malaysian Prime Minister Mahathir, the strongest proponent of an East Asian Economic Group, went on record against an East Asian FTA for the foreseeable future. He forewarned, "In the case of East Asia, we will proceed very, very cautiously."[98]

---

[95] See, for example, comments of former Malaysian Prime Minister Mahathir. "Malaysian Premier in Berlin Says East Asia Not Ready for Free Trade Zone," *Bernama*, reported by BBC Worldwide Monitoring, March 20, 2002.

[96] Tay Eng How, "ASEAN May Become an East Asian Grouping," *Straits Times*, October 12, 2002, *Lexis-Nexis Academic: World News*, online, August 1, 2004.

[97] Takehiko Kajita, "Study Group to Propose Stepped-Up Cooperation in East Asia," *Japan Economic Newswire*, October 13, 2002.

[98] "Malaysian Premier in Berlin Says East Asia Not Ready for Free Trade Zone."

Chapter 12

New Leadership Team, New Approaches toward Taiwan?

Chih-cheng Lo

When commenting on the then upcoming Sixteenth Communist Party Congress during his May 2002 visit to the frontline island of Tatan, Taiwan's President Chen said that, "If China's new leader is pragmatic enough to open a dialogue with Taiwan, Taipei stands ready to talk." How realistic was President Chen's expectation? That is, how will China's Taiwan policy under its fourth-generation leaders differ (if at all) from the approach laid out by their predecessors? What factors came into play in determining the trajectory of future cross-Strait relations after the new leaders took over? When Chen Shui-bian came into power in 2000, despite heavy-handed Chinese efforts to discourage such an outcome, China decided to adopt a "wait and see" attitude.[1] It is now Taiwan's turn to "listen to their

---

[1] See Willy Wo-Lap Lam, "Will Cross-Strait Tensions Ease?" *China Brief* 2, no. 3, Jamestown Foundation, Washington, D.C., January 31, 2002, http://china.jamestown.org/pubs/view/cwe_002_003_001.htm.

words and watch their deeds" as China's fourth generation of leaders attempts to further consolidate its control of power.

The reason why the international community, especially Taiwan, attaches great importance to the generational change in the Chinese Communist Party (CCP) is that China is still an authoritarian society, characterized by the rule of man and not by the rule of law. The forecasting of the much-anticipated Sixteenth Party Congress was marked by mixed anticipations. It was said that President Jiang Zemin would have difficulty preserving his legacy after he retired. Therefore, there were hopes that this leadership change could lead to more pragmatic and creative thinking on the side of the Chinese mainland with regard to the so-called Taiwan issue. Meanwhile, there were also pessimistic views that one should not expect any great changes to take place during the period of succession and consolidation of power.

In light of the fact that China was facing yet another crucial moment and that China attached great importance to ensuring stability as its priority goal, one could expect more continuity than change in China's policy toward Taiwan. Against the backdrop of the evolution of China's Taiwan policy during the 1990s, this chapter examines the problems that the new leadership will face in the years ahead and explains the reason why Taiwan is not a primary concern for Beijing now. The decision-making and policy-formulation processes within the Chinese political system are investigated to elucidate the rationale for the continuation of Beijing's policy during the leadership of Jiang Zemin toward Taiwan. It is contended that, given recent and possible future developments in domestic, cross-Strait, and international environments, the power transfer is unlikely to trigger drastic changes in Beijing's policy toward Taiwan. In other words, Chinese leaders are likely to continue to be preoccupied with their own domestic problems, thereby downgrading the urgency and priority of the Taiwan question. Although the major pillars to Beijing's Taiwan policy likely will remain largely unchanged, it is evident that Beijing has become more skilful and sophisticated in utilizing and modifying its tactics in dealing with Taiwan.

NEW LEADERS FACING OLD AND NEW PROBLEMS

To be sure, the new Beijing leadership must deal with a great number of daunting economic and sociopolitical challenges: economic disparity, the problems resulting from China's accession to the WTO, a rising unemployment rate, rampant official corruption, the restructuring of state-owned enterprises, bad loans, and increased demand for political reform. None of these problems, which could seriously threaten the stability and the very survival of the communist regime, has an easy solution. More importantly, all of these issues were impossible for a new successor to confront independently before consolidating his power. Thus, during the transition period, a collective leadership among the fourth-generation leaders and the continuing but declining influence of the third-generation leaders was expected. Since the successors must concentrate on how to develop China's economy while maintaining its social and political stability, one can speculate that they do not want to be distracted from these priority concerns. Moreover, continued preparations for hosting the 2008 Olympics create a constraining effect on Beijing. For now, it appears that the new leaders are taking a "risk-adverse" attitude toward Taiwan. And from this perspective, it will be unlikely that Taiwan will soon be on the top of the new leaders' agenda, and the probability is that the policy existing under Jiang Zemin will be maintained in the near future.

Of the greatest importance for the new leadership is sustaining China's economic progress and dealing with problems resulting from reform. More importantly, accession to the World Trade Organization has accelerated the momentous socioeconomic changes previously set in motion. Many Chinese express doubt that they will be able to cope with the multiple challenges ahead. For instance, the problem of bad loans has increasingly become a critical issue for the state-owned banks. So, cleaning up the banking system has emerged as an urgent concern for China. A related problem is the reform of the state-owned enterprises (SOEs), many of which must borrow in order to continue operating; indeed, these large and inefficient companies have become a major cause of the state's ongoing budget deficits. Without privatizing SOEs, China will face continuing and even worsening problems of corruption. However, across-the-board privatization and downsizing would undermine the last vestiges of party power and could exacerbate the unemployment problem.

Another serious problem that the new leaders face is the rising inequality among the people of China and increasing dissatisfaction with the status quo. The income gap between rural and urban households, as well as that between coastal and inland provinces, has become ever wider. The unemployment rate is estimated at 26 percent, including registered unemployed in the cities, laid-off workers, and surplus laborers in rural areas.

Moreover, in 2003 alone, over fifty thousand mass demonstrations, with a total of three million participants, were reported. The so-called "three agricultural problems" (*san nong*: agriculture, rural village, and farmers) have become the biggest headaches for leaders in Beijing. The deterioration of rural living standards has created negative spillover effects. To escape impoverishment in the countryside, tens of millions of people have immigrated to urban areas in search of work. This "floating population" has become a serious social and economic problem for China. These severe and growing disparities between the haves and have-nots have resulted in an endemic and accelerating pattern of urban and rural protest that the regime greatly fears. These socioeconomic problems in China are compounded by the gradually deteriorating public confidence caused by rampant corruption and inefficient bureaucracy.

The domestic tension created by China's strategy of "marketizing" its economy while preventing meaningful political change has become gradually evident and serious. While downplaying or even abandoning its communist ideology to validate its continued dominance, the party has no intention to relinquish or reduce its grip on political power. Jiang's notions of the "Three Represents" — that the party should represent advanced productive forces, advanced culture, and the fundamental interests of the broad masses of the people — exemplifies the CCP's effort to justify continued communist rule while embracing a market economy. Witnessing the growing need and demand for opening up the political system, the CCP tried to introduce a bottom-up political reform model of local elections in rural villages. Implementing direct democratic elections at the village level, however, has led to tension between village party branches and the popularly elected village committees. Consequently, this reform seems to have come to a standstill. Despite several years of calls for the upward expansion of village democracy, no significant breakthrough has been made thus far.

Apart from consolidating the long-awaited transfer of leadership power, another matter is whether the CCP's Sixteenth National Congress truly reinvigorated long-stagnant political reforms. There are pressures forcing the party to initiate a limited response to strong social and internal party needs for political reform, the core of which would be internal party democracy. Moreover, reform of the personnel system, streamlining the bloated government bureaucracy, is also badly needed in China. Ironically, local governments, at least, are larger than before. In short, the creation of a real market in China will require the full recognition of private property rights. However, without further constitutional and political reform that places rights to life, liberty, and property above the party and allows for both economic and political freedom, there can be no certainty of such ownership. The tension between the communist autocratic political system and the market capitalist economic system will continue and become even worse.

All these issues point to the conclusion that the new leadership in Beijing is busy with domestic problems for the near future. "Development must be at the service of stability," Jiang said repeatedly in internal sessions with senior cadres. Thus, the new Beijing leadership will devote much time to ensuring sociopolitical stability in the midst of drastic economic changes. Accordingly, to maintain a stable and favorable domestic and external environment conducive to economic development will continue to be the major task and priority for the fourth-generation successors. And due to their seemingly weak power basis, this generation of leaders may rely even more than their predecessors on power sharing and consensus building. Thus, the orientation of the new leaders' external policies, including foreign and cross-Strait policies, will likely be passive and reactive than proactive and innovative. A policy of *tao guang yang hui*, to hide one's real strength in order to buy time for one's own development, therefore likely is to be maintained.

Meanwhile, the strategy of "Great Power Diplomacy" — that China should play a role on the world stage commensurate with its growing economic and military strength and that China should carefully manage its relations with other great powers with which China's strategic interests converge — likely will continue to be upheld by the new leadership as the guiding principle for developing foreign relations. In addition, for the purpose of creating a friendly and peaceful neighboring environment favorable to China's economic modernization, a "good-neighbor policy" is apt to be maintained for the foreseeable future. Examples of Beijing's efforts to dampen the border disputes with land neighbors such as India, Vietnam, Russia, and Kazakhstan have been widely noted. The establishment in June 2001 of the Shanghai Cooperation Organization, which includes China, Russia, Kazakhstan, Tajikistan, Kyrgyzstan, and Uzbekistan, was also an indication of China's strategy of building closer ties with its neighbors. In addition, the Treaty of Good-Neighborliness and Friendly Cooperation, signed between China and Russia in July 2001, further demonstrated Beijing's primary concern. Beijing also displays its quest for stability and cooperation to its southern neighbors. Under the leadership of China, the Boao Forum was established in February 2002 with an aim to promote regional dialogue and cooperation. More importantly, the proposal for a 10+1 (ASEAN plus China) Free Trade Area reveals not only Beijing's economic strategy but also its political gestures.

In short, it is likely that China seeks more continuity than innovation in its external policies. More importantly, China's daunting domestic challenges undoubtedly continue to dominate the political agenda of the new leadership. In order to concentrate on its domestic problems, third-generation successors must sustain a peaceful and favorable external environment. Therefore, one can speculate that China's foreign policies will tend to be more reactive and, in some cases, conciliatory. When it comes to Beijing's Taiwan policy, it is also expected to demonstrate similar features.

THE TAIWAN POLICY OF CHINA'S THIRD-GENERATION LEADERSHIP

It has appeared that the overall process by which Taiwan policy is formulated and implemented has become highly regularized, bureaucratic, and consensus-oriented over time, reflecting the growing complexity of Taiwan policy, the changing nature of leadership authority in China, and the complexity of change on Taiwan. The rapid expansion of cross-Strait economic and cultural ties, the initiation of quasi-governmental bilateral negotiations, and the challenges to Beijing posed by Taiwan's democratic vitality, military capabilities, and diplomatic activities have all increased the number and breadth of responsibilities of various state and party agencies involved in Taiwan affairs.

Perhaps the most important transition in the PRC policy-making process regarding Taiwan during the past two decades took place in the early 1990s, with the departure from the political scene of Deng Xiaoping and his associates as well as the ascension of the so-called third generation of leaders led by Jiang Zemin. While the authority of the Mao- and Deng-generation of revolutionary leaders was derived primarily from their revolutionary credentials, individual prestige, and personal relations, the leadership group that replaced them consisted largely of more pragmatic, bureaucratically-trained technocrats whose authority depended primarily on policy successes, substantive policy expertise, organizational control, and the ability to persuade rather than dictate. This transition "reinforced the trend...toward a more extensive, bureaucratic, and consensus-oriented policy-making process...[which] supplanted the largely top-down, authoritarian, personalistic, and at times ideological pattern of decision-making of the Deng era."[2] Denny Roy made a similar observation:

> Deng's reforms have changed foreign policy-making from what was virtually a one-man dictatorship to a process with greater scope for haggling among

---

[2] Michael Swaine, "Chinese Decision-Making Regarding Taiwan, 1979–2000," in *The Making of Chinese Foreign and Security Policy in the Era of Reform,* ed. David Lampton (Stanford, CA: Stanford University Press, 2001), 308.

bureaucracies and groups representing special interests, although major decisions are still made by a handful of top leaders. Deng's restructuring efforts have also resulted in greater influence for state institutions and less for party institutions, shifting power from ideologues to technocrats.[3]

Indeed, while ideological divisions in the making of foreign policy within the Chinese government are less acute than in the past, bureaucratic politics remains significant for other reasons. As a result of Deng Xiaoping's measures to decentralize the PRC's political system, Jiang Zemin was unable to personally dominate the policy process the way his predecessors did. Furthermore, China's foreign relations have become pluralized because the PRC's linkages with the outside world have become so numerous that they are no longer manageable by a small group of high-ranking officials, let alone by a single paramount leader.[4] Consequently, the various bureaucracies with input into Chinese foreign policy-making have found opportunities to increase their influence, some of which will inevitably be directed toward the pursuit of relatively narrow organizational agendas. In Quansheng Zhao's formulation, the foreign policy-making process has shifted from "vertical authoritarianism," characterized by a dominant leader, a single chain of command, and a unified set of policies, to "horizontal authoritarianism," typified by multiple power centers representing a variety of interests. This has resulted in a less coherent set of policies.[5] Attention now turns from the broad observations made above to more specific aspects of the third-generation leaders' Taiwan policy.

On January 30, 1995, in an important speech entitled "Continue to Promote the Reunification of the Motherland," Jiang Zemin raised an eight-point proposal on the development of ties between the two sides of the Taiwan Strait. Based on the core principles laid out by

---

[3] Denny Roy, *China's Foreign Relations* (London: Macmillan Press, 1998), 64.
[4] Carol Lee Hamrin, "Elite Politics and the Development of China's Foreign Relations," in Thomas Robinson and David Shambaugh, *Chinese Foreign Policy: Theory and Practice* (Oxford: Clarendon Press, 1994), 70–109.
[5] Quansheng Zhao, *Interpreting Chinese Foreign Policy* (Hong Kong: Oxford University Press, 1996), 81.

Deng Xiaoping in the late 1970s and early 1980s, Jiang's "Eight Points" focused primarily on the modalities of cross-Strait discussions leading to reunification. The proposal listed various specific steps for action, such as the convening of a cross-Strait dialogue between equal representatives and an agreement to end hostilities. It also emphasized the need for a phased process of rapprochement and negotiations leading to reunification. Unlike the policy shift from fierce confrontation to the search for peaceful reunification during 1978 to 1982, which reflected Deng's desire to resolve the Taiwan issue swiftly, Jiang's "Eight Points" did not anticipate such speedy reunification. Rather, Jiang's proposal merely sought to forge an agreement on a transitional framework that would stabilize the status quo, facilitate economic exchanges, and generally preempt any permanent separation of Taiwan from the mainland.[6] This was borne out by the fact that Jiang's proposal placed more emphasis on concrete proposals which would lead to a stepped reapprochement between China and Taiwan preceding reunification (such as a cross-Strait summit and signed agreements to end the state of hostility). Moreover, the proposal suggested that, as long as Taiwan would negotiate under the principle that there was only one China and Taiwan was a part of China, Beijing would consider all of Taiwan's concerns.

Jiang's "Eight Points" were formulated in response to various new domestic and external developments confronting the Chinese leadership in the early 1990s. First and foremost, Chinese leaders feared that Lee Teng-hui's apparent efforts to legitimize a "one China, one Taiwan" arrangement could result in the permanent separation of the two. Second, China noticed and was perturbed by an apparent shift in the stance of the United States toward the island, exemplified by Washington's 1992 decision to sell F-16 aircraft to Taiwan and the almost unanimous resolution adopted by Congress demanding a visa for the unprecedented visit by Lee Teng-hui to the

---

[6] Yun-han Chu, "Making Sense of Beijing's Policy Toward Taiwan: The Prospect of Cross-Strait Relations During the Jiang Zemin Era," in *China under Jiang Zemin*, ed. Yun-han Chu and Hung-mao Tien (Boulder, CO: Lynne Rienner, 2000), 205.

United States. Third, the Chinese leadership succession process and, in particular, the rise of Jiang Zemin's influence provided various structural and personal opportunities for policy change. Jiang undoubtedly believed that a peaceful breakthrough on Taiwan would serve to confirm the continuity of his policies with those of Deng Xiaoping, boost his stature among the public, strengthen his position among his colleagues and rivals for power, and defuse concerns within the military over an increasingly independence-minded Taiwan.[7]

The actual procedure involved in formulating the "Eight Points" reflected the above-mentioned extensive process of bureaucratic consultation and consensus building in foreign policy formulation that had emerged in the late 1980s and early 1990s. All members of the new Taiwan Affairs Leading Small Group (TALSG), including the military, were reportedly involved in the formulation process, with each member providing conceptual input and recommendations generated by his bureaucratic system. The actual writing group consisted of Taiwan experts from all the major civilian and military research institutes, whereas the leading role was reportedly played by the Chinese Communist Taiwan Affairs Office/State Council Taiwan Affairs Office (CCTAO-SCTAO), and their heads, Wang Zhaoguo and Wang Daohan, respectively. A draft was circulated to all TALSG members and then to Politburo members for comment. A final draft was produced by October 1994. The draft was then reviewed by the Central Committee General Office (CCGO) Policy Research Office and given final approval by the Politburo Standing Committee (PBSC) soon thereafter. In short, Beijing's Taiwan policy under the third-generation leadership was a product of a factional and bureaucratic consultation and consensus-building process.

Incorporating various agencies' and actors' concerns and policies was also reflected in Beijing's multipronged strategy toward Taiwan. Some observers suggest that the multifaceted strategy used during the 1995–1996 Taiwan Strait crisis was a consequence of the

---

[7] Ibid., 200. Chu states that "formulating a new policy guideline on the Taiwan issue was a strong political statement about the coming of Jiang's era."

rise of a hard-line faction of military leaders and Jiang's opponents within the party who were committed to a more coercive stance toward Taiwan. According to this interpretation, Taiwan's bold actions in April and May 1995 permitted these hard-line forces to wrest control of Taiwan policy from Jiang, who was thus forced to accept the decisions proposed by the hardliners. However, Michael Swaine emphasized that such an interpretation was misconceived, noting that the military seldom dictated Chinese policy in any area, nor did it directly present formal policy recommendations on any issue, including Taiwan. Although the People's Liberation Army (PLA) research and intelligence organs often submitted reports to the Central Military Commission (CMC), such documents did not constitute the position or assessment of the military. On the contrary, the military leadership issued a report on a sensitive issue only if Jiang Zemin requested it. However, Swaine also emphasized the differences between the decision-making processes during crisis and noncrisis periods. During the crisis of the mid-1990s, a larger number of senior party and military leaders became involved in formulating and implementing Taiwan policy than under more routine circumstances. Specifically, key decisions were made during the crisis by the PBSC, in particular, Jiang Zemin, Li Peng, and Liu Huaqing, and not by the TALSG. As a result,

> Some elements of the four-point strategy were doubtless a product of compromises between moderates on Taiwan policy generally within the MFA (Ministry of Foreign Affairs) and the CCTAO-SCTAO and hard-liners (generally within the military). Nevertheless, the decisions arrived at during this crisis period were by and large the consequence of a collaborative policy-making process led by Jiang and not the outcome of a factional struggle.[8]

Still, many Taiwan observers believed that Beijing's strategy of comprising incentives and threats reflected an ongoing internal power struggle between hardliners and moderates in the Chinese leadership. A common interpretation of Chinese foreign policy in the second half of the 1990s went as follows: The military and conservatives in the

---

[8] Swaine, "Chinese Decision-Making Regarding Taiwan, 1979–2000," 322.

party retained a dominant role in the Taiwan policy-making process for many months following the crisis in the mid-1990s, eclipsing Jiang and his moderate supporters within the CCTAO and the Wang Daohan-led Shanghai expert community. It was only in the fall of 1997, after Jiang consolidated his control of the party apparatus and laid the groundwork for the retirement of the two most powerful figures in the PLA (Liu Huaqing and Zhang Zhen), that he was able to regain control of Taiwan policy and resurrect his peace overture. However, following Lee Teng-hui's provocative July 9, 1999 statement that relations between Taiwan and the PRC were relations between two states, and the general downturn in Sino-American relations that had occurred in late 1998 and 1999, hardliners were again able to gain the upper hand.

Such an interpretation, however, distorts an important feature of the Taiwan policy process and leadership relations on this matter.[9] The Chinese leadership as a whole was in agreement on the basic assumptions underlying Taiwan policy. Although political and bureaucratic interests served as a basis for debate in a consensus-oriented policy process, such differences largely arose over timing and emphasis, not fundamental direction. Moreover, Jiang Zemin was able to decisively influence, if not control, the overarching strategy toward Taiwan. At the same time, he could not simply dictate any particular policy course to the senior leadership. He had to "balance the interests and preferences of the major leaders and organizations involved in Taiwan security issues, in particular, those of the People's Liberation Army, on the one hand, and the Foreign Ministry and other civilian officials, on the other."[10] Military leaders at times apparently expressed criticism of what they viewed as overly conciliatory approaches adopted by the Foreign Ministry. Yet the standing PLA leadership did not formally develop and present "positions" on overall grand strategy toward Taiwan. Moreover, as head of the party's Central Military Commission, Jiang served as the primary

---

[9] Ibid., 331.
[10] Michael Swaine and James Mulvenon, *Taiwan's Foreign and Defense Policies: Features and Determinants* (Santa Monica, CA : Rand, 2001), 103.

channel for the expression of the military's views to the senior party and state leadership.

The serious confrontation with Washington that resulted from Beijing's military displays in 1995 and 1996 served to exacerbate the natural contrast in policy preferences between the PLA and the Foreign Ministry. Following the crisis, Foreign Ministry and other civilian entities reportedly stressed the feasibility of containing Taiwan and moving toward attainment of Jiang's "Eight Points" through political and diplomatic means, particularly the improvement of relations with the United States. While in agreement on the ultimate objectives, the military and some hardliners within the party stressed the need to continue developing China's military capabilities vis-à-vis Taiwan.[11] However, these were not mutually-exclusive views, and the above strategy clearly reflected elements of both sets of preferences. In other words, the Chinese military did not dictate Beijing's policy regarding Taiwan, even though military leaders generally had been very attentive to Taiwan policy because of their obvious institutional responsibilities. This attentiveness only increased in the 1990s, as a result of the growing capabilities and pro-independence orientation of the Taiwan leadership.[12]

The apparent revitalization of Jiang's "Eight Points" in the latter half of 1997 (albeit alongside more coercive elements) occurred not because moderates had regained control of the policy-making process, but because significant progress had been made and other events had taken place that permitted a renewed focus on the peace initiative. Three developments were of particular importance: the improvement of Sino-American ties by mid-1997, following Clinton's public affirmation of the "three no's"; the successful reversion of

---

[11] Ibid.

[12] In general, the PLA's most active role in the policy process was limited to (1) providing intelligence and assessments on the domestic situation in Taiwan, the United States–Taiwan and United States–Japan–Taiwan security relationships, and the military balance across the Strait; (2) pressing for support from the civilian leadership for the acquisition of weapons and equipment to more effectively deal with Taiwan-related security contingencies; and (3) applying various types of military pressure on Taiwan.

Hong Kong to Chinese rule, which suggested that Beijing could implement a "one country, two systems" formula without jeopardizing the peace, stability, and economic growth of the formerly separate entity; and the fact that Jiang finally managed to consolidate his control of the party leadership at the Fifteenth Party Congress in the fall of 1997 and his control of the Foreign Affairs Leading Small Group (FALSG) soon thereafter. He was also able to place several of his supporters in the Politburo and in its Standing Committee. This added strength undoubtedly gave Jiang greater confidence in pressing forward with a revitalized peace initiative.

The basic strategy adopted by Beijing described above remained in place under Jiang's leadership. The election of the Democratic Progressive Party's (DPP's) candidate, Chen Shui-bian, to the presidency of the Republic of China (ROC) in March 2000 did not dramatically alter Beijing's strategy, although it produced some tactical modifications and certain new emphases. Beijing was initially very alarmed by Chen's election and sought — both before and immediately after the event — to intimidate Taiwan's citizens and the new ROC government by drawing attention to the grave dangers to cross-Strait peace presented by the DPP's rise to power, and by demanding that the Chen government explicitly renounce its pro-independence platform.

However, China soon adopted a more sophisticated approach with a number of new emphases. First, Beijing increasingly sought to use a "united front" tactic in an attempt to divide Taiwan.[13] By improving ties with a wide range of Taiwan's politicians, businesspersons, and cultural figures and encouraging them to make statements supportive of the "one China" concept, the opening of a political dialogue with Beijing, and other seemingly moderate, anti-DPP positions, it hoped to isolate and presumably weaken support among Taiwan's public for the Chen Shui-bian government. This campaign arguably was strengthened by the continued decline of

---

[13] See, for example, "Ruan Says Beijing Will Continue to 'Divide and Rule,'" *Taipei Times Online Edition*, April 20, 2002, www.taipeitimes.com/news/2002/04/20/story/0000132587.

Taiwan's economy and the accompanying increase in cross-Strait economic links that had occurred in recent years. These developments contributed to an increase in public and business support for greater cooperation with the mainland, as well as an apparent increase in popular support for eventual unification.

Apart from this "united front" strategy, Beijing went even further than during the period of 1997–2000 to present a stance of moderation and flexibility regarding cross-Strait dialogue. Although Chinese officials continued to insist that the Chen government must explicitly affirm its commitment to the notion of "one China" before any official talks could begin (or before the "three links" could be established), they also gave more explicit indications that they did not equate a future "one China" with the government of the People's Republic of China and that they were willing to consider a range of formulas for future reunification. In particular, Chinese officials indicated their willingness to accept the 1992 consensus reached between Taipei and Beijing, in which both sides affirmed the notion of "one China," but reserved their own interpretation of what the concept meant.

Beijing apparently calculated that the Chen administration could be pressured by domestic political opposition, a divided and seemingly paralyzed central government, domestic economic problems, and a more moderate PRC approach to cross-Strait relations to affirm some version of a "one China" concept. Failing that, the PRC leadership apparently believed that Chen would prove unable to govern effectively through his term of office and likely would be replaced by a more flexible government, led perhaps by a Kuomintang (KMT) leader less associated with the more objectionable policies of the Lee Teng-hui government, by James Soong, the leader of the People First Party, or by some type of "moderate" coalition of parties.

In its Annual Report on the Military Power of the PRC made public in July 2002, the Pentagon expressed concern over a disturbing emphasis on military modernization within the Chinese army, which cast a cloud over China's declared preference for resolving differences with Taiwan through peaceful means, especially since "preparing for a potential conflict in the 100-mile wide Taiwan Strait [was] the 'primary driver' for China's accelerating military modernisation."[14] Although constantly professing a preference for resolving the Taiwan issue peacefully, Beijing made clear its interest in seeking credible military options for use of force against potential targets such as Taiwan and to complicate foreign intervention (especially from the United States) in any Taiwan Strait conflict. The Pentagon's first-order concerns included China's buildup of short-range ballistic missiles within range of Taiwan (China is adding missiles at a rate of nearly fifty per year), as well as a recent deal to purchase Russian-made submarines which could be used to cut off Taiwan's sea lanes, limiting what U.S. forces could do to aid Taiwan.

This military buildup might have been a calculated reaction to what Beijing perceived as political trends leading in the direction of Taiwan's independence. The increase in strength of Chen's Democratic Progressive Party following the December 2001 local and parliamentary election, coupled with the prospect of a 2004 reelection of Chen, strengthened the position of hardliners on the mainland who favored a more aggressive policy toward Taiwan during the final days of the third-generation leadership. Also, as the Pentagon Report observed, "The PLA is continuing to develop military capabilities that could expand its options for an armed conflict against Taiwan."[15]

Although it is natural to express concern about China's military buildup, one should not overlook the many areas in which China's military is encountering problems in its modernization. For example, it has had difficulties integrating its air, naval, and land forces in ways that would enable China to conduct sustained, joint-service operations offshore. Second, China still lacks the planes and ships

---

[14] *Annual Report on the Military Power of the People's Republic of China, Report to Congress Pursuant to the Fiscal Year 2000 National Defense Authorization Act,* July 2002, www.defenselink.mil/news/Jul2002/d20020712china.pdf.
[15] Ibid., 47.

needed for a successful amphibious invasion.[16] Besides considering its military capabilities relative to Taiwan, Beijing also has to ascertain the PLA's capability to deter or deny any external intervention on Taiwan's behalf. This is not to mention the potential political and economic costs in terms of China's regional and global interests if it were to wage war against Taiwan. This chapter agrees with former Secretary of State Colin Powell, who said in 2002 that he saw little cause for concern about China's military modernization as long as it did not "reflect any kind of new strategic purpose."[17] In congressional testimony in March 2002, the director of the Defense Intelligence Agency, Admiral Thomas Wilson, said it was doubtful that China would attempt a large-scale attack on Taiwan unless Taipei moved more directly toward independence.[18]

In sum, the critical importance of Taiwan to supreme leadership authority, the changed nature of that authority (i.e., less charismatic, less personal, and more dependent on success of policy), and the overall trend toward the institutionalization of authority led Jiang to center decision-making on Taiwan in a restructured, more powerful TALSG. Under Jiang, the TALSG became a smaller, more efficient policy-making mechanism, including representatives of only the most critical bureaucratic systems involved in Taiwan policy and figures, such as Qian Qichen and Xiong Guangkai, with close ties to core party and military power holders. Although a deliberative PSBC became the ultimate decision-making authority over Taiwan strategy in the post-Deng era, Jiang was able to utilize his chairmanship of the restructured TALSG, as well as his formal and informal interactions with key party and military leaders on the PBSC and CMC, to ensure his control of Taiwan policy. This was most clearly shown in the formulation of the "Eight Points" and the renewed peace overture of 1996–1997.

---

[16] See, for example, the *Annual Report on the Military Power of the PRC*, 49.
[17] "US Eyes Chinese Military Buildup," *MSNBC Online*, Washington D.C., July 12, 2002, http://stacks.msnbc.com/news/779440.asp?cp1=1.
[18] Ibid.

As discussed above, although political and bureaucratic interests served as a basis for debate in a consensus-oriented policy-making process, the Chinese leadership as a whole was in agreement on the basic principles underlying the PRC's Taiwan policy. Indeed, certain core strands of Beijing's foreign policy were constants, having been determined by CCP ideology and historical factors. These included Beijing's longstanding goal of eventual reunification with Taiwan. Although disagreement occurred occasionally, it usually arose over timing and emphasis, not fundamental direction. Debate usually surrounded the means (for example, should there be more focus on "carrots" or on "sticks") rather than ends. As such, efforts to explain the evolution of China's grand strategy toward Taiwan purely in terms of struggles between sharply opposed personal or bureaucratic factions during the leadership of Jiang Zemin "greatly exaggerate the level of contention, overlook the basic consensus among Chinese elites on grand strategy toward Taiwan, and neglect the preponderant influence exerted by Jiang Zemin after 1994."[19] The question now is whether the leadership succession in the PRC following the Sixteenth Party Congress is having or will have a major impact on Beijing's policy toward Taiwan.

NEW LEADERSHIP, NEW OPPORTUNITIES

One must bear in mind that, although Hu Jintao has managed to successfully assume all three key posts within the Chinese leadership — general secretary of the CCP, president of the PRC, and chairman of the CMC — he by no means is the sole actor in Beijing's decision-making process. Collectively, the fourth generation of leaders appears to be less dogmatic and more pragmatic compared to other political elite generations in PRC history. China-watchers agree that the fourth generation of leaders "will jettison ideology for pragmatism, the occasional rhetorical blast notwithstanding."[20] Mostly in

---

[19] Swaine, "Chinese Decision-Making Regarding Taiwan, 1979–2000," 334.
[20] Dexter Roberts and Mark Clifford, "China's Power Shift," *BusinessWeek Online*, February 25, 2002, www.businessweek.com/magazine/content/02_08/b3771018.htm.

their fifties and sixties, they were born too late to have taken part in the communist revolution that helped set the rigid views of their predecessors. Rather, this generation came of age during the chaos of such destructive political campaigns as the Great Leap Forward and the Cultural Revolution. Thus, they may tend to distrust dogma, adopting instead a more moderate stance on issues which does not incite uneasiness within more radical camps: "Political survivors, they know how to keep their heads down and their mouths shut."[21] Wen Jiabao serves as an example. In 1989, he was close to reformist Premier Zhao Ziyang and followed him to meet protesting students in Tiananmen Square. When Zhao was later ousted for being overly sympathetic to the protestors, Wen managed to survive. Wu Guoguang, who once worked with Wen, remembers his former colleague as "a master of handling sensitive issues. His relations with everyone are good."[22]

Given the daunting challenges they face, it is fortunate that the fourth generation is one of the best-educated groups of leaders in modern Chinese history. Unlike their predecessors, many of whom were force-fed a narrow Soviet curriculum, Hu and his contemporaries are receptive to a variety of ideas. For example, during a trip to Europe in 2001, Hu apparently displayed an unusual willingness to listen to his aides. "It was completely different from how Jiang or Zhu deals with their staff," remarked a Western diplomat.[23] On the same trip, Hu demonstrated a keen interest in world affairs and was especially well-versed in Britain's response to economic challenges over the years.

In terms of broad foreign policy, China's fourth-generation leaders will most likely perpetuate the policy of gradually extending Beijing's influence over the rest of Asia. At the same time, they are expected to foster improved relations with the United States. China's new technocrats understand how much China relies on the United States for everything from technology and investment to education

---

[21] Ibid.
[22] Ibid.
[23] Ibid.

visas for the country's many overseas students. As for Beijing's Taiwan policy, the fourth generation may be more flexible in tactics. Before the political transition, there were indications that Beijing might potentially relax some of its positions. When former Vice Premier Qian Qichen gave a speech in October 2002 that appeared to offer a much more conciliatory approach toward Taiwan, both Hu and Zeng were present, a fact featured prominently in news reports.[24]

However, China's new leaders remain only minimally tested in the tumultuous arena of leadership. They have spent most of their careers serving leaders, not serving as leaders with real power. The ability to offend no one may be a prerequisite to rising to China's political peak, but the very caution that helped presumptive heirs Hu and Wen on the way up may turn out to be a handicap in their positions at the helm. A danger exists that these leaders will be reactive and unable to level-headedly deal with the key issues they will encounter.[25]

Also, despite their tendency to be more pragmatic than their predecessors, it is crucial to keep in mind that the fourth generation is just as capable of ruthless behavior as its predecessors. Shandong native, Luo Gan, is held responsible by groups such as Human Rights Watch for widespread abuses, including the vicious crackdown on the Falun Gong spiritual group; and, in the 2001 Strike Hard campaign against crime, Luo oversaw thousands of executions. Hu Jintao himself has shown willingness to adopt a hard-line stance when Beijing's ultimate authority is challenged. In early 1989, during his four-year tour as party secretary in Tibet, Hu responded to protests calling for Tibetan independence by instituting martial law. Scores of Tibetan demonstrators were shot and killed. Granted, some have questioned if Hu should take the blame for these human rights violations. He was a newly-appointed party secretary, the first civilian appointee to hold the leadership post in Tibet, and may have had little choice, being surrounded by "grizzled veterans of the

---

[24] See, for example, "胡锦涛已逐步掌控对台政策" [Hu Jintao has controlled China's Taiwan policy gradually], *Gongshang Times*, February 4, 2002.
[25] "China's Emerging Leaders," editorial, *BusinessWeek Online*, February 25, 2002, www.businessweek.com:/print/magazine/content/02_08/b3771153.htm?mainwindow.

People's Liberation Army (PLA), who, no doubt, had their own ideas on how to handle the Tibetans."[26]

As discussed in the previous section, the new leaders in Beijing undoubtedly will be preoccupied with daunting domestic problems and unwilling to see a tense cross-Strait situation, which would distract them from their domestic agenda. Moreover, Beijing appears to believe that its current policy of carrot-and-stick has begun to bear some fruit and that time is on China's side. It, therefore, may view Taiwan as the least of Beijing's problems. Apparently, unless the new leaders are confident that they can advance significant progress or even achieve a breakthrough in cross-Strait relations, the risk of getting involved in an initiative concerning Taiwan and then having it fail is far too great. It is unlikely that Hu will risk quick concessions to Taiwan while in a period of further consolidating his power. Accordingly, it is unlikely that the new Beijing leadership, whose power is still under development, will come up with any innovative policy toward Taiwan. In the near future, China probably will not change its bottom-line policy toward Taiwan.

More importantly, it still waits to be seen how much authority the fourth-generation leaders will actually wield, especially with regard to Taiwan. This very much depends on how significant a change might take place in the personnel who handle Taiwan affairs. Some third-generation Chinese leaders could maintain the lead in Taiwan affairs long after their formal handover of power to the fourth-generation leaders. In any case, it is unlikely that Hu will modify China's Taiwan policy soon, and personnel familiar with cross-Strait affairs will most probably stay in their positions. Moreover, for the new leaders, consensus building and position compromising will be even more needed in the near future. It should be noted that it took Jiang almost six years (1989–1995) to come up with his "Eight Points." In short, "collective" decision-making is likely to be the case with regard to Beijing's Taiwan policy.

---

[26] John Tkacik, Joseph Fewsmith, and Maryanne Kivlehan, "Who's Hu?: Assessing China's Heir Apparent, Hu Jintao," *Heritage Lectures*, no. 739, Heritage Foundation, February 27, 2002, p. 12, www.heritage.org/library/lecture/lecture/hl739.html.

As mentioned above, Beijing's Taiwan policy has been remarkably consistent at the strategic level. Its basic tenets such as the "one China principle," "one country, two systems," "peaceful unification," and "no renunciation of the use of force against Taiwan" have remained unchanged for two decades. At the tactical level, however, Beijing has periodically adjusted its approaches. Again, with their preoccupation at home, the new leaders' policy toward Taiwan may remain more reactive than proactive. While upholding the above-mentioned principles, China will continue to use a combination of soft and hard policies — military intimidation, economic attraction, political division, and diplomatic strangulation. Moreover, regarding incentives to and pressures on Taiwan's authorities, Beijing will continue to employ a united-front method to create pressures from within and without. In short, among the new leaders, there will be a consistency in principles and elasticity in tactics in China's Taiwan policy. Early moves under the fourth generation, including the Anti-Succession Law, Hu's "four point" statement on Taiwan and the mainland visits of Taiwan opposition camp leaders Lien Chan and James Soong suggest continuity of Beijing's mixed tactics.

CONCLUSION

Hu and fellow fourth-generation cadres, now at the helm, must help China to confront formidable domestic and external challenges. On sensitive issues such as Taiwan, Hu will probably feel a need to show the world that he can stand up if he is to avoid an ugly confrontation with hardliners within and outside the PLA. Undoubtedly, Hu will undergo a tough test in the early years of his tenure. Many predicted that Jiang would hold on to his CMC chairmanship for at least a couple of years. While Jiang's remaining on the CMC meant that his generals were reined in for a while, his refusal to retire completely prevented Hu from wielding his full authority.[27]

---

[27] Willy Wo-lap Lam, "Hu's Visit: More Talk than Progress," *China Brief* 2, no. 10, Jamestown Foundation, Washington, D.C., May 9, 2002, http://china.jamestown.org/pubs/view/cwe_002_010_001.htm.

Although it appears likely that Jiang will continue to have some influence on Taiwan policy-making, any perception of Hu as merely a lightweight is misconceived. Even by January 2002, Hu had launched an informal task force on Sino-American relations, charged with developing long-term strategies toward the United States Congress, China's public relations image in the United States, and Taiwan.[28] Also, many saw Hu's attendance at Vice Premier Qian Qichen's January 24, 2002 speech on Taiwan policy as an indication that Hu had managed to insert himself into the domain of cross-Strait relations.[29]

In closing, fourth-generation leaders are more than likely to follow China's existing Taiwan policy fundamentals encapsulated in Jiang Zemin's "Eight Points" as a basis to make their own policy decisions. It goes without saying that the decisions they make will likely be colored by their own personality traits: their technocratic and reformist outlook, their upbringing during the Cultural Revolution, as well as their pragmatism. Therefore, the fourth-generation leaders probably will not trigger drastic changes in Beijing's policy toward Taiwan. It is reasonable to expect them to exercise much caution and self-restraint, being initially preoccupied with solving domestic problems and consolidating their authority base. How the next decade actually plays out will depend largely on the ability of Hu and his administration to channel the forces unleashed in recent years by economic and political liberalization. Meanwhile, if there is no change in the position of either side of the Taiwan Strait, there will continue to be a political stalemate in relations between Taipei and Beijing. However, cross-Strait economic exchanges and social interactions are growing and expanding rapidly. This could have some effects on either side's policy toward the other. In addition, the increasing military power of the PRC,

---

[28] Miao-Jung Lin, "China's Top Brass Decided on Next Leader, MAC Says," *Taipei Times*, January 21, 2002, www.taipeitimes.com/news/2002/01/21/story/0000120829.

[29] For example, see Zhu Jianling, "胡锦涛逐步介入对台政策" [Hu Jintao gradually moves into Taiwan policy decisions], *China Times*, January 25, 2002.

especially the ever-growing number of missiles deployed along the coast of the Taiwan Strait, could tempt Beijing to adopt a military option to solve the so-called "Taiwan question." In sum, a mixture of optimism and pessimism is warranted regarding the development of cross-Strait relations in the first decade of fourth-generation leadership in the PRC.

Chapter 13

China's Relations with the United States and Japan: Status and Outlook

Robert Sutter

As the People's Republic of China (PRC) entered the new millennium, its relations with the two international powers most important to China's development, the United States and Japan, were troubled. Chinese relations with the United States had zigged and zagged throughout the previous decade as American and Chinese leaders searched seemingly in vain for a suitable equilibrium that would allow relations to develop common ground without major disruption from a wide range of security, economic, and political differences. PRC relations with Japan, the most important ally of the United States in Asia, seemed to be steadily eroding. Pro-China popular sentiment and pro-China political forces in Japan were in decline, adding to strategic, territorial, historical, and other reasons

---

Note: This chapter is a revision of Robert Sutter's paper for the 20th International Conference on Asian Studies, St. John's University, Jamaica, New York, November 16, 2002. The author is grateful to George Chen, T.J. Cheng, Jacques deLisle, and other conference participants for their constructive comments and suggestions.

why future relations appeared more likely to be competitive than cooperative.

The coming to power of the George W. Bush administration in January 2001 shifted American policy toward China and Japan. Striving to solidify the United States-Japan alliance, while treating China with less positive regard than the outgoing Clinton administration, the Bush approach prompted a string of warnings from specialists about increased chances for crisis in United States-China relations, with attendant tensions in China's relations with Japan and elsewhere in the East Asian region.[1] Contrary to those expectations, the Chinese response to the Bush administration policy saw PRC leaders employ pragmatic and moderate measures, seeking to broaden common ground and mute differences with the United States, Japan, and their associates. This opened the way to a marked overall improvement in China's relations with both Washington and Tokyo.[2]

Part of the reason for the shift to greater moderation in China's policy toward the United States and Japan was Chinese leaders' preoccupation with the major leadership transition taking place during the Sixteenth Chinese Communist Party (CCP) Congress in November 2002, and the Tenth National People's Congress (NPC) in March 2003. Seeking to avoid international difficulties as they dealt with sensitive power arrangements among Chinese party, government, and military leaders, outgoing party leader Jiang Zemin and his colleagues maintained a low profile on foreign policy differences and sought

---

[1] Michael Swaine, "Bush Has a Tiger by the Tail with His China Policy," *Los Angeles Times*, Internet edition, June 17, 2002, and Elizabeth Economy, "Take a New Look at a Changing China," *International Herald Tribune*, Internet edition, April 30, 2002. These views also are reviewed in, among other works, Michael Swaine and Minxin Pei, "Rebalancing US-China Relations," *Policy Brief 13*, Carnegie Endowment, Washington, D.C., February 2002; Richard Holbrooke, "A Defining Moment with China," *Washington Post*, Internet edition, January 2, 2002; and David M. Lampton, "Small Mercies: China and America after 9/11," Press Release, Nixon Center, Washington, D.C., January 14, 2002.

[2] John Pomfret, "China Embraces More Moderate Foreign Policy," *Washington Post*, Internet edition, October 24, 2002.

where possible to broaden common ground with important powers such as the United States and Japan. The Chinese leadership transition carried out at the party and government meetings in 2002–2003 handed ostensible leadership power to the newly installed CCP General Secretary Hu Jintao, whose limited foreign policy experience suggested little likelihood of significant change in China's recent and comparatively moderate approach. Meanwhile, Jiang Zemin remained the most important leader in China for the foreseeable future, increasing the chances that his preferred policies toward Washington and Tokyo would be continued.

This chapter first focuses on a review of the evolution of China's approach to the United States, from troubled relations in 2001 to smooth relations in late 2002. It judges that the protracted Chinese leadership transition associated with the Sixteenth CCP Congress supported Chinese moves toward moderation in foreign relations, including ties with the United States and Japan. However, it gives particular stress to the importance of Bush administration policy as a key determinant of the smooth United States-China relationship. The Bush administration approach also is seen to have had an important spill-over effect on China's approach to Japan, the most important ally of the United States in Asia. As in the case of United States-China relations, Beijing shifted to a more moderate approach toward Japan in 2001–2002, although public attention to Chinese differences with Japan continued to some degree. The latter part of the chapter examines this shift toward moderation in recent China-Japan relations. The chapter concludes with a brief, generally optimistic assessment of the outlook for United States-China-Japan relations.

CHINA AND THE UNITED STATES

Troubled Relations, 2001

In 2001, frictions in United States-China relations were deeply rooted and many centered on key differences between the United States and China in Asian and world affairs that seemed likely to worsen given the rise of Chinese power and influence in the face of

American determination and power. The main focus was Taiwan, where PRC strategy in recent years rested on a major buildup of People's Liberation Army (PLA) forces designed to intimidate Taiwan and to deal with Taiwanese and American forces in the event of a military conflict over Taiwan. Leaders in the United States, especially in the new Bush administration, were blunt in warning Beijing of the consequences of military action against Taiwan, and they took a range of actions,[3] unprecedented since the break in official American relations with Taiwan in 1979, to underscore the support of the United States for Taiwan, especially military support.

Meanwhile, military officials and government strategists in the United States also carefully examined the possible broad security implications for the United States of a conflict with China over Taiwan, building American military power in the area and making preparations to counter other Chinese military options. From Beijing's perspective, the increased military preparations and greater support for Taiwan of the United States reinforced Taiwan's tendency to seek greater independence and separateness from mainland China. This was said to increase the danger that Chinese leaders might feel they had no choice other than to use force in order to deter Taiwan's independence and prevent a major failure in the core Chinese interest regarding the territorial integrity and reunification of China.[4]

Rising China also chafed in a regional and global order dominated by American power. China's approach to its neighbors and foreign affairs, in general, was defined and influenced by a mix of

---

[3] Denny Roy, "Tensions in the Taiwan Strait," *Survival* 42, no. 1 (Spring 2000): 76–96, and Bonnie Glaser, "Fleshing Out the Candid, Cooperative, and Constructive Relationship," *Comparative Connections*, CSIS, Pacific Forum [Honolulu] (April-July 2002), http://www/csis.org/pacfor.

[4] United States Department of Defense, *Annual Report on the Military Power of the People's Republic of China, 2002*, http://www.defenselink.mil; US-China Security Review Commission, *Report to Congress, July 2002*, http://www.uscc.gov/anrp02; and Keith Bradshaw, "China Vexed by Glare of US Investigations," *New York Times*, Internet edition, July 26, 2002.

Chinese leaders' strategic objectives and their assessment of power relations and other factors affecting those objectives. Although China's objectives were subject to considerable debate, a middle view summarized them as follows:[5]

- Chinese leaders sought to perpetuate their power.
- They pursued territorial unification, especially concerning Taiwan.
- They sought to modernize China's economy, technology, and military capabilities, and to improve social conditions, while maintaining stability.

In addition, China had strategic objectives that reflected its status as a rising power.

- Chinese leaders sought regional preeminence.

China wanted to be in a position of sufficient strength so that other countries in the region would routinely take China's interests and equities into account in determining their own policies. Beijing wished the PRC to be seen as the leading power in Asia and not as lower in prestige or regional influence than neighbors. It also wished to project power outward, sufficient to counter hostile naval and air power. Further,

- Chinese leaders wanted global influence.

China desired status and prestige among the community of nations. It intended to be a major player in the United Nations (UN),

---

[5] On Chinese leaders' goals, especially as they relate to Asian and world affairs, see among others, Denny Roy, *China's Foreign Relations* (Lanham, MD: Rowman and Littlefield, 1998); Samuel Kim, ed., *China and the World* (Boulder, CO: Westview Press, 1998); David M. Lampton, ed., *The Making of Chinese Foreign and Security Policy* (Stanford, CA: Stanford University Press, 2001); Steven Mosher, *Hegemon: China's Plan to Dominate Asia and the World* (New York: Encounter Books, 2000); and Michael Pillsbury, ed., *China Debates the Future Security Environment* (Washington, DC: National Defense University Press, 2000).

the International Monetary Fund (IMF), the World Bank, the World Trade Organization (WTO), and other key international institutions. It sought to assert its influence on all issues that it deemed important, not only to protect and defend its interests but also to bolster its standing as a major power. Chinese leaders believed that international power and prestige were an extension of national economic and technological prowess, which they intended to develop.

Chinese leaders tended to view China's influence as growing but far from dominant; external and internal factors limited China's assertiveness in world affairs.[6] Chinese perceptions of global trends appeared to be in flux and a matter of considerable internal debate. Chinese leaders and academics, as reflected in official comment, had believed the world was becoming multipolar, with the United States as the single superpower but increasingly less able to exert its will as other countries and regions opposed American initiatives. However, this view had changed sharply in recent years, owing to the striking disparities between the economic performance of the United States and that of other major powers, and also to American leadership in international crises and military campaigns. The Chinese apparently concluded that the world would be unipolar in the near term, with the United States exerting greater influence than Beijing had originally calculated. Chinese leaders often perceived that this influence might not be benign vis-à-vis China's core interests.[7]

Chinese commentary expressed particular concern about the expansion and strengthening of the American alliance structure and the ability of American-led alliances to intervene globally. Chinese officials believed that they must be on guard to counter actions by the United States or its expanded alliance structure that were detrimental to Chinese interests, notably the United States-Japan alliance

---

[6] Wu Xinbo, "Four Contradictions Constraining China's Foreign Policy Behavior," *Journal of Contemporary China* 10, no. 27 (May 2001): 293–302.

[7] Among the best observers of the ebb and flow of Chinese elite views of American power and prospects for a multipolar world, see the quarterly reviews of United States-China relations by Bonnie Glaser in *Comparative Connections,* http://www.csis.org/pacfor.

and implications regarding Taiwan.[8] Chinese officials also were concerned by the upswing in the strategic relations of the United States with Russia, India, and Central Asian countries — nations China had previously looked to as providing a buffer against pressure from the United States and its allies.

Preoccupied with domestic issues of modernization and stability, Beijing primarily was reactive to international developments. Deng Xiaoping had stated that China should not get out in front on key issues but should take advantage of opportunities, and his successors did not explicitly break with this view. However, recent behavior in Asia, in international forums such as the United Nations, World Trade Organization, Asia-Pacific Economic Cooperation (APEC), the ASEAN Regional Forum (ARF), and other arenas showed China increasingly trying to ensure that it was one of the rule-makers for the global environment of the twenty-first century. Beijing also perceived that it must continue to build its military capabilities to be able eventually to back up its diplomacy with the threat of force, especially over the status of Taiwan.[9]

Chinese statements averred that the overall external threat to China was significantly less than it was during the Cold War. Nevertheless, China perceived, or believed it must foster the impression, that internal threats to its stability were often encouraged from the outside. China was convinced that the United States, directly or indirectly, interfered with Beijing's ability to recover Taiwan and maintain control in Tibet and even Xinjiang.[10]

China saw the United States as a competitor, adversary, and partner. Efforts to improve relations with the Bush administration moved in tandem with resistance to the "hegemony" and "power politics" of

---

[8] David Shambaugh, "China's Military Views the World," *International Security* 24, no. 3 (Winter 1999–2000): 52–79, and Thomas Christensen, "China, the US–Japan Alliance, and the Security Dilemmas in East Asia," *International Security* 23, no. 4 (Spring 1999): 49–80.

[9] See among others, Denny Roy, *China's Foreign Relations* (Lanham, MD: Rowman and Littlefield, 1998).

[10] Robert Sutter, *Chinese Policy Priorities and Their Implications for the United States* (Lanham, MD: Rowman and Littlefield, 2000), 39–58.

the United States. State-fostered education in nationalism was accompanied by the growing perception among Chinese that the United States was behind many of China's problems. China perceived that such international organizations as the United Nations, the International Monetary Fund, World Bank, and World Trade Organization were becoming increasingly important to its interests of economic development and political stature but remained dominated by the United States and other Western powers. Japan, South Korea, and other regional players in Asia and Europe could hinder or help China achieve its goals and thus were important to China. Although China also wanted to bolster its status in the developing countries, it was clear-eyed about these countries' secondary relevance to its core interests, except when such issues as recognition of Taiwan and the security of Chinese borders were at issue.[11]

In addition to important differences between the United States and China over Taiwan and the balance of influence in regional and global affairs, another major area of friction in United States-China relations had to do with widespread American pressures to seek change in China's political system. In general, American administration officials eschewed public comment on this issue, although President Clinton and members of his administration were explicit at times in noting a desire to see the end of the authoritarian communist political system in favor of a more pluralistic and democratic one. Officials in Congress, the media, opinion leaders, and others in the United States were not so reticent in calling for change in China's political system. The Tiananmen crackdown of 1989 captured the attention of many Americans, emphasizing the brutality of the PRC regime. Many Americans had worked ever since, to effect political change in China, and broad segments of opinion in the United States supported their efforts.[12]

---

[11] Elizabeth Economy, "The Impact of International Regimes on Chinese Foreign Policy Making," in *The Making of Chinese Foreign and Security Policy*, ed. David M. Lampton (Stanford, CA: Stanford University Press, 2000), 123–150.

[12] Kerry Dumbaugh, "Interest Groups: Growing Influence," in *Making China Policy: Lessons from the Bush and Clinton Administrations*, ed. Ramon Myers, Michael Oksenberg, and David Shambaugh (Lanham, MD: Rowman and Littlefield, 2001), 113–148.

It is hard to exaggerate the impact these efforts had on Chinese leaders. Seeing their political system and power base under constant pressure and attack from various quarters in the United States, they were prone to see United States government motives in a negative light. Even during periods when government leaders in the United States stressed their strong interest in positive and mutually-beneficial engagement with China, Chinese leaders held the view that American policy invariably had ulterior motives. They tended to see the policy of the United States as having two hands: one was the hand of positive engagement, designed to build common ground and pursue relations of benefit to both countries; the other was the usually hidden hand of containment. In the latter case, the view was that American policy was designed to use engagement in ways that would pressure China to change and ultimately bring down the Chinese Communist Party's rule through an incremental process called "peaceful evolution."[13]

Meanwhile, concern in Washington that the Chinese government should conform to a broad range of security, economic, and political norms in accord with American interests had resulted in a wide range of often contentious issues between the two states. Apart from the salient issues noted above, these issues involved clusters of sensitive questions, ranging from Chinese government practices in Tibet and Xinjiang, Chinese human rights practices regarding political dissidents, religious movements, and the Falun Gong movement, to Draconian and abusive family planning practices, unfair trading practices, environmental issues, major security concerns regarding Chinese proliferation of weapons of mass destruction (WMD) and related technologies, and other issues. These concerns dominated the domestic debate in the United States over China policy that raged fairly steadily in the post-Cold War period, despite the general fall-off in American interest in foreign affairs and the neglect that seemed to characterize American relations with many other parts of

---

[13] Wang Jisi and Wang Yong, "A Chinese Account: The Interaction of Policies," in *Making China Policy*, ed. Myers, Oksenberg, and Shambaugh, 269–296, and Sutter, *Chinese Policy Priorities*, 39–40.

East Asia. The debate was widely reported by the American media, which tended to portray the Chinese government and its practices in a negative light, reinforcing already strong skepticism among the American public about the Chinese ruling authorities.[14]

For their part, PRC leaders, seeking to shore up their regime in response to the barrage of American charges and pressures, shifted the regime's still-effective educational and propaganda mechanisms in a more negative direction as far as the United States and its governmental policy were concerned. Exposed to an educational regimen and an official media constantly harping on American "aggression," "power politics," and "hegemonism," especially against China, the Chinese public and elite opinion moved in a decidedly negative direction regarding the United States and its government. Some Western observers saw this as a seedbed for future United States-China conflict.[15]

Bush Administration China Policy

Against the background of deeply rooted differences in United States-China relations, several American specialists were disappointed and dismayed by the toughening of Washington's stance toward China, evident in the first year of the Bush administration. A lack of "vision" produced "a China policy adrift," with no real progress on important issues with China and greater United States-China tensions over Taiwan.[16] Many specialists on Chinese affairs in the United States argued strongly that the Bush administration needed to change its policy in several ways in order to avoid damage to American interests as a result of growing differences and possible confrontation with Beijing, caused notably by the new

---

[14] Kerry Dumbaugh, *China–US Relations*, Issue Brief 98018 (Washington, DC: Library of Congress, Congressional Research Service, February 20, 2003), available via Representative Mark Green's Web site, http://www.house.gov/markgreen.

[15] US–China Security Review Commission, *Report to Congress, July 2001*, chapter 1.

[16] Elizabeth Economy, "Take a New Look at a Changing China," *International Herald Tribune*, Internet edition, April 30, 2002.

administration's tilt toward Taiwan. Some specialists urged that American policy more strictly abide by the three communiqués governing United States–China relations, curb recently expanded American military cooperation with Taiwan, resume active military and other strategic dialogue with the PRC, and seek closer interaction with China's leaders in order to develop a cooperative partnership with them that promoted common ground amid continuing differences. The alternative was seen as an unstable and dangerous United States–China relationship that would be prone to fall into confrontation and conflict for many years to come. Broad American goals of regional peace and development would be impossible to achieve under such circumstances, it was argued.[17]

A somewhat different perspective was offered by specialists who stressed that the antiterrorism campaign after September 11, 2001, added to pressures on the Bush administration to modify differences with China and to seek closer relations through high-level leadership contacts and other means with the Chinese administration.[18] Some in this group of specialists judged that, when a new administration takes power in the United States, it often positions its China policy in ways markedly different and often tougher than its predecessor. Over time, however, China's importance to the United States in various ways usually results in American policymakers' modifying their initially harder line and adopting a stance of overall engagement of China that has been followed to various degrees by all American administrations since the opening to China by President Richard Nixon over thirty years ago.

In contrast with those specialists concerned or even alarmed by the new administration's turn in the policy of the United States toward China, or with those who saw the United States making special efforts to resume engagement with China after an initial hard-line

---

[17] Among other sources, these views are reviewed in, Swaine and Pei, "Rebalancing US–China Relations"; Holbrooke, "A Defining Moment with China"; and David M. Lampton, "Small Mercies: China and America after 9/11."

[18] David Shambaugh, "From the White House, All Zigzags Lead to China," *Washington Post*, Internet edition, February 17, 2002.

period, was the view supported in this chapter that is impressed by the strong advantage and leverage of the United States over China in international power and influence and regarding important issues in United States-China relations. This view is relatively sanguine about the Bush administration's ability to manage this leverage in ways advantageous for long-term American interests, including peace and stability in East Asia.[19]

Proponents of this view tend to see that the experience of the past three decades of American policy in relations with the PRC shows that the leverage of the United States over China regarding American policy toward Taiwan and other issues has increased in the past when American leaders have felt confident in the international position of the United States and in their own domestic position. Strong and confident American leaders during the tenure of Secretary of State George Shultz in the Reagan administration in the mid-1980s were successful in muting Chinese pressure on Taiwan, and American policy toward the island proceeded without significant interruption, despite serious acrimony over the United States-China-Taiwan relationship in the preceding years. Washington's leverage over China appeared strong after the end of the Cold War and the collapse of the USSR undermined the perceived American strategic need for accommodation of Chinese interests over Taiwan and other issues. But Washington's leverage was poorly used as policy was subjected principally to the active domestic debate in the United States over American policy toward China.[20]

---

[19] Robert Sutter, *Grading Bush's China Policy*, PACNET 10, CSIS, Pacific Forum (Honolulu), March 8, 2002. See also, Robert Sutter, "The Bush Administration and US China Policy Debate," *Issues and Studies* 28, no. 2 (June 2002): 1–30.

[20] Among useful sources for coverage of these issues, see Ramon Myers, Michel Oksenberg, and David Shambaugh, eds., *Making China Policy: Lessons from the Bush and Clinton Administrations* (Lanham, MD: Rowman and Littlefield, 2001); David M. Lampton, *Same Bed-Different Dreams* (Berkeley: University of California, 2001); James Mann, *About Face* (New York: Knopf, 1998); Robert S. Ross, *Negotiating Cooperation* (Stanford, CA: Stanford University Press, 1995); and Robert Sutter, *US Policy Toward China* (Lanham, MD: Rowman and Littlefield, 1998).

The Clinton administration eventually came up with a more coherent "engagement" policy toward China in its second term, but lost leverage over China, especially regarding the Taiwan issue, partly because of its perceived need to avoid "swings" in the United States-China relationship over the Taiwan issue and to seek signs of progress in American engagement with China that required cooperation from leaders in Beijing. Not surprisingly, PRC bargainers insisted on concessions in areas of importance to them, notably American relations with Taiwan.[21]

The PRC's ability to bargain and exert pressure on Taiwan and other issues appeared much less with the Bush administration that seemed to seek little in the way of concessions from China and offered little in return. The administration appeared popular at home and powerful and influential in world affairs, with or without Chinese government support. Powers such as Russia and India joined with the European Union and Japan in endeavoring to work hard to join with the United States in key international efforts — notably the war against terrorism.

China continued on a recent trajectory as a rising power — with attendant economic growth, military modernization, and expanding political influence. Nevertheless, Chinese leaders were also preoccupied with difficult leadership succession issues associated with the Sixteenth CCP Congress, and protracted economic and social challenges to China's internal stability. Leaders in Beijing notably sought to preserve advantageous economic contacts in the United States and to avoid the broad and internally wrenching ramifications of any major change in China's policy toward the United States. Seeking an Olympic bid for 2008 and a smooth transition into the WTO added to reasons for moderation. Rapidly growing Taiwan-mainland economic interchange also caused Chinese leaders to become somewhat more optimistic about

---

[21] See among others, Dumbaugh, "Interest Groups: Growing Influence," and Sutter, "The US Congress: Personal, Partisan, Political," in *Making China Policy*, ed. Myers, Oksenberg, and Shambaugh, 79–222.

cross-Strait relations, although the PLA's military buildup opposite Taiwan continued.[22]

The initial adjustments in American policy toward China during the George W. Bush administration involved several steps, many focused on Taiwan, most notably the President's personal pledge on national television in the United States that he would do "whatever it takes" militarily to protect Taiwan in the event of an attack from mainland China. No American president had issued such a strong statement in support of Taiwan's defense since before the ending of the defense treaty between the United States and Taiwan at the time of normalization of United States-China diplomatic relations in the late 1970s. American officials maintained that the President's statement did not represent a change in the policy of the United States toward the PRC and Taiwan, but no American official maintained that the President did not mean what he said, and several senior officials highlighted the President's statement in interchanges with Taiwan officials and other observers.[23]

President Bush also notably departed from the past practice of presidents of the United States while preparing for and carrying out visits to the PRC, by strongly highlighting American support for Taiwan in his rhetoric before and during his China trip in February 2002. Thus, President Bush used his weekly address to the nation just prior to his departure for Asia to hail Taiwan as one of America's notable friends in the region; he equated Taiwan with the Philippines, a formal ally of the United States.[24] In the Japanese Diet during his Tokyo stop prior to visiting Beijing, the President pointedly emphasized American support for Taiwan to the warm applause

---

[22] Among useful assessments of recent Chinese priorities, see Thomas Christensen, "China," in *Strategic Asia,* ed. Richard Ellings and Aaron Friedberg (Seattle: National Bureau of Asian Research, 2001), 27–70.

[23] "US Vows to Do What It Takes to Aid Taiwan Defense," Reuters, April 9, 2002, and Steve Mufson, "President Pledges Defense of Taiwan," *Washington Post,* April 26, 2001, A1.

[24] *Radio Address of the President to the Nation,* White House, Office of the Press Secretary, February 16, 2002.

of the Japanese legislators.²⁵ In China, Mr. Bush repeatedly mentioned the importance of the Taiwan Relations Act and the defense commitment of the United States to Taiwan, while making no public mention of the three communiqués that define the United States-China relationship and are viewed by Beijing as the bedrock of the relationship.²⁶

The Bush administration's initial arms sales package for Taiwan was larger than any since the President's father agreed in 1992 to sell 150 F-16 fighter jets to Taiwan, in a move seen motivated in considerable part by the President's need to woo voters in Texas, a key state in the 1992 presidential race and the location of factories producing the F-16s. The George W. Bush administration provided considerably greater freedom to President Chen Shuibian and other high-level Taiwan officials on several day "transit" visits to the United States, and the Taiwan defense minister was allowed to participate in a business conference in Florida in March 2002, where he engaged in talks with the deputy secretary of defense and other American officials attending the meeting.²⁷

Senior American defense, intelligence, and foreign policy officials repeatedly took aim at the buildup of Chinese missiles and other forces opposite Taiwan, viewing them as a threat to Taiwan and to American forces that could be ordered to help protect Taiwan in the event of a conflict in the Taiwan Strait.²⁸ Although the administration's initial arms package to Taiwan did not contain AEGIS destroyers and their capable missile defense systems, senior American officials warned on the record and in the presence of PRC officials, if

---

[25] "Bush Address to Diet Promotes Security, Trade, Reform," *Japan Times*, Internet edition, February 20, 2002.

[26] Erik Eckolm, "US and China Stay Positive, But Make Little Progress," *New York Times*, Internet edition, February 23, 2002.

[27] For quarterly reviews and chronologies of developments in United States–China relations, see the articles by Bonnie Glaser in *Comparative Connections*, http://www.csis.org/pacfor.

[28] Testimony of CIA Director George Tenet to the Senate Armed Services Committee, March 20, 2002. Testimony of Admiral Dennis Blair to the House Armed Services Committee, March 20, 2002.

the PLA buildup continued, the chances that the United States would provide missile defense systems to Taiwan would increase.[29]

The changes in American policy also involved a notable downgrading in the importance that the United States government placed on relations with China. Though early campaign rhetoric about China as a strategic competitor received heavy media attention, George W. Bush gave relatively little attention to China and foreign policy during the campaign and early months of the administration, and he was careful to reaffirm strong interest in cooperative trade relations and China's entry into the WTO.[30] The administration's approach toward China appeared to be part of a broader effort to improve the power and influence of the United States in world and Asian affairs through American economic and military strength, closer ties with American allies and friends (in East Asia, especially Japan), and new openings with other world power centers, notably Russia and India.[31]

The new President and his team also displayed a view of China that was much less benign than that of President Clinton, who expressed faith that economic development, globalization, and American engagement with China would lead to eventual change in China and greater Chinese interdependence abroad that would benefit the United States. The Bush strategic vision of China was more focused on China as a competitor and strategic adversary, and Taiwan was seen as a key area where these differences played out.[32] In particular:

- China was seen as a rising economic and military power, seeking to confront the United States over Taiwan and over time to ease the United States out of East Asia.

---

[29] Luncheon remarks of Assistant Secretary of State James Kelly at the National Press Club, Washington, D.C., February 27, 2002.
[30] Murray Hiebert, "The Bush Presidency: Implications for Asia," *Asian Update* (New York: Asia Society, January 2001), 5–9.
[31] Ibid., 9–19.
[32] Testimony of CIA Director George Tenet to the Senate Armed Services Committee, March 20, 2002; Testimony of Admiral Dennis Blair to the House Armed Services Committee, March 20, 2002; "Viewing US as Obstacle to Its Rise, China

- China opposed American support for Taiwan, giving top military priority to dealing with the United States in a Taiwan contingency.
- China also opposed the strengthening of the United States-Japan defense alliance and American missile defense plans, and worked against American interests in Asian and world affairs, and in ASEAN Plus Three, the Shanghai Cooperation Group, the UN, and elsewhere.
- Aware of China's continued strong need for workable ties, especially economic ties, with the United States, the new Bush administration was able to set upon a course that appealed to those in the United States who were supportive of Taiwan and critical of the PRC, without risking a breakdown in United States-China relations.

Differentiating China from American allies and friends in Asia, President Bush personally called leaders in Japan, South Korea, and Russia, while Chinese leaders were sent more formal letters. Strenuous administration efforts were made to make certain that the President met personally with the senior leaders of South Korea and Japan before a senior PRC official, Vice Premier Qian Qichen, was allowed to meet with the President in March 2001.[33]

The EP-3 incident of April 1, 2001, led to a sharp downturn in relations. Significantly, the Bush administration did not resort to high-level envoys or other special arrangements often used to resolve difficult United States-China issues, insisting on working through normal State Department and Defense Department channels that did not raise China's stature in American foreign policy. In the strained atmosphere of those months, American officials resorted to a tactic often used by China to show its displeasure with

---

Modernizes Military: CIA," Agence France Presse, March 20, 2002; and United States Department of Defense, *Annual Report on the Military Power of the People's Republic of China, 2002,* http://www.defenselink.mil.

[33] Bonnie Glaser, "First Contact: Qian Qichen Engages in Wide-Ranging, Constructive Talks," CSIS, Pacific Forum [Honolulu] (January–March 2001), http://www.csis.org/pacfor.

foreign governments by ordering all American officials to avoid all but the most essential contacts with Chinese officials in Washington and elsewhere.[34] The recently arrived Chinese ambassador, Yang Jiechi, was largely ignored by official Washington; he made the rounds of Washington think tanks, giving speeches in a carefully moderate tone, emphasizing China's sincere interest to move the relationship forward.[35]

While avoiding compromise in core Chinese interests, PRC leaders endeavored to ensure that Secretary of State Powell's one-day visit to Beijing in late July 2001 went smoothly. Official Chinese media had already begun to muffle the sometimes-strident Chinese media complaints against alleged American hegemony and efforts to contain China that had been common in recent years, and Chinese officials even hinted at a more positive view of the American military presence in the western Pacific. The American side also signaled an interest to calm the concerns of friends and allies in Asia over the state of United States-China relations and to pursue areas of common ground in trade and other areas with the PRC.[36]

The antiterrorism campaign saw an upswing in cooperation, although China was the most reserved among world power centers in supporting the American war against Afghanistan. President Bush's visits to Shanghai in October 2001 and Beijing in February 2002 had as much to do with the strategy of the United States in Asia as with China. They showed an American willingness to meet Chinese leaders' symbolic needs for summitry. However, they sustained a tough American stance on bilateral differences.[37]

---

[34] John Keefe, *Anatomy of the EP-3 Incident* (Alexandria, VA: Center for Naval Analysis, January 2002), 6.
[35] Ambassador Yang spoke at forums at the Brookings Institution and the Woodrow Wilson Center for Scholars, among others.
[36] Nick Cummings-Bruce, "Powell Will Explain Bush's Asia Policy," *Wall Street Journal*, July 23, 2001, A 11. See also, the review of this period by Bonnie Glaser in *Comparative Connections*.
[37] Bonnie Glaser, "Bush's China Policy Shows Change," *Taipei Times*, Internet edition, March 18, 2002, and Sutter, *Grading Bush's China Policy*.

The President was unwavering in his support of the American pledge to provide aid for Taiwan's defense. His views on human rights, religious freedom, and other sensitive issues remained firm. In the nine months prior to the trip, his administration imposed sanctions on China three times over issues involving China's reported proliferation of weapons of mass destruction — more than in the entire eight years of the Clinton administration. The United States Defense Department's Quadrennial Defense Review unmistakably saw China as a potential threat in Asia. American ballistic missile defense programs severely challenged China's nuclear deterrent and intimidation strategy against Taiwan, and rising American influence and prolonged military deployments were at odds with previous Chinese strategy along China's western flank.[38]

Seemingly underlining China's continued low priority for the Bush administration, Assistant Secretary James Kelly's discussion of American relations with East Asia, in testimony to Congress prior to the President's trip in February 2002, contained over three pages of very positive commentary on United States-Japan relations, over three pages of very positive commentary on United States-South Korea relations, over three pages of neutral or positive commentary about other parts of Asia where the President was not visiting, and only two pages of mixed negative and positive comments about China.[39] That China's support in the antiterror campaign registered low on the administration's scale at this time seemed underlined by Pacific Commander in Chief Admiral Dennis Blair's seventy pages of testimony to Congress in March 2002 that highlighted the antiterrorism cooperation and activities of various actors in Asia but ignored mention of China in this regard.[40]

---

[38] "Concern over US Plans for War on Terror Dominate Jiang Tour," Reuters, April 7, 2002, and Willy Wo-Lap Lam, "US, Taiwan Catch Jiang Off-Guard," *CNN.com*, March 19, 2002.

[39] Statement of James Kelly before the House International Relations Committee East Asia and Pacific Subcommittee, February 14, 2002.

[40] Statement of Admiral Dennis Blair before the House Armed Services Committee, March 20, 2002.

The adjustments in the American policy toward China did not elicit much domestic debate in the United States. Debate over China policy-related issues was muffled as a result of American preoccupation with the antiterrorism campaign, which appeared to have much more salient implications for American interests. Mainstream opinion in Congress, the media, and in public opinion remained skeptical of China and more positive regarding Taiwan and American support for Taiwan. American business interests remained a powerful domestic force in favor of avoiding disruptive controversy in United States-China relations, but their concerns appeared to be met by the Bush administration's careful emphasis on maintaining mutually-advantageous economic relations with China, despite differences over other issues.[41]

PRC leaders appeared reluctant to express strong dissatisfaction with Bush administration actions, a marked contrast with Chinese public and private pressure on previous administrations in Washington to tow the line on American relations with Taiwan and other sensitive issues.[42] Responding to strong efforts by Jiang Zemin and his colleagues to stabilize a cooperative relationship with the United States, Japan, and other powers, especially during a period of sensitive leadership transition during the Sixteenth CCP Congress, the Bush administration over time endorsed the pursuit of a "constructive, cooperative and candid" relationship with China. President Bush, in particular, appeared to realize the importance of treating Chinese leaders with respect and acknowledging Beijing's progress in developing the Chinese economy and improving the

---

[41] Among reviews of American domestic debate on China policy, see Dumbaugh, *China-US Relations*.

[42] Pan Zhongying, *Bush Visit and Sino-US Ties*, PACNET 8, CSIS, Pacific Forum (Honolulu), February 8, 2002; "Sino-US Cooperation Vital to World Peace: Tang Jiaxuan," *China Daily*, March 7, 2002; Wang Jisi, "Internal Values Set to Push Sino-US Relations to Maturity," *Lien-Ho Pao* (Taipei), March 19, 2002, 13; Murray Hiebert and Susan Lawrence, "Crossing Red Lines," *Far Eastern Economic Review*, Internet edition, April 4, 2002, and David Lague, "This Is What It Takes," *Far Eastern Economic Review*, Internet edition, April 25, 2002.

standard of living of the Chinese people. He seemed to please Chinese leaders by inviting both Vice President Hu Jintao and President Jiang Zemin for separate visits to the United States in 2002.[43] Other reasons for the shift toward greater American cooperation with China in 2002 included preoccupation of the United States with the war on terrorism and particularly the planned military action against Iraq and the utility of Chinese cooperation in dealing with North Korea's nuclear arms development.

Notably lagging in this resumed American engagement was the Department of Defense. During 2002, American military contacts remained very restricted, while other departments were resuming engagement. In this context, many observers speculated about significant differences among Bush administration officials concerning policy toward China.[44] In broad terms, they viewed Secretary Powell and the State Department leading a wing of the administration seeking to manage differences with China in ways that would avoid disruption and allow for greater development of common ground.

In contrast, Defense Secretary Donald Rumsfeld was seen leading a harder-line approach that gave pride of place to China's ongoing military buildup directed at intimidating Taiwan and dealing with contingencies involving American forces in a Taiwan conflict. This Chinese challenge was seen to have implications for the strategic presence and influence of the United States in East Asia and the western Pacific, and to be part of a broader Chinese effort to spread China's influence at the expense of the United States in Asian and world affairs, using military power, WMD proliferation, and espionage, as well as more conventional economic, diplomatic, and political means. By the end of the year, however, high-level military contacts and exchanges were resumed.

A continuing feature of Bush administration policy toward China in 2001–2002 was to limit requests for Chinese support and assistance,

---

[43] Glaser, "Bush's China Policy Shows Change."
[44] See for example, Shambaugh, "From the White House, All Zigzags Lead to China."

particularly any steps seen as possible "favors" to the United States. As one American official privately noted in an interview in February 2002, "This administration (of George W. Bush) doesn't ask China for much"; he viewed this as a contrast with the previous administration that was seen to be in repeated negotiations with China seeking "deliverables" that would be highlighted during high-level United States-China meetings.[45]

As events developed in 2002, President Bush and other senior American officials reciprocated Chinese leaders' practice of playing up the positive features of the relationship in welcoming Chinese increased support in the antiterrorism campaign, and reportedly sought Chinese assistance in getting North Korea to resume dialogue and ease tensions on the Korean peninsula. They also seemed to please China's leaders when they made clear the administration's displeasure with Taiwan President Chen Shui-bian's August 3, 2002 statement, emphasizing Taiwan's separate statehood and implying an interest in going ahead with a referendum to determine Taiwan's future status.[46] However, there was little sign of strong American efforts to ask for changes in Chinese policies and behavior, or to make concessions by the United States in order to encourage those Chinese changes. American officials were clear about the negative consequences for China flowing from such behavior as the military buildup opposite Taiwan and WMD proliferation activities, and they duly criticized Chinese human rights restrictions.

Prospects for Cooperation

The apparent success of the Bush administration in pursuing stronger ties with Taiwan, eschewing concessions in negotiations with Beijing, and maintaining a smooth and business-like United States-China relationship is no guarantee of future success. In particular, the delicate

---

[45] Interview by author at the Brookings Institution, Washington, D.C., February 12, 2002.
[46] David Brown, "Chen Muddies Cross Strait Waters," *Comparative Connections* (July–September 2002), http://www.csis.org/pacfor.

balance in United States-China-Taiwan relations is easily upset; any of the parties could take assertive actions that could unsettle the current equilibrium. Meanwhile, proponents in the American domestic debate over China policy remain active behind the scenes. Democratic leaders in Congress might see some utility in attacking the Bush administration's handling of China policy in the event of a serious downturn in United States-China relations over Taiwan or other issues. Those American interests pursuing a harder line toward China presumably will seek opportunities to implement their policy agenda once the circumstances appear suitable.[47]

Nevertheless, there is a strong likelihood of continued Bush administration success in pursuing its recent China policy directions. For one thing, the leadership of the United States in world affairs appears unassailable for now, and the relatively low level of attention it devotes to China appears broadly understandable at home and abroad, given the many other U.S. foreign policy concerns. The latter include American leadership in the antiterrorism war, preoccupation with the war in Iraq, and continued conflict in the Middle East. In this context, a Chinese move to strongly protest American policy or to downgrade relations with the United States presumably would not change U.S. foreign policy priorities.

Second, President Bush's reelection by a comfortable margin, despite strong criticism at home and abroad, and the strengthening of Bush's allies in the United States Congress, make it more difficult for the various American interest groups with a focus on issues in American China policy to push that policy in directions inconsistent with the recent Bush administration approach. Some groups have tried to revive issues in the China policy debate, notably commentaries in the *Washington Times* giving play to arguments favoring a tougher stance by the United States toward the alleged threats posed by China, and efforts by pro-Taiwan groups for further demonstrations of

---

[47] Richard Holbrooke, "A Defining Moment with China"; Bill Gertz and Rowan Scarborough, "Inside the Ring," *Washington Times*, Internet edition, April 19, 2002; and Hiebert and Lawrence, "Crossing Red Lines."

American support for Taiwan.[48] They attracted little attention and their impact on the policy of the United States appears small.

Third, the preoccupation of Chinese leaders with other policy priorities appears likely to continue. Recently installed Chinese leaders probably will not seek to carry out a major reevaluation of policy toward the United States, unless pressed by events. Also, they will seek under most conceivable circumstances short of military conflict to preserve China's advantageous economic relationship with the United States.[49]

Policy Formulation and Design

Meanwhile, the Bush administration seems likely to persist with the deliberative approach to decision-making over China policy that on balance worked well in the President's first term. The Bush administration came into office with an approach to China emphasizing both a strong desire to engage China economically and a wariness regarding Chinese strategic intentions. Personalities and leaders within the administration were seen to have varying perspectives on China, with some being viewed as "hard line." However, the administration's handling of a significant crisis with China over the April 1, 2001 EP-3 incident appeared to suggest in the context of many other indicators in other areas of foreign policy that the administration's approach to the PRC probably would remain deliberative.[50]

Major players in American policy — leaders of foreign and defense policy departments and agencies — appeared to have the opportunity to make their positions known in Bush administration leadership sessions, presided over by the President and the Vice President. National Security Council specialists, who put a premium

---

[48] Gertz and Scarborough, "Inside the Ring," and Hiebert and Lawrence, "Crossing Red Lines."

[49] Frank Ching, "China Puts Growth before Reunification," *Japan Times*, Internet edition, April 19, 2002.

[50] John Keefe, *Anatomy of the EP-3 Incident* (Alexandria, VA: Center for Naval Analysis, January 2002).

on professional competence and who appeared to have avoided taking sides in significant issues in the ongoing American domestic debate over policy toward China, backed both. In such a context, advocates of strong positions (i.e., "hardliners") might be able to have their views heard, but those views were placed in the context of a collective decision-making process that made moves to the extreme more difficult under most circumstances. Moreover, the broad foreign and security policy experience of the administration's deliberative body meant that American domestic political interests, seeking to push the administration's policy toward China in one direction or another, probably would be subjected to careful scrutiny as to how such American moves, perhaps advantageous in domestic politics, would impact important foreign policy interests of the United States.[51]

Meanwhile, the overall design of the administration's policy seems broadly to replay the approach used during George Shultz's tenure as secretary of state, assisted at that time by Paul Wolfowitz and supported by Richard Armitage.[52] The policy of the United States seeks to build on American national strength and to nurture relations with key allies, such as Japan, that share American interests and values, and are trusted by American policymakers. It also seeks opportunities for cooperation, and has achieved some marked success with other notable power centers, including Russia and India. China's position as the key focus of American East Asian policy in the previous administration has been reduced. Areas of common ground with China are duly pursued, notably closer economic interaction that is beneficial to both countries. Areas of difference with China are dealt with in a matter-of-fact way, without special treatment or major statements of concern, and as is deemed appropriate from the standpoint of the power and influence of the United States.

---

[51] Glenn Kessler and Peter Slevin, "Cheney Is Fulcrum of Foreign Policy," *Washington Post*, October 13, 2002, A1.
[52] See among others, Mann, *About Face*, 128–130.

The administration expresses appreciation and hope that China has behaved and will behave in ways that will broaden the common ground between China and the United States, and, in particular, that Beijing will change its status as the only large power in world affairs that focuses its growing military buildup on the need to deter and attack American forces.[53] But unlike the previous administration, the Bush administration does not appear to see the need to engage in extensive negotiations with Chinese officials or make concessions to the PRC in order to persuade China to change its behavior.

CHINA'S RELATIONS WITH JAPAN

China's relations with Japan in the first years of the twenty-first century followed a pattern in some respects broadly similar to PRC relations with the United States. The international and domestic circumstances that eventually prompted moderation in Chinese policy toward the Bush administration had a similar effect on PRC relations with Japan. In particular, Jiang Zemin and his senior colleagues appeared reluctant to exacerbate differences with Japan as the PRC leadership continued a major transition to a new generation of senior officials during the Sixteenth CCP Congress in November 2002 and the Tenth National People's Congress in March 2003. They moderated a previous harder line toward Japan, gave pride of place to many positive elements in China-Japan relations, and endeavored to mute differences — a stance reciprocated by Japanese leaders also anxious to avoid difficulties with its powerful neighbor at a time of acute domestic difficulties in Japan.[54] The improvement in China's relations with Japan was less than in China's relations with the United States, however. Unlike in the case of the Bush administration, Chinese leaders were less moderate in

---

[53] "US Military Commander Warns of Cross-Strait Arms Race," Agence France Presse, April 18, 2002, and remarks by Admiral Dennis Blair in Hong Kong, April 22, 2002, http://www.pacom/speeches.

[54] See coverage by *Yomiuri Shimbun* of the December 2002 article by a *People's Daily* editorial writer, arguing against anti-Japan rhetoric in China, http://www.yomiuri.co.jp/newse/20021214wo41.htm.

dealing with differences with Japan, and territorial, historical, and other issues continued to receive prominent attention in Chinese media. On balance, however, Chinese rhetoric was less than in the latter 1990s and was offset by important factors preserving businesslike Chinese relations with Japan.

Differences and Divergence since the 1990s

Japan and China in the post-Cold War period at first adjusted their bilateral relations amicably following the demise of the USSR and its strategic influence in East Asia.[55] Later in the 1990s, however, trends moved in a negative direction, prompting warnings of intensified friction.[56] The rise of China's power and influence in Asian affairs in the 1990s and China's military assertiveness over Taiwan and the South China Sea coincided with a protracted period of lackluster Japanese economic performance and weak political leadership. The past disparity of the economic relationship between the two powers was called into question, adding to ongoing differences over territorial, strategic, historical, and economic issues, and strengthening mutual wariness and antipathy.[57]

---

[55] Michael Armacost and Kenneth Pyle, "Japan and the Engagement of China," National Bureau of Asian Research, *NBR Analysis* 12, no. 5 (2002): 1–43, and June Teufel Dreyer, "Sino-Japanese Relations," *Journal of Contemporary China* 10, no. 28 (August 2001): 373–385. James Przystup provides quarterly reviews of China-Japan relations in *Comparative Connections,* http://www.csis.org/pacfor. See also, sources and discussion in Robert Sutter, *Chinese Policy Priorities and Implications for the United States* (Lanham, MD: Rowman and Littlefield, 2000), 79–96.

[56] See notably, Yoichi Funabashi, "New Geopolitics Rages over Various Parts of Asia," *Asahi Shimbun,* January 15, 2002, and Michael Green, "Managing Chinese Power: The View from Japan," in *Engaging China,* ed. Alastair Iain Johnston and Robert Ross (London: Routledge, 1999).

[57] See among others, Christopher Howe, *China and Japan. History, Trends, Prospect* (Oxford: Oxford University Press. 1996); Ming Zhang and Ronald A. Montaperto, *A Triad of a Different Kind: The United States, China, and Japan* (London: Macmillan Press, 1999); and *Asia's Global Powers: China-Japan* (Canberra: East Asian Analytical Unit, Government of Australia, 1996).

With the collapse of the Soviet Union, Japanese opinion targeted China's rising power as the key long-term security concern. China's size and remarkable economic growth were widely seen to undercut Japan's leading economic role in Asia. Rising Japanese nationalism, change in Japanese leadership generations, and Beijing's loss of moral standing in Japan diminished past Japanese willingness to accommodate Chinese demands on historical and other issues.[58] In May 2002, Japanese public perceptions of the Chinese government were affected by the unrelenting Japanese media focus on Chinese security personnel forcibly removing North Korean asylum seekers from the Japanese consulate in Shenyang China at that time.[59]

Longstanding Chinese concerns about Japan's impressive military capabilities increased as a result of American-Japanese agreements since 1996, broadening Japan's strategic role in Asia to include Japanese naval deployments in the Indian Ocean.[60] A Japanese-American-Australian strategic dialogue in 2002 elicited repeated Chinese inquiries and expressions of concern.[61]

Following the collapse of communism, Chinese leaders appealed to nationalism and the sense of China as having been victimized by foreign aggressors in the past. Publicity focused heavily on Japan, by far the most important foreign aggressor in modern Chinese history, exacerbating popular Chinese antipathy toward Japan.[62] In this context, Chinese officials resented Japan's cuts in aid

---

[58] See a particularly articulate example of this line of thinking, Yoshihisa Komori, "Rethinking Japan-China Relations: Beyond the History Issue," a paper presented at the Sigur Center for Asian Affairs, George Washington University, Washington, D.C., December 5, 2001.

[59] James Przystup, "The Good, the Bad and...Japan-China Relations," *Comparative Connections* (April–June 2002), http://www.csis.org/pacfor.

[60] For example, see Tian Peiliang, "Nationalism: China and Japan," Chinese People's Institute of Foreign Affairs (Beijing), *Foreign Affairs Journal*, no. 63 (March 2002): 63–83.

[61] Robert Sutter, "Programs in Australia, May 27–30, 2002," a trip report to the United States Department of State Bureau of Public Diplomacy, June 2002 (available on request via sutterr@georgetown.edu.)

[62] Tian, "Nationalism: China and Japan."

and Japan's greater reluctance to accommodate China over historical and other issues.

Heading the list of signs of heightened Sino-Japanese antagonism and friction were the seemingly competing proposals by China and Japan in late 2001–early 2002 to establish free trade arrangements with the ten Southeast Asian nations in ASEAN, the Association of Southeast Asian Nations. Japan also was showing more support for Taiwan and for stronger American backing of Taiwan during the Bush administration, including active dialogue by senior Japanese defense and foreign policy officials with their American counterparts over China-related issues, including Taiwan.[63] Chinese officials were concerned that the planned Japanese-American-Australian strategic dialogue might focus on Taiwan contingencies.

Other evidence included the first significant cutbacks in Japanese aid to China since the normalization of relations in the 1970s (overall Japanese aid to China in 2001 represented a 17 percent decline over aid provided in 2000).[64] Also important were stepped-up Japanese efforts to improve security, aid, and other relations with India and other nations on China's southern and western flanks, including strong Japanese aid efforts for Pakistan and Afghanistan. In the face of China's steadily increasing economic ties and political influence in South Korea, Japan also made efforts to improve ties with Seoul, attempting to ease differences over historical, trade, and other issues.

A closer look at the two powers' recent approaches to one another and other issues indeed underscored China's growing influence and greater activism, and Japan's relative decline. Consultations with dozens of Japanese media, academic, government, business,

---

[63] "Tokyo-Taipei Links 'Good' Despite Damning Reports," *Asia Times*, Internet edition, March 29, 2002. A Bush administration official with responsibility for relations with Japan reported on the active American-Japanese dialogue regarding China during a background briefing in March 2002.

[64] James Przystup, "Smoother Sailing Across Occasional Rough Seas," *Comparative Connections* (January–March 2002), http://www.csis.org/pacfor.

and other opinion leaders in four Japanese cities in May 2002 reflected a deepening Japanese anxiety over Japan's uncertain future in the face of China's continued remarkable economic growth and expanding military power and influence. Combined with an expected continued stagnation in Japan's economic growth and a perceived "hollowing out" of Japanese manufacturing relocating to China, the rise of China meant that the United States and other world powers would inevitably devote less attention to Japan and be more attentive to China in the future, according to Japanese opinion leaders. They said they were at a loss to define an appropriate policy for Japan to deal with these expected adverse developments.[65]

Recent Moderating Factors in China-Japan Relations

The recent smooth United States-China relationship has gone far toward determining whether Sino-Japanese relations are cooperative or conflictive. The close United States-Japan security alliance and the prevailing Chinese view of Japan as a junior partner to the United States superpower regarding key Chinese security concerns in Asian and world affairs suggest that, as Beijing decides to maintain smooth and businesslike relations with the United States, it likely will be prepared to work pragmatically with Japan as well. Indeed, Chinese pre-occupation with leadership succession associated with the Sixteenth CCP Congress and other sensitive internal issues appeared to reinforce the proclivity of Jiang Zemin and his senior colleagues to keep relations with Japan as well as the United States on a positive footing. Japanese Prime Minister Koizumi for his part took a number of steps to reinforce positive elements in Japan-China relations. However, bilateral Sino-Japanese issues continued to intervene, causing divergence in Chinese approaches to Washington and Tokyo, but several important determinants argued for the maintenance of a degree of stability in Sino-Japanese relations.

---

[65] Robert Sutter, "Programs in Japan, May 21–24, 2002," a trip report to the United States Department of State Bureau of Public Diplomacy, June 2002 (available on request via sutterr@georgetown.edu.)

Indeed, recent trends in Sino-Japanese relations showed a variety of strong and often growing factors that served to offset and neutralize the serious differences noted earlier. Sino-Japanese relations were unlikely to be close under foreseeable circumstances, but their differences were likely to be bounded by important constraints and imperatives. A cautiously optimistic outlook for Sino-Japanese relations added to the likelihood of overall smooth Sino-Japanese-American relations over the next few years.

A comprehensive assessment of Sino-Japanese relations fairly quickly gets beyond expressions of angst and signs of friction to focus on strong and often growing areas of mutual interest, and the strong external forces that are likely to dampen any nascent rivalry between China and Japan for some time to come.[66] Perhaps of most importance, both the Japanese and Chinese governments are domestically focused, and continue to give top priority to the economic development of their countries, which they believe require a prolonged, peaceful, and cooperative relationship with their Asian neighbors, notably one another. In particular, the challenges posed by difficult domestic issues dealt with at the Sixteenth CCP Congress and delicate relations with Taiwan and the United States are likely to preoccupy Chinese leaders for the foreseeable future. Chinese interest in antagonism or confrontation with Japan would appear low under these circumstances.

The Japanese government, meanwhile, has closely aligned its foreign policy with that of the United States. In Asia, this has led to strong Japanese government support for strengthening the United States-Japan alliance, working closely with South Korea and the United States in dealing with North Korea, and firm economic and military backing for the American-led war against terrorism in Afghanistan and elsewhere. Japanese deployment of naval forces to

---

[66] Armacost and Pyle, *Japan and the Engagement of China*; Dreyer, "Sino-Japanese Relations"; and Przystup's quarterly reviews of China-Japan relations in *Comparative Connections,* www.csis.org/pacfor. See also, sources and discussion in Sutter, *Chinese Policy Priorities,* 79–96, and Robert Sutter, "China and Japan: Trouble Ahead?" *Washington Quarterly* 25, no. 4 (Autumn 2002): 37–49.

the Indian Ocean was a strong signal of support. Japan hosted the world donors' conference on postwar aid to Afghanistan and is a major provider of aid to Afghanistan, India, and Pakistan, among others in the region.

Prime Minister Koizumi has sought consultations with China about Japan's expanding military activities, and has endeavored to mute signs of rivalry in Sino-Japanese relations. He was one of the few heads of government to participate actively in the China-hosted Boao Forum on Hainan Island on April 12, 2002. Koizumi stressed that Japan, "as a friend of China," supported Chinese reform and openness. He added that, while "some see the economic development of China as a threat, I do not." He saw "the advancement of Japan-China economic relations, not as a hollowing out of Japanese industry, but as an opportunity to nurture new industries in Japan and to develop their activities in the Chinese market."[67]

Indeed, China depends heavily on Japan for economic assistance, for technology and investment, and as a market for Chinese goods; Japan is increasingly dependent on China as a market, source of imports, and offshore manufacturing base. Two-way trade for the first six months of 2004 grew 30 percent over the comparable period in 2003 and reached $78.7 billion, according to Japanese statistics. [68]

Personnel exchanges between Japan and China have grown markedly. Tens of thousands of Japanese students visit or study in China each year. Government-sponsored exchange programs abound, and even if they do not always promote positive feelings, they probably do promote more realistic mutual perceptions.

Looking at external forces, no other government in Asian affairs would benefit from or seeks to promote greater Sino-Japanese friction. This includes the Bush administration, which has been careful to balance its strong pro-Japanese slant with reaffirmation of continued

---

[67] Przystup, "The Good, the Bad, and...Japan-China Relations."
[68] Przystup, "Smoother Sailing Across Occasional Rough Seas," and James Przystup, "Not the Best of Times," *Comparative Connections* (July–September 2004), http://www.csis.org/pacfor.

interest in closer mutually-beneficial relations with China, designed in part to sustain regional peace and stability. Meanwhile, because the United States remains the dominant military and economic power in the region, the United States-Japan alliance has resulted in a marked asymmetry in recent Japanese and Chinese perceptions of competition and rivalry. While Japanese elite and popular opinion is more focused on China as a future concern, Chinese elite and popular opinion is much more preoccupied with the United States as a possible concern; Japan's role is seen as secondary, the junior partner in one of the American alliances and security arrangements that affect Chinese interests. Given the Chinese focus on dealing with the more important concern posed by the United States, one result that works against Sino-Japanese rivalry is that Chinese officials at times have sought to avoid disputes with Japan and have tried to woo Japan away from close alignment with the United States and toward positions more favorable to China.[69]

OUTLOOK FOR CHINA'S POLICY TOWARD THE UNITED STATES AND JAPAN

The assessment of recent Sino-Japanese-American relations shows that American power and influence has grown, and Japan's influence arguably has grown as it has linked Japan closely with the United States on key security issues. China's overall power and influence continues to grow as well, but it has faced setbacks in efforts to curb American influence in its southern and western flanks, while Russia's shift from close alignment with China to more focus on relations with the United States and the West has undercut China's strategic position vis-à-vis the United States to some degree. Beijing has felt compelled to absorb what, under other circumstances, would be seen as unacceptable affronts regarding the support of the United States for Taiwan and other sensitive issues by the

---

[69] David Pilling, "China and Japan Look to Restore Relations," *Financial Times*, Internet edition, April 3, 2002, and Kwan Weng Kim, "China-Japan Ties Lack Spontaneity," *Straits Times*, Internet edition, April 5, 2002.

Bush administration, and to see its priority in American Asian policy decline from its premier position during the Clinton administration.

The reasons Beijing has gone along with the less-than-satisfactory recent trends are not only that it would be counterproductive to try to resist them actively. PRC leaders also have crucial domestic issues to attend to, and China would have few if any allies were it to attempt to confront the United States superpower and its main Asian ally under current circumstances.

Perhaps of more importance, a lower PRC profile allows Beijing to continue the steady increases of its economic and military power — China's "comprehensive national power," according to Chinese pronouncements. This, in turn, incrementally increases Chinese influence all around its periphery, including in Taiwan, which is increasingly attracted by the economic opportunities on the mainland. A cooperative and pragmatic attitude toward the United States and Japan also sets the stage for incremental improvement in relations. Beijing and Washington and Beijing and Tokyo have many areas of common ground that have not been well developed. Leaders in all three capitals are pragmatic enough to do so, even though key differences will persist. This incremental improvement is more likely to succeed in developing better relations than the unrealistic images of "strategic partnership" that characterized rhetoric in the past but resonated poorly with various interests in the respective countries.

Contributing Authors

Alice D. Ba is an Assistant Professor of Political Science in the Department of Political Science and International Relations, University of Delaware, Newark, Delaware. Her publications and research have focused on ASEAN-China relations and Asia's evolving regionalisms. Professor Ba's co-edited volume, *Contending Perspectives on Global Governance*, is published by Routledge Press.

Deborah Brown is an Associate Professor in the Department of Asian Studies at Seton Hall University, South Orange, New Jersey. She has authored, edited, and co-edited eight books on East Asian political affairs and also contemporary religion, including *Religious Organizations and Democratization: Case Studies from Contemporary Asia* (M.E. Sharpe, 2005). Her research has centered on Hong Kong in transition, electoral and other elements of democratization in Northeast Asia, and the role of religious organizations in democratic transition and consolidation in Northeast and Southeast Asian societies. From 1997 through 2003, she was the managing editor of the *American Asian Review*; presently, she is the managing editor of the *Taiwan Journal of Democracy*. Her many articles have appeared in both scholarly journals and the popular media, internationally.

Tun-jen Cheng is a Class of 1935 Professor in the Department of Government at the College of William & Mary, Williamsburg, Virginia. He previously taught at the University of California, San Diego, and was a visiting scholar at the University of Tsukuba, Japan, and an associate visiting professor at the University of Michigan, Ann Arbor. His primary interests are in comparative political economy and East Asian development. He has published numerous journal articles and book chapters, co-authored *Newly Industrializing East Asia in Transition*, and co-edited *Political Change in Taiwan, Inherited Rivalry, The Security Environment in the Asian-Pacific*, and *New Leadership, New Agenda*. Professor Cheng is the director of the Pacific Asia Program and chair of the East Asian Studies Program at William & Mary. He was editor-in-chief of the *American Asian Review*, 2001–2003, and currently is editor of the *Taiwan Journal of Democracy*.

Jacques deLisle is a Professor of Law and a member of the faculty of the Center for East Asian Studies at the University of Pennsylvania in Philadelphia. He is also the director of the Asia Program at the Foreign Policy Research Institute. He has published numerous articles and book chapters that focus on legal reform and the politics of economic reform in contemporary China, the law and politics of Hong Kong's reversion to China and post-reversion Hong Kong, relations between the United States and the People's Republic of China (PRC), the PRC's approach to sovereignty, international law, and international relations, and the law and politics of Taiwan's international status. He has been a visiting professor at the National University of Singapore and the University of Aveiro, a visiting researcher at universities in the PRC, and a consultant to foreign-assisted law reform programs in China. He is a member of the National Committee for U.S.–China Relations and a contributing editor for *Orbis*. He previously served in the Office of Legal Counsel, United States Department of Justice, where his responsibilities included China-related legal matters and United States foreign relations law.

Bruce J. Dickson is a Professor of Political Science and International Affairs at George Washington University, Washington, D.C. His research and teaching focus on political dynamics in China and Taiwan, especially the role of political parties in the process of political change. His most recent book is *Red Capitalists: The Party, Private Entrepreneurs, and Prospects for Political Change* (Cambridge University Press, 2003).

Joseph Fewsmith is a Professor of International Relations and Political Science and the director of the East Asia Interdisciplinary Studies Program at Boston University in Massachussetts. He is the author of four books: *China Since Tiananmen: The Politics of Transition* (Cambridge University Press, 2001), *Elite Politics in Contemporary China* (M.E. Sharpe, 2001), *The Dilemmas of Reform in China: Political Conflict and Economic Debate* (M.E. Sharpe, 1994), and *Party, State, and Local Elites in Republican China: Merchant Organizations and Politics in Shanghai, 1880–1930* (University of Hawaii Press, 1985). His articles have appeared in such journals as *Asian Survey, Comparative Studies in Society and History, The China Journal, The China Quarterly, Current History, The Journal of Contemporary China*, and *Modern China*. In addition to his other positions, Professor Fewsmith is also a research associate of the John King Fairbank Center for East Asian Studies at Harvard University.

Edward Friedman is a Professor in the Department of Political Science at the University of Wisconsin, Madison. He has been doing research in poor parts of rural China since 1978. His co-authored book, *Chinese Village, Socialist State* (Yale University Press, 1991) won the Association of Asian Studies (AAS) prize as the best book of the year on modern China. It has been translated into Chinese and has received strong reviews. The sequel, *Revolution, Resistance and Reform in Village China*, was published in 2005 by Yale University Press.

Amy E. Gadsden recently received her Ph.D. from the University of Pennsylvania, after completing her thesis on legal reform in early twentieth-century China. From 2001 to 2003, Ms. Gadsden served as a special adviser in the Bureau of Democracy, Human Rights and Labor in the United States Department of State. Previously, she was the deputy director of the International Republican Institute's China program. Ms. Gadsden has written multiple articles on grass-roots political change and the prospects for democratic reform in China and consults regularly for organizations doing rule of law and development work in China. In 2004, Ms. Gadsden served as a consultant to the United Nations Office of the High Commissioner for Human Rights and the United Nations Development Programme.

Xiaobo Hu is an Associate Professor of Political Science at Clemson University in Clemson, South Carolina. He specializes in comparative political economy of transition, property rights, regulatory policy, China studies, and United States-China relations. Professor Hu has been a National Fellow of the Hoover Institution at Stanford University, Public Policy Scholar at the Woodrow Wilson Center, and Research Fellow of East Asian Studies at the National University of Singapore. His most recent publications include *China after Jiang* (Stanford University Press, 2003), co-edited with Gang Lin.

Yanzhong Huang is an Assistant Professor at the John C. Whitehead School of Diplomacy and International Relations at Seton Hall University, South Orange, New Jersey, where he also serves as the director of the school's Center for Global Health Studies. His teachings and research interests cover Chinese politics, global health, and international security. He has written articles on Chinese politics, political economy, and public health that have appeared in the *Journal of Contemporary China*, *Harvard Health Policy Review*, and *Harvard Asia Quarterly*. He is a member of the National Committee on U.S.-China Relations. In summer 2005, he was a visiting fellow at the Center for Strategic and International Studies (CSIS) in Washington, D.C.

K. Thomas Liaw is Chairman of the Department of Economics and Finance and Professor of Finance at the Peter J. Tobin College of Business at St. John's University, New York. His work in the areas of investment banking, capital markets, risk management, and asset management has been widely published. Through his consulting practice, he has been an adviser to several companies, including Polaris Securities Group and RiskVal Financial Solutions, Inc. He also serves as a board member of the Chinese American Academic and Professional Society. Professor Liaw is the president of the Chinese American Academic and Professional Society for 2005. In addition, he is a board member of the State Bancorp, Inc., and its wholly-owned subsidiary, the State Bank of Long Island.

Yawei Liu is Director of the Carter Center's China Village Elections Project and Associate Professor of American History at Georgia Perimeter College. He is a member of the Board of Association of Chinese Professors of Social Sciences in the United States and serves on the editorial board of the *American Review of Chinese Studies*. Also, he is the editor of China Elections and Governance (www.chinaelections.org), a Web site sponsored by the Carter Center that concerns political and social issues of China. He has authored numerous articles on Chinese grass-roots elections. Professor Liu was a member of the Carter Center delegations to monitor Chinese village, township, and county elections from 1997 through 2004. He also has observed elections in Nicaragua, Peru, and Taiwan. Yawei Liu earned his doctorate in American History at Emory University.

Chih-cheng Lo is an Associate Professor of Political Science at Soochow University and the Executive Director of the Institute for National Policy Research. From May 2000 to February 2002, he was chairman of the Research and Planning Board of the Ministry of Foreign Affairs, Taiwan. He also served as secretary-general of the Taiwanese Political Science Association (1997–1998). His research interests center on East Asian security, cross-Strait relations, and United States foreign policy. Professor Lo's most recent publications include "Taiwan," in *Arms Procurement Decision Making II* (Oxford University Press, 2001); "Taiwan: The Remaining Challenges," in *Coercion and Governance* (Cambridge University Press, 2001), and *Challenges of Civilization in the 21st Century*, co-edited with Hung-mao Tien (Council for Cultural Affairs, Taiwan, 2001).

Robert Sutter has been a Visiting Professor in the School of Foreign Service at Georgetown University since August 2001. During his government career of thirty years, he specialized in Asian and Pacific Affairs and United States foreign policy. Since 1970, he has held adjunct faculty positions with Washington-area universities, including Georgetown, George Washington, and Johns Hopkins, in addition to the University of Virginia. He has published thirteen books, the most recent of which is *The United States and East Asia: Dynamics and Implications* (Rowman and Littlefield, 2003).

Index

AEGIS destroyer 387
   missile defense systems 387
Afghanistan, American war in 390
American markets 235
   China's access to 235
ASEAN-China Free Trade Area (ACFTA) 289, 291, 311, 312
   Beijing's proposal for 289
   Framework Agreement on Economic Cooperation 312, 345
   significance of 311
ASEAN-China trade 331
ASEAN Expert Group on Economic Cooperation 330, 332
ASEAN Plus Three 389
ASEAN Regional Forum (ARF) 313, 379
ASEAN's own free trade area (AFTA) 319
ASEAN-4 economies 331
   China's trade with 331
Asian financial crisis 255, 298, 327
Asia-Pacific Economic Cooperation (APEC) 315, 379

Association of Southeast Asian Nations (ASEAN) 311, 316, 317, 325, 328, 330, 333
   concerns of 325
   economies 316
   competition from China 316
   loss of investor confidence 328
   palm oil and China-ASEAN relations 333
   post-Asian financial crisis 317
   response to ASEAN concerns 330

Baoshi Town 202
   People's Congress in 203
   public election in 202
Beijing municipality 73
   domestic market disintegration, and 73
Beijing regime 104, 106, 143, 150, 159, 288, 290, 324, 351, 358, 368, 370
   and ASEAN diplomacy 324
   authoritarian regime 136, 150, 159

414 Index

CCP patriots in 104
and cyberspace strategy 136
elections 196
and IT revolution 136
and its challenger 290
participation in IT-based economic growth cycle 143
and PRC-Taiwan cases 288
problems faced by 351
and Taiwan policy 358, 368, 370
fourth generation 368
2008 Olympics, constraining effect on 351

Bo Au Forum 354
B-shares 254
bulletin-board sites (BBS) 147
Bush administration 375, 382, 393, 394
China policy 382
continuing feature of 393
prospects of cooperation during 394
Buyun elections (*see also* elections, China) 202, 209, 210, 211, 218, 219, 223, 224, 225
and China's political reform 224
expansive opinion survey 210
monitoring 223
nomination rule 219
Organic Law of the Villager Committees of 1987 186, 213
and people's democratic awareness 211
roving boxes and proxies 223
second elections 215, 220, 221
secret polling booth 221
steering committee 220
success of 225

Canadian Sparkice 152
capital import boom 239
Carter administration 234
human rights themes 234

Carter Center 189, 222
Central Commission for Disciplinary Inspection (CCDI) 195
Central Committee General Office (CCGO) Policy Research Office 358
Central Military Commission (CMC) 37, 359
Che Guevara 114
Chen Shui-bian administration 363
China (*see also* People's Republic of China) 27, 28, 31, 43, 51, 53, 55, 57, 58, 59, 60, 74, 78, 86, 94, 97, 98, 107, 120, 135, 136, 137, 138, 140, 141, 144, 148, 150, 151, 167, 171, 179, 181, 186, 190, 197, 199, 222, 229, 233, 236, 241, 251, 264, 266, 269, 292, 293, 294, 297, 298, 299, 300, 301, 302, 304, 313, 315, 316, 319, 332, 333, 349, 350, 351, 352, 354, 355, 364, 367, 373, 375, 380, 398, 399, 406
administrative reform 74
agricultural sector 333
partial liberalization of 333
and ASEAN exports 332
WTO-plus liberalization 332
and rich-poor gap 97
and United States 375
troubled relations 375
and WTO (*see also* World Trade Organization) 229
as potential market of ASEAN goods 313
banking 302
domestic regulations 302
industry reformation 302
foreign banks 300
local currency business 300
nonperforming loans (NPLS) 302, 306
bilateral agreement with Australia 299

bureaucratic authority in a market economy 27
casino capitalism 98
comprehensive national power 406
corruption and political patronage 53
corruption in decline 53
distribution of FDI in 140
economy (*see* Chinese economy)
electoral reform effort (*see also* elections, China) 190
Enron-like problems 167
export-oriented enterprises 241
foreign policy 367
  making of 356
good-neighbor policy 354
government (*see* Chinese government)
grass-roots democracy in 186
industrial goods 301
  trading and distribution rights 301
information technology in (*see also* Chinese government) 135, 136, 141, 150
  Golden Bridge 137
  as major IT producer 138
infrastructure 137
institutionalization 28
Internet users and computer hosts 144, 148
  circuit switch to block international Internet traffic 151
  government monitoring and sanitizing 150
  political risk of 141
  threat to political control 136
local state corporatism 171
  under Mao 97
    party-sponsored mass mobilization 47
marketing, strategy of 352
military assertiveness 399
new diplomacy 197

new leadership from Sixteenth Party Congress 74
new security concept 315
new structure 171
opened economy and decentralization 171
policy process 71
  fragmented authoritarianism model 71
political capitalism 55
political control, problem of 46
political culture 101, 102, 105, 121
  conflicting identities 101
  conflicting nations of 105
  methodology and studies 101
  political contestation, methodology of 101
  political dynamics, mechanisms of 101
  post-Jiang era 101
  projections 121
political patronage 57, 58, 59, 60
  nomenclatura system 57
  objective criteria 60
  paoguan phenomenon 57
  party bosses 57, 58, 59
  personalized selection process 59
political reality in 78
  coercion and repression 78
political reform 190, 199
political succession 27, 33, 46
  impact of 27
political system 93, 350, 380
  decision-making and policy-formulation 350
politics 183, 205
  control over SOEs 183
  institutional-bureaucratic 256
  and post-Cold War United Nations Security Council 264
post-Jiang 102

post-Mao economic reform 169, 173, 180
  decentralization limited 169
  entrepreneurial skills 173
  high-quality products, competition for 180
post-Mao era 47, 48, 49, 81, 103, 136, 143
  band-wagon politics 49
  CCP and people 81
  Chinese nation, sufferings of 103
  decentralization 48
  decrying Maoist, for children rebels 103
  efforts for IT development 136
  political legitimacy in 143
  reformist leadership 240
  reforms 53, 55, 100
    China's body politic 55
    market-oriented economic transition 53
    societal chasm 100
  state rebuilding 49, 51
post revolutionary generation (see postrevolutionary generation, China's)
red-brown coalition in 120
reform and institutionalization 31, 72
reform era in 94
  coalition 23
  domestic reform 232, 280
regime institutionalization 51
  reinstitutionalization 27
regional multilateralism 313, 315
regions in 107
short-range ballistic missiles 364
socioeconomic problems in 352
SOEs 351
  privatizing of 351
state corporatism 181
Taiwan issue 350
Taiwan policy 349, 355

tariff reduction 297
telecommunications 300
third-generation leadership 355
trade-linked strategy 251
traditional socialist approaches 236
two-track economy 98
villages in 43
voter registration (*see also* elections, China) 222
West, non-Han 107
WTO accession 32, 269
  membership 266
  progress toward 294
  postaccession 277
  sneaky protectionism 277
China Daily 213
China Everbright Group 304
China-Japan relations (*see also* Sino-Japanese relations) 373, 398, 402
  economic relations 404
  moderating factors in 402
China policy of United States (*see also* United States) 395, 396, 405
  outlook toward United States and Japan 405
China Telecom 151
China-United States relations (*see also* Sino-American relations) 373
Chinese Academy of Social Sciences (CASS) 92, 214
Chinese bureaucracy 49, 50, 53, 61, 67
  accountability responsiveness and state effectiveness 61
  bureaucratic overexpansion 67
  policy enforcement problems 61
  political and institutional landscape 49
  public financing problems 67
  upward accountability 61
Chinese Central Television (CCTV) 214
  Golden Lands 214

Chinese Communist Party (CCP) 28, 33, 38, 40, 41, 43, 51, 75, 77, 78, 79, 80, 84, 85, 86, 87, 90, 99, 122, 123, 133, 135, 146, 162, 163, 168, 350, 353
  approach to state-society relations 78
  as an effective patronage machine 80
  cadres, revolutionary 47
  Central Committee 201
    Circular No. 12 201
  closure of the political market in 163
  conflicting imperatives 38
  constitution as basic norm of conduct 28
  corrupt politics 163
  decentralization without accountability 133
  democratic centralism 41
  early reform period 28
  elections 186
    compulsory voting 186
  factionalism, personal 38
  and Falun Gong members' protest 135
  Fifteenth Party Congress 37, 206
  Fourteenth Party Congress 174
  forces threatening China with destabilization 122
  Guiding Principles for Political Life Within the Party 28
  importance to the generational change in 350
  information technology and 135
  key interests 77
  leadership 123
  legitimate political organization 79
  managing cadres 61
  membership and career goals 80
  problems of 38
  quinquennial party congresses 42
  rectification campaign 43
  reinstitutionalization of system 33
  red capitalists 85
  regime 152
  representation 86
  and Satellite-based TV broadcasts 146
  Sixteenth Party Congress 51, 353
    new leadership 51
  strategy of adaptation 84
  Tammany Hall 33
  Three Represents 77, 86
  Three Stresses (*sanjiang*) 43
  transformation of 40
  vanguard of the proletariat 87
  Wayabao Conference (1935) 90
  widespread corruption 162
Chinese Consumer's Association 70
Chinese culture 107
Chinese economy 31, 173, 318
  development of 267
    automobile industry 267
    crony capitalism 181
    enterprises 239
    foreign exchange deficits 239
    Enrons 181
    Enron-like problems 167, 171
    Enron-omics 167, 180, 181
      roots of 167
  interests in Southeast Asia 319
  law-breaking or corruption 173
  market orientation 31
  legal-national authority 32
  financial crisis of 1997-1999 316
  financial markets 293
    deregulation of 304
    market regulatory functions 72
    modernization of 93
  proposal for 318
  non-SOEs 181
  reform economics 119
    polarization without immiserization 119
  reforms 72, 86, 168

418 Index

basic market economy 72
decentralized structure of 168
Chinese elections (*see also* elections, China) 185, 188, 191, 195, 196
  activists 189
  Civil Affairs election organizers 187
  direct, open elections 186, 196
  evolution of 185
  exercises in democracy 196
  Guozuo Village 185
  haixuan, or sea election 188
  liang piaozhi 188
  mock election (*moni xuanju*) 188
  multiday training seminars 188
  party elections 195
  private voting booths 187
  secret ballot voting (*mimi tou piao*) 187, 188
  transition in 167, 179
  township 191
  village level, direct 189, 191
  voter registration 222
Chinese enterprises 171, 235
  under American trade laws 235
Chinese exports 279, 288
  safeguards against 279
  Taiwan's nontariff barriers to 288
  textile 279
Chinese federalism 171
  decentralization of authority 171
Chinese government 149, 150, 154, 155, 156, 276, 307
  approach to IT risk management 155
  comprehensive legal framework 150
  counter-measures to forestall cyber activism 154
  cyberspace police 157
  efforts to combat bureaucratic dishonesty 149
  legal-institutional resources, shortage of 276
  local governments 170
    local business, major partner in 170
  officialdom 52, 59, 60
    booty capitalism 52
    cronyism, nepotism, and favoritism 60
    money promotion 59
    political campaigning 205
  open-end mutual funds 307
  software encryption techniques 156
  two-tiered IT network structure 150
Chinese industry 281
Chinese laws 273
  nontransparency 273
Chinese society 96
  and party membership 96
Chinese state apparatus 47
Chinese struggle 106
  data on diverse communities 106
Chinese succession, elite 36
  generational succession 36
  feudal practice 36
Chongqing 130
Cisco 151
Civil Affairs officials 187, 189
  and foreign NGOs 189
Civil society 96
  emergence and strengthening of 96
Clientalism 45
Cold War 312, 316
Communist Taiwan Affairs Office/State Council Taiwan Affairs Office (CCTAO-SCTAO) 358
Comprehensive Economic Partnership (CER) 338
Corruption Perceptions Index (CPI) 54
crony capitalism 182
Cultural Revolution 28, 31, 34, 47, 48, 81, 82, 125, 244, 367
  class struggle policies 81
  end of 47
  generational succession 31

professional-based bureaucrats 48
retirement norms 31
Czarist Leninist institutions 103
    importing of 103

Dahl, Robert A. 95
    increased participation within elite circles 95
danwei (work unit) 41
    erosion of 41
decentralization policies 167
    Chinese-style Enron problems (*see also* Chinese economy) 167
decision-making authority, China 168
    separation of party and government administration 168
democracy 211
    democracy movement, student-led 245
    evolutionary democratization 191
        in South Korea and Taiwan 191
    intraparty (*dangnei minzhu*) 194
    grassroots 188
    village 190, 353
        upward expansion of 353
democratic politics 224
    prodemocracy political activists 8
Democratic Progressive Party (DPP) 362
    election of candidate 362
Deng Xiaoping 30, 34, 48
    economic reforms 34
    model 39
    party-state dualism 48
    period 30
    theory 92
Dengist reformers 237
    against Hua 237
    against petroleum faction 237
Doha meeting 299
Doje Cering 191
    and village elections 191
domestic industries 278
    protection of 278

East Asian Free Trade Area (FTA) 327, 343
    FTA fever 337
    FTA proposals 341
        with ASEAN 341
    creation of 343
East Asian confidence building 345
elections, China (*see also* Chinese elections)
    township elections 191, 221
        campaigning 221
        multiple voting 222
        township magistrate 192
    urban areas 193, 194
        electoral reform 194
        revitalizing elections in 193
    urban committee elections 193, 194
        shequ weyuanhui, or community committee 193
    urban direct elections 193
    village elections 186, 189, 190
        evidence of democratization 190
        xuanju guancha, or election monitoring 188
    villager committee elections 213
        political and economic dynamics 213
    voter identification 222
        verification of 222
Engels, Friedrich 117
    Dickensian inhumanity 117
Enron Corporation 165
Enterprise for ASEAN Initiative (EAI) 339
European Union (EU) 297
    transition period 297

Falun Gong 111, 368
    crackdown on 111
    demonstrations of late July 1999 111
    movement 66, 381

financial services industry 299, 306
  implications for 306
  regulatory changes in 299
floating population 281
Ford Foundation 187
Foreign Affairs Leading Small Group (FALSG) 362
foreign direct investment (FDI) 138, 139, 304
  in China 139
  in Chinese life insurance companies 304
foreign investors 254
  B-shares 254
foreign markets 251
  openness of 251
Foreign Trade Law 269
  enterprises' rights 269
Foster and Goodman 137
  top-down approach to IT development 137
fragmented authoritarianism model 71
Freedom House scale 149

General Agreement on Tariffs and Trade (GATT) 229, 236, 242, 291, 293
  international economic regime 291
  membership 242
  observer status 236
  parties and norms 236
  pursuit of 242
global and regional relations 312
  uncertainty of 312
globalization 32
  China's accession to WTO (*see also* World Trade Organization) 32
Golden Card system 154
Golden Dragon project 154
Google-China 151
Great Leap Forward 367
Great Power Diplomacy 354
  strategy of 354

haixuan, or sea election (*see also* Chinese elections *and* elections, China) 188
  open candidate selection process 188
Hebei, village, southern 106
Henan 114, 131
  AIDS crisis 114
  HIV victims 131
houxuan jianmian, or candidate meeting 188
hukou (household registration) system 41, 223
Hu Jintao 29, 97, 99, 100
  reforming ruling party 99
  rich-poor gap, closing of 100
human capital, new 171
  bureaupreneurial class 171
Human Rights Watch 368
Huntington, Samuel P. 95

information technology (IT) (*see also* China, information technology) 135, 141
  encryption technology 159
  revolution 136, 137, 145
    call for civil liberty 145
    under Jiang Zemin and Zhu Rongi 137
    threat to political control 136
institutionalization 45
  and Hu Jintao 45
  transfer of power 45
insurance 303
  life insurance companies 306
    in China 306
intellectual property rights (IPR) 295
international economic regime 245
international isolation, threat of 313
International Monetary Fund (IMF) 378
International Republican Institute (IRI) 187

Internet 155
  and authoritarian regime 155
  and e-mail links 145
  and Falun Gong's protest 145
  internal tension and line struggle 155
  security, policy for 158
  service providers (ISPs) 150

Japan-China Free Trade Area (FTA) 338
Japanese-American-Australian strategic dialogue 400
Jiang Zemin 39, 84, 99, 121, 258, 357, 361
  Eight Points 357, 361
    revitalization of 361
  politics of personalism 39
  reform agenda 121
  role-based administratve CCP 99
  successors 10, 97
  Three Represents 39, 87, 89, 90, 92, 258, 352,

Kuznets curve 118

Leninist regimes 126
  super-patriotism 126
life insurance companies, China 304, 306
Li Hongzhi 111

Mahathir Mohamad 326
  and East Asian cooperation 326
Mao Zedong 34, 103, 126
  Great Leap Forward 34, 103
  post-Great Leap Forward 126
  revolutionary generation 34
Mao era 43, 76, 83, 103, 116, 120
  ideological issues 76
  ideological mobilization and coercion 83
  Leninist state system 116
  Nanjing massacre 103
  policies 120

Mao Zedong Thought 92
Marxism 92
  sinicization of 92
Marxism-Leninism 29, 30
  Marxist-Leninist doctrine 29
Marxist tradition 30
  reformers and conservatives 30
Max Weber 55
Mexican-Chinese negotiations 299
Ministry of Civil Affairs (MCA) 186, 187, 189
  secret ballots 187
Ministry of Foreign Affairs (MOFA) 338
Ministry of Foreign Trade and Economic Cooperation (MOFTEC) 243
Ministry of the Information Industry (MII) 282
Ministry of Post and Telecommunication (MPT) 153
Ministry of Public Security (MPS) 152
Minxin Pei 129, 131
Most Favored Nation (MFN) 232, 295
  trade privileges 232
Mueller, Milton 137

national character studies 102
National People's Congress (NPC) 39, 192
  and foreign election specialists 192
newly industrialized countries (NICs) 182
Nikita Khrushchev 91
North American Free Trade Agreement 320
nuclear secrets, accessing U.S. 298

People's Action Party (PAP) 159, 161, 162
People's Court 59
People's Insurance Co. of China (PICC) 303
People's Liberation Army (PLA) 376
  major buildup of 376
  research and intelligence organs 359

People's Procurate 59
People's Republic of China (PRC) (*see also* China) 198, 229, 236, 238, 373, 406
  electoral reform in 198
  Great Leap Outward 236
  laws and policies 238
  leaders 406
Politburo Standing Committee (PBSC) 39, 358
post-Leninist discourse 125
postrevolutionary generation, China's 34, 35, 36
  bureaucratic ladder, rung-by-rung 34
  Jiang Zemin 34
  single *xitong* (system) 36
  systems builders 35
postsocialism 116
  dog-eat-dog cynicism 116
post-Tiananmen period 38, 264
  communist or socialist ideology 264
  political atmosphere of 38
power sharing 353
  and consensus building 353
property rights 168
  separation of 168
  proxy voting 223
Public Security Bureau (PSB) 152

Reagan administration 384
Red Guards 34
  younger members of fourth generation 34
regional culture analysis 131
Religious Affairs Bureau Regulations 44
Republic of China (ROC) (*see also* Taiwan) 362
rural government debts 69
  ballooning of 69
rural migrants 112
Russian communist imperium 105

securities 305
Severe Acute Respiratory Syndrome (SARS) crisis 63, 280, 336
Shanghai-Beijing split 110
Shanghai Cooperation Organization (SCO) 110, 323, 389
  China's initiation with Central Asian neighbors 323
Shortage Economics 180
Sichuan People's Congress 215
  four-point decision 215
Singapore 159
  and Confucian ethics 104
  government 104
  and information flow 159
  and multiculturalism 104
  Muslims in 104
Sino-American relations 361
  improvement of 361
Sino-Japanese relations 401
  and signs of friction 401
Sixteenth Congress of the Chinese Communist Party (*see also* Chinese Communist Party) 38, 39, 46, 51, 77, 84, 136, 294, 349, 353, 374
  leadership transition 374
  lifting the ban on private entrepreneurs 84
  political report of 39
  Three Represents slogan 77
socialist construction 47
  tasks of 47
socialist political civilization 40
  building of 40
social protests 33
social stability 132
Special Economic Zones 239, 252
  coastal enclave 239
state apparatus 69, 71
  bureaucratic fragmentation 71

coordination and regulation, problems of 71
dysfunctional fiscal system 69
state corporatism, local 169
state-owned commercial banks (SOCBs) 302
state-owned enterprises (SOEs) 165, 167, 179, 351
  centrally-planned economy 179
  corporate practices, flaws in 167
  future of 165
  restructuring of 351
stock market 307
  in China 307
Strike Hard campaign against crime 368
succession, generational 38
  professional civil service 38
succession politics 41
Sun Life Assurance of Canada 304
swap markets 239

Taikang Life Insurance, Beijing 304
Taiwan 350
  China's policy toward 350
Taiwan Affairs Leading Small Group (TALSG) 358
Taiwanese 113
Taiwan leadership 361
  pro-independence orientation 361
Taiwan policy 349, 355
Taiwan Strait crisis 358
Tan, Zixiang 137
tao guang yang hui, or hide strength to buy time for development, policy 354
Teledisic 147
Tenth National People's Congress (NPC) 374
Three Gorges Dam 119
Three Represents (*see also* Jiang Zemin) 39, 87, 89, 90, 92, 258
  Jiang's notions of 352

Tiananmen Square 255
  crackdown 31, 186, 189, 294, 313, 380
  reversal of Zhao Ziyang's reforms 31
  demonstrators 87
  economic downturns associated with 255
  and GATT members 294
township and village enterprises (TVEs) 167
township cadre corps 205
Trade Act 234
trade barriers 296
  nontariff 296
Trade and Investment Framework Agreement (TIFA) 340
Trade Related Intellectual Property (TRIPs) 271
Trade-Related Investment Measures (TRIMs) 270

United Nations (UN) 377
United States 246
  ballistic missile defense program 391
  China policy 395, 396, 405
    adrift 382
    domestic debate on 395
    formulation and design of 396
  China's MFN trading privileges with 246
  Congress 297
  Defense Department 391
    Quadrennial Defense Review 391
  East Asian policy 397
  foreign policy 234, 381, 389
    major players 396
United States-Japan defense alliance 389
  strengthening of 389

value added tax rebates 275

Wang Changjiang, Central Party School 88, 91
Wan Runnan 87
Wang Shaoguang 129, 131
weapons of mass destruction (WMD) 381
Weberian terminology 27
Wen Jiabao 183
  and new management regulation 183
World Trade Organization (WTO) 137, 293, 229, 264, 265, 268, 284, 287, 314, 378

Cancún meeting 287
China's accession 32, 294, 306
China's economic restructuring 306
consequences in 268
membership 264, 265
  credible candidate for 265
  pursuit of 264
mission creep 284

Xiangzhen Luntan (Town and Townships Tribune) 188

Yahoo-China 151